Exploring Tessellat

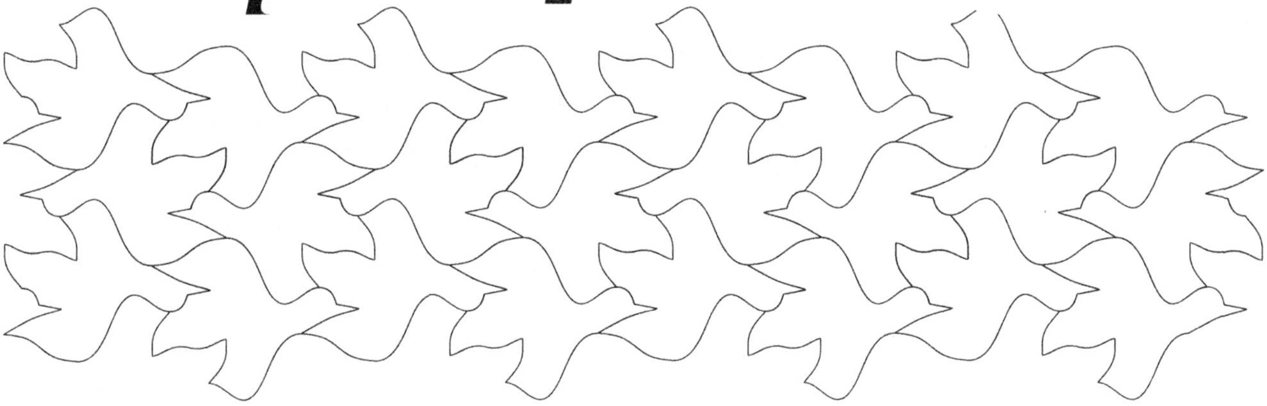

A Journey through Heesch Types And Beyond

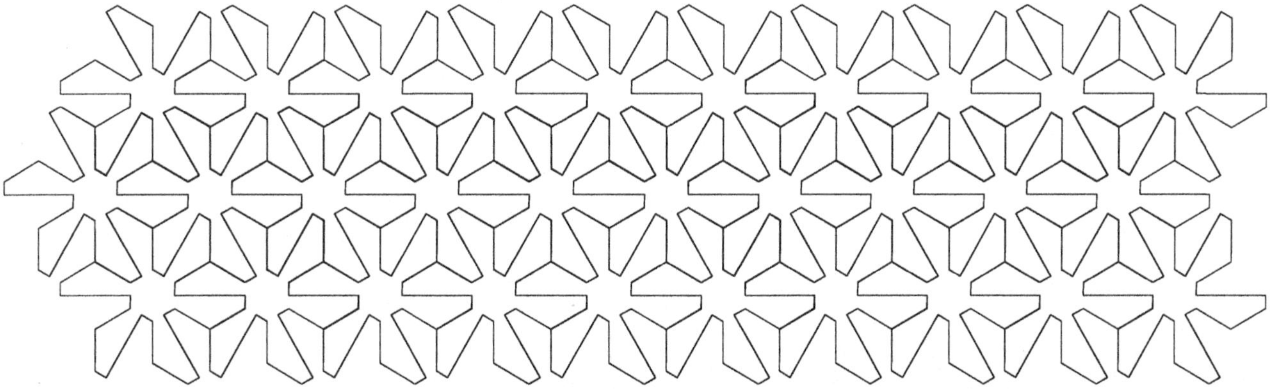

Robert Schenk

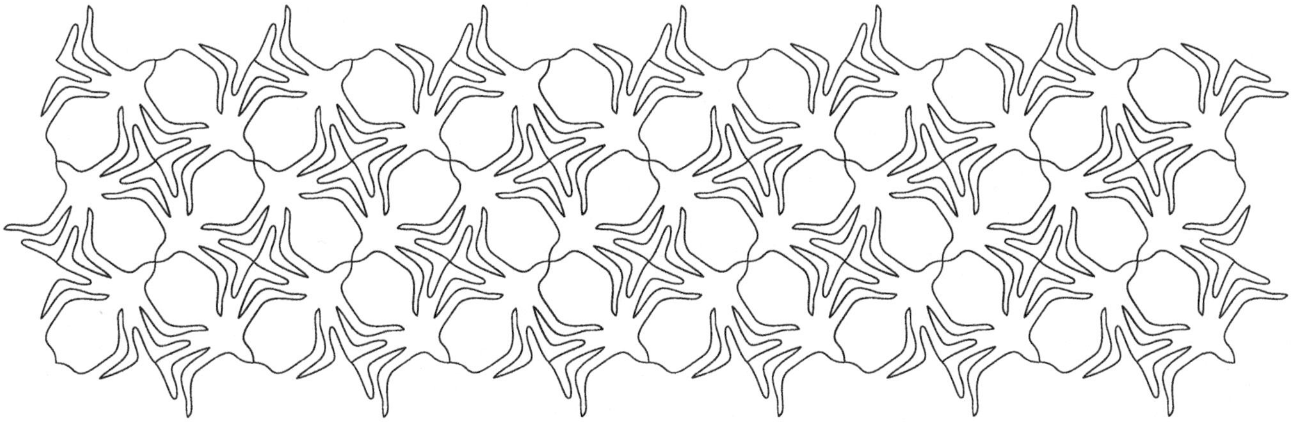

Exploring Tessellations: A Journey through Heesch Types And Beyond is a new work, first published by IngrimayneType in 2015. version xvi

IngrimayneType

ingrimayne.com

ISBN: 978-1515115304

Contents

Introduction

Many years ago I combined two interest, computer programming and typeface design, to developed a maze construction kit. Computer programs generated mazes that were displayed with special typefaces that I designed. It did not take long to realize that using tessellations, shapes that fit together with no gaps or overlaps to fill the plane, was a way to display mazes in a visually interesting way.

In 2015 while working on *Holiday Mazes*, I discovered the program *TesselManiac!*, a successor and improved version of the once-popular program *TesselMania*. I used it in designing a few pages of *Holiday Mazes* but also found interesting tessellating patterns that did not fit that book. Playing with the program, I began for the first time to seriously study the various Heesch types. (German mathematician Heinrich Heesch [1906-1995] showed that all single-tile tessellations that meet certain criteria can be sorted into 28 types and those types are named after him.) As I played with the program, I decided to see how many of Heesch types I could use to create a shape that was recognizable as a bird standing on the back of another bird. Eventually I found designs for 17 of them and that exercise was the genesis of this book.

Many people who are interested in tessellations arrive at the topic via symmetry because tessellations are a subtopic of the study of symmetry. Quilters, for example, find that symmetry is the key to designing visually interesting quilt patterns. Patterned squares can be arranged in many ways but not all give pleasing results. In my case, the process was reversed: I started with tessellations and they led me to trying to understand symmetry. There is no reason to repeat my mistake so we begin this tessellation adventure by looking at symmetry.

Next we will explore how Heinrich Heesch categorized tessellations. With one exception, each of the 28 Heesch types will be illustrated with at least one bird pattern. All will also have examples of other patterns, many of which I used in maze books. Standing-bird tiles will illustrate 17 of the types. Because these shapes are similar, they illustrate how these Heesch types differ. Ten of the other 11 types are also illustrated with at least one birdlike shape. For each type there is an explanation of how edges are related with translation, rotation, and glide moves. We will pay attention to the valence, which is the number of lines meeting at each intersection or vertex, and to how many tiles form what is called a translation unit, a group of tiles that can fill the plane without rotation or flipping.

An alternative classification of tessellations was developed by Grünbaum and Shepard who found that there were 93 classes of isohedral tilings. These classes include the Heesch types and also some Heesch types with restrictions on how edges are formed. In sorting the various patterns I have used in the past, I was surprised by how many of them fit into these restricted classes. Some of the 93 classes force edges to be straight and allow flips that violate the Heesch types. Next, discussions of various themed tessellations, including tessellating arrows, crosses, letters of the alphabet. Near the end of the examination of alphabet tessellations, there is a short discussion of non-isohedral or anisohedral tilings. Following are two sections that grew out of an attempt to see how many different puzzle pieces with a given edge would tessellate.

The most famous name in the field of tessellations is M. C. Escher (1989-1972), a Dutch artist who created scores of beautiful prints and drawings based on tessellating animals and humans. An Escher-like tessellation is one that resembles a real-world object rather than being an abstract, geometrical shape. I found most of the Escher-like tessellations illustrated in these pages by playing with programs such as *TesselMania* or *TesselManiac!*, by trial and error in *Fontographer*, or by thinking through designs on paper. I have tried to acknowledge when my tile has relied on a method used by others and have largely omitted designs that are fairly accurate reproductions of designs of others. I have undoubtedly omitted credit that is due on some of these designs. I do not make the same claim for abstract, geometrical tiles. In some cases I have copied what I considered well-known patterns that have been independently discovered many times.

Disclaimer: The study of tessellations is a branch of mathematics. Mathematicians speak about the subject in ways that require more mathematical knowledge than I have. This book attempts of unravel a few of the insights of mathematicians and to illustrate them with examples. I am not an expert on the subject of tessellations and this account almost certainly contains significant errors. I found and corrected many errors in the process of preparing this book, some of which are described in the text, and I doubt that I found and corrected all of them. Please excuse whatever typos remain; I corrected many but know that some remain.

Robert Schenk
September 2015 (with updates)

The journey is not ended. In addition to several small revisions since October 2015, there were major revisions in January and May of 2016 that broke the book into parts, adding many pages to the material that is in the "Explorations" chapters. I also corrected many mistakes but undoubtedly missed many and also introduced new ones.

I. Symmetry

The discovery that all two-dimensional repeating patterns could be classified into just 17 groups was made by a Russian mathematician in the late 19th century and rediscovered by a Hungarian mathematician in the early 20th century. However, symmetry has been used since mankind began making decorative patterns. Examples for many or all of these groups can be found in the decorative work of people from around the world, including ancient Egypt, pre-Columbian America, and medieval Arabia. One does not need to know the mathematical details of symmetry to enjoy it or to create it.

These symmetry classes are called wallpaper groups or crystallographic groups and they are composed of four elements. Suppose that we have a tiling or pattern that stretches to infinity. If we can make a copy of it and slide it right or left, up or down, or diagonally and have it reproduce itself, so that the copy after the move is identical to the original, we have translational symmetry. All 17 wallpaper groups have translational symmetry in at least two directions because this classification system is based on the assumption that the patterns periodically repeat. Group p1 has only translational symmetry.

Instead of sliding the copy, suppose we rotate it around some point. If the copy after some degree of rotation reproduces the original, the pattern has rotational symmetry. A "6" in the name of the group indicates there is symmetry after a rotation of 60°. A "4" in the name indicates symmetry after a rotation of 90°. A "3" occurs if there is symmetry after a rotation of 120° and a "2" indicates symmetry after a rotation of 180°. Patterns can be rotated around more than one point and they may have different types of rotational symmetry depending on the point of rotation. The common name only include the highest rotational number.

The third type of move is a mirror reflection. It is a flip over a line and if the group has an "m" in its name, it has this move. The fourth type of move is a called a glide reflection. It consists of a flip and then a slide along the axis of the flip and is indicated with the letter "g". (I have not yet found a clear explanation of why two groups begin with a "c".)

Patterns can be broken down into fundamental units, or alternatively, a pattern is built up from smaller units that have the same size and shape but not necessarily the same orientation. There are several mathematical or geometric regularities when moving these units. Two rotations or two flips give a result that can be reached by one rotation. A rotation and a flip give a result that can be obtained with a flip over the appropriate line. Both reflections (mirroring) and glide reflections are flips and flips change the handedness of a fundamental unit. Left becomes right and right becomes left. In contrast, a rotation does not change the handedness of the unit. Fundamental units that are symmetrical do not have handedness because one side is the mirror image of the other.

The 17 Groups

The first step in identifying the symmetry group of a pattern is to determine the highest order of rotation. There are only five possibilities: no rotation, twofold rotation or a rotation of 180°, threefold rotation or a rotation of 120°, fourfold rotation or rotation of 90°, and sixfold rotation or rotation of 60°. The second step is to determine if the pattern is mirrored. A pattern can have no mirrors or mirror lines in one, two, three, four, or six directions. Determining the order of rotation and the type of mirroring limits the possible groups to not more than three. Use of the table below can then determine the type.

Guide to Identifying The 17 Wallpaper Groups

Rotation:	Mirror Reflections? No	Yes
None	Glide Reflection? No: p1 Yes: pg	Glide Reflection? No: pm Yes: cm
180°	Glide Reflection? No: p2 Yes: pgg	Reflections in Two Directions? No: pmg Yes: Rotation off Mirrors? No: pmm Yes: cmm
120°	p3	Rotation off Mirrors? No: p3m1 Yes: p31m
90°	p4	Mirrors at 45°? No: p4g Yes: p4m
60°	p6	p6m

(Adapted from tables at en.wikipedia.org/wiki/Wallpaper_group and euler.slu.edu/escher/index.php/Wallpaper_Patterns.)

There are several naming schemes for the 17 symmetry groups. The most commonly used is the crystallographic notation, which has short and full versions. There is also a fairly recent notation that mathematicians like, the orbifold notation that is based on topology. The table below contains these three notations. In addition to these, others have been proposed.

Short	Full	Orbifold
p1	p1	0
pg	pg	xx
pm	p1m1	**
cm	c1m1	x*
p2	p211	2222
pgg	p2gg	22x
pmg	p2mg	22*
pmm	p2mm	*2222
cmm	c2mm	2*22
p3	p3	333
p3m1	p3m1	*333
p31m	p31m	3*3
p4	p4	442
p4g	p4mg	4*2
p4m	p4mm	*442
p6	p6	632
p6m	p6mm	*632

The orbifold notation stresses the centers of rotation. The table indicates that all symmetry groups that have rotational symmetry have more than one center of rotation. An x indicates that a glide reflection is needed to form the group. An asterisk indicates that the group has reflection. The numbers before an asterisk are centers of rotation that are not on intersections of lines of reflection and the numbers after the asterisk indicate centers of rotation that are on intersection of mirror lines. For example, the p4g group has orbifold notation of 4*2 indicating the centers of 90° rotation symmetry lie off mirror lines but the centers of 180° rotation symmetry lie on intersections of mirror lines. (I do not fully understand orbifolds. They are part of advanced mathematics.)

Groups without Rotational Symmetry

We begin by looking at the four groups that have no rotational symmetry, illustrating them with a pattern of feet.

p1

The simplest pattern simply repeats an asymmetric unit at regular intervals. It is called p1.

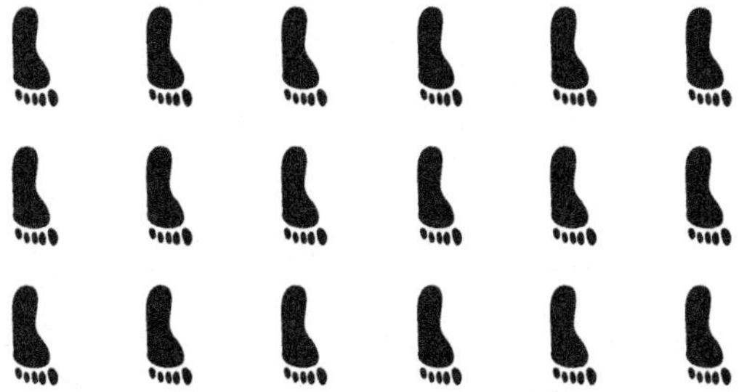

A p1 pattern does not have to consist of a single motif. The pattern below is also p1. Three-fourths of the feet are facing downward, so there can be no rotational symmetry. The odd rows and columns have glide reflection but the even rows and columns have mirror reflection, so there is no overall mirroring or glide reflection. A block of four feet makes up the fundamental unit that repeats periodically throughout the pattern.

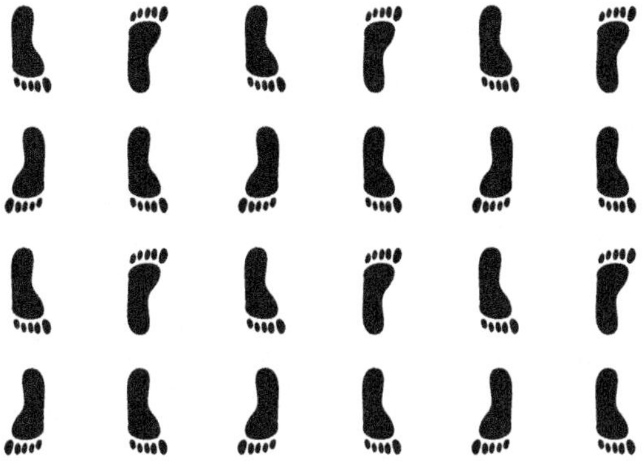

The orbifold notation of 0 for this group indicates it has no rotational, reflective, or glide reflective symmetry.

pg

Slightly more complex is the pg group. It takes a copy of the fundamental unit, flips it, and then moves it along the line over which it was flipped. In the first example the foot is flipped over the horizontal midpoint of the original unit and then moved along that line. There is also a line of glide reflection between rows that generates the next row in the pattern.

A more common way of illustrating pg with feet is to use the pattern that results when people walk, shown below. The left foot is flipped over a line that is to its right and then moved forward a bit. Similarly the right foot is flipped over a line to its left and moved forward a bit. There is also a line of glide reflection to the right of right feet and to the left of left feet. The flip transforms right feet into left feet and right feet into left feet.

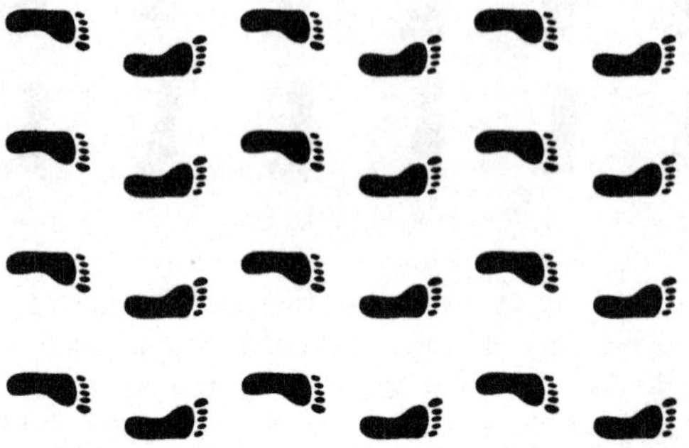

The orbifold notation of xx for this group indicates it has only glide reflection symmetry. There are two parallel guide reflection lines, one through the feet and another between them.

pm - p1m1

In the pm group the two parallel guide lines of the pg group are replaced with two parallel lines of reflection. In the example below the symmetry is over the vertical lines that separate the columns of feet. The lines of reflection also act as guide-reflection lines; glides from one row create the next row. Reflection could also be over horizontal lines, in which case the feet in a column would be toe to toe and heel to heel and the rows would all have the same element. (This alternative is not illustrated.)

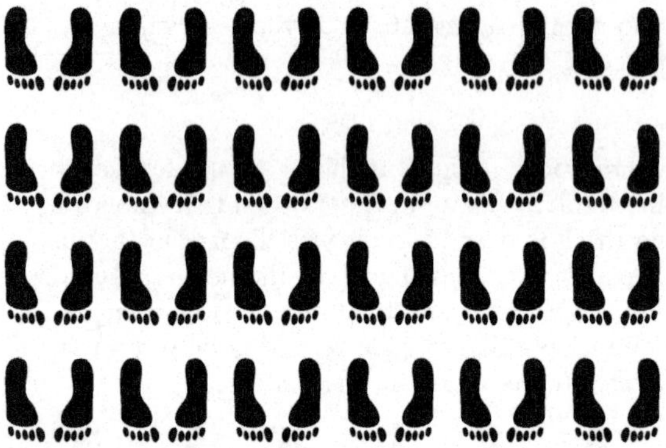

The orbifold notation of ** for this group indicates it has only reflective symmetry.

cm - c1m1

In the pm group lines of mirror reflection are also lines of glide reflection. The cm group has lines of glide reflection that are not lines of mirror reflection. The lines of glide and mirror reflection are parallel and alternate. In the arrangement below the lines of reflection go between the feet that are not paired correctly and the guide lines create the walking pattern of feet.

The glide lines create a staggered pattern that is evident in most cm patterns. Below is another way of arranging feet in a cm pattern.

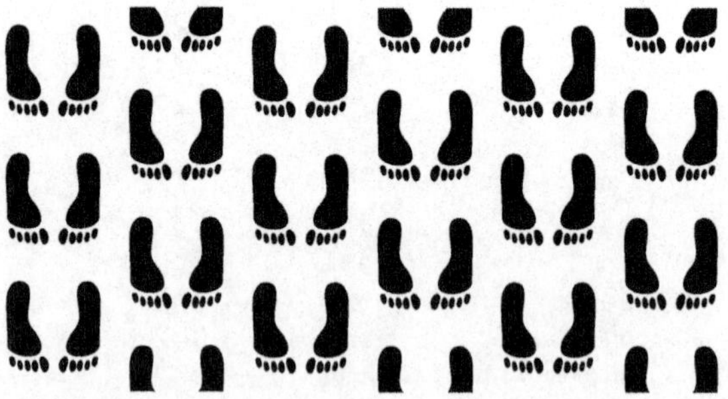

The staggering is less obvious in the pattern below. You should be able to see that a vertical line of mirror reflection runs between columns of feet and a vertical line of glide reflection runs through the feet.

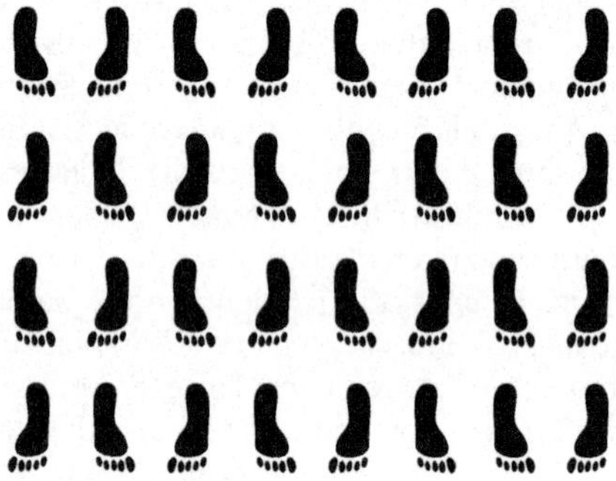

The orbifold notation of x* for this group indicates that it has both mirror or reflective symmetry as well as glide reflective symmetry.

Twofold Symmetry

p2 - p211

There are five groups with rotational symmetry that is only twofold, more groups than any other order of rotation has. Two of the five groups have no mirroring and three have mirroring. The simplest group, the p2 group, has only rotational symmetry. The basic unit is repeated after being rotated 180°. Although it has a superficial resemblance to the pg pattern in that both use only two orientations of the base unit, it differs in that all the elements—feet in the example below—have the same handedness (right in the example below) while the pg pattern has both left and right feet.

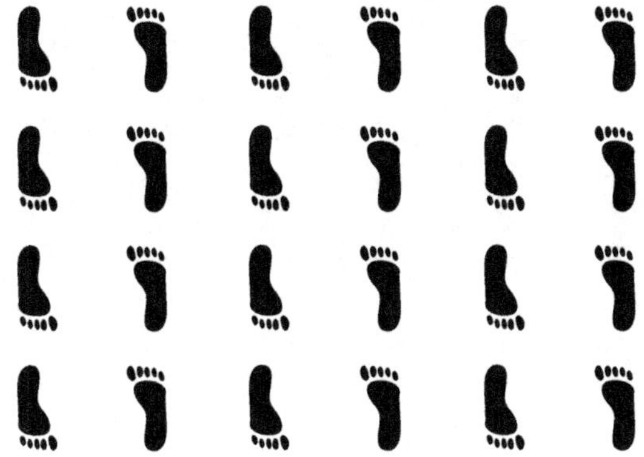

Below is an alternative way of forming a p2 pattern with the same basic unit. The centers of rotation in both cases are the midpoints between the original foot and its rotated counterparts. If we think of a grid with each foot centered in each box of the grid, the centers of rotation are at the corners of the boxes and the midpoints of two of the sides.

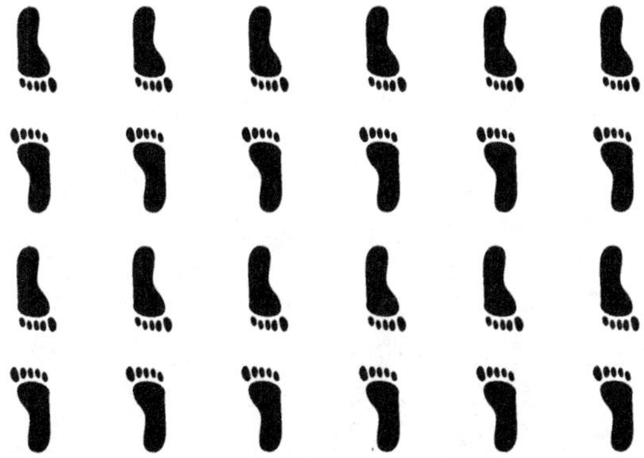

The orbifold notation of 2222 for this group indicates that it has four centers of rotation. In the pattern above there are two in each column between heels and between toes and two between columns between four heels and between four sets of toes.

pgg - p2gg

The pgg group flips a copy of the foot along a horizontal line and move it along that line, then flips another copy along a vertical line and moves it along that line. That yields three elements. The fourth element can be formed in three ways, all giving the same result. It can be formed by rotating a copy of the original element 180° over a point midway between the second and third elements, it can be formed by flipping a copy of the second element over a vertical line and moving it along that line, or it can be formed by flipping a copy of the third element over a horizontal line and moving it along that line. The end result is two left feet and two right feet.

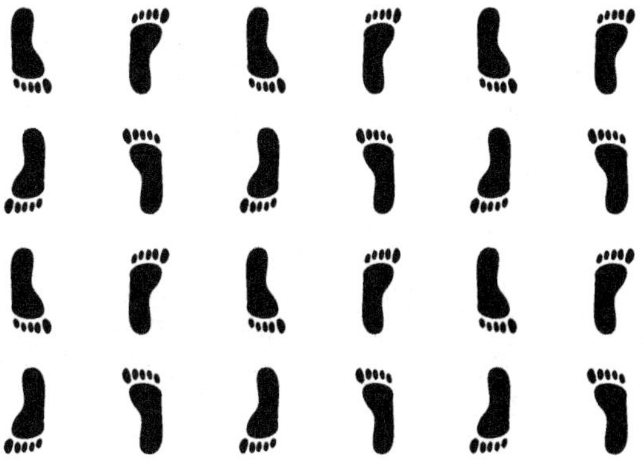

Below is an alternative way to arrange the same shapes in a pgg manner. The vertical flip over and glide along the horizontal line is the same, but the horizontal flip and glide is done over and along a vertical line midway between pairs of feet. The two centers of rotation remain in the centers of boxes formed by the lines of glide reflection.

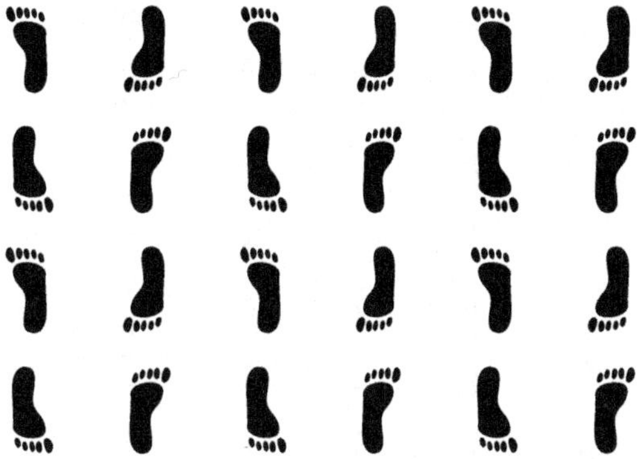

The orbifold notation of 22x for this group indicates that there are two centers of twofold rotation and that there is also glide reflection.

pmg - p2mg

The pmg group has mirror symmetry over lines in one direction and glide reflection over lines that are perpendicular to the lines of mirror symmetry. In the example below, the lines of mirror symmetry are vertical between pairs of right and left feet. The axes of glide reflection are horizontal lines between the rows of feet. Points of rotation symmetry are on the glide lines midway between the mirror lines.

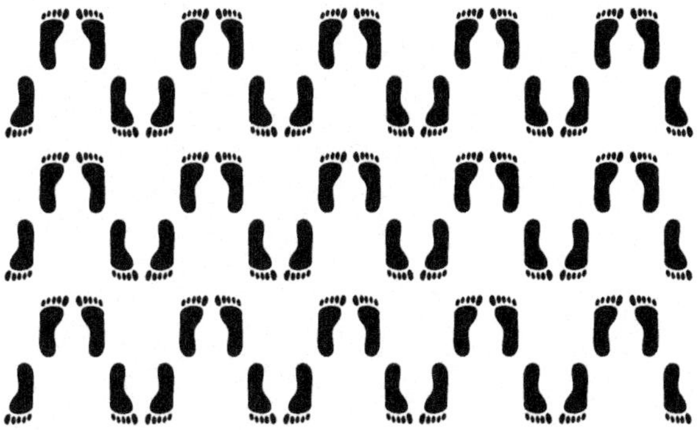

The orbifold notation of 22* for this group indicates that there are reflections and two centers of twofold rotation that do not lie on intersections of reflection lines.

pmm - p2mm

The pmm group has reflection in two directions that are perpendicular to each other. In the example below, the arrangement gives horizontal and vertical mirroring. Starting with a single foot, a copy is mirrored horizontally and another copy is mirrored vertically. The fourth element can be formed in one of three ways, all giving the same result. It can be a copy of the original element rotated 180°, or a copy of the second element mirrored vertically, or a copy of the third element mirrored horizontally. Centers for 180° rotational symmetry are at the intersections of the lines of symmetry.

The orbifold notation of *2222 for this group indicates that there are four twofold rotations and that all four lie on intersections of lines of reflection.

cmm - c2mm

Like the pmm group, the cmm group has mirroring in two directions that are perpendicular to each other. Unlike the pmm group, the cmm group has staggering, which means that it has lines of glide reflection that are parallel to the lines of mirror reflection. The lines of glide reflection and the lines of mirror reflection alternate in a mgmgmg sequence. In the example below, the lines of mirror symmetry go through the center of the blocks of four feet and the lines of glide reflection frame the blocks. The points of 180° rotational symmetry are at the intersections of two mirror lines or two glide reflection lines. The intersections of the mirror lines with the glide reflection lines are not centers of rotational symmetry.

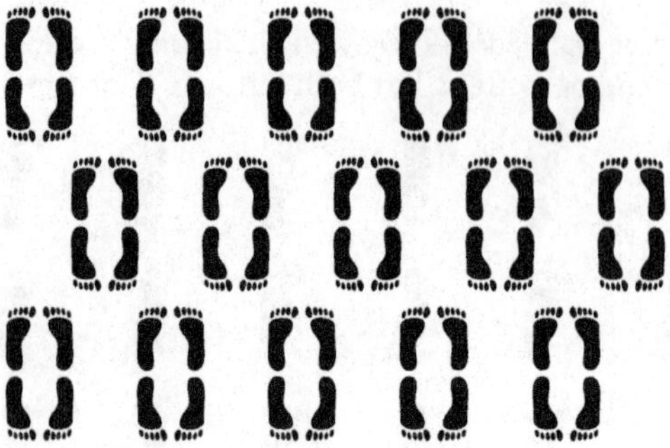

The orbifold notation of 2*22 for this group indicates that there are three centers of twofold rotation, two of which lie on intersections of lines of reflection. (I do not understand why the notation is not 22*22.)

Threefold Rotational Symmetry

p3

There are three groups that have rotational symmetry that is only threefold rotational or symmetry when rotated 120°. The easiest to identify is group p3, which has no mirroring.

The orbifold notation of 333 for this group indicates there is no mirror reflections and that there are three centers of 120° rotational symmetry. The center in the middle of the heels is easiest to see. There is another between the three sets of toes and the third is centered between three outer sides of feet.

p3m1

Distinguishing between groups p3m1 and p31m takes a bit of practice. In addition to threefold rotational symmetry, both have threefold mirroring, that is, they mirror over three axes that are at 120° angles from one another. The easiest way to distinguish the two is to plot all the lines of mirror symmetry and also all the points of rotational symmetry. If the points of rotational symmetry all fall on the intersections of the lines of mirror symmetry, the type is p3m1. If some of them fall off those lines, the type is p31m. To make an example with feet, we need to start with two feet that are mirrored as in the pattern below.

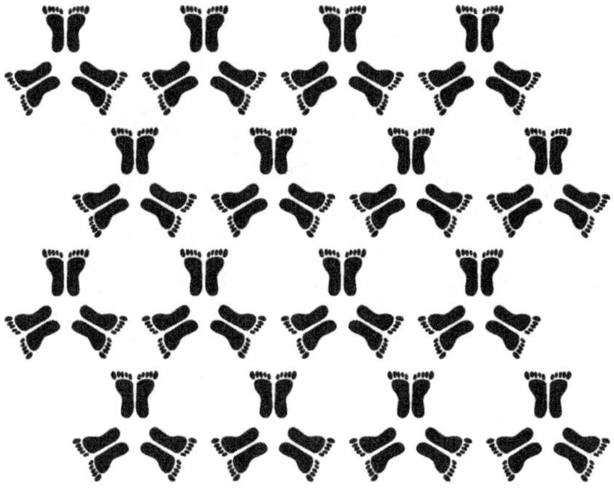

The orbifold notation of *333 for this group indicates there are three centers of rotation and all three lie on intersections of lines of reflection. The centers are in the center of the six heels, in the center of the toes, and in the center of the white space.

p31m

The lines of symmetry in the example below are at noon and the even hours. These lines intersect in the center of the heels and this is a center of threefold rotation. If the odd hours are indicated with straight lines they will meet in the center of big toes and this is a center of threefold rotational symmetry that is not on a line of reflection.

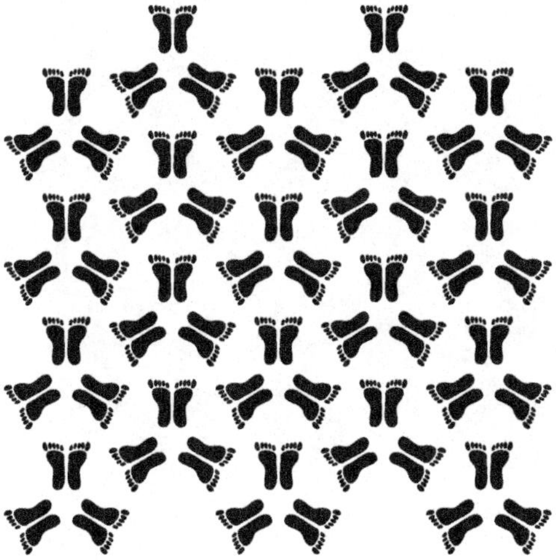

The orbifold notation of 3*3 for this group indicates one center of rotation lies off the intersections of mirror lines and the other lies on the intersections.

If we superimposed a grid of hexagons on the p3m1 and p31m patterns above, lines of reflection would bisect the corners of the p3m1 hexagons and the edges of the p31m hexagons.

Fourfold Rotational Symmetry

p4

There are three groups that repeat when rotated 90°. The p4 group has no mirror symmetry and the other two do. In addition to centers of 90° rotational symmetry, the p4 group has an equal number of centers of 180° rotational symmetry. In the example below, centers of 90° rotational symmetry are located where the four heels come together and also where four sets of toes come together. The centers of 180° rotational symmetry are halfway between centers of fourfold rotation.

The orbifold notation of 442 for this group indicates there are two centers of fourfold rotation and one center of twofold rotation and there is no reflection.

p4m - p4mm

Both p4mg and p4mm have mirror symmetry over two axes that are perpendicular to each other. p4mm also has symmetry at 45°, so that there are four lines crossing at the points of intersection. At these points where four lines of reflection cross and only at these points are the centers of 90° rotational symmetry. The intersections of two mirror lines mark the locus of centers of twofold rotational symmetry. Designs using p4mm symmetry, which are popular with quilters, often have a cross pattern in them.

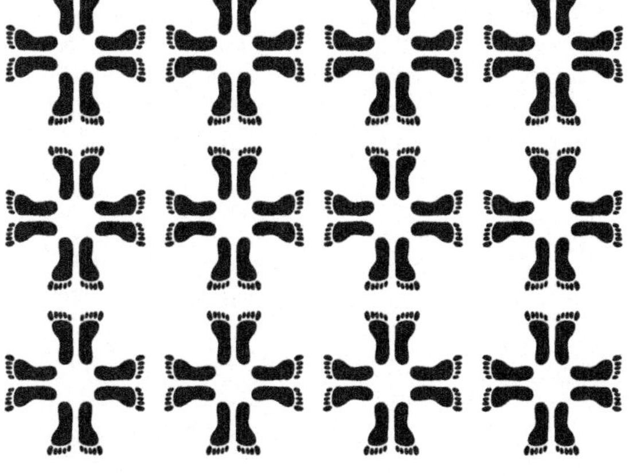

The orbifold notation of *442 for this group indicates that all centers of rotation lie on intersections of reflection lines.

p4g - p4mg

Many of the p4mg patterns have an obvious weave pattern in them. The intersections of the lines of mirror reflection are points of 180° rotational symmetry. However, the p4mg pattern also has lines of glide reflection that alternate with the lines of mirror reflection, and the intersections of the lines of glide reflection are the points of 90° rotational symmetry.

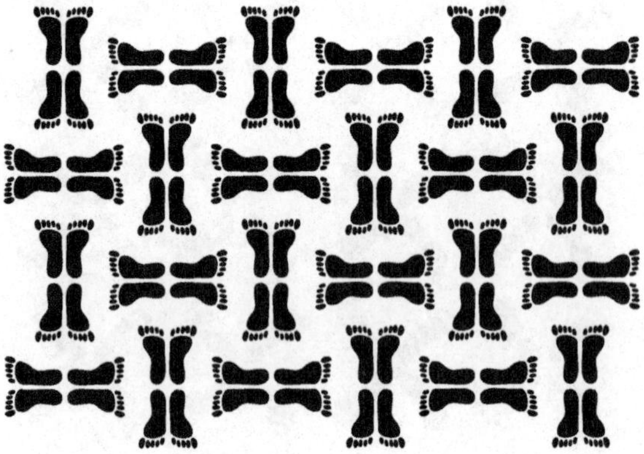

The orbifold notation of 4*2 for this group indicates that the centers of fourfold rotation lie off intersections of reflection lines and centers of twofold rotation lie on them.

Sixfold Rotational Symmetry

p6

There are only two groups with sixfold rotational symmetry or symmetry with rotations of 60°. One group, the p6 group, has no mirror symmetry and the other has it in abundance. In addition to sixfold rotational symmetry, both groups also have threefold and twofold rotational symmetry. In the example below, the center where the six heels come together is the point of rotation for 60°. There is threefold rotational symmetry where three sets of toes come together and twofold rotational symmetry midway between centers of threefold rotation, or alternatively, midway between centers of sixfold rotation.

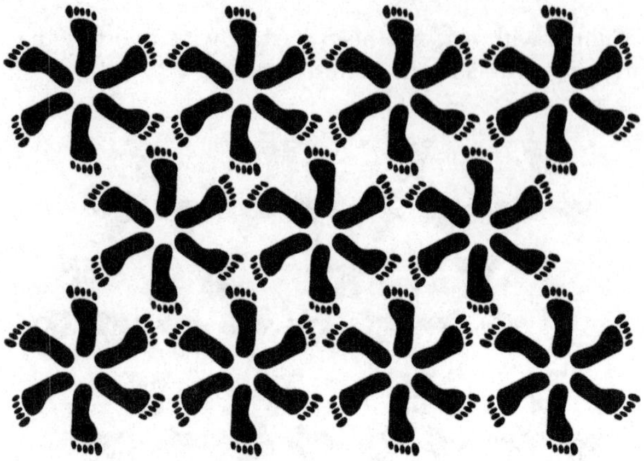

p6m - p6mm

In patterns with p6m symmetry, there are six symmetry lines that pass through the center of the basic unit and they divide the unit into twelve equal parts. Think of the unit as a clock face. At the center of the clock face, six lines cross and there are also intersections of three and two lines between clock faces. For example, midway between each of the floral patterns is a location where two lines cross. The points where six lines cross are points of 60° rotational symmetry, where three lines cross are points of 120° rotational symmetry, and where two lines cross are points of 180° rotational symmetry. The p6 group has an identical set of points of various rotational symmetries, but they are harder to locate because it has no lines of reflection.

The orbifold notation of 632 for p6 and *632 for p6m reflect these arrangements of rotational symmetry and mirror reflection.

Of the 17 groups, ten of the full names have an "m", indicating mirroring. The 28 Heesch types use only the seven types of symmetry that have no mirroring. Discussion of tessellations with mirroring will wait until the introduction of isohedral classes. In the next two chapters the symmetry group will be included with Heesch types and isohedral classes.

II. The 28 Heesch Types

The Heesch classification system uses letters to indicate how each edge is manipulated and these letters are the same as those used in the wallpaper groups. A translation or T moves a copy of one edge to the opposite, parallel edge. A glide or G flips a copy of an edge over an axis and then moves the copy along that axis to another edge. The axis line connects the midpoints of the two edges. There are several C moves. The plain C or center-point rotation has one half of an edge rotated 180° to form the other half. There are also corner rotations of 60°, 90°, and 120° and these are respectively C6, C4, and C3 rotations.

Sometimes center rotations and glides look quite similar, as can be seen in some of the following pages. Although the edges may look similar, the C and G moves arrange the tiles differently. In the bird tessellation patterns that follow this page, a center rotation will always position the same part of the bird on the two sides of a line—bills with be next to bills, wings next wings, etc. A glide move will put different parts of a tile next to each other—front to back, bottom to top, etc.

Heesch types are isohedral, which means that there is one tile shape and one tile size, that the tile fits together with copies of itself to fill the plane with no gaps or overlaps, and that the tile plays the same role throughout the tiling. The last item means that pairs of adjacent edges remain the same throughout the pattern. The Heesch classification also requires that all sides be shapeable—no reflections over straight lines are permitted. None of the Heesch types requires a tile to have either rotational or mirror symmetry.

Type TTTT (IH41) p1

The simplest tessellation is a Heesch type TTTT tessellation of a parallelogram. The top edge is repeated on the bottom edge.

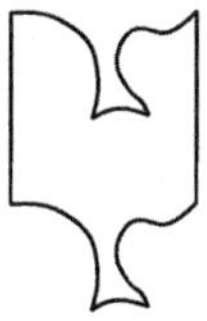

The right edge is repeated on the left edge.

When we put the two together we have a bird that tessellates. M. C. Escher had a type TTTT tessellating bird formed in the same way.

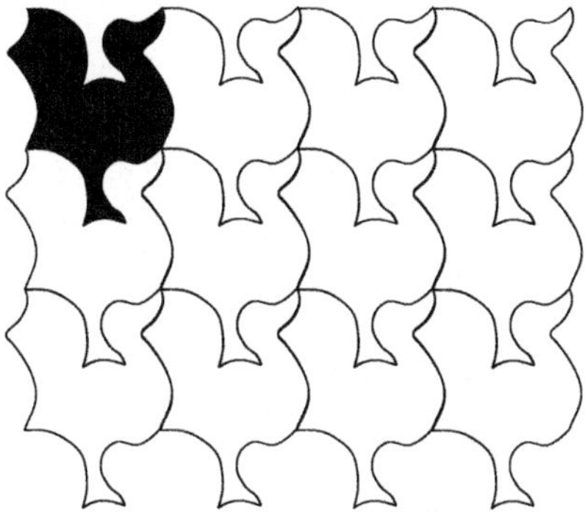

Below is a TTTT version of storks.

These flying birds were inspired by flying birds I found on the Internet, though they were not type TTTT.

A few minor changes and they are owls.

Below is a swarm of some kind of menacing insects. Escher did something similar but with antennae cutting the wings.

Although type TTTT is very simple, I have had difficulty finding interesting tiles that fit it.

Type TTTTTT (IH1) p1

Related to type TTTT is type TTTTTT in which each tile has six neighbors. Opposite edges must be of the same length and parallel. Type TTTT can be seen as derived from type TTTTTT by having one pair of opposite edges shrink to zero.

In exploring tessellations I tried to form standing birds in as many of the Heesch types as I could. I succeeded in all 17 types that have translated or glided edges. Below is an example for type TTTTTT. Notice that each vertex three lines converge. In contrast, type TTTT had vertices with four lines converging. The way that lines meet at the vertices is known as *valence* and is one of the clues that can be used to identify the Heesch type of a tessellation.

When I started playing with *TesselManiac!*, I did not pay enough attention to that possibility that the starting template might not identify the final result. The standing duck below was designed using the TTTT template in *TesselManiac!* and was meant to illustrate that type. However, in trying to get a more realistic duck by lifting the top of the wing to raise the bottom of the tail, I overlapped lines and the resulting tile has six neighbors, not four. It is a TTTTTT type.

Below is another example of a TTTTTT type that was intended to be a TTTT type. This flying duck was created in the TTTT template of *TesselManiac!*. But note that at each vertex three lines converge and each tile has six neighbors, indicating type TTTTTT

This lizard tiling is another TTTTTT pattern that was created in the TTTT template of *TesselManiac!*.

Below is a reworked version.

A slight modification to the TTTT flying insects converts them to type TTTTTT.

s it a girl holding a candle or a guy playing a guitar? Either way, it is a TTTTTT type, as is the second one.

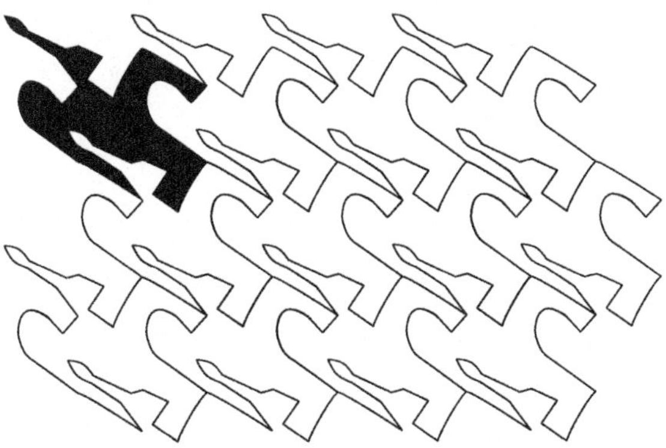

Type TGTG (IH43) pg

The TGTG type is slightly more complex than the TTTT type and the difference between them can be illustrated with the stork tessellation below. It has the same edges as the stork tessellation shown in the discussion of type TTTT. The left and right edges are translated. The top edge is moved to the bottom but before it is moved, it is flipped. (This shape was suggested by a tessellation of Makato Nakamura.) As a result of the flip, the tiles in a TGTG pattern have two orientations rather than the single orientation in the TTTT type.

Below is another standing bird tessellation formed in the same way. The TT edges are the front and back of the bird while the GG edges are top and bottom. Notice how the bottom is a flipped version of the top. The basic shape of this type is also a parallelogram. Notice that at each vertex four lines come together, a property that nine of the eleven quadrilateral tessellation types share.

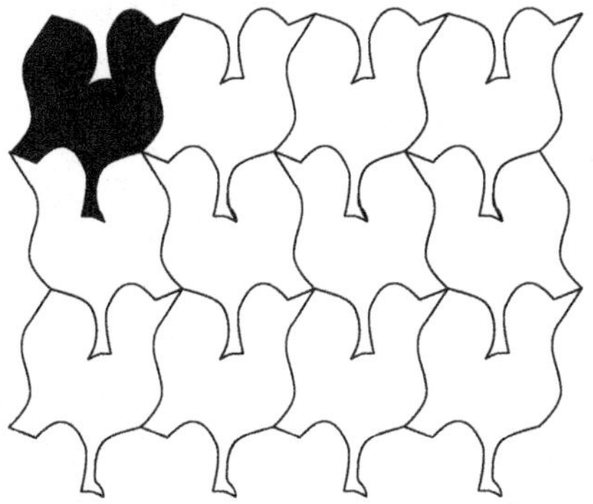

The pattern below is also a TGTG type but is different from the one above in the way the bird is drawn. The top and bottom of the bird are on the TT edges. It is still a TGTG type because the Heesch identification always begins with a T if there is a T edge. (If there is no T edge, it will begin with a C if there is a C edge. The other edges follow in clockwise order.)

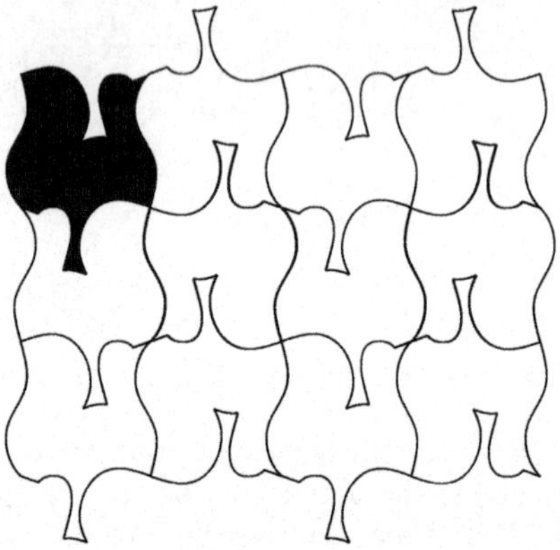

Others have found similar flying bird patterns.

The front and back of the bug below are the translated edges. The legs are glided. Notice how the top edge is moved to the bottom and then flipped. As a result, every row is a flipped version of the previous row.

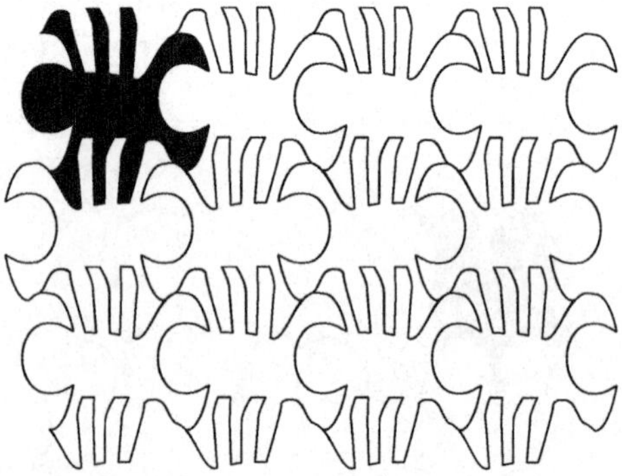

Type TG1G2TG2G1 (IH3) pg

Type TGTG can be seen as derived from hexagonal type TG1G2TG1G2. Type TG1G2TG1G2 has a pair of translated edges and two pairs of glided edges. Type TGTG results when one of the pairs of glided edges is shrunk to zero.

In this bird of type TG1G2TG2G1, the top of the image is repeated on the bottom, the T part. The upper right side is flipped vertically (over a horizontal line) to form the upper left side, and the lower right side is also flipped vertically to form the lower left side.

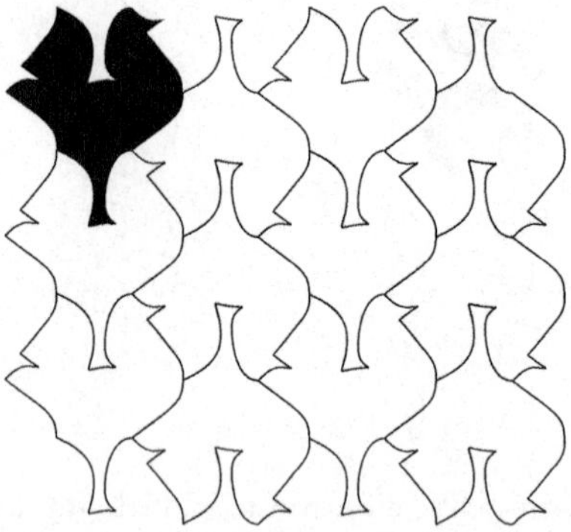

Below is a rearrangement of the hexagonal TG1G2TG2G1 type, dropping the legs from one of the G edges rather than from a T edge. The tile for this pattern was not designed using a TG1G2TG2G1 template but from a TGTG template in *TesselMania*. Sometimes the end result hides the starting point of either *TesselMania* or *TesselManiac!*.

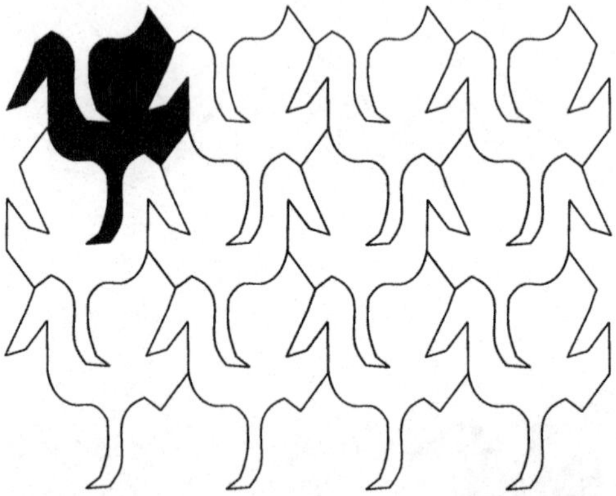

The pattern below almost looks like TGTG but there is a hint of additional edges where the top of the wing touches the top of the head. It was created using a hexagonal TG1G2TG2G1 template in *TesselManiac!*. The lines were manipulated so that one of the G pairs was almost eliminated.

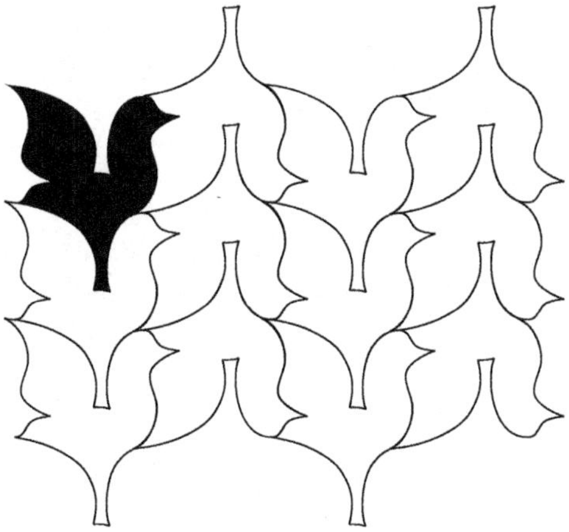

I originally thought that the design below was an illustration of the TGTG type because I designed it in that template. However, it touches six adjacent birds so its correct type is TG1G2TG2G1.

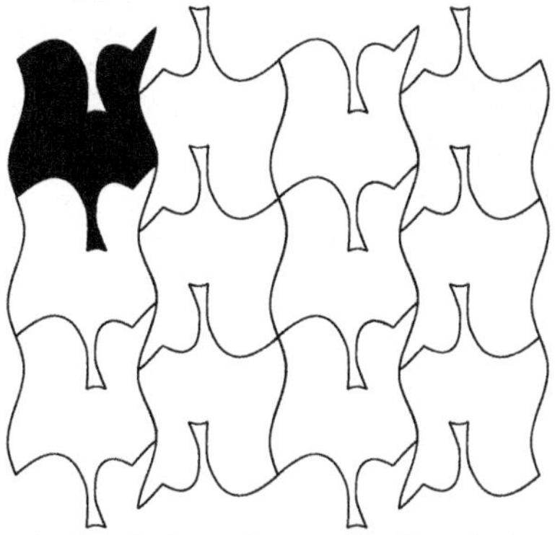

This next design is based on a similar design by Escher. The translated edges are the breast and lower back of the bird.

Below is an attempt to tessellate jackrabbits with very small TT edges (the tip of the nose).

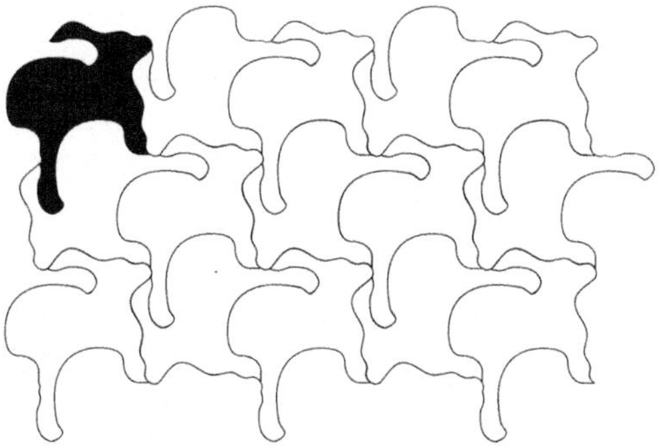

Shrinking one pair of GG edges results in type TGTG. Shrinking the TT edges results in type G1G1G2G2, which can also be obtained by shrinking the TT edges of the next type, TG1G1TG2G2.

Type TG1G1TG2G2 (IH2) pg

Type TG1G1TG2G2, like type TG1G2TG2G1, has a pair of translated edges and two pair of glided edges, but arrangement is different. In these TG1G1TG2G2 type birds the top of the tile is repeated on the bottom. The first pair of GG edges is on the front of the bird, and the top half of the front is flipped horizontally (over a vertical line) to form the bottom half. The same is done on the back. The translation block is two.

In these dead birds the TT edges are very small.

The chalices in this pattern can also be arranged to form a TTTTTT pattern.

The pattern below was an attempt to create mermaids for *The Big Book of Little Princess Mazes*. It is a six-edged tile that is TG1G1TG2G2.

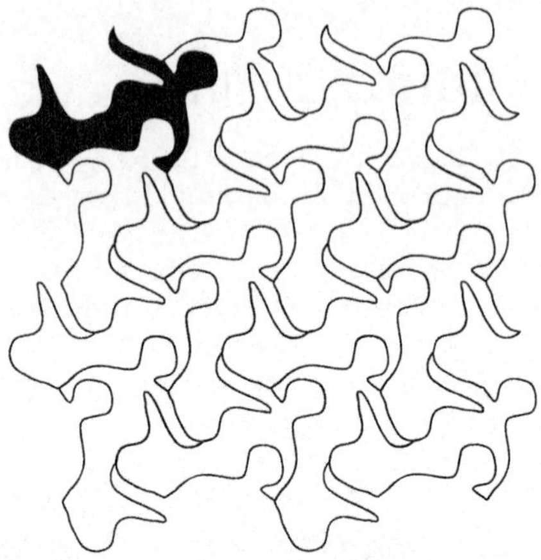

The TG1G1TG2G2 type has yielded several interesting designs, including sharks, boats, and hands.

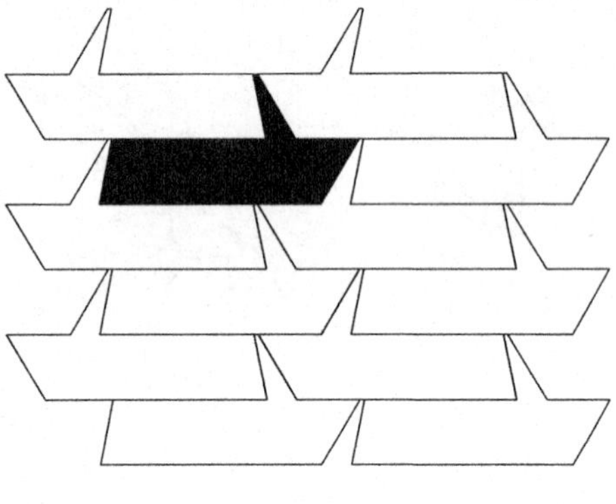

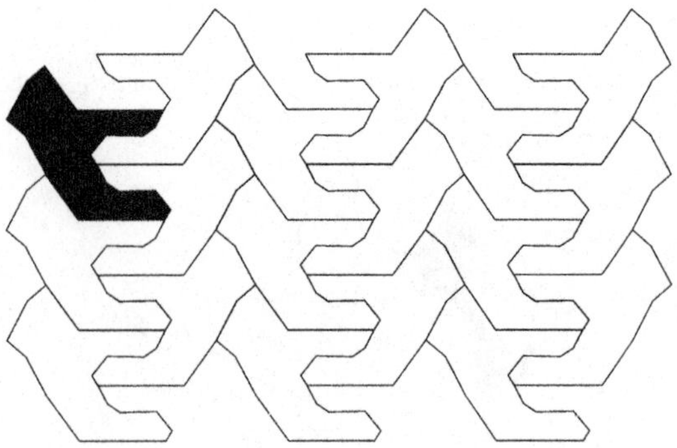

Type G1G1G2G2 (IH44) pg

If the TT pair in either type TG1G1TG2G2 or TG1G2TG2G1 shrink to zero, the result is type G1G1G2G2. Standing birds that are made using glided sides that are adjacent have a very different look from those made with sides that are opposite. The template shape, the shape with straight lines connecting the vertices, can be a kite or an arrowhead. Shape the first G1 edge and find the midpoint between its two endpoints. Draw a line connecting the two points where the G1 and G2 edges will meet and then draw a parallel line through the midpoint of the G1 edge. Copy the shaped G1 edge, flip the copy over the parallel line, and move it along this line until it fits. Repeat for the G2 edges. (Alternatively, the top of the quadrilateral is shaped then flipped and rotated to form one edge with the bottom and other edge formed with a similar shape, flip, and rotation.)

Escher used type G1G1G2G2 in a number of designs. Months after I designed the above birds, I found a vaguely similar Escher design from 1938.

Very similar patterns of stylized fish can be formed from CCCC and CCGG.

Flying birds are one of the more common tessellations. Here are examples using G1G1G2G2.

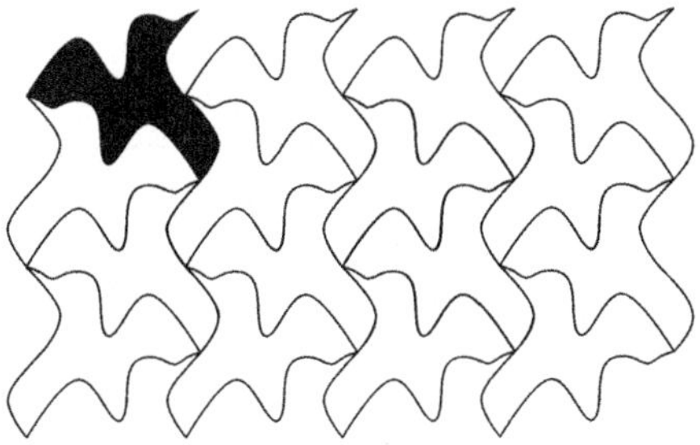

For something different, here are some donkeys that fit the type.

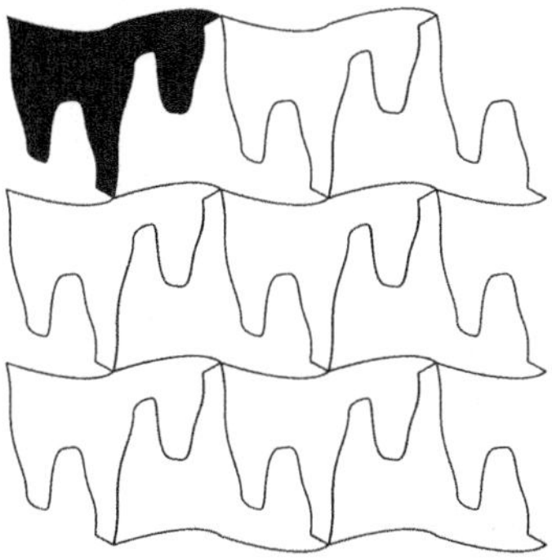

Identification Hints

At this point you may be a bit overwhelmed by technical information. Let us pause for hints on how one can identify Heesch types.

The first step in identifying the Heesch type of a tessellation is to count the number of edges of a tile, which gives the number of adjacent pieces. Be careful because edges can be very short.

It is also helpful to figure out what the translation unit of a shape is. A translation unit or translation block is the smallest group of tiles that can be used to fill the plane with no rotation or flips. In Heesch types it is the number of different orientations that the tile has in the pattern. Knowing just the translation unit narrows the possible Heesch type:

One: TTTT; TTTTTT
A Pair: CCC; TGTG, TCTC, G1G1G2G2, CCCC; TCTCC; TCCTCC, TG1G2TG2G1; TG1G1TG2G2
Three: C3C3C3C3; C3C3C3C3C3C3
Four (2x2): CGCG, G1G2G1G2, CC4C4; C4C4C4C4; CC4C4C4C4, CG1G2G1G2; CG1CG2G1G2;
(4x1): TCTGG; TCCTGG
(other four): CGG; CCGG
Six: CC3C3, CC6C6; C3C3C6C6; CC3C3C6C6

Knowing the number of edges (rows below) and the translation unit (columns below) limits possible Heesch types to at most four:

	1	2	3	4	6
Triangle	0	1	0	2	2
Quadrilateral	1	4	1	4	1
Pentagon	0	1	0	3	1
Hexagon	1	3	1	2	0

Heesch and his coauthor Otto Kienzle showed that there are nine main types of tilings and that the other 19 types can be derived from them by shrinking edges. For example, type TTTTTT becomes type TTTT when one of the pairs of TT edges shrinks to zero. Types TTTTTT and TTTT form a family and each of the other eight main types also has a family. All members of a family share both the size of the translation unit and the symmetry or wallpaper group.

The table on the next page, adapted from a table by Heesch and Kienzle, shows how the 19 "degenerate" types are related to the nine main types. Two of the families do not have hexagonal members but have as their main type pentagonal members. All types to the right of the main type can be derived from the main type but are not necessarily derivable from other types to their left.

Along the top axis is notation giving the valence of the tiling. For example, 4444 means that at each vertex of a tile four edges converge. The number of vertices equals the number of edges. While a valence of 4444 does not narrow possibilities much, there are a few valences that are unique and several that are unique to the translation block.

Type TCTC (IH47) p2

The base shape of a TCTC tessellation is also a parallelogram because the TT edges must be equally long and parallel. In these bird tiles the top and bottom are the TT edges and the front and back are the CC edges. The top half of each C edge is rotated 180° to form the bottom half. With a C move, like faces like—bird fronts face bird fronts and bird backs are butted against bird backs. Notice that if you take two front-to-front pieces (or two back-to-back pieces), you can use them to fill the plane with no rotations or flips.

# Edges:	6	5			4			3		
Valence:	333333	63333	43433	44333	6363	6434	4444	666	884	12,12,3
Translation Block:										
1	TTTTTT						TTTT			
2	TCCTCC						CCCC	CCC		
				TCTCC			TCTC			
2	TG1G1TG2G2						G1G1G2G2			
2	TG1G2TG2G1						TGTG			
3	C3C3C3C3C3C3				C3C3C3C3					
4			CC4C4C4C4				C4C4C4C4		CC4C4	
4	TCCTGG			TCTGG			CCGG			
4	CG1CG2G1G2						CGCG	CGG		
			CG1G2G1G2				G1G2G1G2			
6		CC3C3C6C6				C3C3C6C6		CC6C6		CC3C3

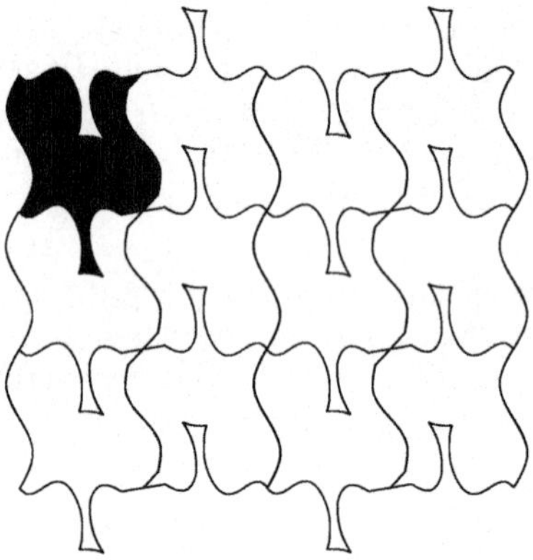

The pattern of bats is quite similar to the birds above. If you draw straight lines connecting all the vertices, you will cut the C edges into two equal parts.

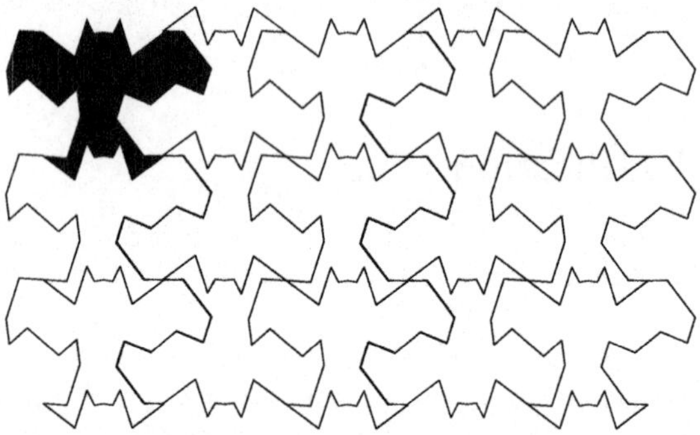

The pattern below may be a better illustration of type TCTC because the C edges are emphasized and the way they fit with the rotation is clearer.

I am not sure where this pattern came from. I may have found the idea on the Internet.

A simple pattern of ducks fits type TCTC.

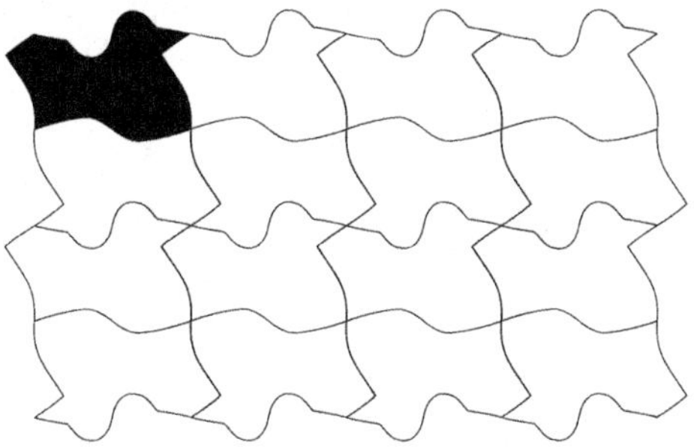

When I was trying to find tessellating letters, I stumbled on this decorative letter F. I realized that slight modification made it into the head of a monster or perhaps a dinosaur. (Both can also be tiled as CGCG.)

Both translated edges and glided edges are paired, that is, the cannot exist independently of a copy. In contrast, C edges are not paired. As a result, all Heesch types with an odd number of edges (3 or 5) must have at least one C edge.

Type TCCTCC (IH4) p2

Type TCTC can be seen as a degenerate case of type TCCTCC when two of the CC edges, one on each side of the TT pair, shrink to zero.

In the example below of a TCCTCC type, two of the C edges are very small, the one that forms the top of the bill and the one that forms the back of the tail. If they shrank until the tip of the tail met the tip of the tail and the tip of the bill met the tip of the bill, this tile would become type TCTC. Type TCCTCC is the third and final hexagonal type that has a translation unit of two.

The bird below is a TCCTCC tessellation tile developed with the TCTC template in *TesselManiac!*. The top and bottom of the bird are the TT edges. The beak-to-beak edges and the tail-to-tail edges are small and straight which often happens when a TCCTCC tile is developed in the TCTC template of *TesselManiac!*.

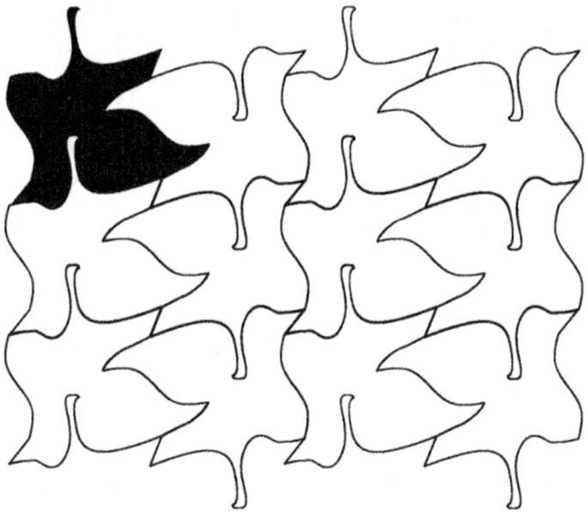

Skydivers or superheroes?

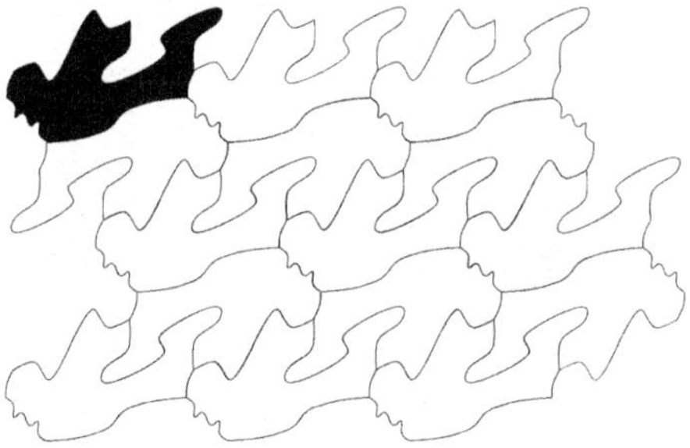

Below are a horse tessellation and a sheep tessellation of type TCCTCC.

Type TCCTCC has been extremely productive in producing tessellating letters. Later in the book there is a whole alphabet composed of letters that fit the TCCTCC type. Here are a few that were not needed there.

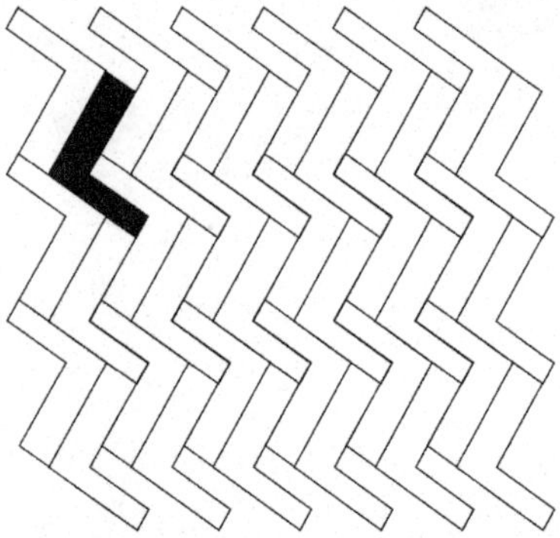

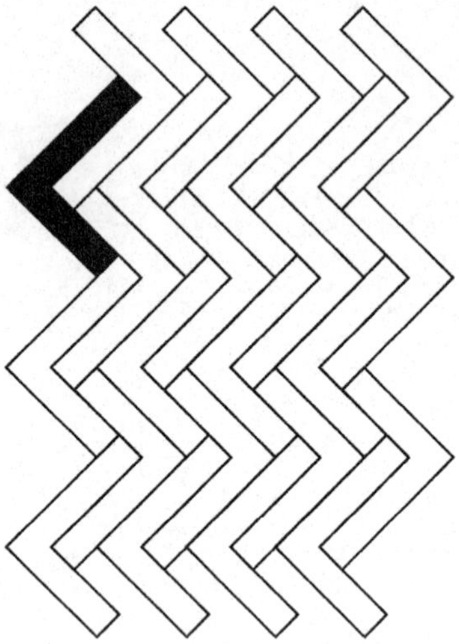

These octopuses were derived from simpler patterns shown latter.

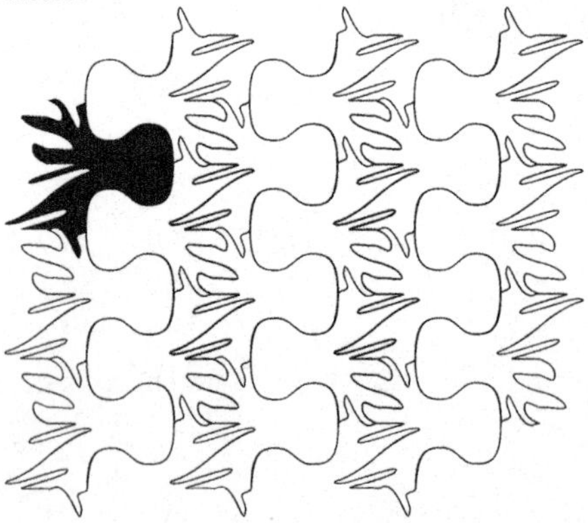

Type TCTCC (IH23) p2

The TCTCC type, like the TCTC and TCCTCC types, has a translation block of two. It is the only Heesch type for which there are no Escher examples.

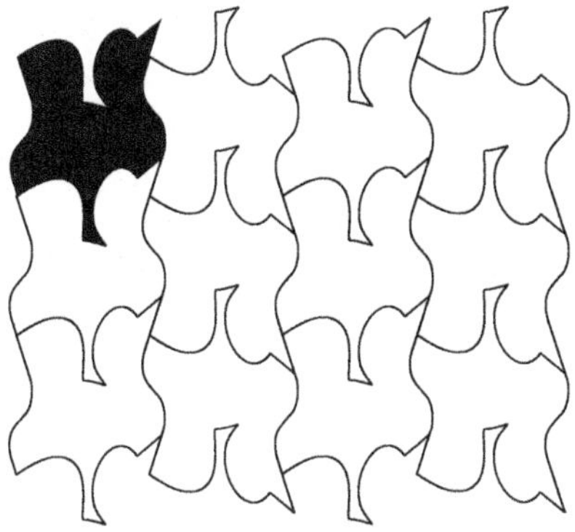

In this pattern of whales, the TT edges are on the left and right, the CC edges form the tail of whale, and the C edge is the top of the whale

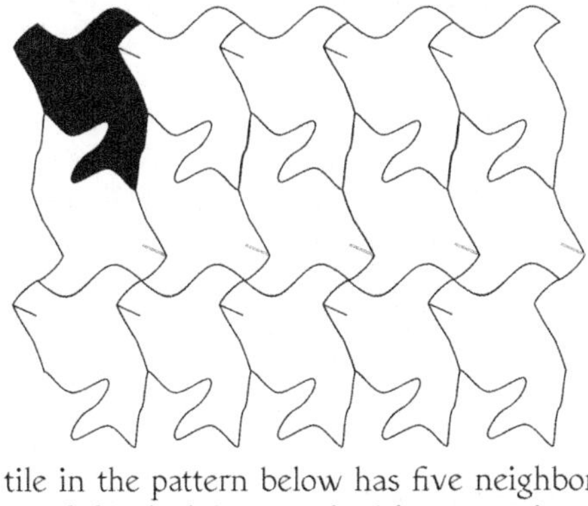

Each tile in the pattern below has five neighbors and the front of the duck is moved without rotation or a flip to form the back of the duck. Hence, it is pentagon type with a TT in it. The top of the duck is rotated 180° to form the adjacent part of the neighboring bird. Look at the bottom. Front of the duck is adjacent to front and back of the duck is adjacent to back, so this is a Heesch TCTCC type.

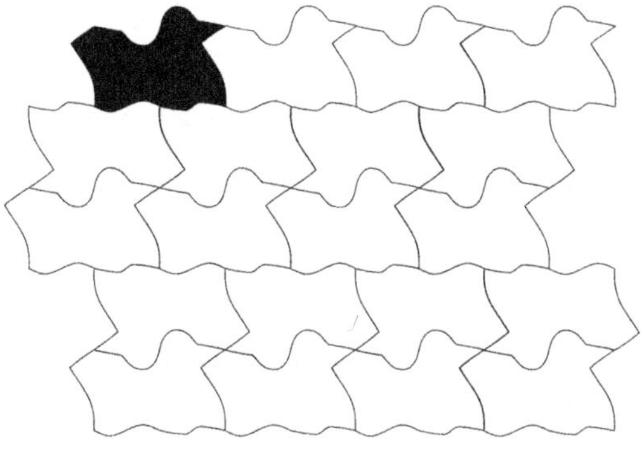

Of course there are also flying birds possible with the type.

I used type TCTCC extensively when tessellating letters of the alphabet. Below are three examples. Straight sides have central-point rotation if they place part of the tile next to the same part after it is rotated 180°.

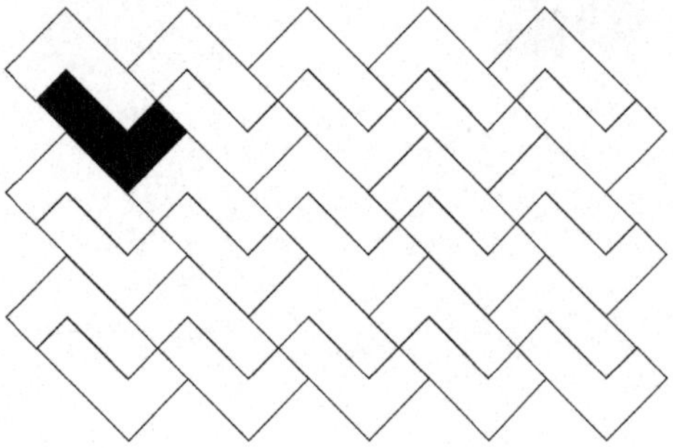

Type CCCC (IH46) p2

If the TT edges of type TCCTCC shrink to zero, what is left is type CCCC. The CCCC type can be any quadrilateral. In the patterns below each edge has a different length and opposite edges are not parallel. The translation block is two.

Below are some crude elephants formed with CCCC.

My interest in using tessellations for mazes is, as far as I know, unique. Others who find tessellations interesting include artists following the lead of M.C. Escher, mathematicians and their students who find interesting geometrical properties hidden in them, and quilters who find that tessellation patterns provide visually interesting designs for their quilts. Quilters have created a number of cat tilings. Below is one that I found on the Internet. My only contribution to it was to skew it a bit so that it would not drift—that it aligns in perfectly vertical columns and perfectly horizontal rows. Apparently the drift is not a problem for the quilters. The design is an excellent example of the CCCC type.

The letter F can be fit into a CCCC pattern.

Type CCC (IH84) p2

Because a triangle has no opposite sides, there are no T moves in triangle tessellations. Of the five triangle types, three, including the CCC type, have vertices of six but only the CCC type has a translation unit of two. The picture of flying geese may remind you one of Escher's prints showing interlocking flying geese—it is one of his most famous. However, Escher's geese have two different shapes so they are not true tessellations of a single tile.

Horse heads can be made with the CCC type.

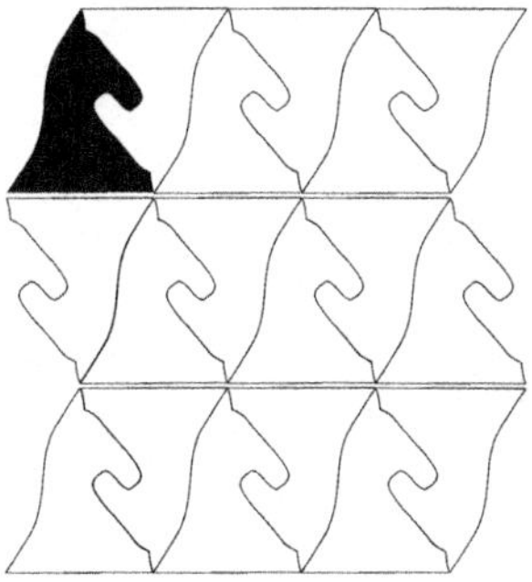

These musical notes are an interesting pattern of type CCC. Connect the vertices with straight lines and you should be able to see how each edge has a different central rotation.

Type CGCG (IH51) pgg

The CGCG type can be any quadrilateral with two opposite edges of equal length. Notice that on the C edges front is adjacent to front and back to back. Also notice that it takes four pieces of the pattern to form a translation unit, a block of pieces that will fill the plane with no rotations or flips.

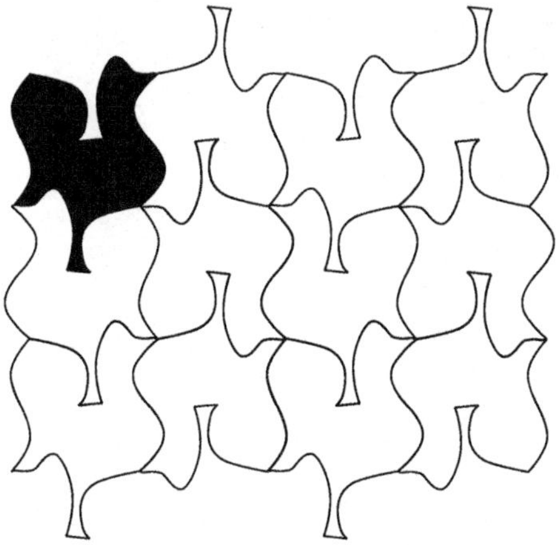

I drew a pattern of tessellating octopuses while doodling in a classroom about fifty years ago. Obviously they did not get digitized until fairly recently. Notice that the CC edges have different lengths. Only the GG edges need to have the same length.

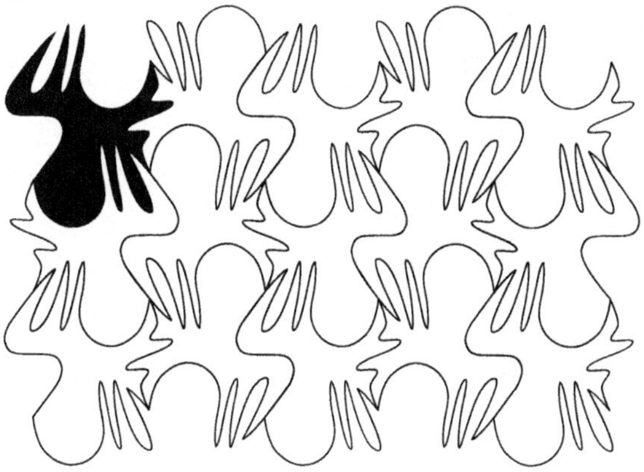

I stumbled on this hammer design while playing in *TesselMania* a few years ago.

Below are two versions of a lady in a long dress. Notice how the front of the figure is flipped to form the back. These are the glide edges.

In the pattern below, the heads are on glide edges and the arms are on C edges.

Type CG1CG2G1G2 (IH6) pgg

The CGCG type can be seen as derived from hexagonal type CG1CG2G1G2, which also has a translation unit of four. In the pattern below, one pair of GG edges is used to make the feet and back of the bird while the C edges form most of the right and left sides. A very short G2 pair completes the tile. If the short G2 edges were shrunk to zero, the tiling would be type CGCG.

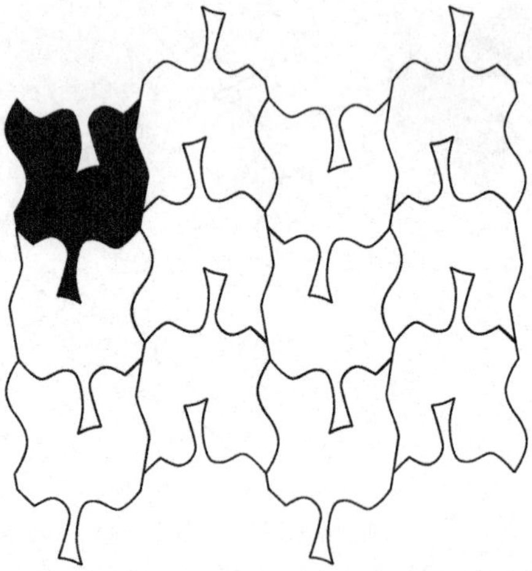

Instead of making the G2 edges small, the design below makes the C edges small. You can see them in the tops of the beaks and in the part of the tails that overlap.

The stork below of type CG1CG2G1G2G was constructed in *TesselMania* using a template for a G1G2G1G2 type. Both C edges are straight lines, a common result when a more complex type is constructed using the template of a simpler type.

These stylized interlocking doves belong to the CG1CG2G1G2 type.

Like many of the birds in this section, these hands were designed not in the CG1CG2G1G2 template of *TesselMania* but in its CCGG template. To get the index finger to look better, I overlapped lines. CCGG is a "degenerate" case of CG1CG2G1G2.

The tip of the finger that touches the thumb is an edge so the tile below is hexagonal and the type is CG1CG2G1G2. If the very short edge was shrunk to zero, the type would be CGCG.

Below are several more examples of standing birds that are type CG1CG2G1G2 though some were not intended to be of that type.

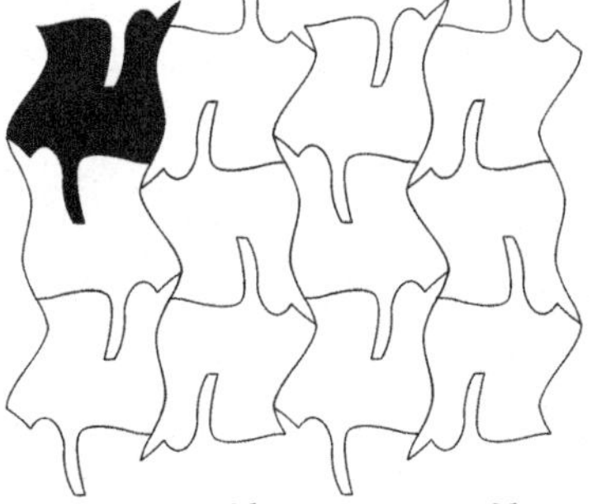

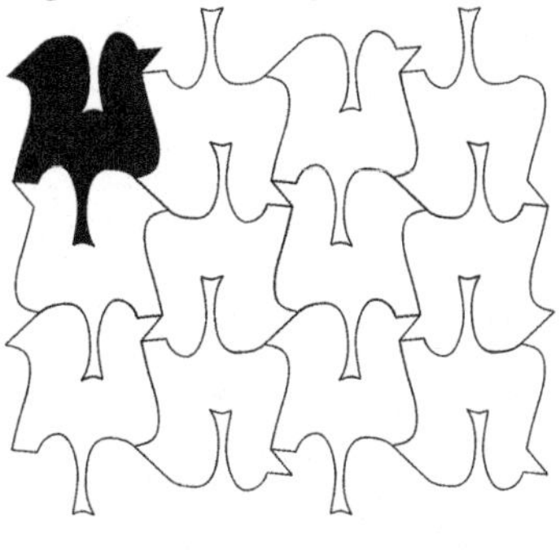

These letter Ts are also CG1CG2G1G2.

Type CG1G2G1G2 (IH27) pgg

If one of the C edges of the CG1CG2G1G2 type shrinks to zero, the result is type CG1G2G1G2, one of five pentagonal Heesch types. The CG1G2G1G2 type, like the CG1CG2G1G2 type, has a translation block of four, but the vertices are different: 43433. This first tiling of standing birds has the C edge on the top of the tail.

The C edge could also be placed on the bill, as it is in the tiles below.

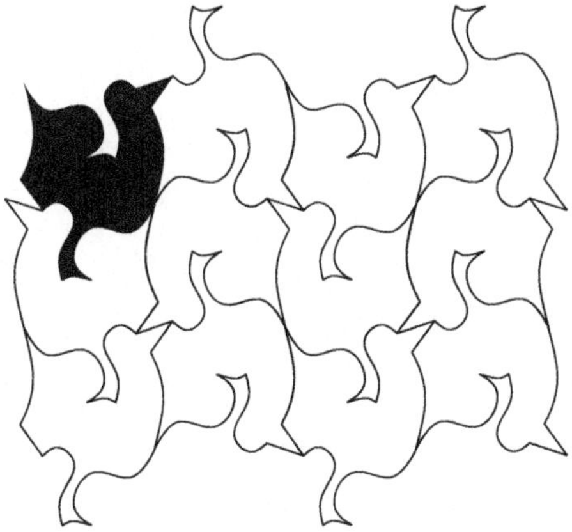

Each tile below is surrounded by five other tiles, which indicates this is a pentagonal type. The straight back edge of the wing is adjacent to itself in the pattern, which indicates that it is a C edge. The pattern is a CG1G2G1G2 type that was created in the G1G2G1G2 template of *TesselManiac!*.

Below are two more examples of flying birds using CG1G2G1G2.

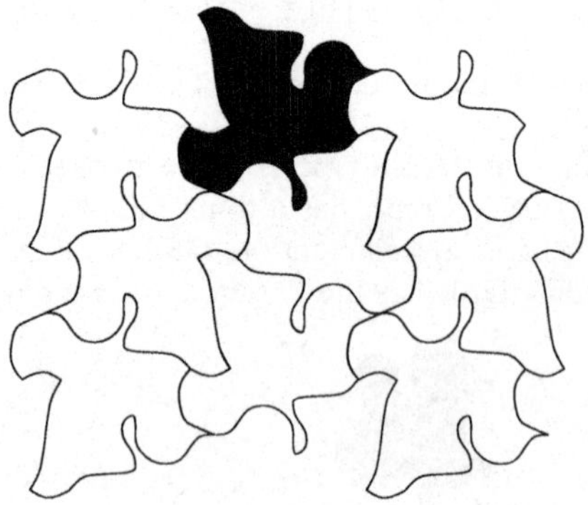

These fish were found by playing with *TesselManiac!*.

Type G1G2G1G2 (IH52) pgg

If the C edges in type CG1CG2G1G2 shrink to zero, the result is type G1G2G1G2. The translation unit for this type is also four, but unlike the CGCG type, bird fronts face bird backs. The base shape of the type is a rectangle. The top of the tile is flipped horizontally to form the bottom and one side is flipped vertically to form the other side.

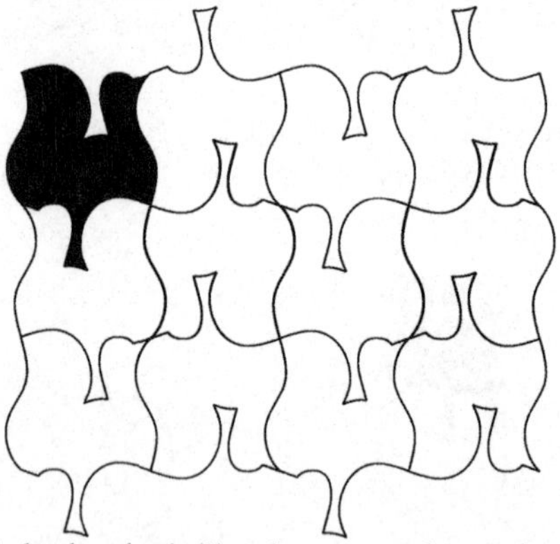

These birds that look like they were drawn by a child are a good illustration of the G1G2G1G2 type.

A reworking of the TGTG bugs produces a G1G2G1G2 version with a little stinger to help see how they are flipped.

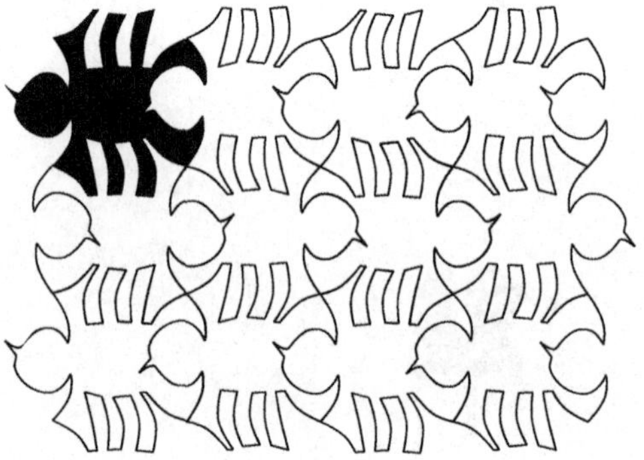

Type CCGG (IH53) pgg

Type CCGG can be derived from type CG1CG2G1G2 by shrinking the G1 pair to zero. It can also be derived from type TCCTGG (discussed below) by shrinking the TT pair to zero.

In this CCGG type tessellation of a standing bird, the front of the bird is kept the same as in the G1G1G2G2 example. The shape of the tile is very similar to the G1G1G2G2 tile but the way the shapes align is different. The translation block has four elements instead of the two that the G1G1G2G2 type has.

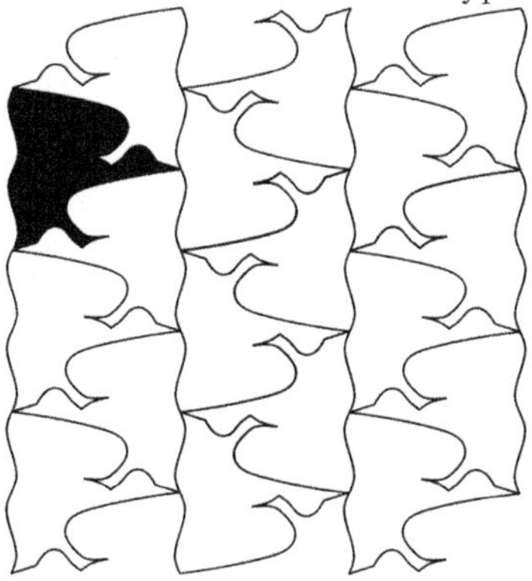

The pattern of eagles standing on the heads of other eagles is a more visually appealing pattern than the one above and is the best example of this type that I have.

The picture below shows a way to create flying birds with type CCGG.

Maybe these are also birds.

Type CGG (IH86) pgg

The same bird shape used with types CCGG and G1G1G2G2 can, with slight modification, be used for the CGG type, one of five Heesch types that is based on a triangle. Like the CCGG type, the translation block has four elements. Six lines converge at each intersection. Because the adjacent GG edges must be equally long, the base polygon for this type is an isosceles triangle.

I have very few CGG types in my specimen book of maze fonts because it does not fit my maze construction set well. I never developed a system to display triangular-celled mazes that have a translation block of four. I can make mazes from these types, but it takes a few extra steps to do so.

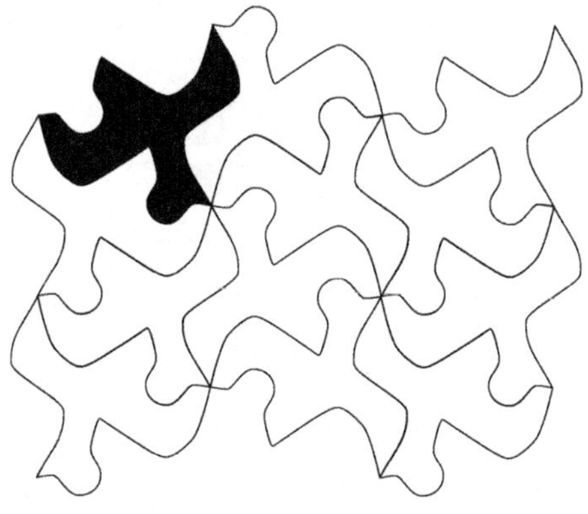

Notice how in the above pattern of flying birds the tiles are arranged at each vertex: two bills, two tips of the left wing, and two tips of the right wing are present and opposite. Below is a very different looking pattern of flying birds that is also CGG.

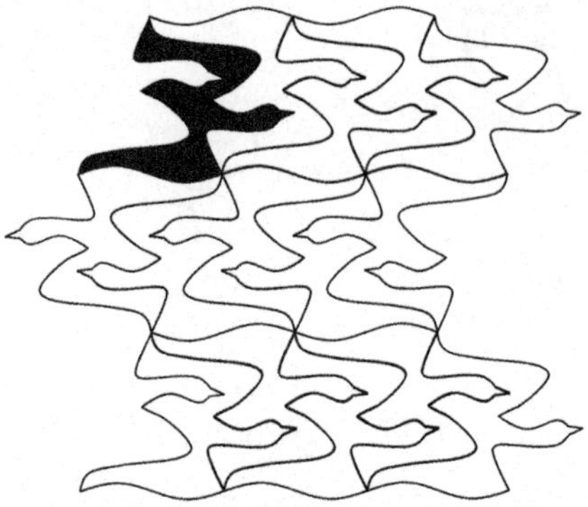

Type CGG can be not only be derived from type CG1CG2G1G2 by shrinking a C edge and the G1 pair to zero, but also from the TCCTGG type by shrinking the TT pair and one of the C edges to zero.

Various animal heads can be formed using this type.

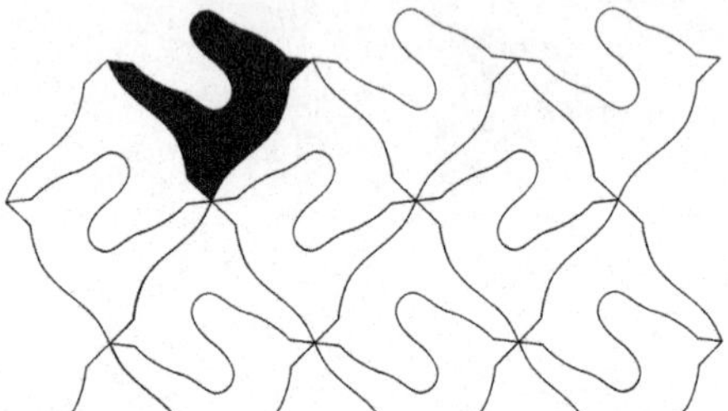

Type TCCTGG (IH5) pgg

A type TCCTGG tessellation has the tile in four different orientations strung out in a 4x1 pattern. It seems to be capable of producing many interesting tiles that tessellate but because a column or row of four does not match well with the requirements of my maze construction set, I avoided it.

The four-by-one translation block can be seen in the birds below. The back of the bird contains the central-rotation edges and the front of the bird contains the two glide edges.

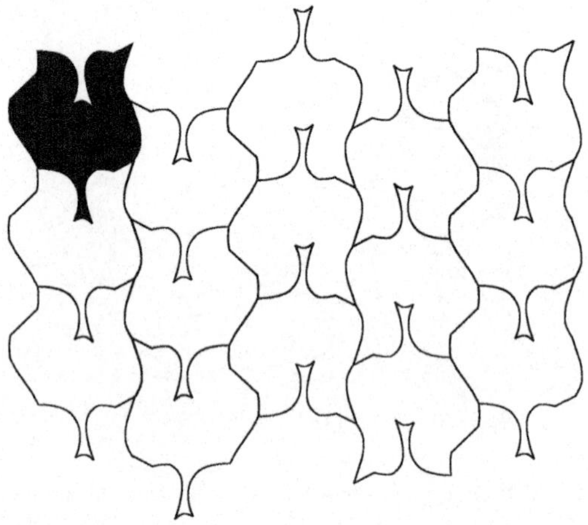

Below the head of the fish has the CC part and the tail the GG part of the tile.

Below is what I consider a moderately successful effort at tessellating hands. It was designed in the CCGG template of *TesselMania* but I pulled up the edge of the index finger line to overlap the edge of the palm and that made the tile hexagonal, a TCCTGG type. Notice that the columns contain the tile in the same orientation while the rows have four orientations before repeating.

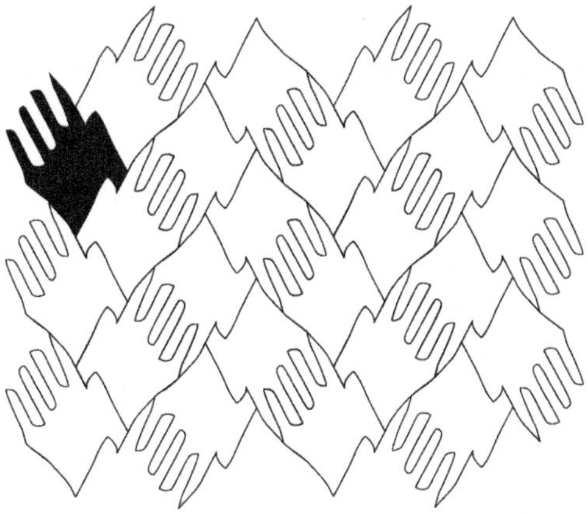

These goats have rather crude legs as did the horses illustrating TCCTCC. In all three cases the legs are formed with center-point rotation. TCCTGG types have a translation block of four in a row (or column depending on how the pattern is oriented). The goat heads are oriented in four different ways.

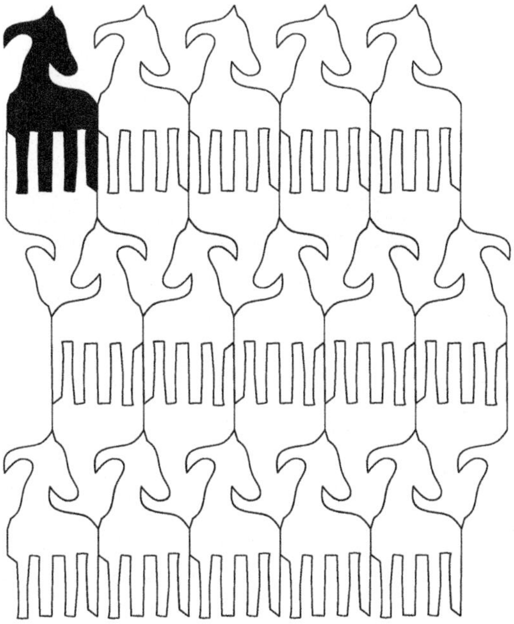

The goats have the heads formed at the GG end of the tile and the feet formed at the CC end. In contrast, the dogs below have the heads formed at the CC end and the feet formed at the GG end of the tile.

As noted above, types CCGG and CGG can be derived from type TCCTGG as well as from CG1CG2G1G2.

Type TCTGG (IH25) pgg

If one of the C edges of the TCCTGG type shrinks to zero, the result is type TCTGG. It also has a translation block of four strung out in a line, a 4x1 block.

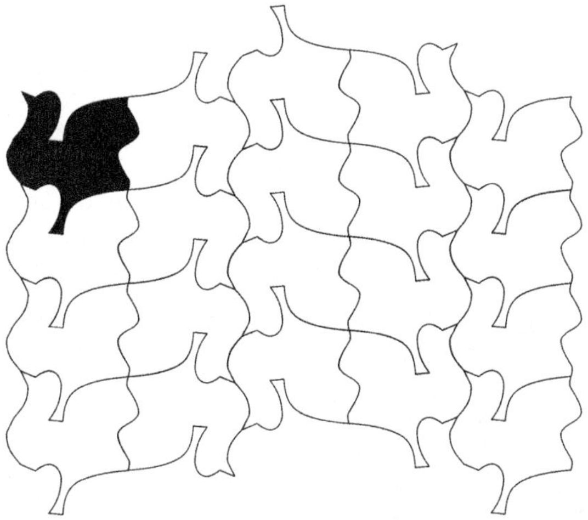

The ducks below are similar to those in the TCTCC section but the bottoms are a little different. Bottom fronts are adjacent to bottom backs. Rather than the direction of ducks alternating row by row, they alternate every two rows. The bottoms of the ducks are GG edges and the Heesch type is TCTGG with a translation unit that is a column of four.

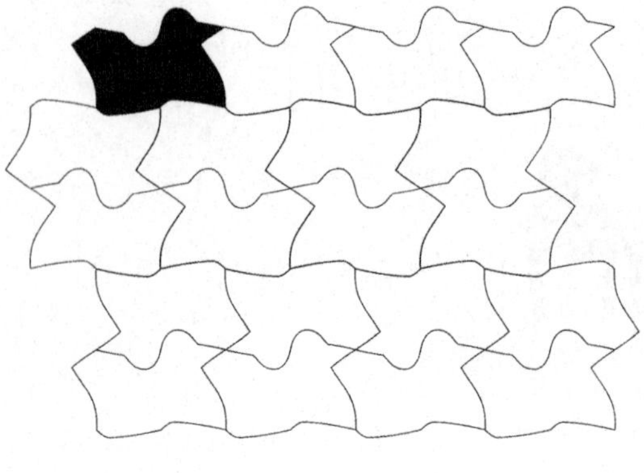

Below is a different attempt to make swimming birds using type TCTGG.

Here are flying birds done with type TCTGG.

Type C3C3C3C3C3C3 (IH7) p3

With type C3C3C3C3C3C3 we encounter corner rotations. Corner rotations have paired edges of the same length. A copy of one edge is rotated to produce a second edge. The number indicates the angle of rotation: 3 indicates an 120° rotation, 4 indicates a 90° rotation, and a 6 indicates a 60° rotation.

These flying birds illustrating type C3C3C3C3C3C3 form a translation block of three. The tile has three pairs of adjacent edges. For each pair one edge is rotated 120° to form the other edge.

Below is a C3C3C3C3C3C3 type that I think resembles a motorcycle rider without a motorcycle.

The simple tiles of type C3C3C3C3C3C3 can combined to form a larger C3C3C3C3C3C3 tile.

Type C3C3C3C3 (IH33) p3

In type C3C3C3C3 edge one is rotated 120° to form edge two and edge three is also rotated 120° to form edge four. This is the only four-edged tile that has a translation unit of three and a valence of 6363.

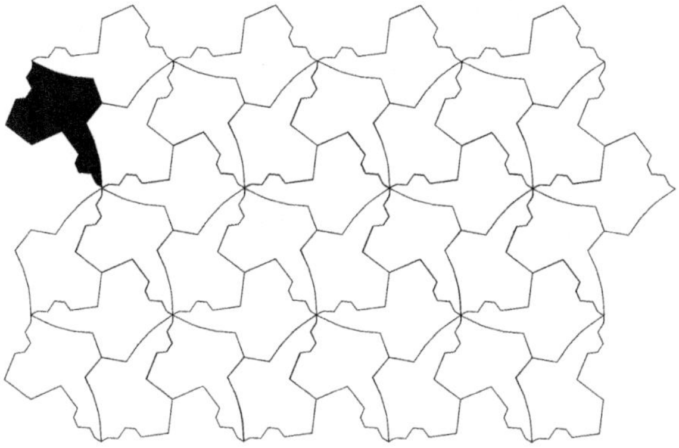

I found that I could use patterns built with this type for mazes by fitting them into the slots I used for triangle-celled mazes. The key was realizing that the two sets of lines converging at each of the three-line nodes not only made up the entire pattern but that they could be broken in a way that allowed passages similar to breaking the walls of triangles.

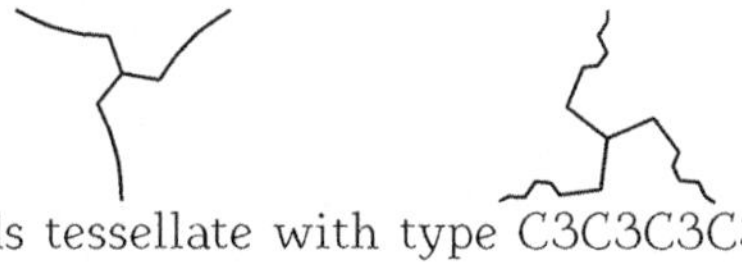

Horse heads tessellate with type C3C3C3C3.

A nesting-hen pattern is made up of these two segments.

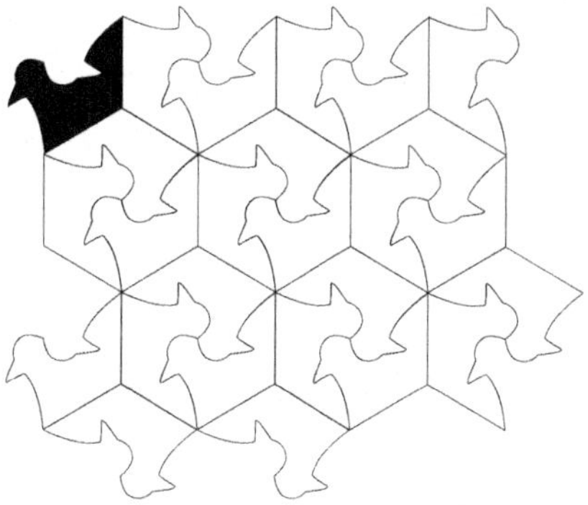

Puzzle pieces or dollar signs?

With a lot of imagination you might see dragons in these tiles.

Type CC4C4C4C4 (IH28) p4

The pentagonal type CC4C4C4C4 is part of a family of three types. Type C4C4C4C4 results when the C edge is reduced to zero and CC4C4 results when one of the C4 pairs is reduced to zero. All three family members have translation blocks of four.

The C edge in this type CC4C4C4C4 pattern of soaring birds is in the tail. If it shrunk to zero, you would get a pattern of type C4C4C4C4 and there is a very similar soaring-birds pattern pictured later in the book.

Like the design above, if the C side is shrunk to zero, one can obtain a very similar-looking tile that is C4C4C4C4.

This next pattern was an attempt to tessellate boots.

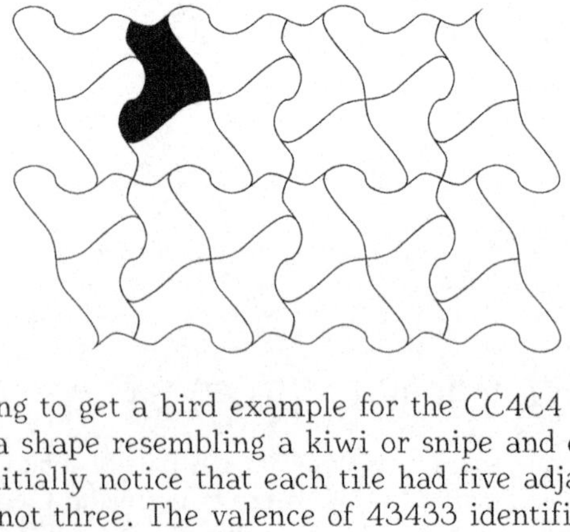

Trying to get a bird example for the CC4C4 type, I got a shape resembling a kiwi or snipe and did not initially notice that each tile had five adjacent tiles, not three. The valence of 43433 identifies it as a CC4C4C4C4 type.

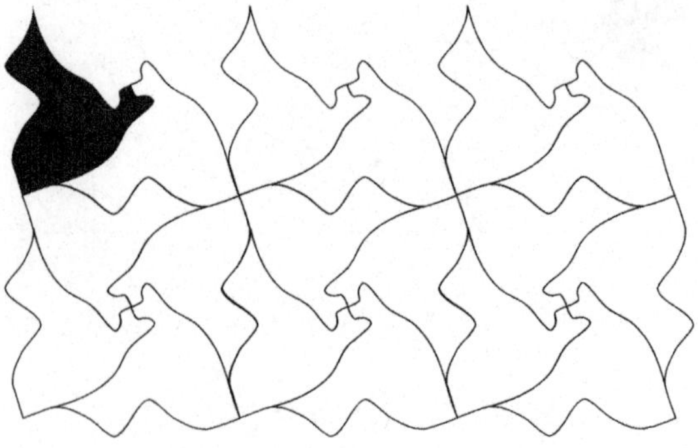

The pattern of axes was created in the same way.

Type CC4C4C4C4 provided many letter tessellations. Below is a letter shape formed with the CC4C4C4C4 type that was not needed later in the book where letter tessellations are discussed.

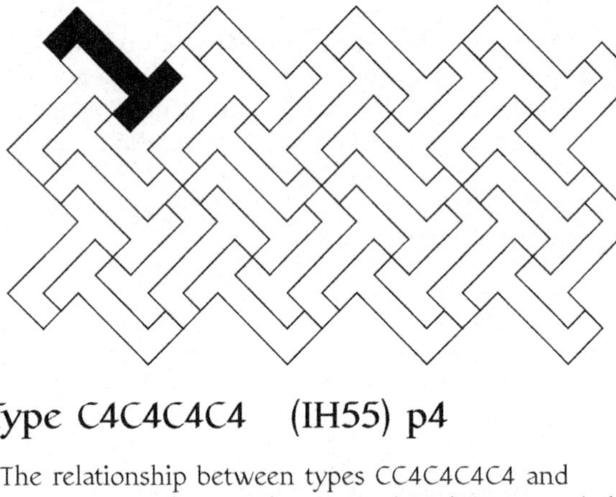

Type C4C4C4C4 (IH55) p4

The relationship between types CC4C4C4C4 and C4C4C4C4 can be seen by comparing the pattern below with the similar one above. In the one below the C edge has been eliminated but the other edges are the same.

The base geometric form for the C4C4C4C4 type is a square. Edge one is rotated 90° to form edge two and edge three is also rotated 90° to form edge four. Like the CC4C4C4C4 type, the C4C4C4C4 type has a translation block of four.

Here is an attempt to make lizards using this type.

These dogs were created using the C4C4C4C4 template in *TesselMania*.

I like this shape because of the pattern of circles it creates when it tessellates as type C4C4C4C4.

Type CC4C4 (IH79) p4

The base shape of the CC4C4 type is an isosceles right triangle. In the swimming bird pattern below, the bottom of the bird is rotated 90° to form the front of the bird. The hypothenuse segment forms the back of the bird and because it is a C segment, the back of one bird forms the back of the adjacent bird. The CC4C4 type is the only Heesch type with a vertex with eight converging lines.

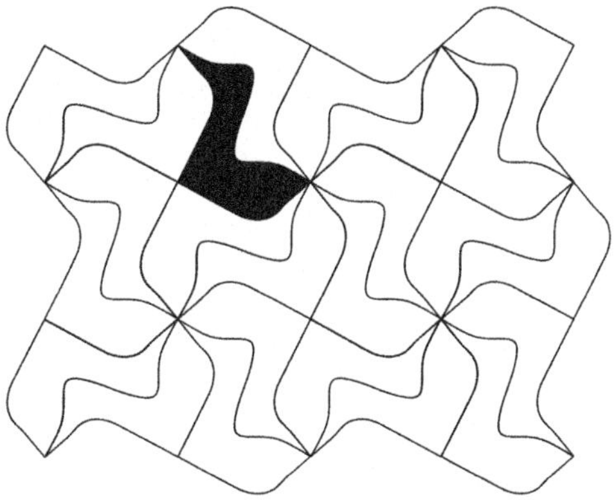

Below are more CC4C4 birds:

Below are two horse tilings that illustrate CC4C4.

Type CC3C3C6C6 (IH21) p6

Type CC3C3C6C6 is the other main family member that has five adjacent tiles, not six. There are three other types that can be derived from it.

Six birds in the tiling below pivot around a common point, the result of the C6 pair in the type CC3C3C6C6. Note the valence is 63333, which is unique to a CC3C3C6C6 tiling.

In this next flying bird pattern the C or central-point-rotation edge is the front edge of the longer wing.

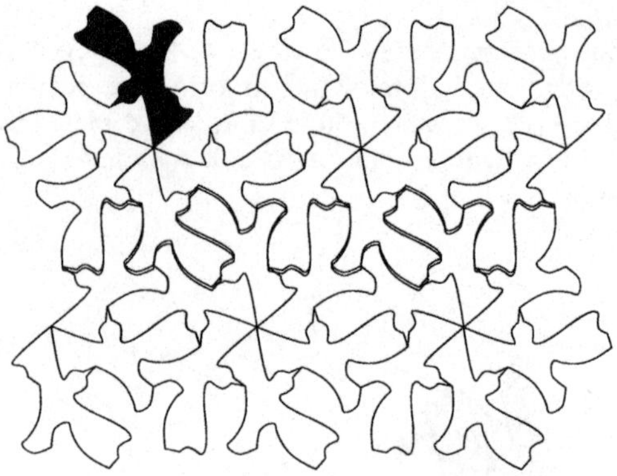

Below the bird beaks are the center of C6 rotation.

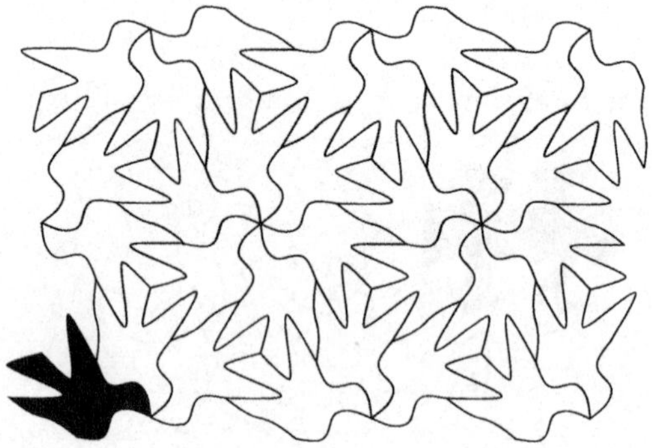

Below is a similar-looking tiling, but notice that the C edge forms a different part of the bird.

Next is a tiling of swimming ducks. Combining two can give a flying duck, but this shape does not tessellate by itself.

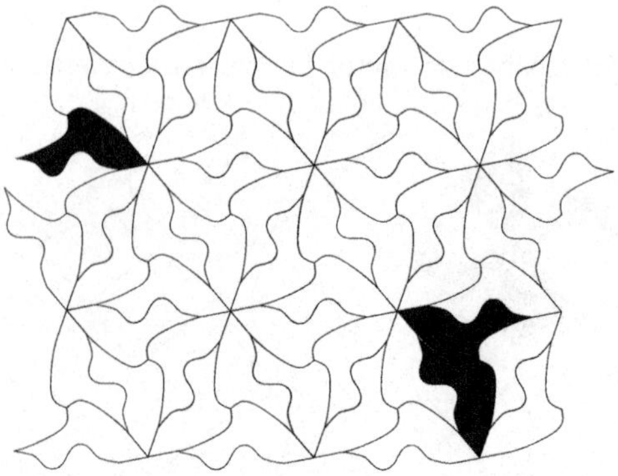

In the swans below the heads are formed with C6 edges. The C3 edges are short. The C edge forms the back bottom of each bird.

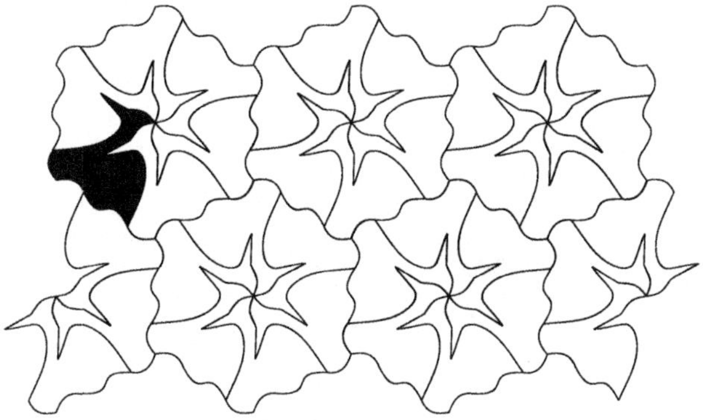

Here is a tiling that I used for mazes. What I liked about it was that three of the tiles form a triangular tile of type CCC with identical edges and a block of six of them form a hexagonal figure with identical edges.

Type C3C3C6C6 (IH31) p6

The swimming swans shown below use the same C6 edges as those used to illustrate CC3C3C6C6. The C edge has disappeared and the C3 edges are formed to suggest feet.

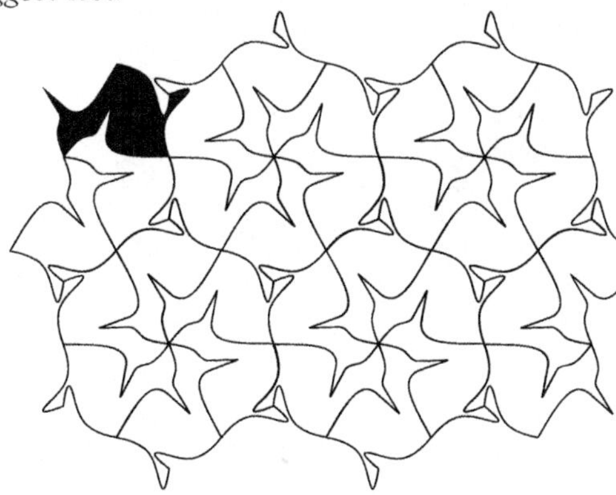

Below is a C3C3C6C6 flying bird pattern similar to the one used to illustrate CC6C6. It is the only four-edged tile with a translation unit of six and the only four-edged tile with a valence of 6434.

This next pattern illustrating type C3C3C6C6 has standing birds but they are not standing on the backs of other birds.

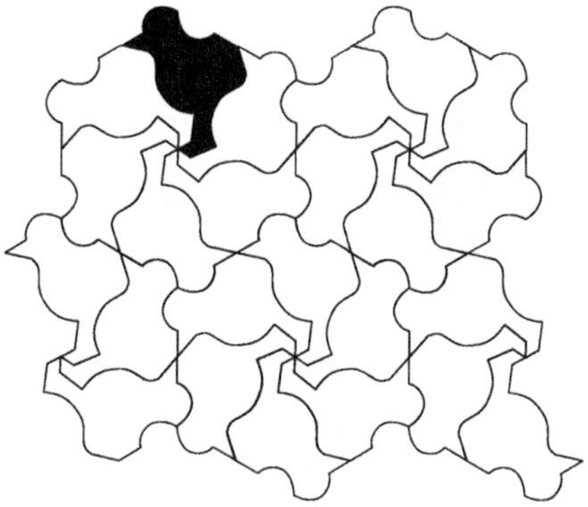

In the pattern below the two C6 edges are kept straight. You can see that they meet at a vertex with six lines converging. The two C3 edges are shaped and they meet at a vertex with three lines converging. If we take a block of six with C3 edges forming the outer edges, we have a shape that is TTTTTT with all edges formed identically with central rotation. A group of three tiles with C6 edges forming the edge makes a triangle.

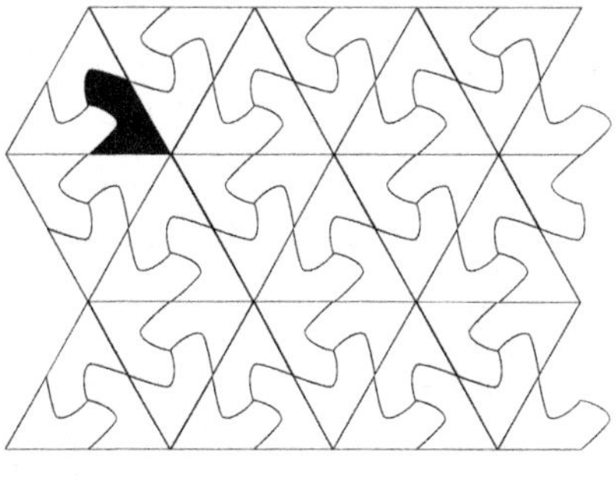

I primarily used this type in geometric tilings such as the next pattern of chevrons. Twelve C3 edges form a regular hexagon and six C6 edges form a type CCC tile with all edges identical.

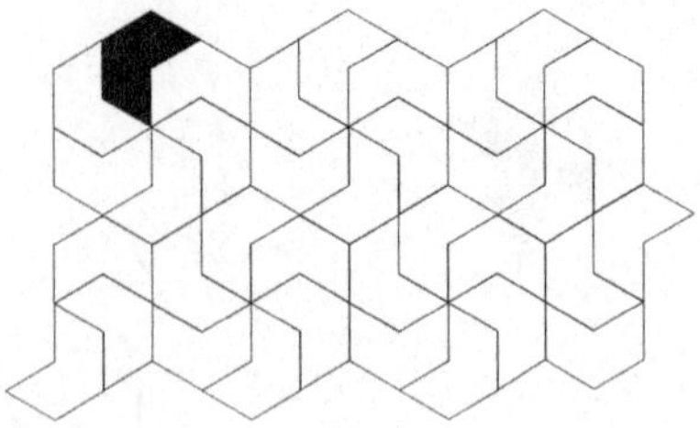

Type CC6C6 (IH88) p6

The CC6C6 type is one of three with all vertices of six, but it is the only triangular type with a translation block of six.

The swans below keep the head shape of the swans of two previous types, but the bottom is formed with a C edge.

In the birds below the tail end of the bird is rotated 60° to from the top of the bird. The bottom of the bird is the C edge.

Below is a different pattern of flying birds.

This unusual pattern keeps the C edge of CC6C6 tile straight and shows that the CC6C6 type can be seen as arising from cutting a regular hexagon into six isosceles triangles.

These chairs not only recline but also tessellate.

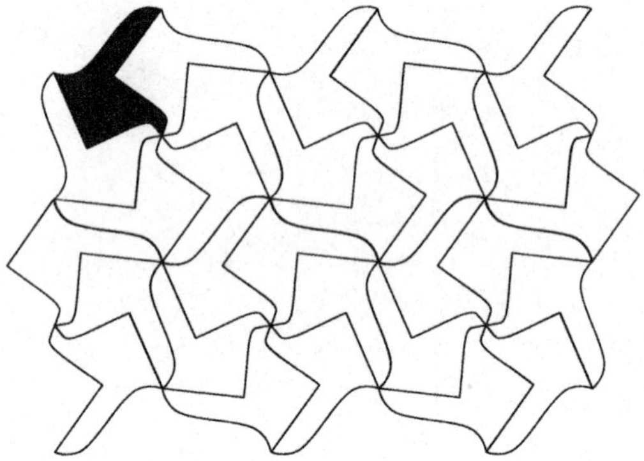

Type CC3C3 (IH39) p6

Getting interesting shapes from the CC3C3 type is challenging and I have not found a convincing bird tile. The CC3C3 type is the only Heesch type with a vertex of twelve converging lines. With imagination, this tiling could be of swimmers or mermaids.

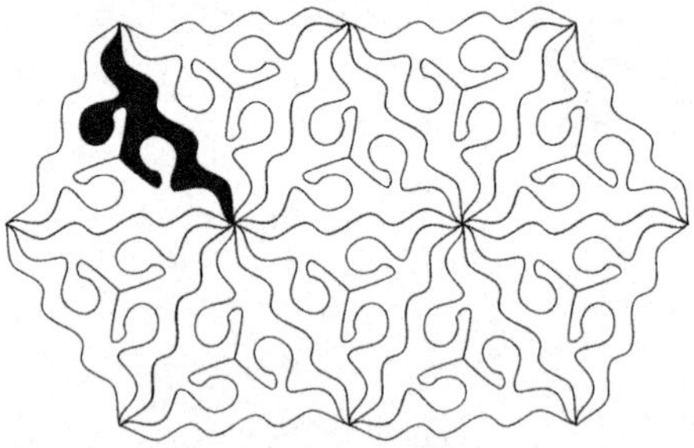

The tile in the next pattern could be a dinosaur.

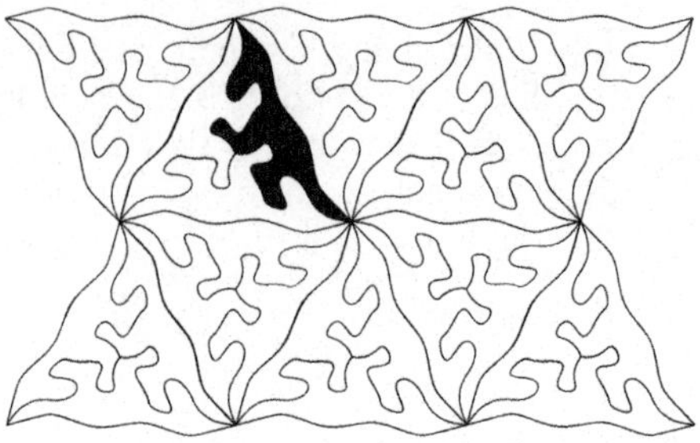

Wallpaper Group	Hexagonal	Pentagonal	Quadrilateral	Triangular
p1	TTTTTT		TTTT	
p2	TCCTCC		CCCC	CCC
		TCTCC	TCTC	
p3	C3C3C3C3C3C3		C3C3C3C3	
p4		CC4C4C4C4	C4C4C4C4	CC4C4
p6		CC3C3C6C6	C3C3C6C6	CC6C6
				CC3C3
pg	TG1G1TG2G2		G1G1G2G2	
	TG1G2TG2G1		TGTG	
pgg	TCCTGG	TCTGG	CCGG	CGG
	CG1CG2G1G2		CGCG	
		CG1G2G1G2	G1G2G1G2	

A leaf on a thorned twig fits CC3C3 and makes a pleasing pattern.

We have now visited all 28 Heesch types. We have avoided tiles that have mirror or rotational symmetry but will visit them in the next section.

In addition to the Heesch type, the headings have included the isohedral class (the topic of the next section) and the symmetry group. All members of a Heesch family share the same symmetry group as the table above indicates.

Some Notes on Shapes

A template shape is the shape of the polygon obtained by connecting the vertices of a tile with straight lines. There are regularities in template shape in some of the Heesch types. These regularities occur because, except for central-rotation moves, tessellation moves are paired. For pairs to match, they need to be equally long and often positioned in a certain way. All TT pairs must match in length and be parallel to each other. The GG pairs must be equally long but do not in most cases need to be positioned in predetermined ways. The C3, C4, and C6 edges must have a match of the same length and be set at a predetermined angle.

These restrictions force certain template shapes. Among the five triangle-based types, four of the five must be isosceles triangles. The two equal legs of the CC6C8 type meet at a 60° angle, those of the CC4C4 type meet at a 90° angle, those of a CC3C3 type meet at a 120° angle, and those of a CGG type can meet at any angle. The CCC type can be any triangle.

The eleven quadrilateral types are not as orderly. Three of them have completely rigid template shapes. C4C4C4C4 must be a square. C3C3C3C3 must be a rhombus (a parallelogram with equal edges) with opposite angles of 120°, which implies that the other two angles must be 60°. The C3C3C6C6 type has one pair of equally long adjacent edges meeting at 120° and the other pair meeting at 60°, which implies that when the vertices are connected with straight lines, the other two angles will be right angles.

A square is a special case of a rectangle and a rectangle is a special case of a parallelogram. The template shape of the G1G2G1G2 type is a rectangle. The three types with TT edges, TTTT, TCTC, and TGTG, all have template shapes that are parallelograms. Opposite edges are equally long and parallel.

The G1G1G2G2 type has one set of adjacent edges equal to each other and also the other set of adjacent edges equal to each other. Imagine an isosceles triangle with a button on the midpoint of the base. The button can be pushed toward the top giving us an arrowhead shape, or it can be pulled away from the top giving us a kite shape. In both cases the template has a symmetry that the shaped figure will lack. The template shapes of the CGCG and CCGG types are only lightly restricted. Two opposite edges of the CGCG type must be equally long, while two adjacent edges of the CCGG type must be equally long. Finally, there are no restrictions at all on the CCCC type. It can be based on any quadrilateral.

Describing the shapes of the various pentagonal and hexagonal types is as tedious as reading them. Here is the short version. Whenever there are TT edges, you say that an opposite pair must be of equal length and parallel. Say that all the matched GG pairs must be equally long. For the C3, C4, and C6 edges, say that the adjacent pairs must have the same length and be separated by the predetermined angle. You do not have to say anything about the C edges because they can be of any length and they do not match another edge.

Isohedral

When a tiling is isohedral, all the tiles are in the same symmetry group. An obvious example of a tiling that has multiple symmetry groups is a tiling that has two shapes, such as the octagon and square tiling below. Each octagon has eight neighbors, four octagons and four squares, and each square has four neighbors, all octagons.

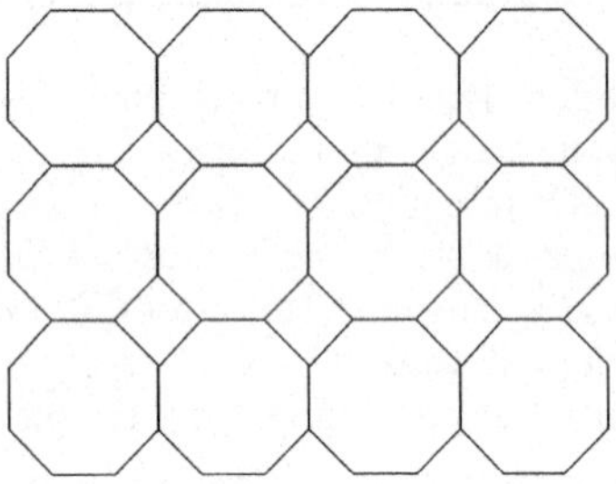

Tiles of the same shape can also be from different symmetry groups. A common example is the pattern of rectangles below. The middle brick in each trio has four neighbors and the end bricks have six neighbors. With rotations, flips, and slides, the pattern can be exactly reproduced with any end brick in exactly the same position as any other end brick. However, there is no way to reproduce the pattern exactly with flips, rotations, and slides so that any end brick will be in same position as any middle brick. End bricks and middle bricks play different roles in the tiling because they are different symmetry classes. This tiling is not isohedral.

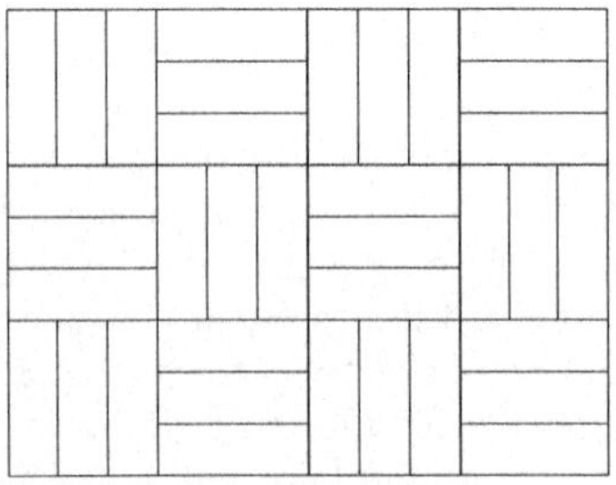

Arrangement Matters

Shape alone does not determine Heesch type; arrangement matters. Compare the way the geese are arranged in the top part of the pattern with the way that they are arranged in the bottom part. In the three top rows the tails of the birds reverse each row while in the three bottom rows they are the same row by row. The translation block in the top four rows is four while the translation block in the bottom four rows is only two. The pattern at the top is CGG while the pattern bottom is CCC. The shapes are the same but the top birds are rotated and flipped to fit together while those on the bottom are only rotated to fit.

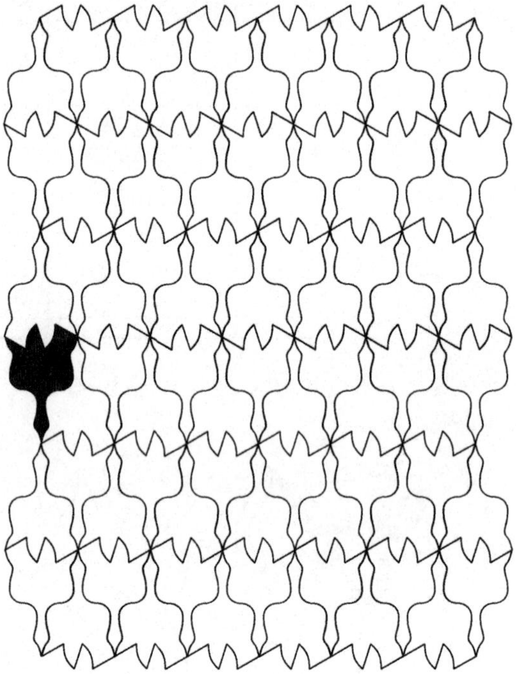

One of the features of edges with central rotation is that the edge can play any role, not just the role of a C edge. All of the Heesch types can be formed only using edges with central rotation.

The tile below has the vertices of a square with all edges formed with identical central rotation. Naturally it tiles as a CCCC type. (In the next section we will meet this kind of tiling as IH69.)

The tiling below shows the shape in a CGCG type. Two of the edges act as C edges but two others act as G edges. When a C edge is mirrored, it is also glided.

Below the same tiles as above are arranged with no edges acting as C edges. In the next section we will meet this pattern as an IH71 tiling.

This tiling was given as an example of type TCTGG.

It can be rearranged to illustrate TG1G1TG2G2.

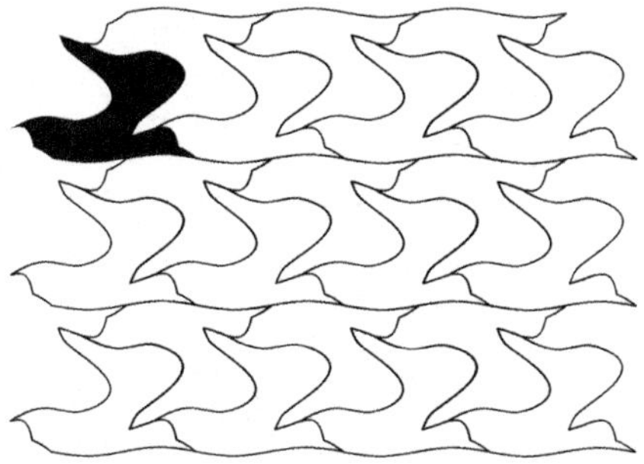

In this case each half of the edge with center-point rotation reflects over its midpoint, allowing each half to act as a part of a pair of G edges.

A few years ago I developed a pattern that resembled a clasping hand or a fist that is clenching another fist. I do not recall the process by which I came to this pattern, but I liked it because it fit into a narrative I had for one of my maze books. It is a CCCC type with each edge different and one edge left straight.

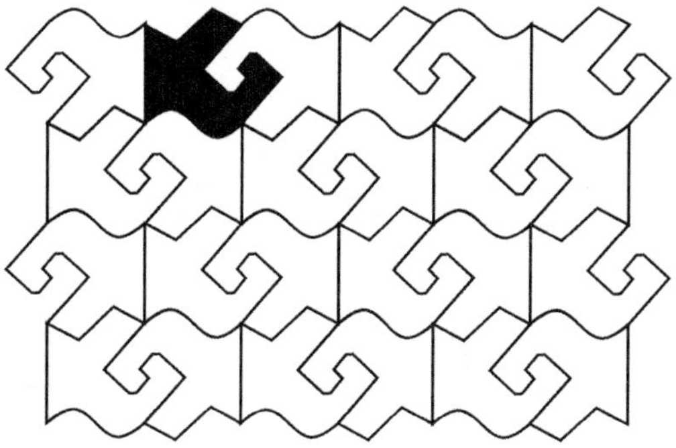

Playing with the design, I gave the top and bottom edges the same shape, a central-rotation shape, and flipped it as if it were a glide edge. As a result the tiles could still fit together as they had in the original pattern, with a translation block of two, but they could also fit together in a new way, with a translation unit of four. In that pattern they were arranged as a CGCG type, shown in the bottom two rows.

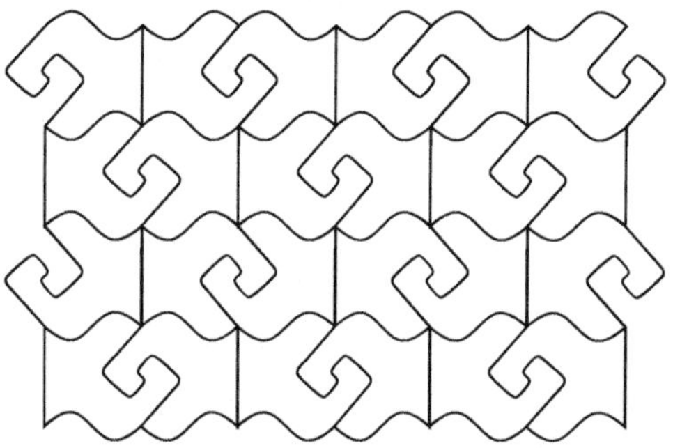

When I was trying to find tessellating letters of the alphabet (described later) I modified these shapes a bit to get the letter T. It also fits in two patterns. (The CCCC tiling is in the top two rows and the CGCG tiling is in the bottom two.)

There are two more ways to arrange the clenched-fist tile. In the image below notice that the tile is reflected or flipped, not rotated, over the straight edge, so the tiling cannot be a Heesch type. Also, sometimes the bottom of the thumb is adjacent to another thumb but sometimes it is adjacent to the top of the fist. Because edges do not have a single pairing throughout the tiling, the tiling is not isohedral but *anisohedral.* (However, the tile itself is isohedral because it can fit into isohedral tilings.)

Eliminating the straight edges and combining pairs of adjacent tiles yields the second tiling shown above. It has six edges, all formed with central rotation and is a CG1CG2G1G2 type. The clasping edge is the G1G1 pair. The C edges are where two tops of fists are adjacent and where two thumbs are adjacent. The G2 edges are where top of fist is adjacent to bottom of fist. The CG1CG2G1G2 tiling has a translation block of four but this tiling appears to have a translation block of only two. The disappearance of two of the block is due to the symmetry of the tile. Because the right side mirrors the left side, a flip over a horizontal line appears to give the same result as a rotation of 180°.

This tile can also be arranged as a TCCTCC tiling, shown below. The translated edges are arranged in a diagonal running from lower left to upper right.

When the tile in the TCCTCC arrangement is bisected along its axis of symmetry, it forms a slightly different anisohedral tiling. Both have the same translation block of four in a row, but the ways in which the row is moved to form additional rows are different.

Below is a tiling of a stylized butterfly formed in the same way as the hexagonal tiles above. All edges are center-point rotation and two side edges are formed identically and mirror each other. The other four edges are identical to each other and each is glided vertically and horizontally. (A different version of this tiling is on the copyright page.)

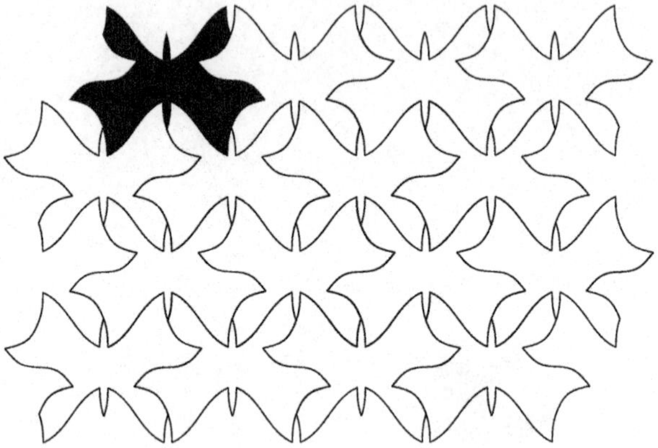

Below is the same tile in a TCCTCC tiling.

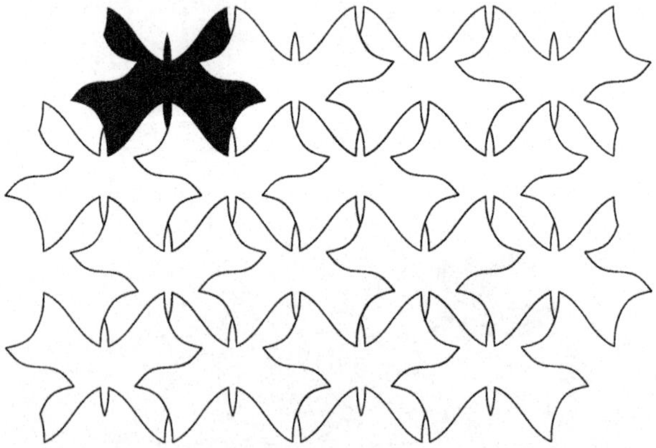

About one sixth of the outline determines the rest. These tiles seem to be hypersymmetric, that is, the tiles have symmetry that the tiling does not have. They cannot be created easily with *Tesselmaniac!.*

Isohedral Classes of Grünbaum and Shepard

IH1 Heesch TTTTTT p1
IH2 Heesch TG1G1TG2G2 pg
IH3 Heesch TG1G2TG2G1 pg
IH4 Heesch TCCTCC p2
IH5 Heesch TCCTGG pgg
IH6 Heesch CG1CG2G1G2 pgg
IH7 Heesch C3C3C3C3C3C3 p3
IH8 RestrictedH TTTTTT p2
IH9 RestrictedH TGGTGG pgg
IH10 RestrictedH TTTTTT p3
IH11 RestrictedH TTTTTT p6
IH12 *RestrictedH TG1G1TG2G2 cm
IH13 *RestrictedH TCCTCC pmg
IH14 2 of 6 fixed cm
IH15 2 of 6 fixed pmg
IH16 2 of 6 fixed p31m
IH17 2 of 6 fixed cmm
IH18 RestrictedH TTTTTT p31m
IH19 6 of 6 fixed p3m1
IH20 6 of 6 fixed p6m
IH21 Heesch CC3C3C6C6 p6
IH22 1 of 5 fixed cm
IH23 Heesch TCTCC p2
IH24 1 of 5 fixed pmg
IH25 Heesch TCTGG pgg
IH26 3 of 5 fixed cmm
IH27 Heesch CG1G2G1G2 pgg
IH28 Heesch CC4C4C4C4 p4
IH29 1 of 5 fixed p4g
IH30 2 of 4 fixed p31m
IH31 Heesch C3C3C6C6 p6
IH32 4 of 4 fixed p6m
IH33 Heesch C3C3C3C3 p3
IH34 RestrictedH C3C3C3C3 p6
IH35 4 of 4 fixed p3m1
IH36 *RestrictedH C3C3C3C3 p31m
IH37 4 of 4 fixed p6m
IH38 1 of 3 fixed p31m
IH39 Heesch CC3C3 p6
IH40 3 of 3 fixed p6m
IH41 Heesch TTTT p1
IH42 2 of 4 fixed pm
IH43 Heesch TGTG pg
IH44 Heesch G1G1G2G2 pg
IH45 2 of 4 fixed cm
IH46 Heesch CCCC p2
IH47 Heesch TCTC p2
IH48 4 of 4 fixed pmm
IH49 2 of 4 fixed pmg
IH50 1 of 4 fixed pmg
IH51 Heesch CGCG pgg
IH52 Heesch G1G2G1G2 pgg
IH53 Heesch CCGG pgg
IH54 3 of 4 fixed cmm
IH55 Heesch C4C4C4C4 p4
IH56 2 of 4 fixed p4g
IH57 RestrictedH CCCC/TTTT p2
IH58 2 of 4 fixed pmg
IH59 RestrictedH G1G1G2G2 pgg
IH60 4 of 4 fixed cmm
IH61 RestrictedH C4C4C4C4 p4
IH62 RestrictedH CCCC p4
IH63 4 of 4 fixed p4g
IH64 2 of 4 fixed pm
IH65 4 of 4 fixed pmm
IH66 *RestrictedH TCTC pmg
IH67 2 of 4 fixed cmm
IH68 *RestrictedH G1G2G2G1 cm
IH69 *RestrictedH CCCC pmg
IH70 4 of 4 fixed p4m
IH71 *RestrictedH C4C4C4C4 p4g
IH72 4 of 4 fixed pmm
IH73 RestrictedH C4C4C4C4 p4g
IH74 *RestrictedH CCCC cmm
IH75 4 of 4 fixed p4m
IH76 4 of 4 fixed p4m
IH77 3 of 3 fixed p6m
IH78 2 of 3 fixed cmm
IH79 Heesch CC4C4 p4
IH80 3 of 3 fixed p4m
IH81 1 of 3 fixed p4g
IH82 3 of 3 fixed p4m
IH83 1 of 3 fixed cm
IH84 Heesch CCC p2
IH85 1 of 3 fixed pmg
IH86 Heesch CGG pgg
IH87 3 of 3 fixed p3m1
IH88 Heesch CC6C6 p6
IH89 3 of 3 fixed p31m
IH90 RestrictedH CCC p6
IH91 1 of 3 fixed cmm
IH92 3 of 3 fixed p6m
IH93 3 of 3 fixed p6m

(The table and the explanations rely on information from the website freespace.virgin.net/tom.mclean/index.html. The website seems to have disappeared but is mirrored as of September 2016 at www.jaapsch.net/tilings/mclean/index.html.)

III. The Isohedral Classes

The Heesch types do not include all possible isohedral patterns. In the Heesch classification all edges must be shapeable, which eliminates reflections over an edge because reflection over an edge requires that the edge be a straight line. The complete classification of isohedral tessellations—tilings composed of identically shaped and sized tiles that cover the plane with no overlaps or gaps with the tile having the same set of adjacent neighbors throughout the pattern—was developed by Branko Grünbaum and Geoffrey Shepard in their book *Tilings and Patterns* (Freeman, 1987).

In examining symmetry and Heesch types we have seen that designs that appear very different from one another can be classified as belonging to the same group. The starting point for Grünbaum and Shepard in enumerating isohedral classes is that all isohedral tilings can be reduced to topological equivalents of the eleven Laves tiles. If after transforming a tiling by stretching and bending the edges, the tiling still has the same vertices, number of edges, and the same neighbors on each edge, the new tiling is topologically equivalent to the old one. In a Laves tiling the angles at each vertex are equal, so a vertex of three will have angles of 120°, a vertex of four will have angles of 90°, etc.

Grünbaum and Shepard begin their analysis by marking each Laves tile with indicators of rotational and/or reflective symmetry. Using these indicators they letter the sides to show whether or how symmetry will force restrictions on the edges. They call this lettering the "tile symbols." A tile with no symmetry is lettered $a^+b^+c^+$ etc. up to f^+ for a hexagonal tile. If the tile has rotational symmetry, a letter or letters will repeat; $a^+a^+a^+a^+$ is a square-based tile with fourfold rotational symmetry (which requires that all edges be formed identically). If a tile has reflection, the sign changes; $a^+b^+b^-a^-$ is a tile with mirror reflection over a diagonal. If a letter has no sign, it reflects over its middle; abab would be a square- or rectangle-based tile with both vertical and horizontal reflection over the midpoints of the edges.

Grünbaum and Shepard explain in some detail how they mark the square. The square can have eight symmetries. It can have no symmetry at all, twofold rotational symmetry, fourfold rotational symmetry, reflection over one pair of opposite edges, reflection over both pairs of opposite edges, reflection over one diagonal, reflection over both diagonals, and reflection over both diagonals and both pairs of opposite edges. Each case yields a different type symbol. In order they are $a^+b^+c^+d^+$; $a^+b^+a^+b^+$; $a^+a^+a^+a^+$,; ab^+cb^-; abab; $a^+b^+b^-a^-$; $a^+a^-a^+a^-$; and aaaa.

Grünbaum and Shepard then see what sequences of letters in adjacent tiles, the "adjacency symbols", result in a consistent pattern. If an a^+ edge is next to a b^+ edge in one place, it must always be next to the b^+ or else the pattern will not work. From this they find 93 pairings of tile and adjacency symbols, which they call the "incidence symbols", that work. A few simple rules determine the shape of edges. If a signed letter is adjacent to the same signed letter (a^+ next to a^+), the edge has center-point rotation (an S edge). If an unsigned (unoriented) letter is next to a different unsigned letter (a next to c), the edge reflects over its midpoint (a C edge). If a signed letter is next to a different signed letter (b^- next to c^+), the edge is an asymmetric edge (a J edge). In other cases (a^+ next to a^-, a next to a) the edge is a straight line. Shared edges must be identically formed. Except for flips over straight lines, their classification has no additional ways to form tilings than those used in the Heesch types. However, symmetry allows some of their classes to simultaneously fit multiple Heesch types.

Twenty-one of the 93 classes required all edges be straight, resulting in grids of squares, rectangles, and other simple geometric shapes. Some look identical if they do not have interior markings and most of the 21 are ignored below. Twenty-eight are the familiar Heesch types. Another twenty fit Heesch categories with tiles that have reflective or rotational symmetry. The other twenty-four have some lines that are shapeable and others that are unshapeable straight lines. Some of these twenty-four still fit Heesch types because their straight lines are or can be viewed as edges of central rotation or translation.

The table at the start of this section gives some basic information about the 93 isohedral classes. The letters at the end of each entry in the table indicate the symmetry class of the tiling. The ordering is based on the valence of the tiling. If there are six vertices with three lines converging at each, which is true of all the six-edged tilings, the notation is 3^6. Each group corresponds to a Laves tiling.

3^6	IH1-IH20
$3^4.6$	IH21
$3^3.4^2$	IH22-IH26
$3^2.4.3.2$	IH27-IH29
3.4.6.4	IH30-IH32
3.6.3.6	IH33-IH37
3.12^2	IH38-IH40
4^4	IH41-IH76
4.6.12	IH77
4.8^2	IH78-IH82
6^3	IH83-IH93

TesselManiac! gives both the Heesch type for each of its templates and also the isohedral class (IH) number. In addition to the 28 Heesch types, *TesselManiac!* has templates for eight restricted Heesch types that have mirror symmetry, that is, one half of the tile is a mirror image of the other half. These eight are indicated with an asterisk in the table. Most of the twelve restricted Heesch types that lack templates in *TesselManiac!* can be formed using *TesselManiac!* by combining tiles of other types and ignoring interior lines.

In unrestricted Heesch types, one half of the tile determines the whole tile. In the restricted types less than one half of the outline determines the rest. In many it is one-fourth determining the whole (one-sixth for hexagonal types), but it can be as little as one-eighth or even one-twelfth.

In trying to make sense of these isohedral classes, I realized that whenever a tiling had mirror symmetry that was shared by the tiles themselves, a bisection of the tiles and tiling (or in one case a trisection) would generate another tiling that had an isohedral class:

IH12 → IH22 (cm)
IH13 → IH24 (pmg)
IH14 → IH45 (cm)
IH15 → IH49 (pmg)
IH17 → IH26 → IH54 (cmm)
IH17 → IH67 → IH54 (cmm)
IH18 → IH16 (trisection)→ IH30 (p31m)
IH36 → IH38 (p31m)
IH64 → IH42 (IH64 also fits IH42) (pm)
IH66 → IH50 (pmg)
IH68 → IH83 (cm)
IH69 → IH85 (pmg)
IH71 → IH81 (p4g)
IH73 → IH29 → IH56 (p4g)
IH74 → IH91 → IH78 (cmm)
?? → IH58 (pmg)

This table includes all isohedral classes with mirroring and also all classes with both straight and shapeable edges. Also, none of rightmost tilings fit Heesch types but all the others can be made to fit the Heesch classification. Ten other totally shapeable isohedral classes have tiles with rotational symmetry. The discussion that follows will examine the isohedral types in the order they are in the above table and then continue with the ten in which the tiles have only rotational symmetry.

(The mystery of IH58 will be explained below. An appendix summarizes many of the connections between classes and types.)

IH12 & IH22 (cm)

This flying bird is an example of isohedral class IH12, a six-edged tile with one pair of opposite edges formed with central symmetry (head and tail of the bird) and the other four edges all shaped the same (the rest of the bird). It can be seen as a special case of type TG1G1TG2G2 with the G2 edges mirrored images of the G1 edges (or *vise versa*). Because of its symmetry it is also a TTTTTT type and a single tile forms the translation unit.

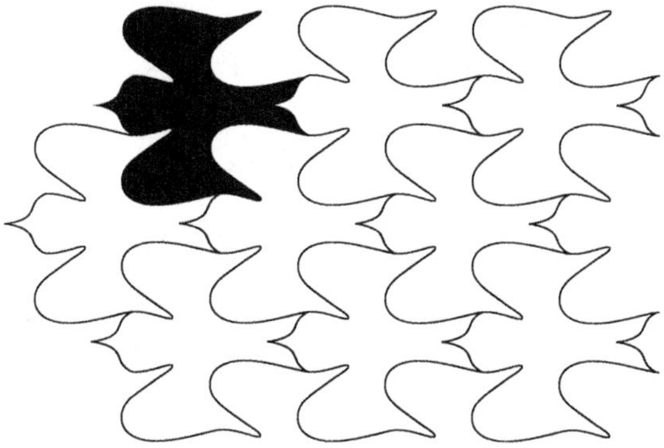

I used this soaring-bird pattern several years ago in a maze book.

I designed this ant tilings several years ago, probably using *TesselMania.*

Below is a slightly different version of the ant design.

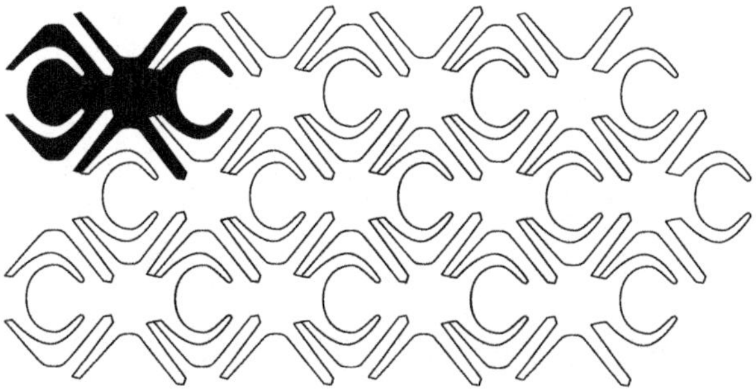

In preparing this book I sorted the various patterns that I have used in various maze books. I had not realized how much I had relied on IH12 tessellations.

The cup or chalice patterns below are very simple. Flipped, they becomes bottles or vases.

I used this next pattern in a maze book to represent lobsters.

The next three were created using the IH68 template of *TesselManiac!.*

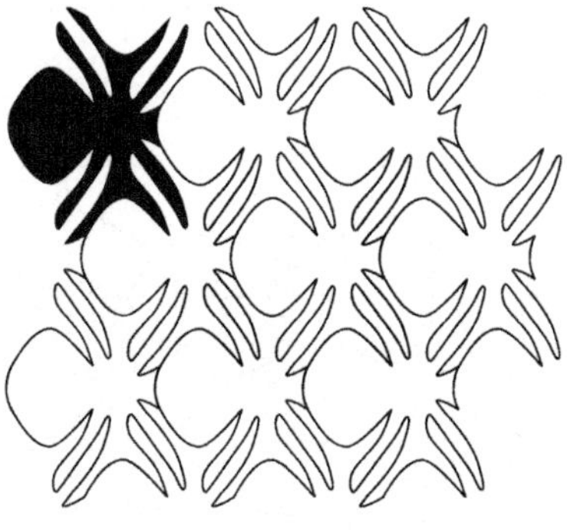

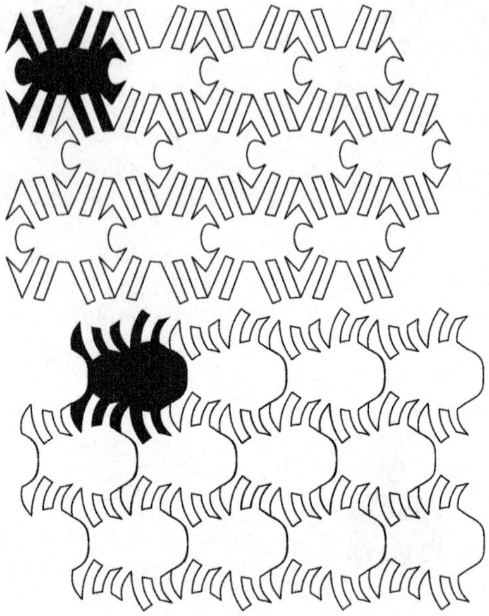

The next tile is similar to first illustration of IH12. With just a few changes the flying birds becomes angels.

Bisecting a class IH12 tiling yields a class IH22 tiling. In the figure below the top two rows have a hexagonal tile that fits the criteria for class IH12. In the bottom two rows it is cut in half and that tiling is IH22. Because the bisection results in a reflection over a straight line, IH22 does not fit any Heesch type.

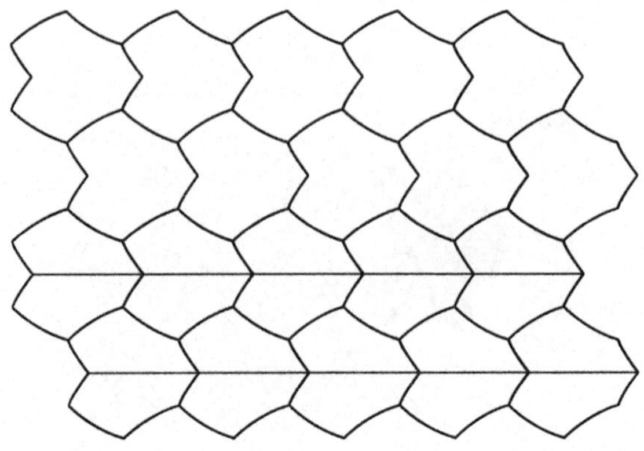

IH22 is a pentagonal type similar to type TCTGG but the C edge is replaced with a straight and unshapeable line and the tile is flipped over this line rather than rotated around its midpoint. Below is an example that is derived from the standing birds that were used to illustrate the TCTGG type. It was constructed before I realized that IH22 could be seen as a bisection of IH12. The translation block is two instead of four.

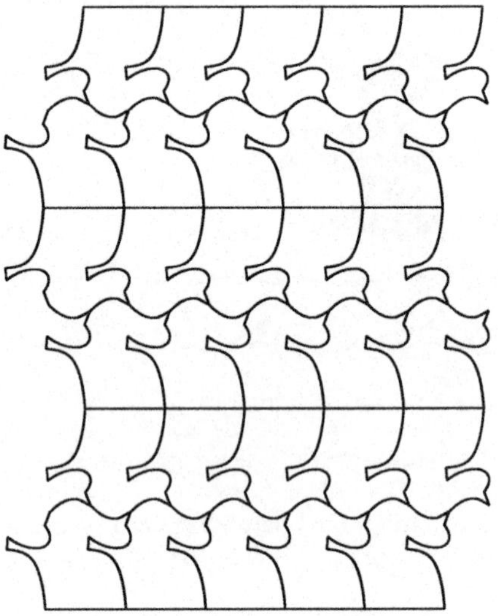

Last is an example that came from trying to tessellate letters. The tile used here can be arranged in many different tilings, but with the flip over the long, straight side, this arrangement is an example of IH22.

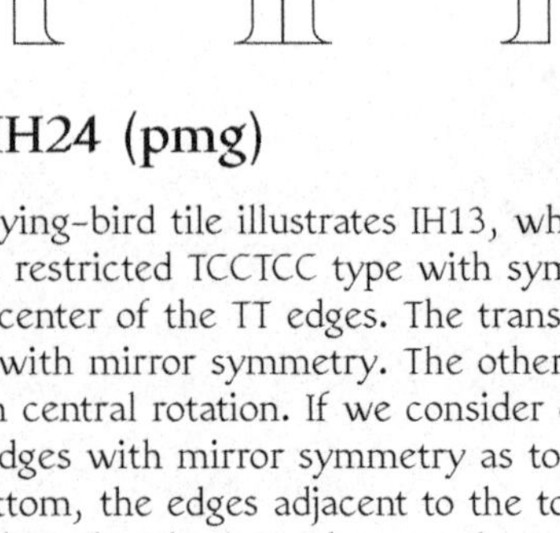

IH13 & IH24 (pmg)

Another flying-bird tile illustrates IH13, which can be viewed as a restricted TCCTCC type with symmetry around the center of the TT edges. The translated edges are formed with mirror symmetry. The other edges are formed with central rotation. If we consider one of the translated edges with mirror symmetry as top and the other as bottom, the edges adjacent to the top are identically shaped and mirrored as are the two edges adjacent to the bottom.

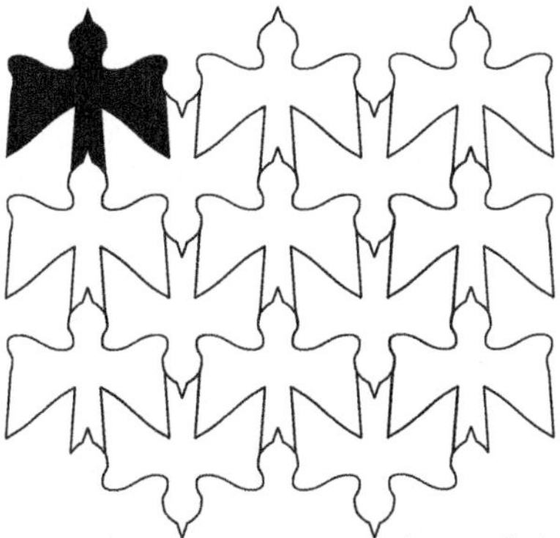

Below is another example with the front of the wings given more length and the back of the wings less.

This animal head fits the class. Mirroring an edge with center-point rotation glides it. In addition to fitting the TCCTCC type, IH13 tilings also fit types TG1G2TG2G1 and CG1CG2G1G2. As can be seen in these examples, the translation block is two.

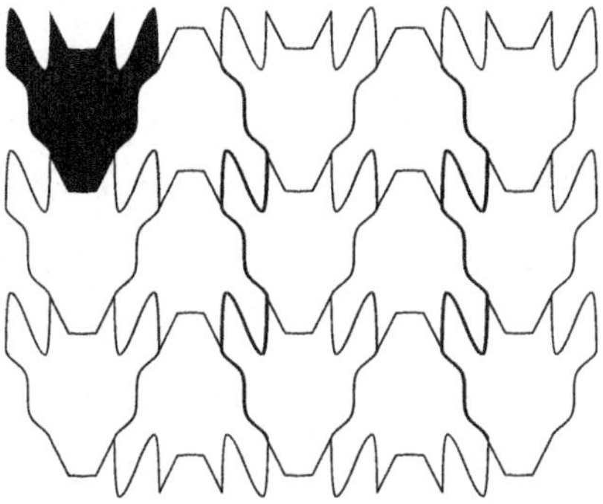

Below is an attempt to make insects that fit class IH13.

The figures resemble motorcycle riders on invisible motorcycles.

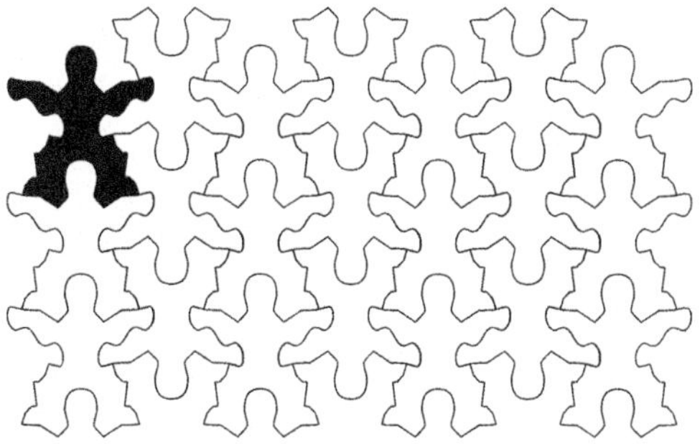

The tiling of wagons below appears as if the translation block is a single tile, which suggests type TTTTTT, but opposite edges do not line up correctly. If we connect the vertices with straight lines, we get a coffin shape. The wheel edges have center-point rotation, so it is type TCCTCC. However, the coffin shape suggests that it could also be TG1G2TG2G1, and it is. It could also be CG1CG2G1G2 where the G1 edges are the straight sides, the C edges are the long wheel edges, and the G2 edges are the short wheel edges. It fits the requirement for isohedral class IH13.

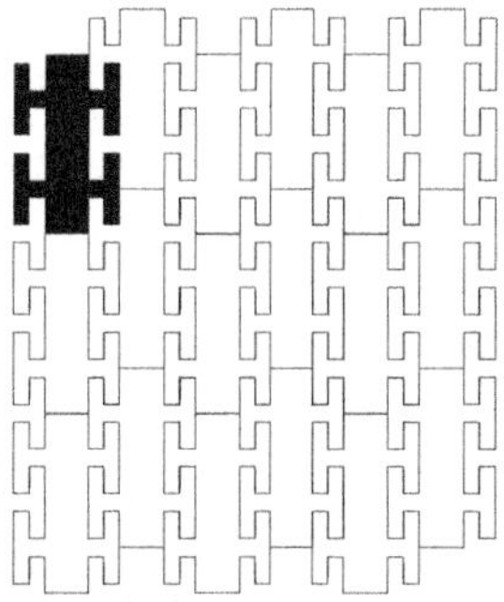

Bisecting a IH13 tiling on its axis of symmetry results in a class IH24 tiling. At the top of the figure below is an IH13 tiling and below it is the bisected result, the IH24 tiling. This tiling does not fit the Heesch classification because the bisecting line can only be a reflection line. It has a translation block of four.

If the tile is rotated over the midpoint of its straight side, it becomes the pattern below with a pentagonal tile that fits the TCTCC type.

When doing letter tessellations, I found tilings for G, P and F that satisfy the conditions for IH24. In all these examples the TT part of the tile is a straight line, but it does not have to be straight to meet the requirements of the class.

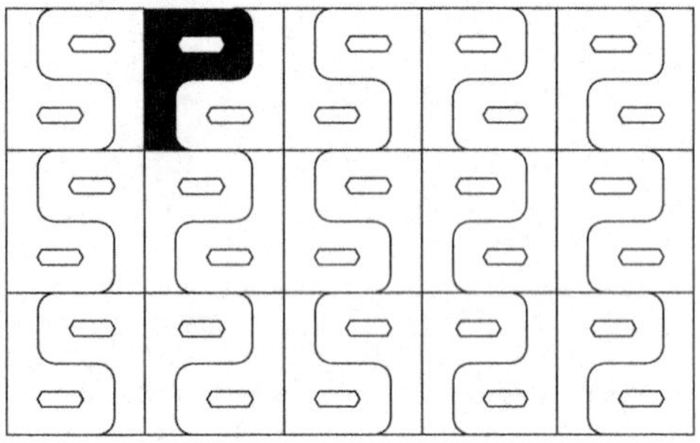

If the four C edges of IH13 are identical, the class is still IH13 but the tiling will also fit TG1G1TG2G2 and TCCTGG and the tile can fit TTTTTT. If the TT edges of this tiling are made straight, the tiling becomes class IH17.

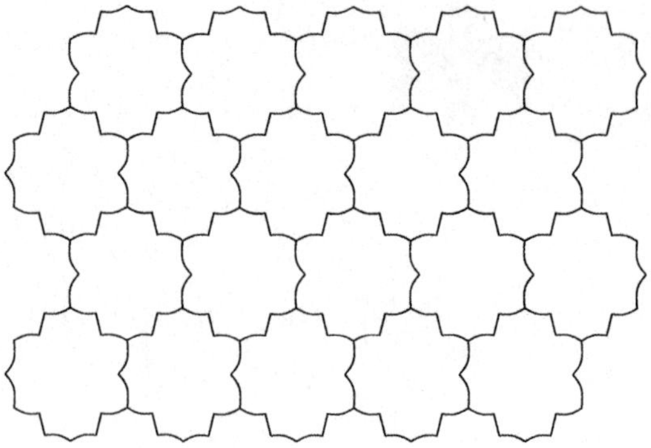

IH14 & IH45 (cm)

The tilings below illustrate IH14, which can be considered a special case of TG1G2TG2G1. Two opposite edges are straight and unshapeable; they are the TT edges. The edges on either side of the first T edge are shaped identically because they are related with a glide. This half tile is then mirrored to form the other half. As a result of the symmetry of the original glide and then the mirroring, each edge is translated to its opposite edge and the resulting tiling is also of type TTTTTT and the translation block is one.

Notice that there are two ways of placing the straight edges relative to the shaped edges to get the IH14 tiling.

Below is another example of the class.

These moths are an example of a shape that both fits class IH14 and resembles a real-world object.

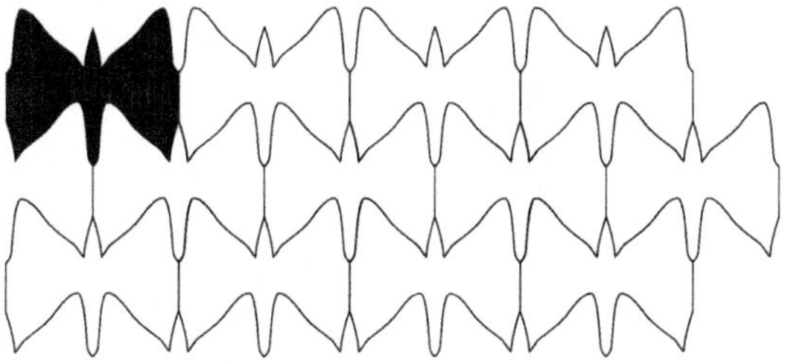

Another way of viewing this class is that it is a TG1G2TG2G1 type with reflection symmetry on the diagonal between G1G2 and G2G1. It can only have that symmetry if the TT edges are straight and all the G edges are identically shaped.

If the straight sides of this tile shrink to zero, this tile will become a member of the IH68 class. In *TesselManiac!* it can be created using the IH68 (G1*G2G2G1*) template and pulling up a line to form a straight edge. These gingerbread men were created in this way.

Bisecting a IH14 tiling along the diagonal that is the line of reflection yields an IH45 tiling. IH45 resembles a CGCG type with the C edges forced to be straight and parallel though not of equal length and the tile is flipped over these sides. The translation block is two. IH45 does not fit any Heesch type.

IH15 & IH49 (pmg)

As in IH14, IH15 has two opposite edges that are straight and unshapeable. The other four edges rotate around their center point and the edges above the straight pair are mirrored as are the edges below the straight pair. If the straight sides of this tile shrink to zero, it joins class IH69. IH15 fits types TCCTCC, TCCTGG, and TG1G1TG2G2; when an edge of central rotation is glided, it results in a mirror image. The translation unit for this class is two.

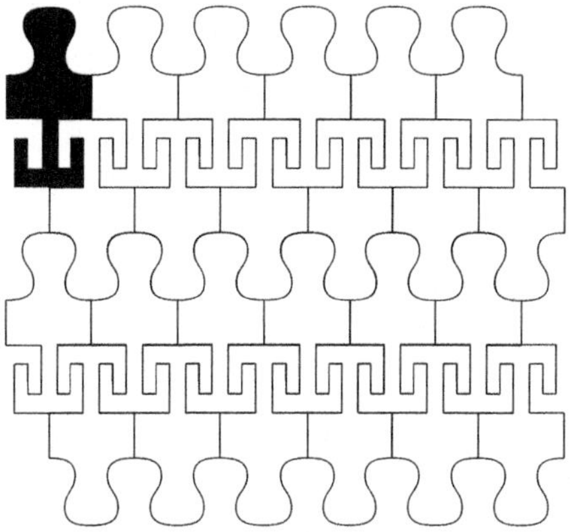

A frog-like shape illustrates the class with something other than a geometric form. If the straight edges shrink to zero, the tiling will become class IH69. In *TesselManiac!* IH15 can be created using the IH69 (C*CC*C) template and pulling up a line to form a straight edge.

The IH15 tiling below was also formed in the IH69 template of *TesselManiac!* but lines were overlapped giving it six neighbors. The two very short segments at the ends of the wings are T or translation edges, and the other edges are C edges that are mirrored over a diagonal, unlike IH13, which is mirrored over the middle of the TT edges.

The rolling pin tile or shape used as an example for IH17 led to a variety of other tiles, all done without *TesselMania* or *TesselManiac!*. I realized that I could change one end and the shape would still tessellate. There followed some designs that did not resemble much of anything, such as these two.

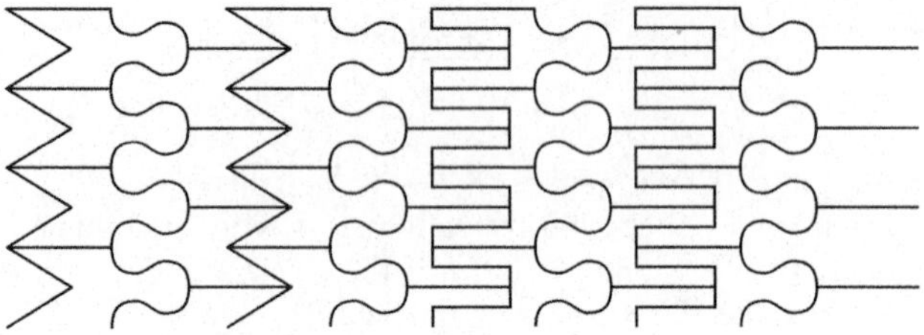

However, it was only a short step from them to clothespins, something a lot of people once used.

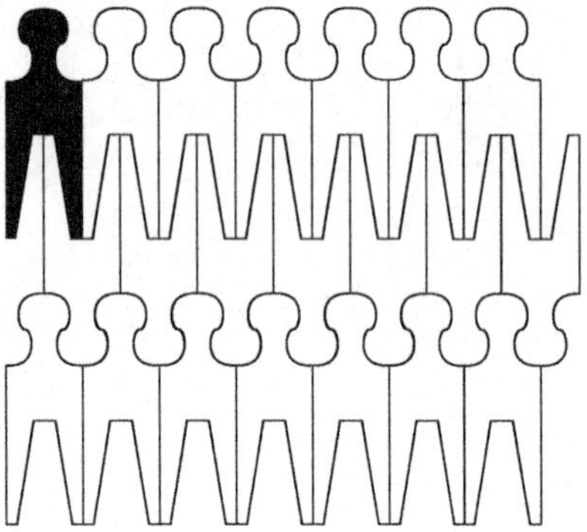

Altering the rounded edge a bit and pointing the other edge resulted in garden spades. Minor alterations led to arrowheads.

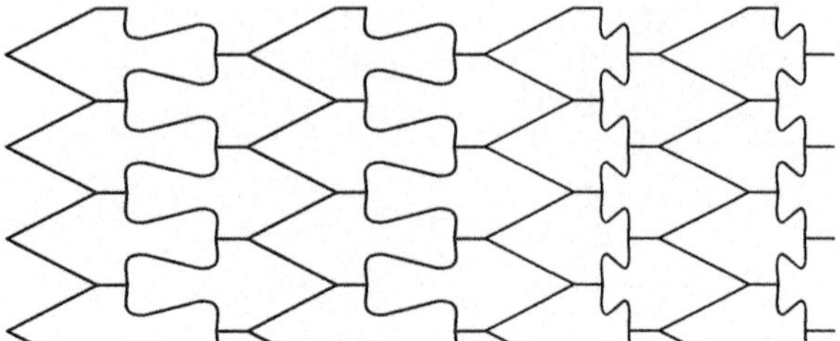

One of the early variations resembled a two-tined fork. Why not four tines?

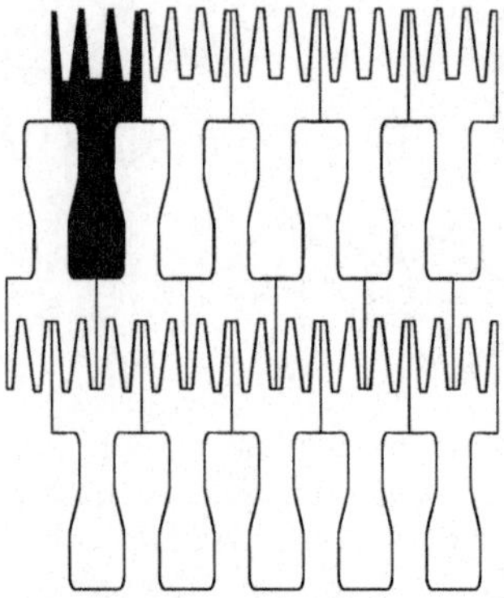

When I showed a design derived from this one to a relative, she said it reminded her of a deer head. I had not seen that, but why not? The moose was followed by something more cow like. The shape of the face did not look right, so I thinned it. All of these shapes fit into various maze books.

When I was working on a maze book about trains, I thought I could alter the pattern to make tessellating rails. Actual railroad rails, however, will not tessellate—the gap is much larger than the top of the rail. However, a bit of alteration resulted in goblets. The foot of the goblet is thick because I wanted to make passages through it.

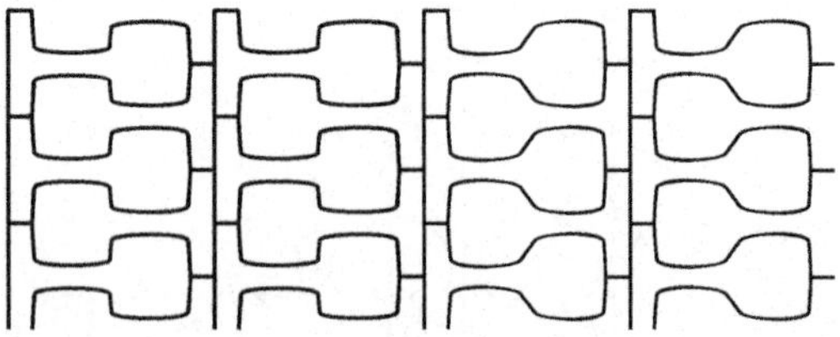

From goblets to wine glasses is an easy transition

These rockets or bombs are a simple shape that fits this class.

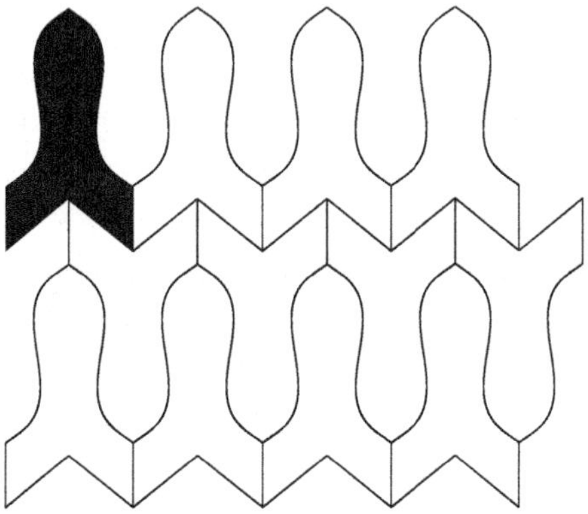

These birds in flight have more shaped edges.

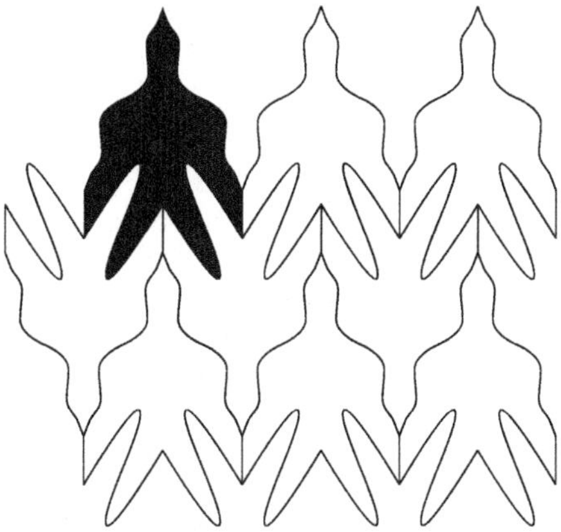

More of my letter tessellations fell into the TCCTCC type than any other, and a number of them fit this class, some of which kept one pair of central-rotation edges straight.

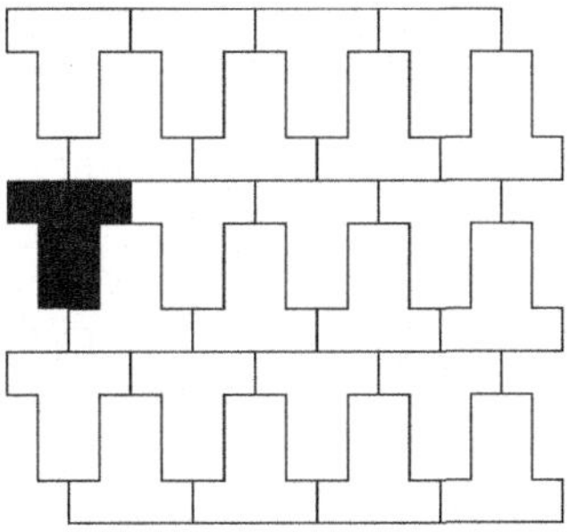

Bisecting IH15 tiles on their axis of symmetry results in IH49 tilings. (See the discussion of IH58 for an exception.) The template shape is a trapezoid. The two parallel edges are straight and the two other edges have central rotation but are not shaped in the same way. The translation block is four. With the flip over a straight line, the IH49 class does not fit in the Heesch classification. IH15 is shown on the top and IH49 on the bottom of the figure below.

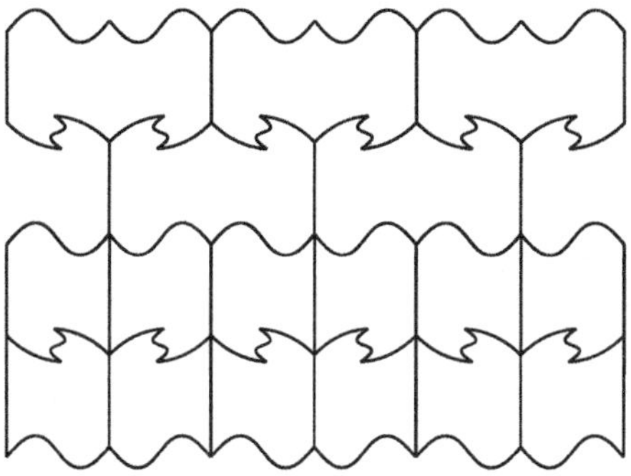

Notice that as in the case of IH14 there are two ways that the straight edges can be placed with shaped sides to form the IH15 tile; the bisecting lines and the original straight edges can be swapped. The same is true of the next class, IH17.

Several letter tessellations used in maze books fit the IH49 class, including tilings of F, J, L, and P. The letter L is the easiest letter to tessellate, and there are also many possible ways to tessellate the letter F.

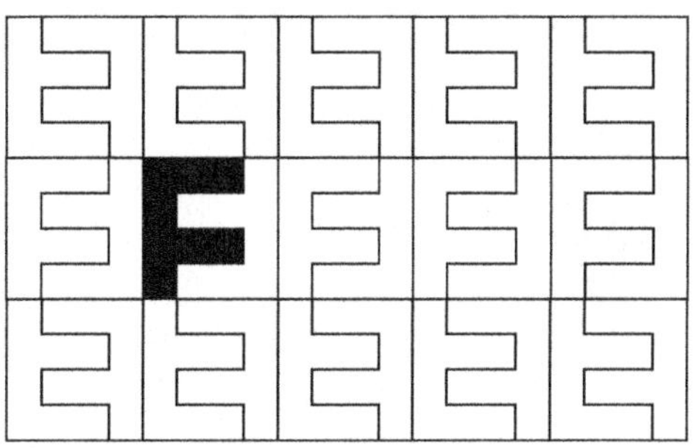

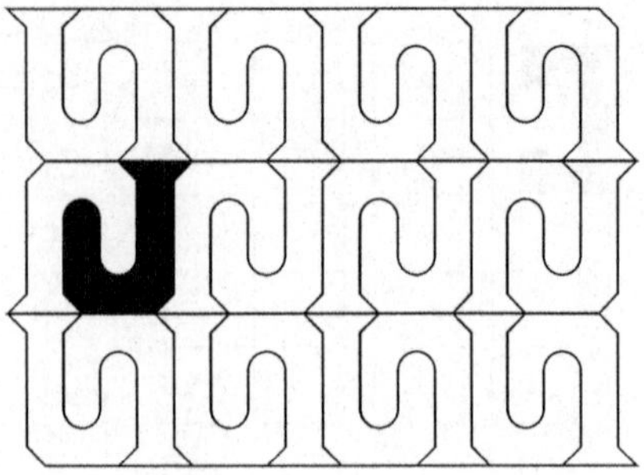

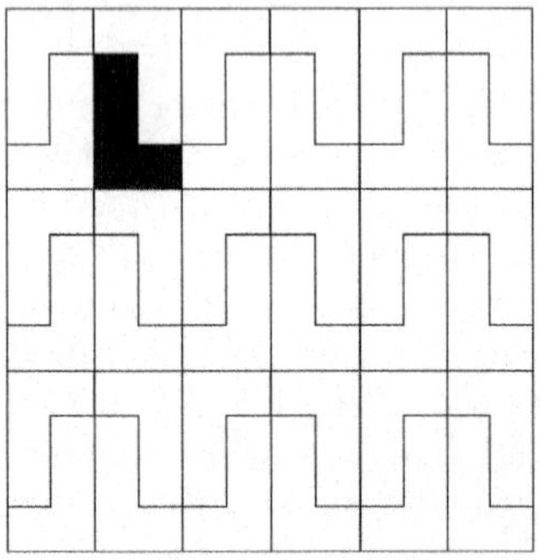

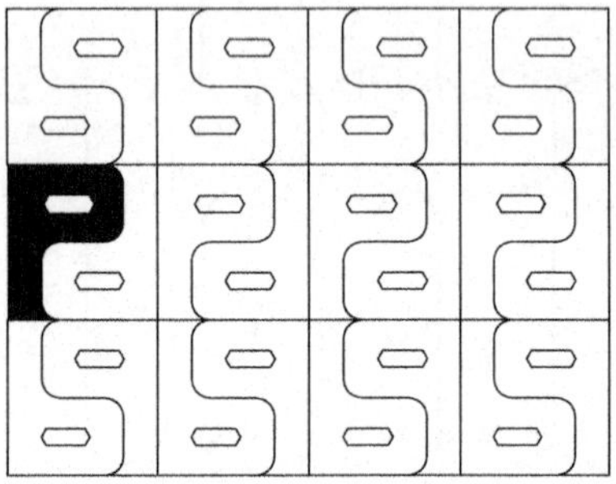

Both class IH13 and IH15 are special cases of TCCTCC with two mirrored pairs of edges formed with center-point rotation. In IH13 these edges mirror so that they also fit as type TG1G2TG2G1 and in IH15 they mirror so that they also fit type TG1G1TG2G1. As the two edges that are not formed with center-point rotation shrink to zero, both IH13 and IH15 merge to class IH69.

IH17, IH26, IH67, & IH54 (cmm)

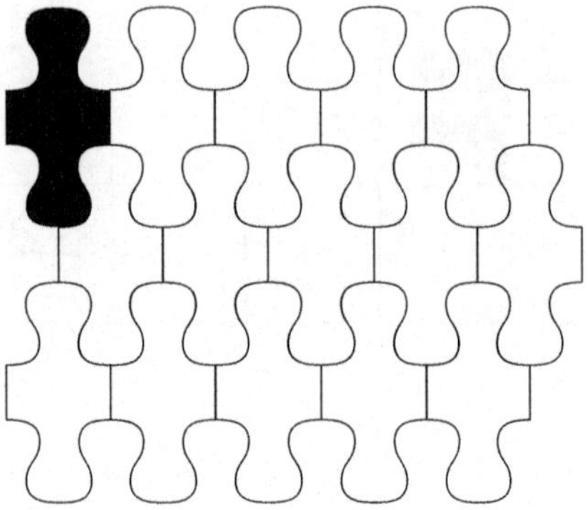

I stumbled on the simple pattern shown above many years ago and struggled to find a way to fit it into one of my maze books. It was not until working on this book that I came to appreciate how special it is. It is clearly a TTTTTT type, but it much more. Flipping it horizontally or vertically or rotating it 180° returns the original shape. It fits six of the seven hexagonal Heesch types.

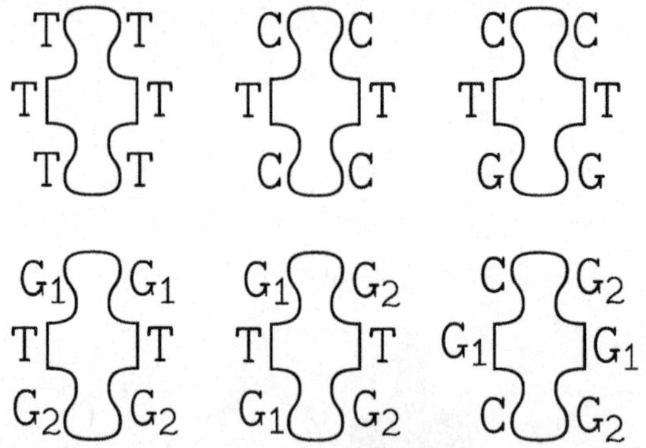

IH17 can be considered a special case of isohedral classes IH8, IH9, IH12, IH13, IH14, and IH15 because it fits their less restrictive criteria. Like class IH15, IH17 is a constrained type TCCTCC in which the TT edges are unshaped and the tile is mirrored so that one CTC half is the mirror of the other CTC half. Unlike IH15, all the C edges are shaped in the same way. If the straight sides of this tile shrink to zero, this tile will become a class IH74 tile. In *TesselManiac!* IH17 can be created using the IH74 (C*C*C*C*) template and pulling up a line to form a straight edge.

The IH17 pattern below can be used to make challenging and visually interesting mazes. Note that the tile has mirror symmetry both horizontally and vertically; the IH15 class is only symmetrical in one of the ways.

Although I did not realize it at the time, I used IH17 tessellations of several letters when I was doing maze books of tessellating letters. Below is an example of the letter I. A design for the letter H can be made with the same structure but with different dimensions and a different orientation.

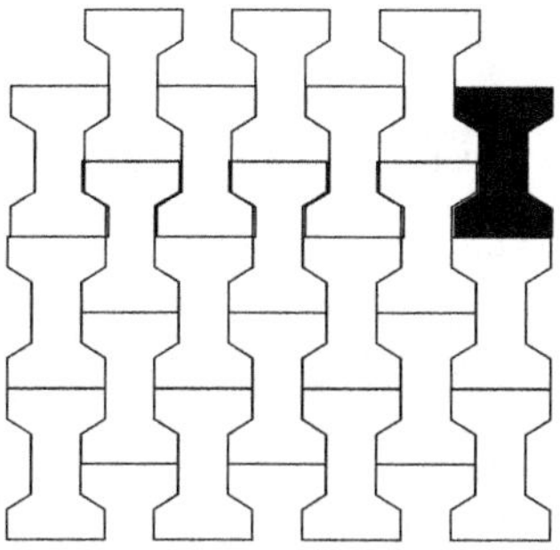

The restrictions of IH17, like those of IH8 (discussed later), give a TCCTCC tile the symmetry so when it is rotated 180° it reproduces itself, making it also a TTTTTT tile.

IH26 can be seen as the bisecting of a tile of class IH17 through the midpoint of the straight sides. In the example below, IH17 tiles are on the left and IH26 tiles are on the right.

IH26 is a pentagonal TCTCC type with two parallel straight edges providing mirror symmetry that it would not have if they were shaped. The two CC edges are identically shaped and mirrored. The tile is flipped or rotated over the third straight edge—because of symmetry, a flip and a rotation give identical results. As a result, the tiling can be put into the Heesch classification. The goblets and wine glasses below illustrate the class with tiles that resemble real-world objects.

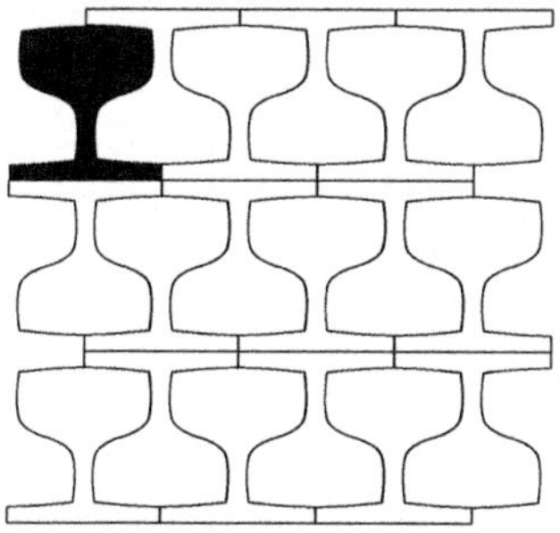

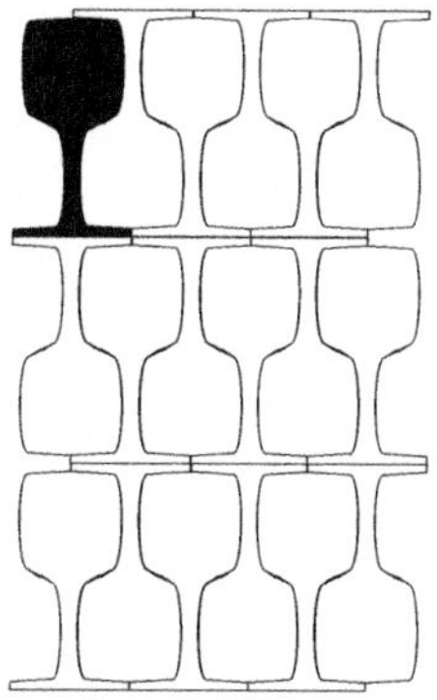

Below are two examples of IH26 that came from attempts to tessellate letters of the alphabet.

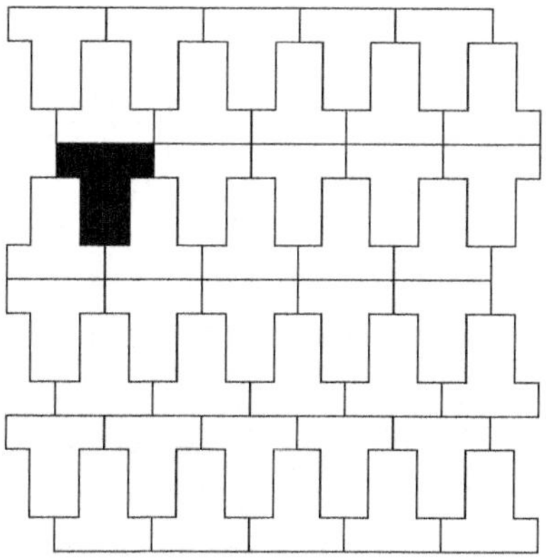

If instead of bisecting an IH17 tiling on the line of reflection that runs through the straight TT sides, we bisect it along the line of symmetry that connects opposite corners, the result is a tile of class IH67. IH67 is based on a trapezoid with top and bottom straight and unshapeable. The tile can be flipped over these sides. The other two edges have central rotation and are mirrored. Two similar isohedral classes are IH58 and IH49, but the shaped edges are mirrored in IH67, translated in IH58, and are unrelated in IH49.

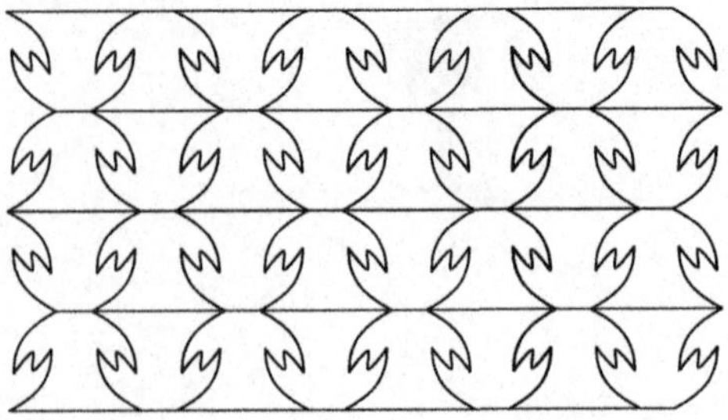

Because the IH17 tiling has both horizontal and vertical symmetry, flips over the straight lines give the same results as rotations of 180°. As a result, IH67 tilings can fit into the Heesch classification system as CCCC types.

Because both IH26 and IH67 tilings retain reflection symmetry, they in turn can be bisected. The result is captured in the IH54 class. IH54 is a quadrilateral class with only one edge shapeable and that with central rotation. The two adjacent edges to this C edge are straight and parallel, though not necessarily the same length. They meet the fourth edge at 90°. The tile is flipped over all three straight sides and the translation block is four. It can be formed as the quartering of a class IH17 tile along its lines of symmetry.

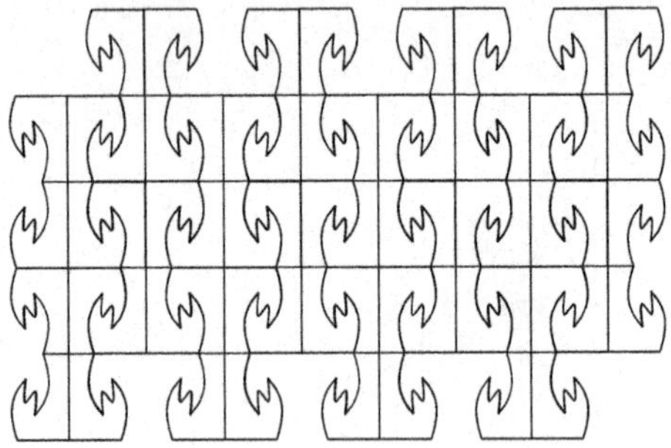

Several letter tessellations used in maze books fit class IH54 including tilings of E, G, and L.

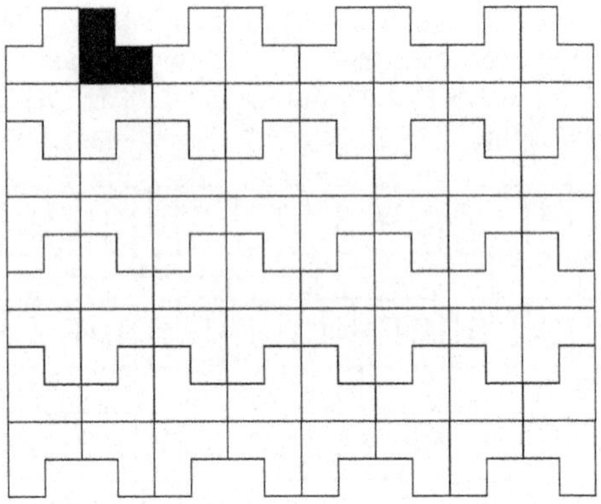

In working on this book, I discovered that I had not used the criteria of this class to arrange tiles of letters F and P. I correct my omission below. Each has three fixed straight edges and one edge of central rotation, so they are not Heesch types. They fit the IH54 class.

This section has been long and involved, so here is a figure that summarizes it.

The top two rows are IH17 tilings. The next two rows, with a line bisecting through the straight sides, are IH26 tilings. IH67 tilings, with the bisection through vertices, are shown below the IH26 tilings. The final two rows show IH54 tilings and one can see that these are bisections of both the IH26 and IH67 tilings as well as a quartering of the IH17 tilings.

IH18, IH16 & IH30 (p31m)

The IH18 class is a more restricted variant of IH10 (discussed later) and can be Heesch type TTTTTT, C3C3C3C3C3C3, or TG1G1TG2G2. It has the vertices of a regular hexagon with all edges having identical central symmetry. The tile is mirrored around the center of opposite edges. As in IH11 (also discussed later), one-twelfth of the outline determines the whole.

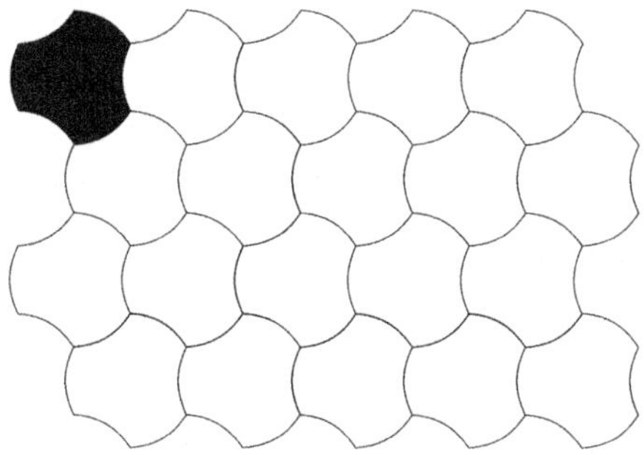

The symmetry of this class allows for decorative patterns. Some have a flower-like look.

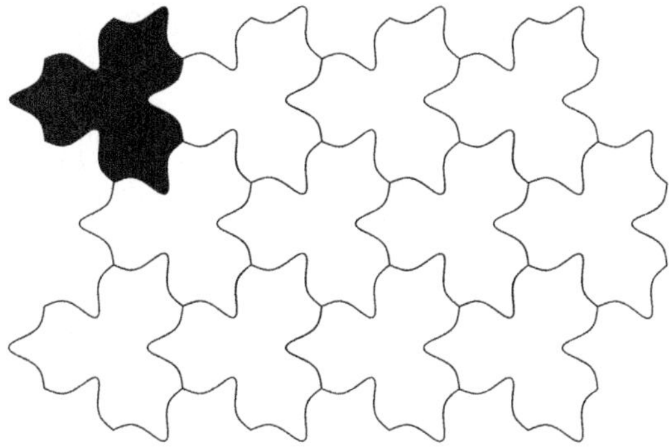

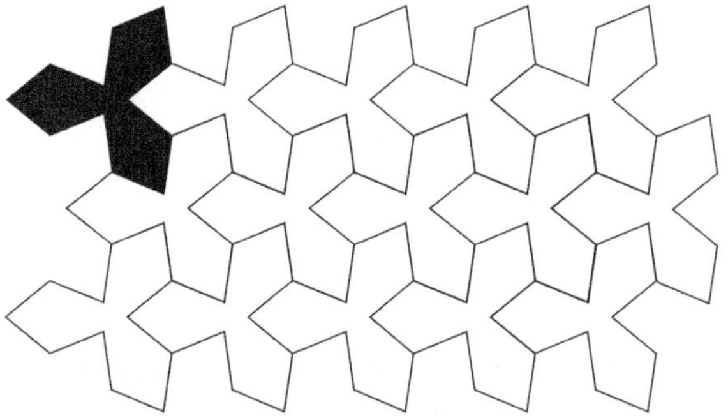

(Some of these shapes in this section may have come from the Grünbaum and Shepard book.)

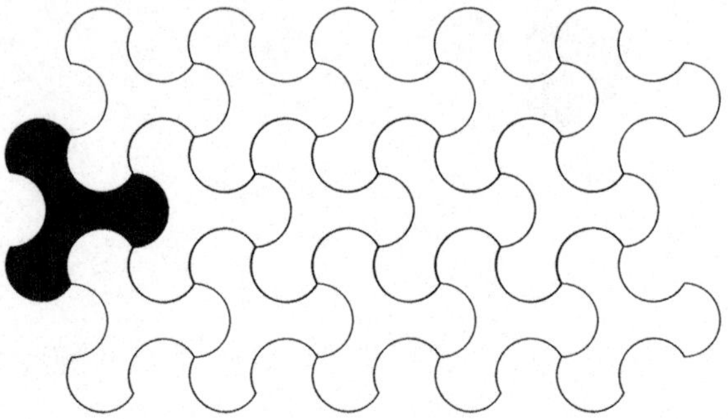

The IH18 class takes artistic talent to design in *TesselManiac!*. Use the C3C3C3C3 template and draw one edge with central symmetry. Three tiles are then combined into one by eliminating the other unshaped edges.

Trisecting an IH18 tessellation results in a tiling that is IH16. Below are the two ways of trisecting the flower-like tiling shown earlier. IH16 tilings are type C3C3C3C3C3C3 in which one pair of adjacent edges is straight and unshapeable. The other four edges all have the same shape with one pair mirrored to form the second pair.

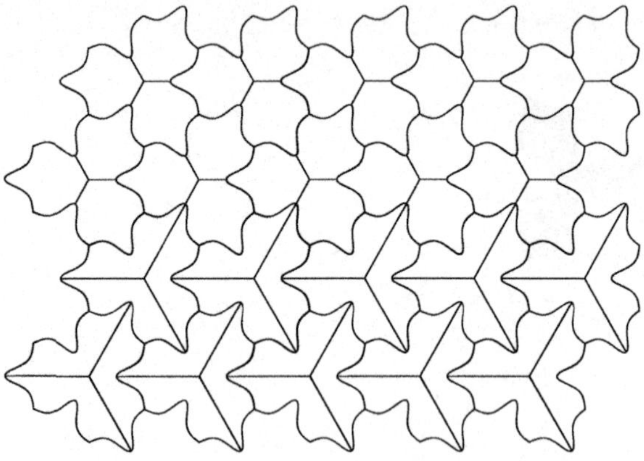

If the straight sides are small, it may be hard to see that there is a trisection of another tiling.

Tilings that are IH16 can be created in *TesselManiac!* with the mirrored C3C3C3C3 type (IH36) by overlapping lines. The tiles have mirror symmetry and if they are bisected, the result is a tiling of class IH30. An example is shown below in the last two rows with IH16 tilings above it. Obviously an IH30 tiling can be seen as the division of an IH18 tiling into six parts with cuts along the lines of reflective symmetry.

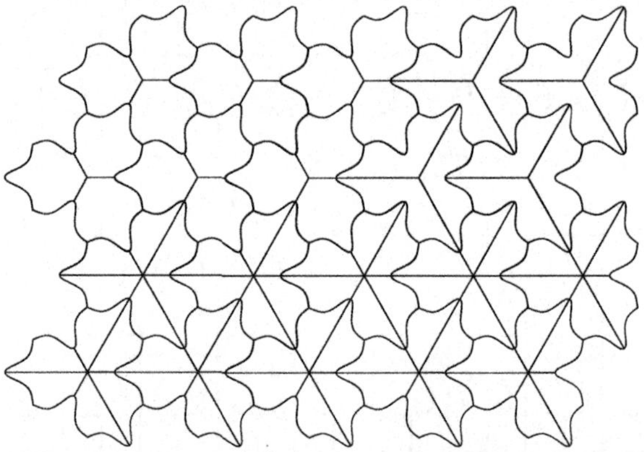

IH30 is similar to C3C3C6C6 in that it has vertices of 3464 and opposite angles of 120° and 60°. It is different in that the edges adjacent to the 60° angles do not need to be the same length. The translation block is six. While IH16 fits as a Heesch type, the IH30 class does not.

The picture below uses the same tiles as the example given for C3C3C6C6 earlier. If the six tiles surrounded by the shaped edge are combined, the result would be a hexagonal tiling of isohedral class IH18.

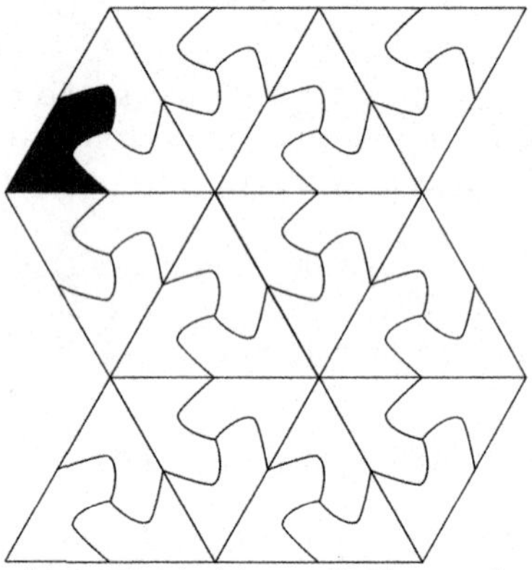

What results when IH18 is bisected? The result will satisfy the IH22 class but when the bisection line of a IH22 tiling is removed, the results will not necessarily be IH18. They will be IH12, which suggests that IH18 is a restrictive case of IH12, as it in fact is.

IH36 & IH38 (p31m)

The template shape for IH36 is a rhombus with 60° and 120° angles. All edges are shaped the same with one C3C3 pair mirrored over the longer axis to form the other pair. The translation cluster is three.

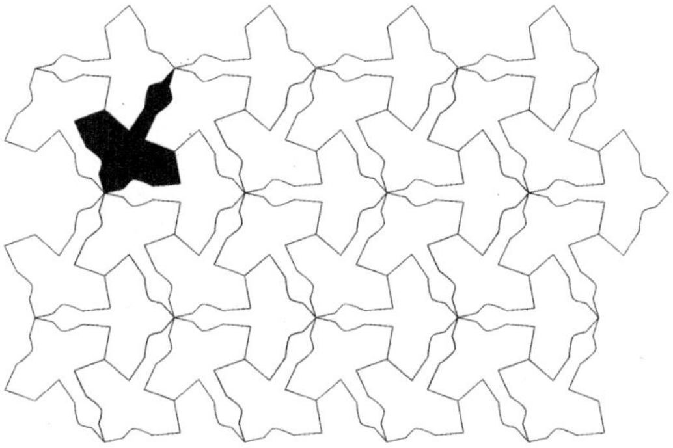

Below are four more examples, two of reptiles or amphibians and two of bugs.

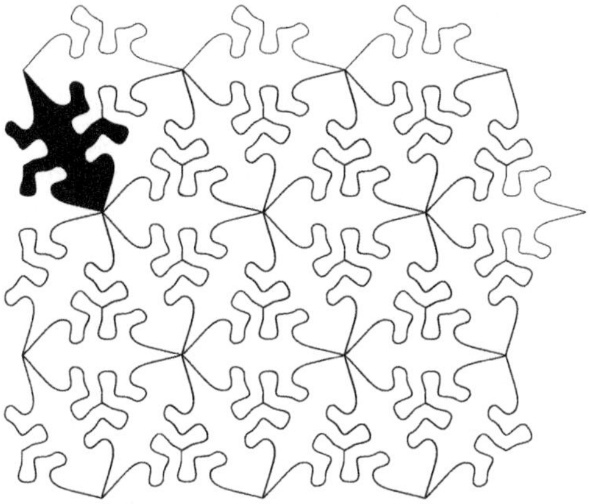

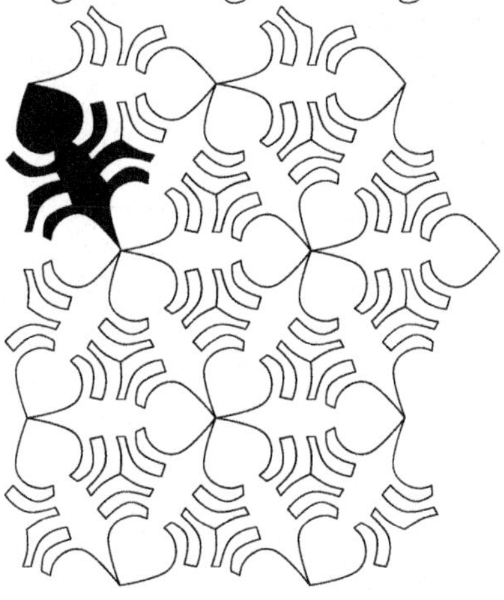

Here is another example, with the edges formed with central rotation. The same tile will illustrate IH69.

Next is a decorative but not very realistic rendition of airplanes.

IH38 results when an IH36 tile is bisected along its axis of symmetry. The translation cluster is six. Below IH36 is shown in the top rows and IH38 on the bottom.

The template for IH38 is an isosceles triangle with a 120° angle between the two equal edges. The tile is flipped over its base that is straight and unshapeable. It does not fit the Heesch classification system.

IH64 & IH42 (pm)

Class IH64 can be seen as a tightly restricted type TTTT tiling. Two opposite edges are straight and unshapeable. The other pair is identical with central symmetry. The template shape is a rectangle. Because of central symmetry, class IH64 also fits type TGTG. Several of my letter tessellations fit this class, including a letter E (which could be a 3 if flipped).

In the example below the midpoint of the horizontal edges is a location of a line of symmetry. Bisecting these tiles would result in another tiling that is also IH64. However, a further bisection would then result in a tiling that is IH42. So bisecting an IH64 tiling can result in another IH64 tiling but further bisection will eventually end in an IH42 tile.

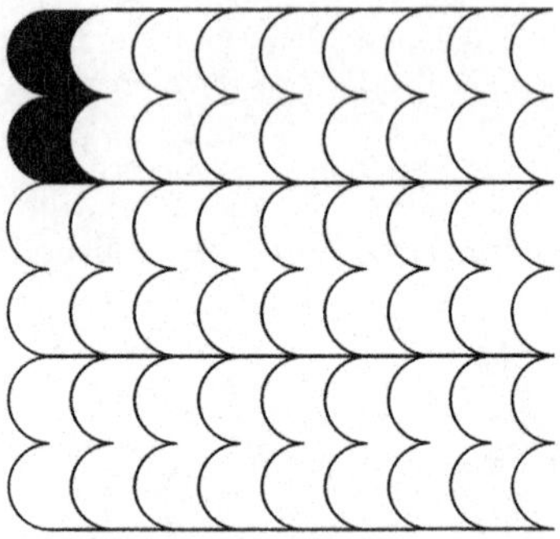

Below is an example of IH64 on the left with its bisection that is IH42 on the right. We will refer back this figure in the discussion of IH58.

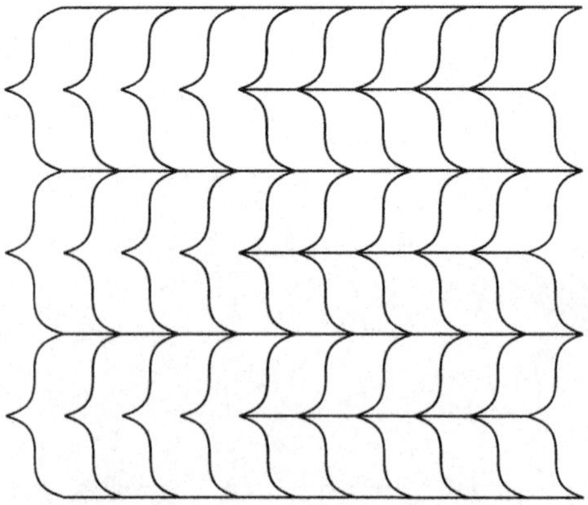

The IH42 template is a parallelogram with two translated edges and two opposite edges straight and unshaped. The tile is mirrored over the straight edges, resulting in a translation block of two.

IH64 fits into the Heesch system because its straight edges can be viewed as edges of translation. IH42 does not fit because its edges can only be interpreted as lines of reflection.

IH66 & IH50 (pmg)

A long-legged owl illustrates isohedral class IH66. IH66 can be viewed as a restricted Heesch type TCTC with the TT edges having central symmetry and the two CC edges identically shaped and mirrored. Class IH66 can also be considered a restricted case of three other Heesch types. Because an edge with reflective symmetry will appear the same whether it is translated or glided, IH66 fits CGCG. Because mirroring an edge with central rotation glides it, IH66 fits TGTG. Because both opposite pairs of edges can be seen as glided, IH66 fits G1G2G1G2. In both the CGCG and G1G2G1G2 cases, the symmetry of the tile reduces the translation block from four to two.

Below are more examples.

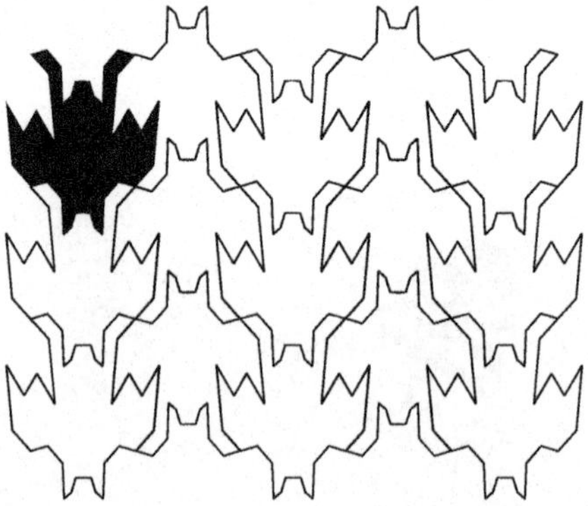

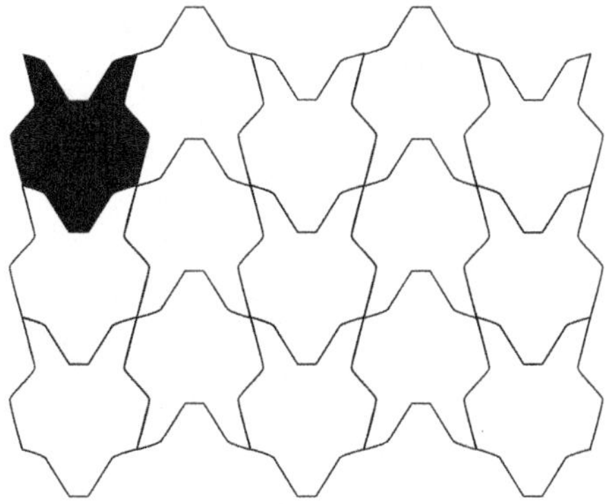

I have found making interesting tilings with this type to be difficult as the examples show.

Below is an airplane with a odd tail.

Human figures formed as the next two tiles have very short legs.

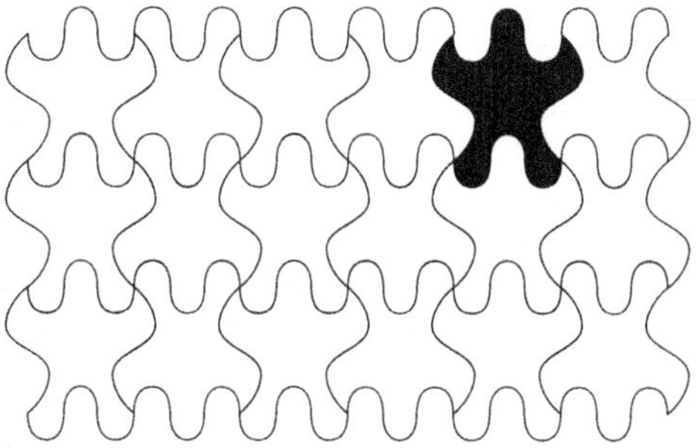

These spider-like (or octopus-like) tiles are another example of isohedral class IH66.

A way of viewing the IH50 class is that it takes an IH66 shape and bisects it along the line of symmetry. It is not a Heesch type because the straight line can be nothing other than a reflection line. The IH50 class is based on a parallelogram with three edges shapable. The edge opposite the unshapeable edge has center-point rotation and the other two edges are translated. The translation block is a row of four. Below the IH66 tiling forms the top and the IH50 tiling forms the bottom of the illustration.

Below is another example of IH50 with a tile that resembles a duck on the water.

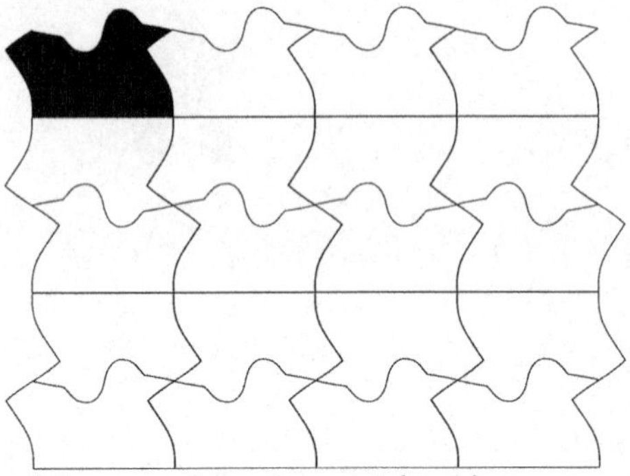

If we slide rows along the straight sides, we can get a pattern with tiles having five neighbors. Most tilings formed with such a slide will not be isohedral.

IH68 & IH83 (cm)

IH68 can be viewed as a Heesch type G1G1G2G2 with all edges shaped the same and mirrored over the diagonal where the G1 and G2 edges meet. Because of the symmetry, the translation block is one, which means it is also a TTTT type.

Below are two moth or butterfly tilings that fit the class. The second one is formed in the same way that Escher formed a tessellations that he called dragonflies.

These spider-like tiles fit the class.

Below is a simple IH68 turtle.

A shape that looks realistic and fits the class is that of a leaf. Here are two examples.

Because IH68 has a line of symmetry from one corner to the opposite corner, bisecting the tiles and tiling along that line will result in three-edged tiles that belong to the IH83 class in the isohedral classification of Grünbaum and Shepard. The IH83 class is based on an isosceles triangle with two glide or G edges and one edge straight and not shapeable. The translation block is two.

The first image below is a IH68 tiling with an IH83 tiling below it. The IH83 tiling resembles baby birds waiting to be fed. These tiles are flipped and do not fit the Heesch classification. If instead they were rotated 180°, they make a CGG (IH86) tiling and this is shown in the second image. If the straight edges are removed in the second image, the tiling will be class IH59.

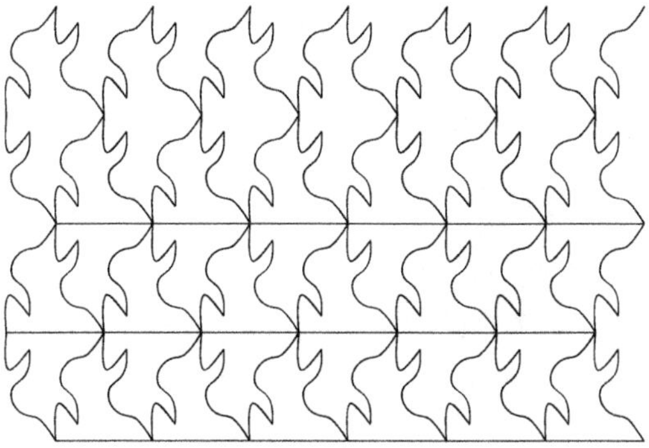

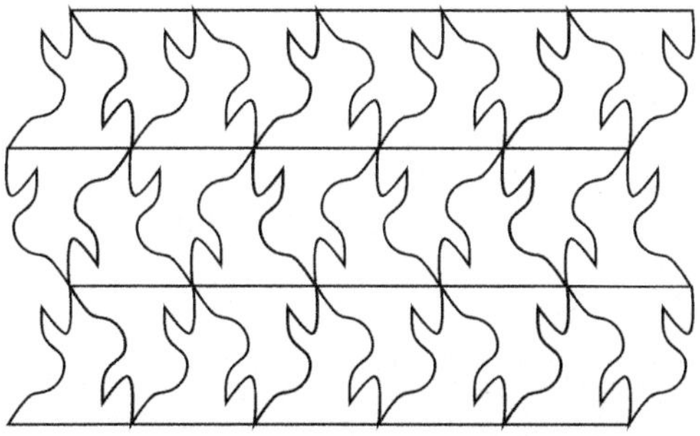

My maze construction kit makes mazes from triangular cells with a translation block of two. Making mazes from triangular cells with a translation block of four requires some extra steps. As a result, when I had a triangular design that could be either flipped or rotated over a straight side, I flipped it.

Below is another example in which a tile fits into either a IH86 pattern (top four rows) of a non-Heesch IH83 tiling (bottom four rows). Note that if we took out the straight lines, the top four rows would fit class IH59, a G1G1G2G2 type with all edges shaped the same but without mirroring. The bottom part would be a member of IH68 class, a mirrored G1G1G2G2 type with all edges shaped in the same way.

IH69 & IH85 (pmg)

IH69 can be seen as a quadrilateral of type CCCC with one half of the shape the mirror image of the other half. This restriction forces one pair of adjacent edges to be identically shaped and the other pair of adjacent edges to also be identically shaped. IH69 also fits G1G1G2G2 and CCGG types because mirroring an edge shaped with central rotation is the same as gliding it.

Mechanical birds or airplanes also can fit this class.

This moth-like shape provides a good example of the IH69 class.

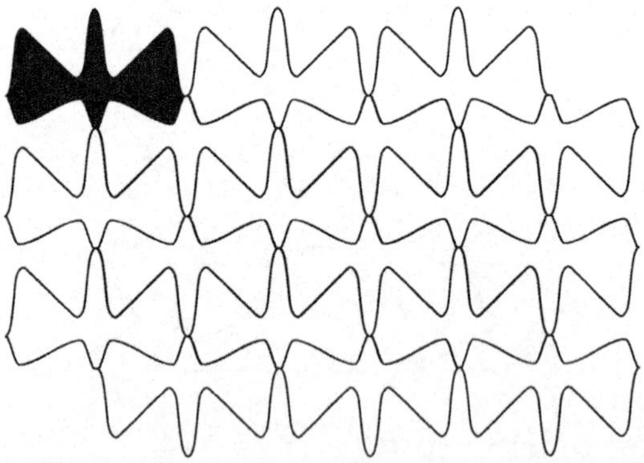

In addition to birds, fish can be constructed that fit this class, though these eyes are not symmetrically placed. The outlines have symmetry across the diagonal but the eyes violate that symmetry. Escher designed very similar-looking fish that were G1G1G2G2 but without mirror symmetry.

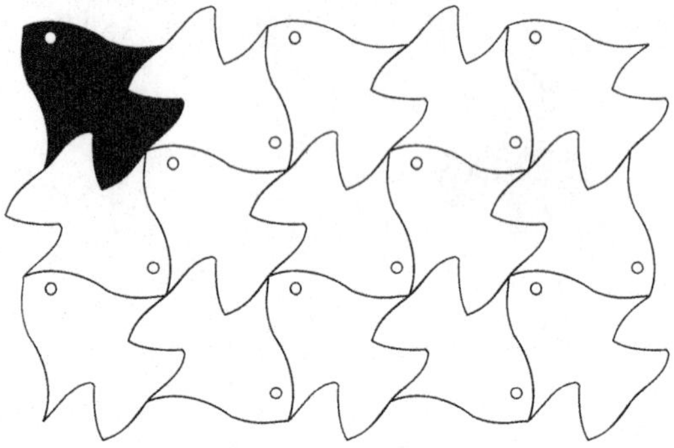

Here is another tiling of a fish shape.

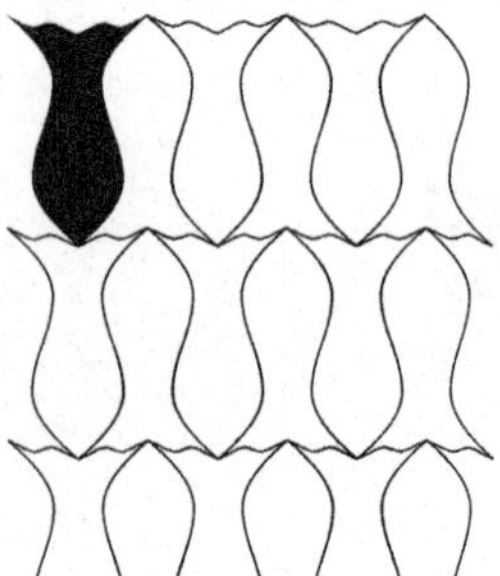

The positioning of these chess pieces and their symmetry puts them in the IH69 class.

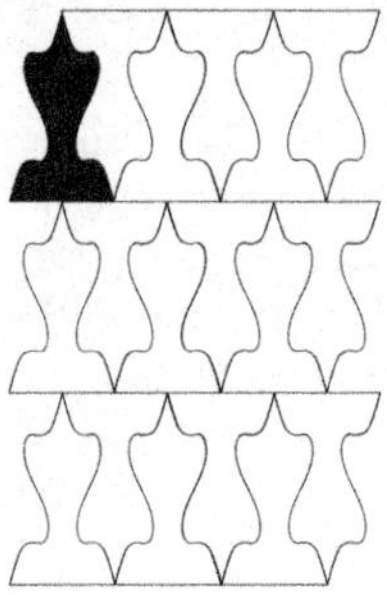

The tile in this next pattern can also be fit together in a different way to illustrate IH36. All edges have the same shape in this tile.

The trident is a simplified soaring bird.

When constructing *The Big Book of Little Princess Mazes,* I wanted a shape that looked like a trident because I had a section about a mermaid. I modified the shape above to make a trident castle for the mermaid to call home.

Below are some human-like shapes that fit the class.

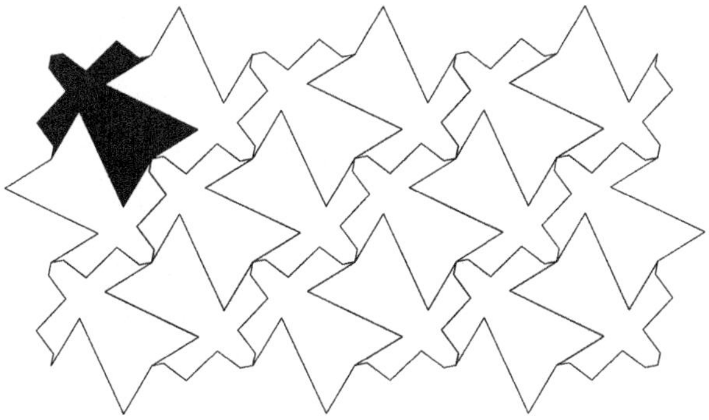

The next shape resembles a bell.

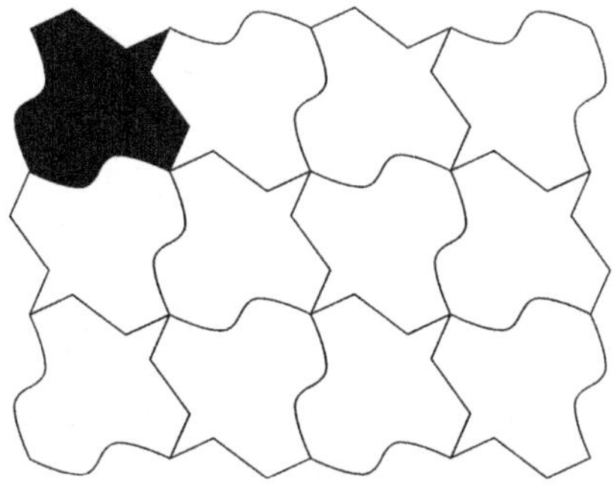

A way of viewing the IH85 class is to see it as a bisection along the axis of symmetry of an IH69 class tiling. Below the full IH69 tile is the symmetrical crab-like shape at the top left. It is a Heesch CCCC type with symmetry across a diagonal. The right edge of the top rows and the third and fourth rows have an example of the IH85 class.

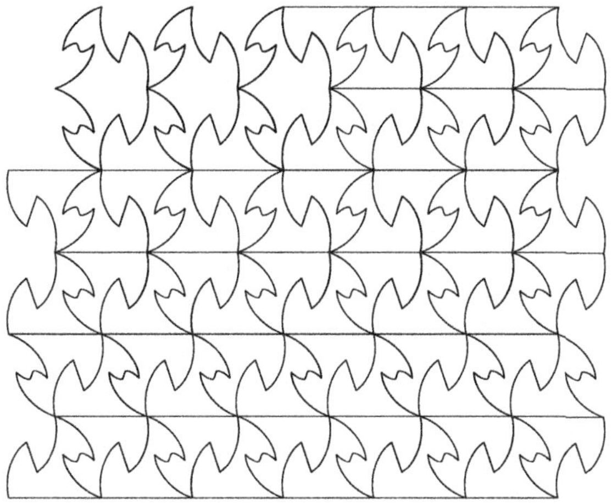

IH85 is similar to the CCC type, but with one of the C edges an unshapeable straight line. If the tile is rotated around the midpoint of this straight side, the result is pattern that is a Heesch CCC type and this is shown in the bottom half of the figure above. (Removing the straight line gives a pattern that fits IH57, discussed later.) When the tile is flipped over the straight side to form IH85, the result does not fit the Heesch classification.

IH71 & IH81 (p4g)

IH71 mirrors over a diagonal. It is a both a Heesch type C4C4C4C4 with all edges shaped the same and a G1G2G1G2 type with all edges shaped the same. Its base shape is a square and the translation unit is four.

Even though the soaring bird used to illustrate this type superficially resembles the soaring bird used to illustrate IH69, the way the tiles fit together is completely different. (In contrast, the similarity between this soaring bird and the one to illustrate CC4C4C4C4 earlier is due to family connection.)

Below is a more decorative version of the design.

A number of people have constructed realistic-looking turtles that fit the IH71 specifications. Here is my effort.

I have always had difficulty finding tessellating lizards. Below is a stylized lizard that fits the class.

With six legs the tile resembles a bug.

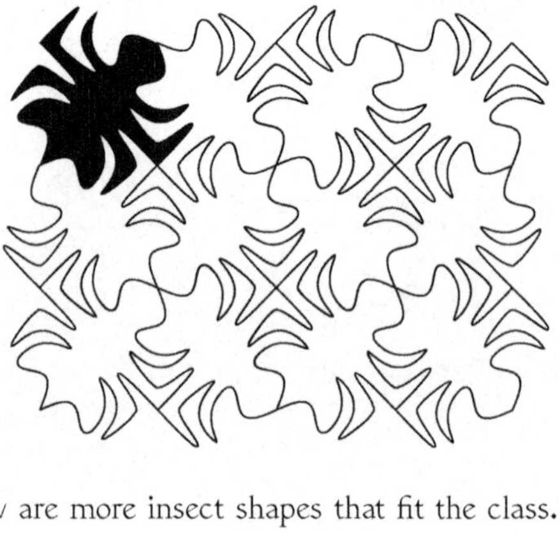

Below are more insect shapes that fit the class.

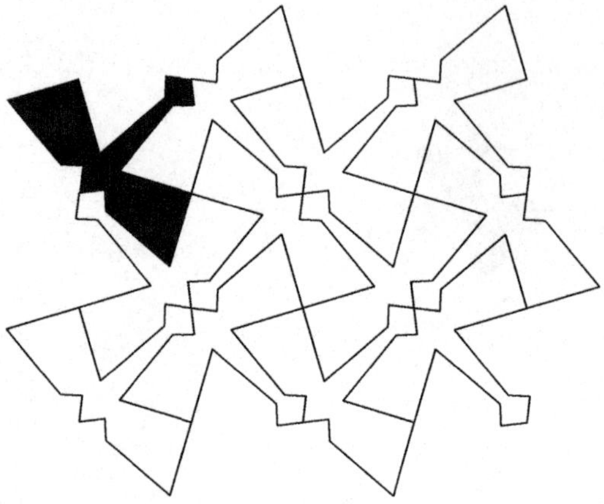

Planes can be formed that fit this class.

The stylized maple leaf is a common example of this class. This shape has been used by many quilters.

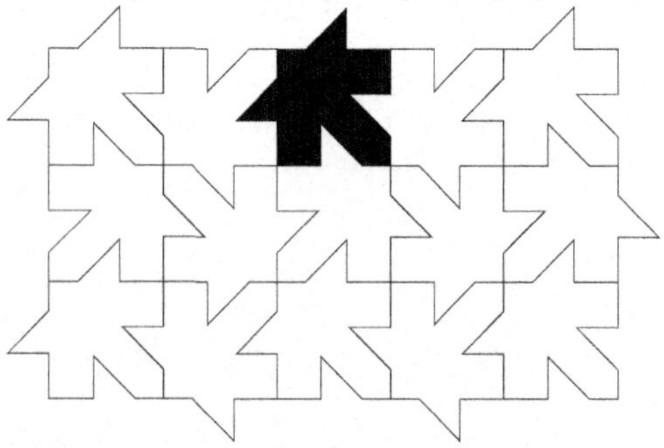

Below is a decorative example of the class.

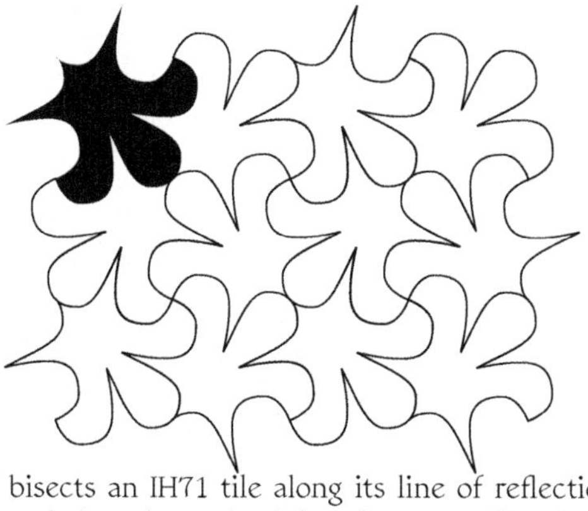

IH81 bisects an IH71 tile along its line of reflection. The translation cluster is eight. The IH71 tiling is shown on the top of the figure and the IH81 tiling is shown on the bottom.

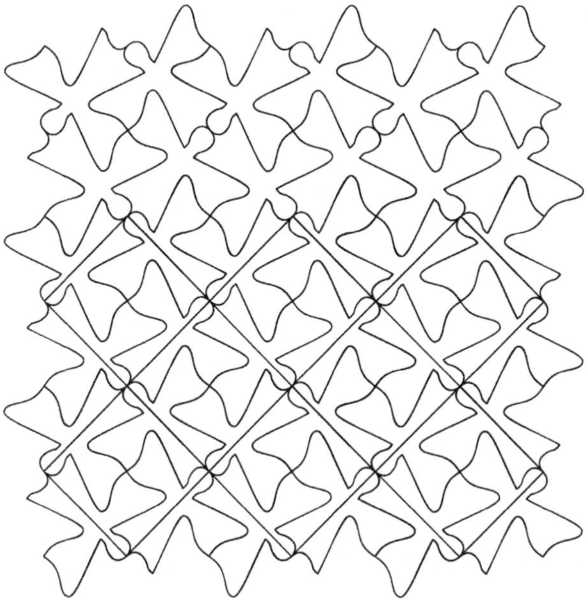

The template for class IH81 is an isosceles triangle with a right angle between the two equal edges. The tile is flipped over its base that is straight and unshapeable and the tiling does not fit the Heesch classification.

IH73, IH29 & IH56 (p4g)

IH73 is a variant of IH61 (a special case of C4C4C4C4 with all edges shaped the same, discussed later) with the further restriction that all edges are symmetrical around their middles. It is mirrored around the center of both the top/bottom edges and left/right edges; one-eighth of the shape determines the whole.

Variations of the moth-like shape below are a common tessellation design. Like the pattern above, it is a special C4C4C4C4 type with the tile possessing both left/right symmetry and top/bottom symmetry.

A common tessellation of the letter I fits this class, along with decorative variants. I used the pattern below in a maze book not to represent the letter I but to represent bones.

Below are two more examples of the class.

IH73 cannot be exactly created in *TesselManiac!* because *TesselManiac!* does not have the drawing tools to line up points or segments so they are exactly centered. Because of central symmetry, this class also fits the Heesch G1G1G2G2 type in addition to the C4C4C4C4 type.

To construct an IH29 tiling, bisect an IH73 tiling on either axis of reflective symmetry. Because of the two-way symmetry of IH73, IH29 can be seen as a Heesch type. Rotation around the midpoint of the straight edge gives an identical result as reflection over that line. IH29 can be viewed as a pentagonal type CC4C4C4C4 with all the C4 edges identically shaped and the C edge left straight. In the figure below, the original IH73 tiling is at the top. Below it are the two ways that it can be cut into IH29 tilings. One has the shape of brackets and the other resembles the shape of a letter T. Because of symmetry, the move over the straight side can be either a reflection or a rotation.

The IH29 tiles still retain symmetry so they can be bisected to form another tiling, which results in the IH56 class. The IH56 tiling is shown at the bottom of the figure above and forms a tiling of letter Ls. The tile has two straight sides that meet at a 90° angle and two edges that are formed as C4C4. The tile is flipped over the straight sides, resulting in a translation block of eight. IH56 cannot be seen as a Heesch type. By bisecting IH29, IH56 quarters IH73.

Below is a five-edged bug of type CC4C4C4C4. It was created in the IH71 template of *TesselManiac!*, but then instead of letting the heads meet at a vertex as in the mites above, the vertex was pinched creating a new edge where the heads meet. It is an Escher-like example of IH29.

IH74, IH91 & IH78 (cmm)

IH74 is a special case of Heesch type CCCC with all edges shaped the same and mirror symmetry over both diagonals. A single tile forms the translation unit and the base shape is a rhombus, a parallelogram in which all edges are of equal length. One-eighth of the outline determines the whole.

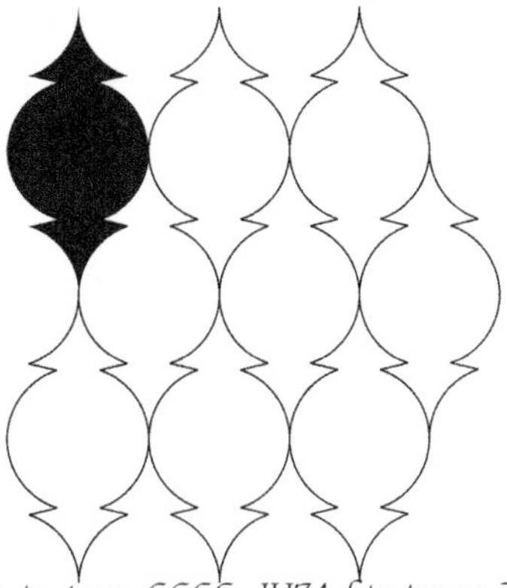

In addition to type CCCC, IH74 fits types TTTT, TCTC, CCGG, and G1G1G2G2. It is what results if type IH68 is formed with edges of central rotation.

IH74 is also what results when the straight edges of IH17 shrink to zero.

A way of viewing the IH91 isohedral class is that it takes a tile of class IH74 and cuts it in half along a diagonal. Because IH74 is mirrored over both diagonals, cutting along either will give a tile that fits the criteria for IH91, though the shapes differ for each diagonal, as shown in the figure below.

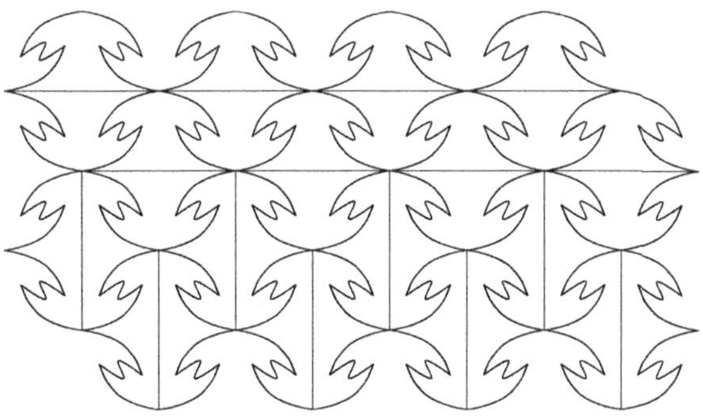

The template shape for IH91 is an isosceles triangle. The two equal edges are shaped with central rotation and they are mirror images of each other. A glide move of a central-rotation edge is equivalent to mirroring it, so this part of the tile is both CC and GG. The last edge is a straight, unshapeable edge and the tile is rotated or flipped over this edge—it does not matter because symmetry gives the same result for either.

If the straight, translated sides of class IH26 shrink to zero, the result is IH91.

Because IH91 retains reflection symmetry, it can be bisected. The resulting tiling is in isohedral class IH78, which has a triangular template with two straight, unshapeable sides and one edge of central rotation. Obviously it can also be viewed as a quartering of IH74 along its two lines of reflective symmetry. It has a translation block of four and is not a Heesch type.

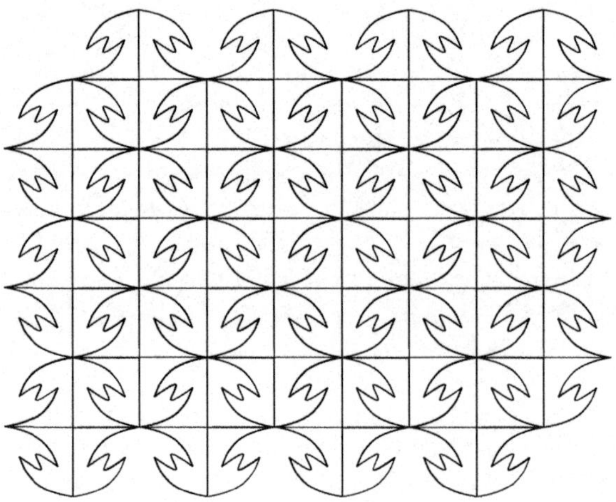

IH58 (pmg)

With IH58 we leave tiles that have mirror symmetry and begun examining isohedral classes in which tiles have rotational symmetry.

In class IH58 opposite edges are of equal length and parallel. One pair of opposite edges is unshaped and the other pair has central rotation that is translated. It seems similar to a TCTC type but the tile is flipped over its straight lines, not rotated or translated. The translation block is two. It does not fit a Heesch type.

Class IH58 resembles several other isohedral classes. Classes IH49 and IH67 also have a pair of unshaped opposite edges and a pair formed with center-point rotation, but the shaped pair in IH67 is mirrored and the pair in IH49 is unrelated. Class IH42 has a pair of straight opposite edges and the other pair translated, but the translated pair need not have central rotation. The tile of IH58 can be fit as class IH57 if it is rotated over its straight edges, but as IH58 it is flipped over those edges.

The introduction to this unit noted that IH58 had no obvious parent class. If we combine two tiles by eliminating a straight edge, we see that the tile can fit in two different ways. In one way the tiling is quadrilateral and and becomes class IH64 with pm symmetry and does not necessarily have edges formed with center-point rotation. (See the illustration for IH64 and IH42.) The template shape is a chevron, but to get pmg symmetry the base tile must be rotated, yielding a pattern similar to that shown below. It has two straight edges and four that are shaped identically. Although the four identical edges may suggest a relation to IH17, it is actually a special case of class IH15. It has pmg symmetry and it fits the same three Heesch types that IH15 does. The top pair of edges is shaped identically to the bottom pair, but they are not related by translation, glide, or rotation, so they function independently in the same way that two differently formed pairs do.

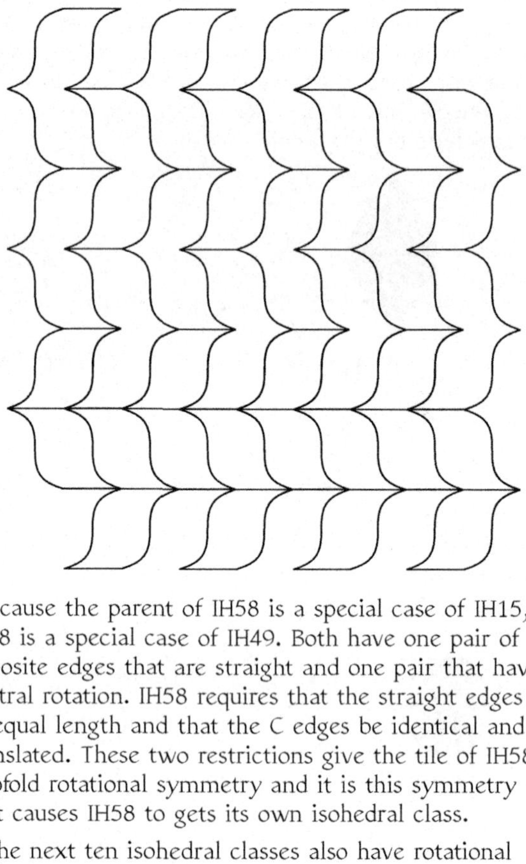

Because the parent of IH58 is a special case of IH15, IH58 is a special case of IH49. Both have one pair of opposite edges that are straight and one pair that have central rotation. IH58 requires that the straight edges be of equal length and that the C edges be identical and translated. These two restrictions give the tile of IH58 twofold rotational symmetry and it is this symmetry that causes IH58 to gets its own isohedral class.

The next ten isohedral classes also have rotational symmetry but are unlike IH58 in that all of their edges are shapeable.

IH8 (p2)

Isohedral class IH8 can be seen as a TTTTTT type in which all edges are formed with center-point rotation. Its opposite edges are equally long and parallel. It also fits type TCCTCC in which any pair of opposite edges can serve as the TT part of the tiling. Because rotating the tile 180° gives back the same shape, the translation unit is reduced to one. It takes effort to find visually interesting tiles and patterns that do not have additional symmetry. Many everyday objects have mirror symmetry but few have two-fold rotational symmetry.

The wagon shape we met in discussing IH13 can be arranged in a different way, shown below. If we connect vertices with straight lines, we get an asymmetrical hexagon with opposite edges having the same length. Since all edges have central rotation, it fits both TTTTTT and TCCTCC as well as isohedral class IH8. Tiles with similar properties can be obtained by connecting two IH17 tiles by erasing the straight edge that separates them.

In preparing this book, I discovered that I had used this class of tile often for letter tessellations. Here are shapes of the letters S and Z that fit the class.

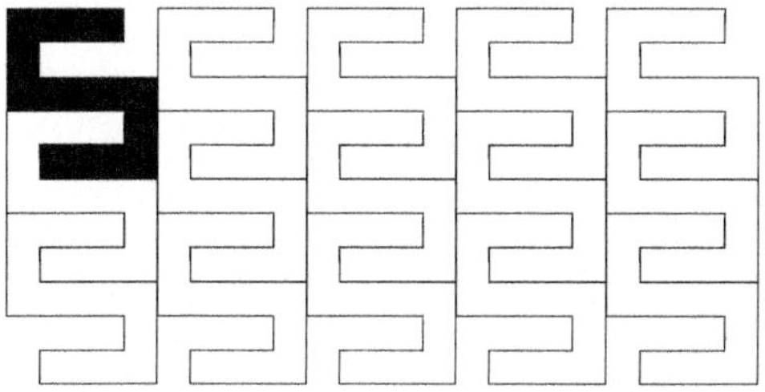

IH8 tiles can be constructed in *TesselManiac!* with the template for the TCTCC type, combining two tiles into one by eliminated the final C edge.

IH9 and IH59 (pgg)

IH9 is a six-edged tile that is a special case of both TG1G1TG2G2 and TG1G2TG2G1. Its opposite edges are parallel, with one pair (the TT pair) equal at one length and formed with central-rotation. Because each of the other four edges is glided both vertically and horizontally, flipping the tile horizontally gives the same result as flipping the tile vertically. Like IH8, the IH9 tile has twofold rotational symmetry.

The third and fourth examples come from my efforts to find ways to tessellate the letters of the alphabet.

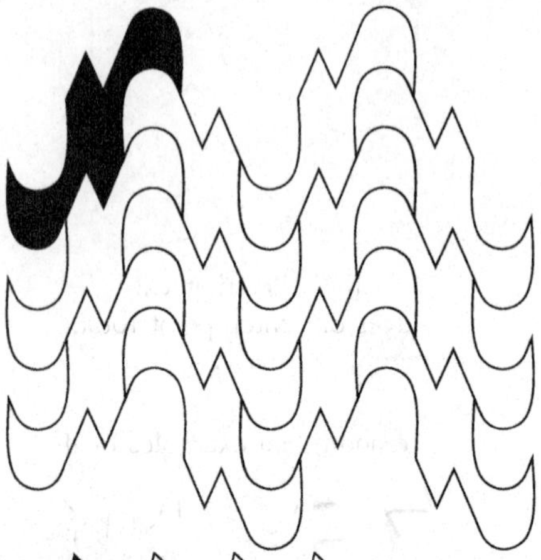

IH9 can be constructed in *TesselManiac!* using either the CGCG or CCGG template and eliminating one of the C lines, thereby combining two tiles.

IH59 is a degenerate case of IH9 in which the TT edges have shrunk to zero. It is based on a restricted rhombus of Heesch type G1G1G2G2 with all edges identical. It fits type G1G1G2G2 in two ways. Like the IH9 tile, the IH59 tile has twofold rotational symmetry.

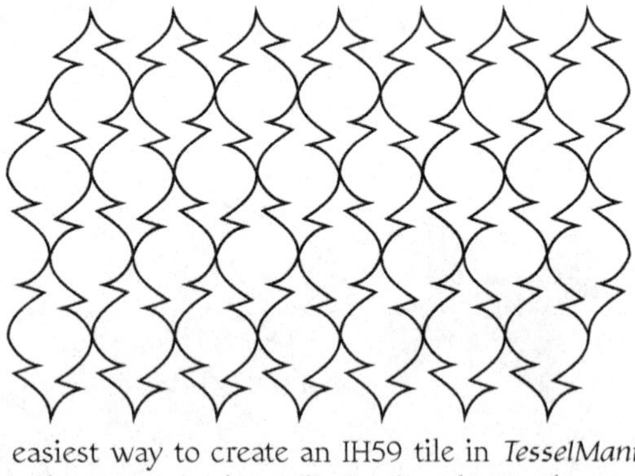

The easiest way to create an IH59 tile in *TesselManiac!* is with the CGG template, eliminating the C edges to join two tiles. IH68 is also a restricted G1G1G2G2 type with all edges shaped the same, but it mirrors over the diagonal and IH59 does not.

IH10 (p3) & IH34 (p6)

IH10 is a restricted regular hexagonal type with identical edges. It satisfies both Heesch types TTTTTT and C3C3C3C3C3C3. IH34 is a restricted rhombus with 60° and 120° angles of Heesch type C3C3C3C3. All four edges are identically shaped. Edge one is rotated 120° to form edge two, edge two is rotated 60° to form edge three, and edge three is rotated 120° to form edge four. The translation block is three and one configuration of that block will form an IH10 tile, as the figure below illustrates.

As the figure illustrates, the IH10 tile has threefold rotational symmetry and the IH34 tile has twofold rotational symmetry. Below are two more examples of class IH10. (A later section will show that there are many ways to arrange the common edge on the framework of a regular hexagon. Only one of the arrangements satisfies IH10.)

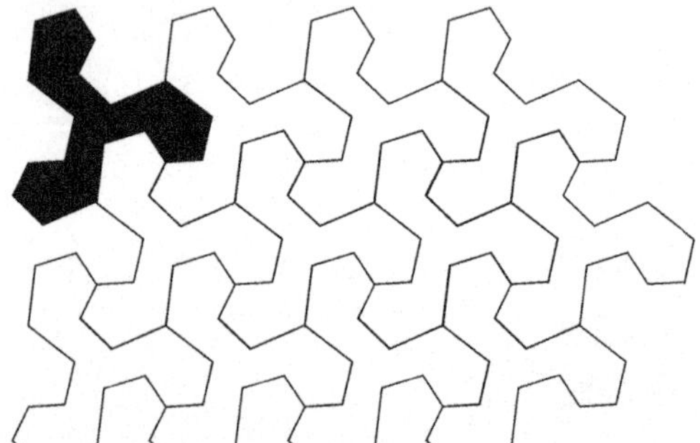

IH10 can be created in *TesselManiac!* with the C3C3C3C3 template, combining three tiles into one by eliminating the edges that form the borders between these three tiles. IH34 can be created using *TesselManiac!* with template type CC6C6 and eliminating the C line, combining two tiles. (IH34 is the one tiling that could be said to be C6C6C6C6.)

Here are two more examples of class IH34. You should be able to see the IH10 shape that a cluster of three could form in the first example. In the second example, where the edges are all formed with central rotation, the cluster of three forms our next class, IH11.

IH11 & IH90 (p6)

IH11 is a restricted hexagon with all six edges identically formed with central rotation. Each edge is rotated 120° to form its neighboring edge. It is a special case of IH8 but it easily leads to more visually interesting tiles than those in IH8. It also satisfies the criteria for C3C3C3C3C3C3 (in two ways) and TTTTTT. The pattern used here was suggested in the freespace.virgin.net website mentioned earlier, and the shape of the edge is used in a number of other tiles that illustrate the isohedral classes. In this class only one-twelfth of the outline determines the entire tile.

There are seven other tiles that will tessellate formed with identical edges of center-point rotation on the template of a regular hexagon. They are discussed later in the book.

Below are some additional examples of IH11.

The tile of IH11 has sixfold rotational symmetry. IH11 tiles can be created in *TesselManiac!* in at least two ways. One way is with the CC6C6 template using only the C edges. It can also be done with the C3C3C6C6 template using only the C3C3 edges and eliminating the C6C6 edges. Both ways combine six tiles into one.

IH10, IH11, and IH18 each fit C3C3C3C3C3C3 in two ways. Each takes an edge, rotates 120°, and repeats the process until the figure is formed. IH10 uses an asymmetric edge, IH11 uses an edge with center-point rotation, and IH18 uses an edge with center-point mirroring.

IH90 is the only restricted triangle in the isohedral classification with all edges shapeable. It is a Heesch CCC type with all edges identical. Each edge is rotated

60° to form the next edge. A block of six of the tiles can form the shape of an IH11 class hexagon, and the shape of the tiles in the example below was chosen to illustrate this feature. The tile of IH90 has threefold rotational symmetry.

The pattern below can be used to make visually intriguing and challenging mazes.

IH90 can also be seen as a special case of CC6C6 where any adjacent pair can be the C6C6 part and any edge can be the C edge.

Below are three more examples.

IH90 tiles can be created in at least two ways in *TesselManiac!*. One way is with the CC3C3 template using only the C or central-rotation edges. The C3C3 edges are eliminated, combining three tiles into one. The other way is to use the C3C3C6C6 template using only the C6 edges. Eliminating the C3C3 edges combines three tiles into one.

Not every CCC type with identical edges belongs to class IH90. In the example below each edge is not a 60° rotation of adjacent edges. These tilings are discussed later in the book.

Translation blocks in the figure above form two IH74 tilings.

IH57 (p2) & IH62 (p4)

IH57 is a restricted parallelogram of Heesch type CCCC, TCTC, and TTTT. All edges have central-point rotation with opposite edges identical giving it twofold rotational symmetry. IH62 has a square template with all four edges shaped with the same central-point rotation giving it fourfold rotational symmetry. IH62 is simultaneously type CCCC, TCTC, C4C4C4C4 and TTTT. Examples of both IH57 and IH62 are shown together below to illustrate how the types differ. In IH62 one-eighth of the outline determines the whole.

IH57 can be created using the *TesselManiac!* template for TCTC and eliminating the C lines between tiles, combining two tiles into one.

The greater symmetry of IH62 makes it the more attractive pattern of the two. Here is an IH62 design that is common among quilters.

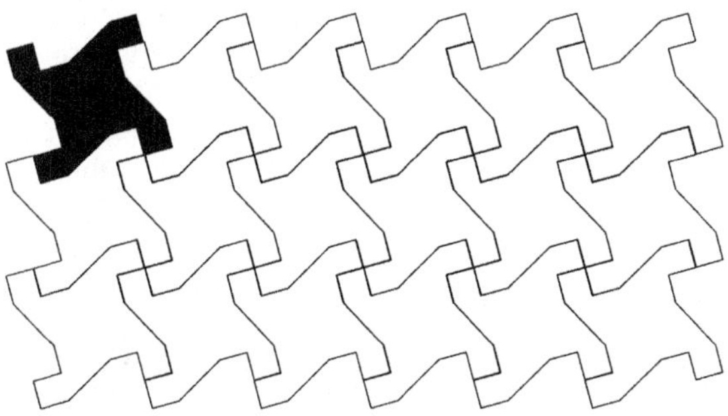

The pattern below was useful when I wanted to suggest waves on the ocean in a maze book.

The tiling below came from tessellating the letter L with a CC4C4C4C4 pattern, shown on the bottom.

IH74 and IH62 both have four identically shaped sides of central rotation. A later section, "Identical Symmetrical Edges", will show that IH62 is one of four tiles possible when all edges of a square template are formed identically with central rotation.

IH62 can be created in *TesselManiac!* with the template for C4C4C4C4 using only one set of C4C4 pairs. The other pairs are eliminated, combining four tiles into one.

If the tile is formed as a rhombus with identically shaped edges as in the example below, it reverts back to IH57 because the tile has only twofold rotational symmetry.

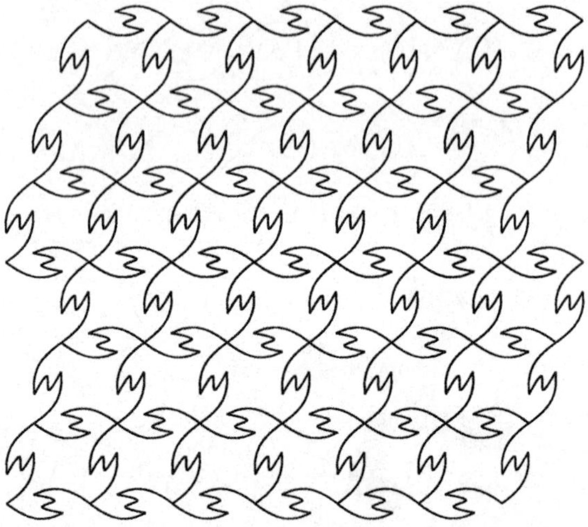

IH61 (p4)

IH61 is a restricted square of Heesch type C4C4C4C4 with all edges identical. Edge one is rotated 90° to form edge two, edge two is rotated 90° to form edge three, and edge three is rotated 90° to form edge four, so it fits C4C4C4C4 in two ways. The IH61 tile lacks the mirroring of the IH71 tile but it has twofold rotational symmetry that Heesch type C4C4C4C4 (IH55) does not have. Even though the IH61 tile has more symmetry than the IH55 tile, the IH61 and IH55 classes have the same overall symmetry of p4.

IH61 can be created in *TesselManiac!* using the CC4C4 template and dropping the C section to unite the two tiles. If opposite sides of an IH61 tiling (top four rows below) are flipped, the result is an IH59 tiling (bottom four rows below). Both have twofold rotational symmetry. Note that the reverse works only when the IH59 tiling is formed on a square template.

A translation block of four has the outline of an IH62 tile with four identical edges formed with center-point rotation.

Final Notes

An isometry is a transformation in which an original image and its transformed image are congruent. For a single tile there are only three types of isometries possible: the identity, rotations, and reflections.

Grünbaum and Shepard use letters and numbers to designate the various isometries. If their isometry symbol begins with the letter "c", it indicates a rotation isometry with the number telling how many degrees it is rotated to reproduce the original. The c1 transformation indicates that the figure must be rotated 360°, which means that it is the identity transformation or that the tile has no symmetry. A designation of c2 indicates the tile has twofold rotational symmetry, c3 indicates it has threefold rotational symmetry, and similarly for c4 and c6. If the isometry begins with the letter "d" it has reflection symmetry and the number after it indicates how many axes of reflection it has. Some tiles can have reflection over either an edge or a diagonal or over different diagonals. To distinguish these, the designation adds (s) for short and a (l) for long. A designation d1(s) is a either a hexagon or square that reflects over the midpoint of one set of opposite edges or a rhombus that reflects over its short diagonal. A designation d3(l) indicates a hexagonal tile that reflects over all three sets of opposite vertices. If a tile is reflected over more than one axis, it will also have a predetermined rotational symmetry so there is no need to add a symbol indicating rotational symmetry.

To derive their isohedral classes, Grünbaum and Shepard listed all possible isometries for each Laves tile. They give tile symbols to each possibility and use these tile symbols to determine what adjacency symbols result in consistent pairings. The tile symbol for the c1 symmetry is $a^+b^+c^+$ etc. All the Heesch types have this sequence as do 14 of the 15 tiles that cannot fit into a Heesch type. (They are IH22, IH24, IH30, IH38, IH42, IH45, IH49, IH50, IH54, IH56, IH58, IH78, IH81, IH83, and IH85. Classes IH26, IH64, IH67, and IH91 can tile with a flip or in a Heesch pattern.) The exception, IH58, has twofold rotational symmetry with tile sequence $a^+b^+a^+b^+$. In the table on the next page, the Heesch types are not listed—they are the missing numbers. None of what I called the restricted Heesch classes is in a c1 row because these classes all have some tile symmetry. In the final column showing tiles with all edges straight lines, the items marked with an "m" must have an interior marking to lower their symmetry to the appropriate level. (IH72 does not need marking because it can be represented by a tiling of rectangles.)

In their illustrations of the 93 classes, Grünbaum and Shepard show that some of the isohedral classes are bisections or trisections of other classes. IH24, IH26, IH38, IH50, IH83, IH85, IH91, and IH78 are pictured with the same shaped edges as their "parent" tilings (pages 288-290 in Grünbaum and Shepard). However, IH22, IH45, IH49, IH54, IH67, IH16, IH30, IH42, IH52, IH29, and IH56 are pictured with different shaped edges than their "parent" tilings. The text does not mention that most tiles formed with both shaped and straight edges are related to other tiles.

Grünbaum and Shepard illustrate how edges are related not just with incidence symbols but also with what they call adjacency diagrams. These do not always indicate how in fact the tiling is formed. For example, for class IH8 the adjacency diagram indicates that each edge has central rotation, which suggests the tile can be formed as CCCCCC.

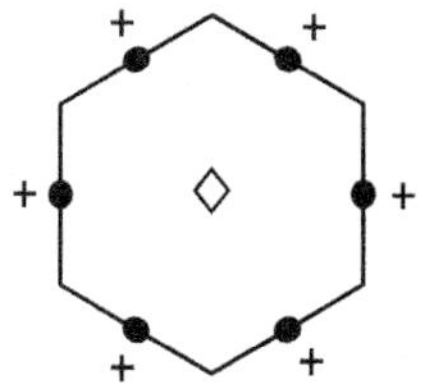

However, if we mark the edges of a class IH8 tile and arrange it as a CCCCCC tiling, we get the result below.

Notice that the edge symbols do not pair up properly. The IH8 tiling must be formed as either TCCTCC or TTTTTT for the symbols on the edges to pair properly.

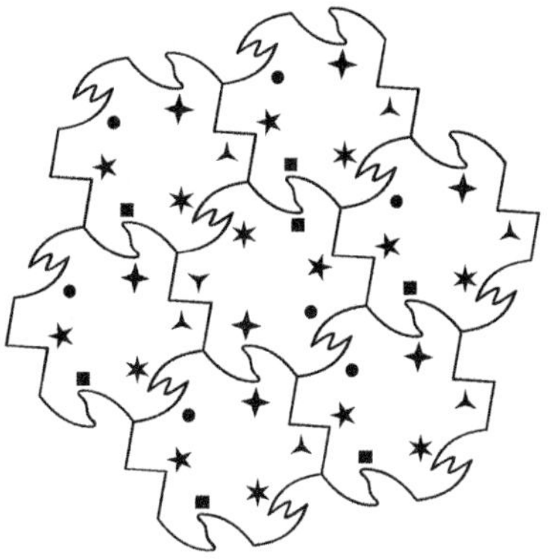

Grünbaum and Shepard's adjacency diagram for IH17 is shown below on the left. The rhombus at the center indicates it has twofold rotational symmetry and the fact that it is filled indicates there is reflective symmetry as well. The short horizontal and vertical lines show the axes of reflective symmetry. If the tile with edges marked is flipped over the straight edge, we get the result on the left. No consistent pairing is possible with the flip. In this case as well as in several others (IH14, IH15, IH16, and IH29), the straight edges are needed for symmetry and are not meant to serve as lines of mirror reflection.

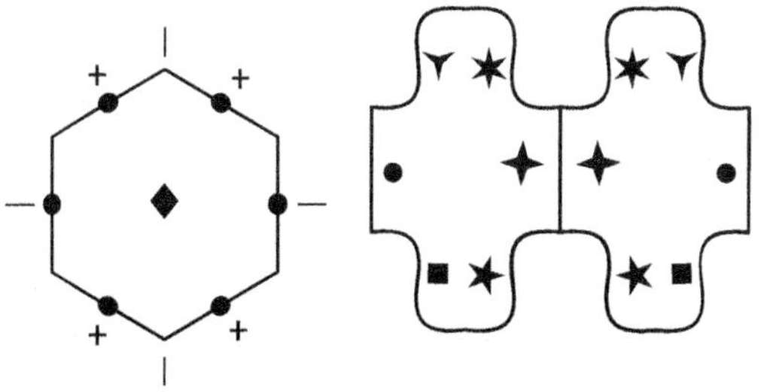

In addition to incidence symbols and adjacency diagrams, Grünbaum and Shepard state that the classes could be differentiated with symbols of how edges are formed and related. They do not pursue this method, but it is the method used by Tom McLean in his exposition of isohedral types. His original website at freespace.virgin.net/tom.mclean/index.html has disappeared but is mirrored as of September 2016 at www.jaapsch.net/tilings/mclean/index.html.

The discussion of the isohedral classes noted that some classes could be seen as bisections or trisections of other classes. The same is true of the classes that have unshapeable edges. IH37 can be formed by trisecting IH20. Bisecting IH37 can yield IH40 or IH93 depending on whether it is cut on the short or long diagonal.

Further Breakdown of Grünbaum and Shepard's Isohedral Classes

Vertices	Isohedral Classes	Tile Symmetry	Restricted Heesch	Some Edges Straight	All Edges Straight
3^6	1-7	c1			
	8-9	c2	8, 9		
	10	c3	10		
	11	c6	11		
	12-13	d1(s)	12, 13		
	14-16	d1(l)		14, 15, 16	
	17	d2		17	
	18	d3(s)	18		
	19	d3(l)			19m
	20	d6			20
$3^4.6$	21	c1			
$3^3.4^2$	22-25	c1		22, 24	
	26	d1		26	
$3^2.4.3.4$	27-28	c1			
	29	d1		29	
3.4.6.4	30-31	c1		30	
	32	d1			32
3.6.3.6	33	c1			
	34	c2	34		
	35	d1(s)			35m
	36	d1(l)	36		
	37	d2			37
3.12^2	38-39	c1		38	
	40	d1			40
4^4	41-56	c1		42, 45, 49, 50, 54, 56	48m
	57-61	c2	57, 59, 61	58	60m
	62-63	c4	62		63m
	64-67	d1(s)	66	64, 67	65m
	68-71	d1(l)	68, 69, 71		70m
	72-73	d2(s)	73		72
	74-75	d2(l)	74		75m
	76	d4			76
4.6.12	77	c1			77
4.8^2	78-81	c1		78, 81	80m
	82	d1			82
6^3	83-88	c1		83, 85	87m
	89-90	c3	90		89m
	91-92	d1		91	92m
	93	d3			93

The numbers not listed in the last three columns are the Heesch types. All are in the c1 rows.

Bisecting IH40 or IH93 yields IH77. IH77 is the only tile with vertices of 4.6.12 that will tile the plane. It forms a grid of triangles with angles of 30°, 60°, and 90°. Below are illustrations of IH20, IH37, IH40, IH93, and IH77.

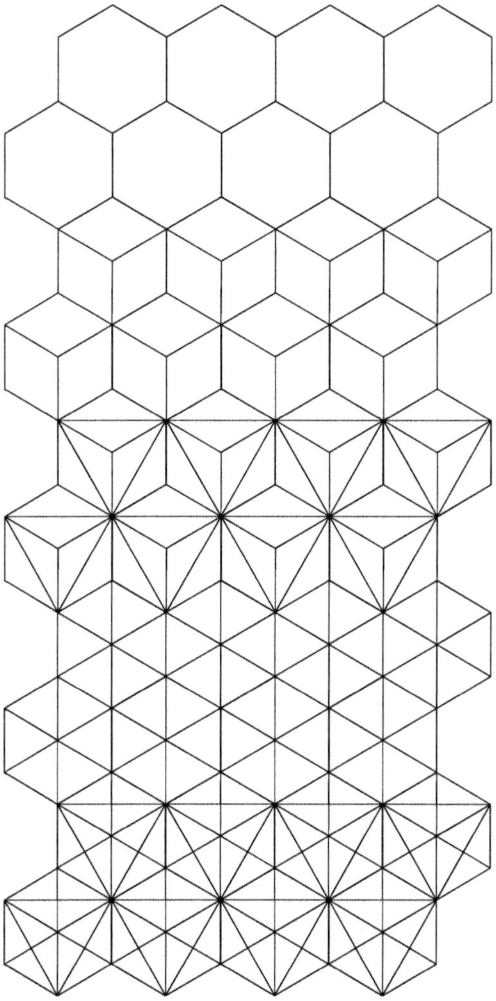

Bisecting IH76 (squares) yields IH82 (right isosceles triangles) and a further bisection of IH82 yields another IH82 tiling.

The shape with the $3^4.6$ vertices appears to allow a d1 variant but if it is formed, an unsigned edge will face a signed edge and the tiling cannot be consistent. If that symmetrical shaped is bisected, the result is anisohedral with one set of tiles with five neighbors and the other set with four.

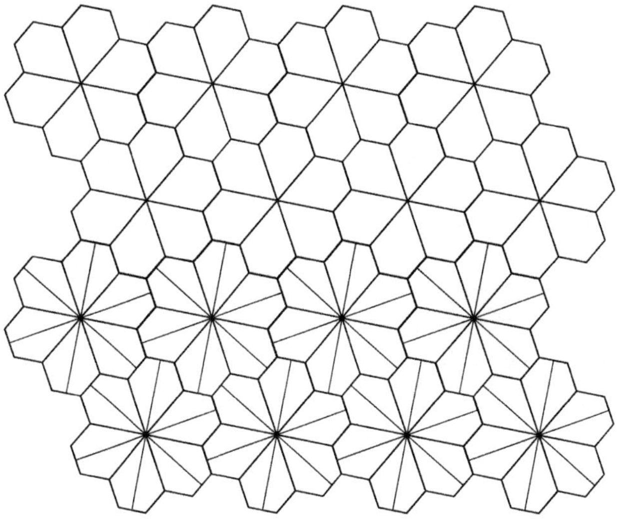

If you want to know more, Grünbaum and Shepard's book, *Tilings and Patterns*, is one of the very few sources available. Their discussion of this topic is detailed and challenging. It contains nuances that I still do not understand.

(Sometime in the 1990s I was browsing through a bookstore in Chicago and I found a box of the Grünbaum and Shepard books, all very cheap. This was the fate of books that did not sell well enough to keep in inventory—the excess was sold off to a book seller. I noticed that the book had a lot of illustrations that might be useful as designs in maze making, so I purchased a copy for a dollar or two. I did not pay much attention to the text—it was at a level of mathematics that I did not want to learn—but the illustrations were very useful. It did not have Escher-like tessellations, but it had decorative geometric tessellations and repeating patterns that were not tessellations. Unfortunately, when I thought I had exhausted all that I could get from it, I either donated it to a sale or I packed it away in some place that I no longer remember. As I was finishing an early draft of this book, I had brief access to the book via interlibrary loan and that brief access significantly changed how I ordered this section. Since then I have purchased another copy of the book and it has influenced subsequent revisions.)

IV. Themed Examples

Arrows

Most people who play with *TesselManiac!* will quickly stumble on the very common arrow pattern shown below. It can be formed in four templates, those for CCCC, CCGG, G1G1G2G2 and mirrored CCCC or C*CCC* (IH69).

One feature of the design is that the shaft can be any length and the arrows still tessellate.

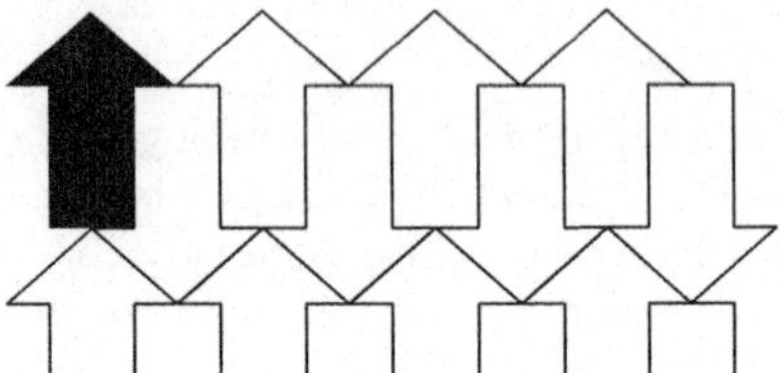

Putting fletching on the arrows requires only minor adjustments. The tile is still mirrored.

An elongated fletched arrow almost looks like a real arrow. Almost—the section of feathers must equal the length of the shaft without feathers. However, this shape or a very similar shape is used for pointing arrows, so the design is familiar.

Another mirrored arrow shape can be created with the mirrored C3C3C3C3 (IH36) template in *TesselManiac!*.

If we manipulate the design above by overlapping some lines, we get a C3C3C3C3C3C3 hexagonal tile that is mirrored, an IH16 class tile.

If we then eliminate the lines that we overlapped, we get this hexagonal shape of a three-way arrow that fits the IH18 class. All edges have the same central symmetry.

I kept some of the non-symmetric arrow tessellations that I found with *TesselMania* and *TesselManiac!* because

I thought they might be good patterns for mazes. The tile below has six neighbors, so it is hexagonal. Some of the tip is adjacent to the corresponding part in a neighbor, as is the longer edge of the tail. These are C or central-rotation edges. The other four are G or glide edges. Going clockwise, you should get CG1CG2G1G2. The G2 edges are the short edges at the end of the tail and on the head of the arrow.

We could also solve the type by noting that there are only two hexagonal tilings with translation units of four, TCCTGG and CG1CG2G1G2. The former has its block strung out in a four by one arrangement, not a two-by-two block as we have here. Hence it must be CG1CG2G1G2.

The pattern below looks similar, but each tile has only five neighbors. The long edge of the shaft of the arrow is rotated around to face itself, so this edge is a C or central-rotation edge. The others are G or Glide edges. Starting with the C edge, we can count off the type as CG1G2G1G2. Here the translation block count is not as useful as above because three of the five pentagonal types have translation blocks of four. (These two arrow patterns show how CG1G2G1G2 results when a C edge of type CG1CG2G1G2 is eliminated.)

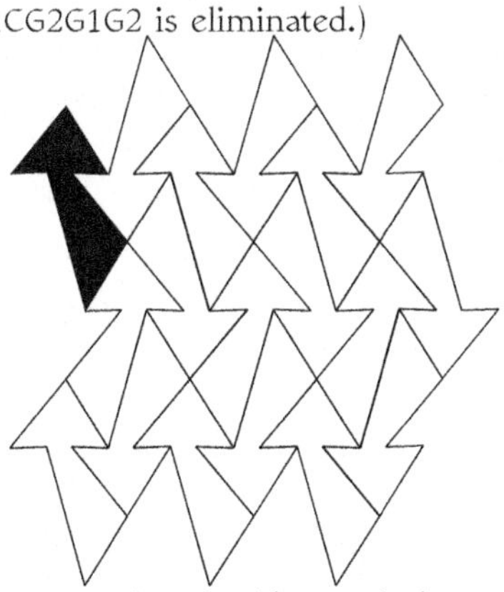

This next pattern gives itself away in its translation block, which is four in a row. Each column keeps the same orientation. There are only two Heesch types with this pattern, TCTGG and TCCTGG. Each tile has five neighbors, so it is TCTGG. The T edges line up in the columns and are short and straight.

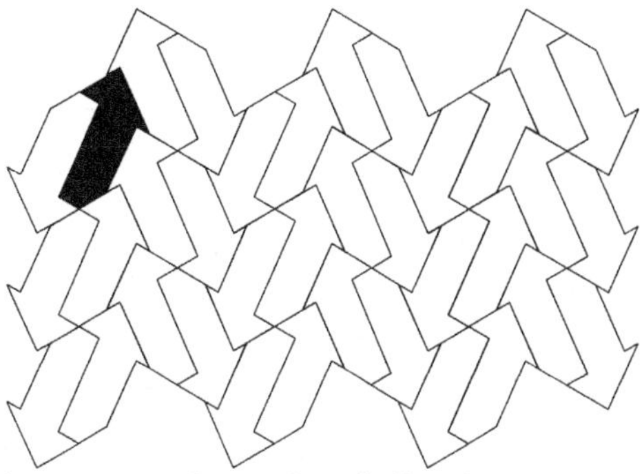

Another pattern that makes challenging mazes but is not attractive visually is the distorted arrow pattern shown below in which each tile has three neighbors. The elongated Z shape is a center-rotation edge and the other two edges, which are identically shaped, are G edges so the pattern is CGG.

Although it has symmetry with the top mirrored on the bottom, this next tile is not an especially attractive arrow and appears to be nothing more than a type TTTTTT design. However, there are two ways it can be aligned, as the next image shows.

The bottom cannot be TTTTTT. It can be TCCTCC and since it has mirror symmetry, it is also isohedral class IH13. That should lead us to reevaluate the top of the pattern, which can be a mirrored TG1G1TG2G2, or class IH12. In both of these cases the base design has an hourglass shape.

It is not possible for any star shape to tessellate. When playing with star patterns, I found that a modified six-sided star would tessellate by inverting one of its points. Of course then it is no longer a star. This shape has the same properties as the arrow discussed above. When the tiles are arranged with a translation block of one, they are class IH12 and simultaneously types TTTTTT and TG1G1TG2G2. If every other row is flipped, the translation block is two and they are class IH13, a mirrored type TCCTCC.

Below are two more TCCTCC type tiles that form arrows, though in different ways. Both also fit class IH13.

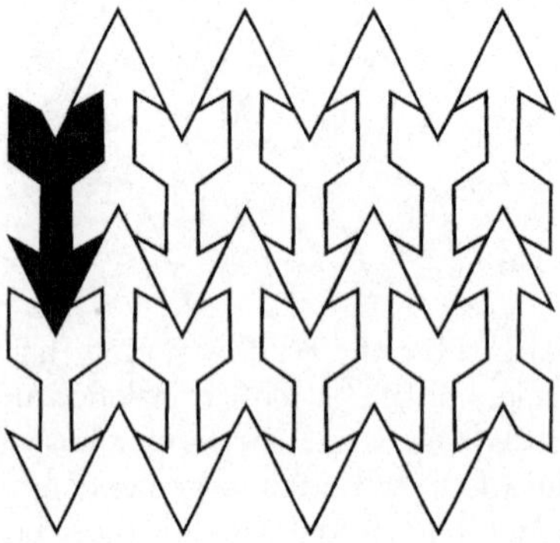

Crosses

The cross tiling created from five squares is well-known. It has a translation block of one so it obviously is a TTTT type. However, it also satisfied three other types: CCCC with all edges alike but no symmetry, TCTC, and C4C4C4C4 with all edges alike. It is also an example of isohedral class IH62. Although the cross shape has both horizontal and vertical reflection, the tiling has neither. It does not have symmetry across the diagonals nor across the midpoint of an edge.

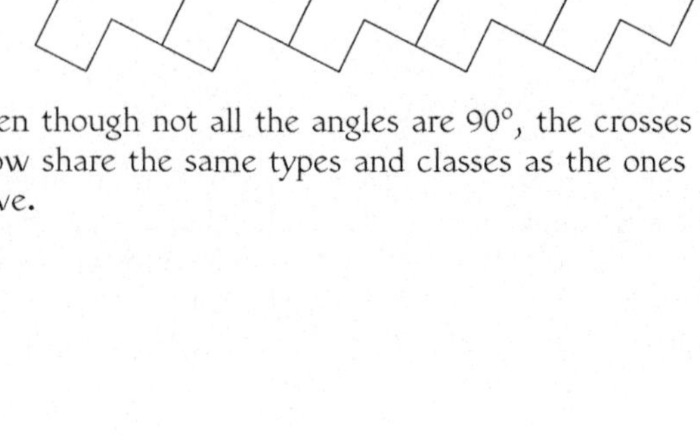

Even though not all the angles are 90°, the crosses below share the same types and classes as the ones above.

The pattern below is obviously TTTTTT because each tile has six neighbors and it has a translation block of one. However, it can also be TCCTCC, TCCTGG, TG1G1TG2G2, TG1G2TG2G1, and CG1CG2G1G2. It has the same properties as the roller pin design that illustrates IH17.

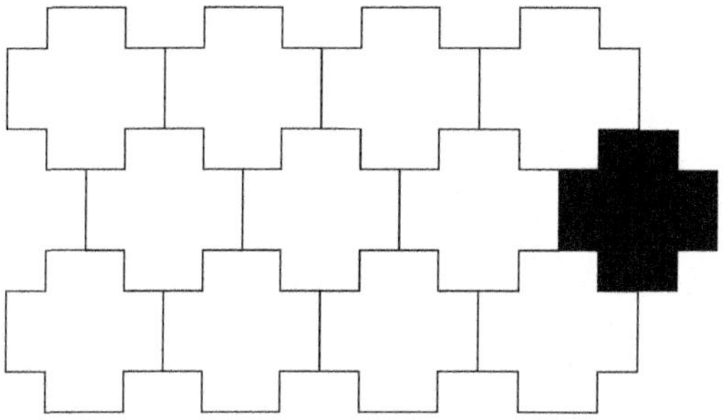

Some crosses have one of the four arms longer than the others, which gives them a letter T shape or the shape of the Christian cross. Below are two patterns of these crosses, the first a CG1CG2G1G2 type and the second a pentagonal type TCTCC. One of the features of the second one is that the longer arm can be of any length (but it does have to be longer).

Crosses appear as a translation block in many tessellations. Below is a pentagonal type CC4C4C4C4 in which a block of four forms a cross. (There are different blocks of four that form irregular hexagons.)

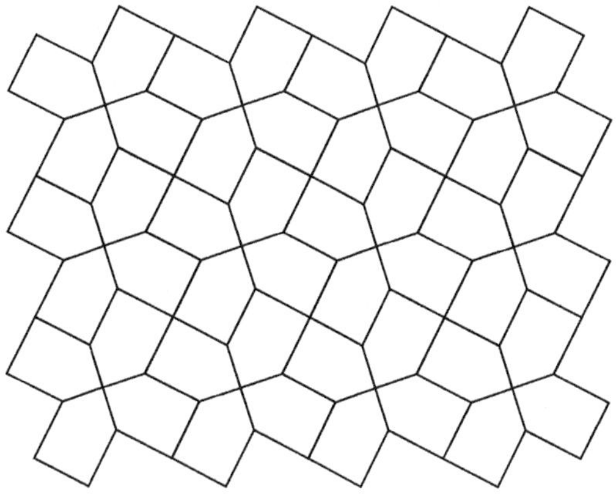

Blocks of two of these CCC triangular-based tessellations also form crosses.

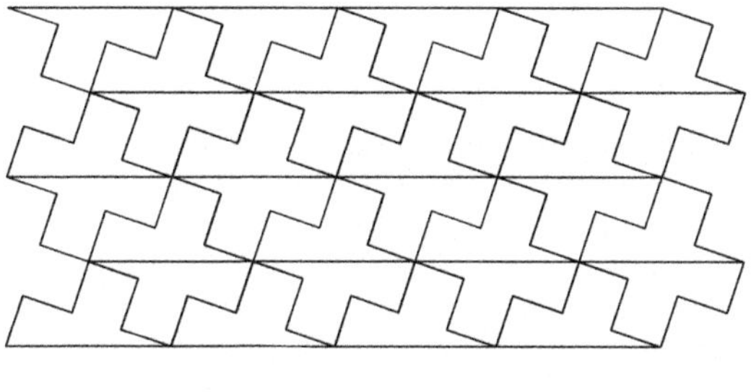

Using the same shape but with a different arrangement also forms crosses. These triangular-based tiles are CC4C4 types. Arrangement of tiles, not their shape, often determines type.

These upright Zs are type C4C4C4C4. Selecting the right block of four will reveal a cross.

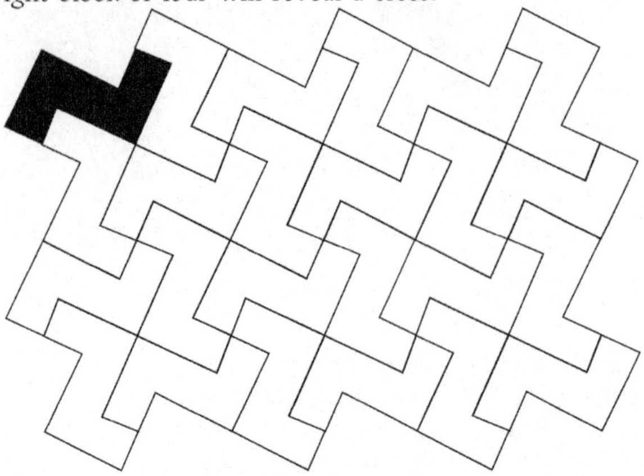

Below is still another way to subdivide a cross with a tile that is C4C4C4C4. This tile can be set into other patterns to form other shapes.

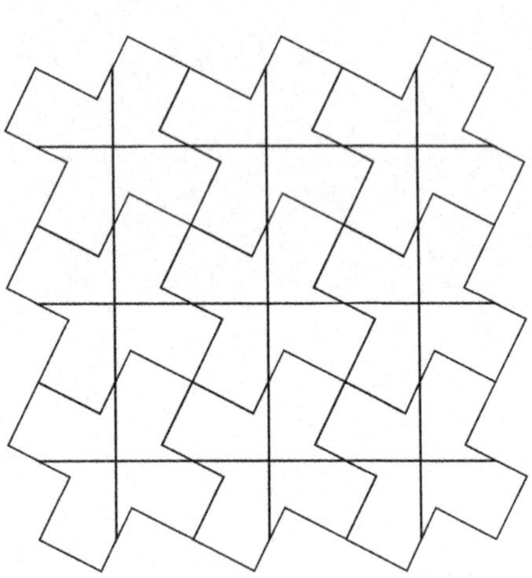

Below is a design that I found on the Internet. Escher knew of it. It may not look like a cross, but it is a modified cross. If the flat roofs in the cross are replaced with peaked roofs, this is the resulting figure. It is type TTTT. Tiles that have symmetry that is not carried over to the tiling have been called hypersymmetric. This tiling has been used as an illustration of the concept.

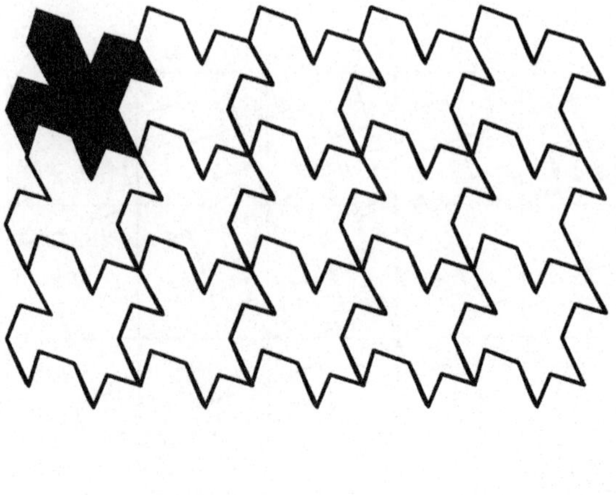

Tri Hex

The simple tile made by fusing three regular hexagons should be very familiar. This simple shape is highly symmetrical and can be arranged in at least four different tilings. Shape does not necessarily determine the Heesch type. Often the arrangement does.

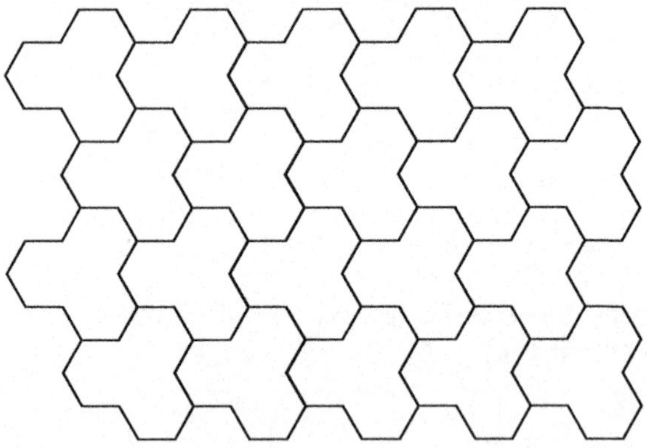

In the arrangement above the tile is clearly a type TTTTTT tessellation that illustrates the highly symmetrical IH18 class in which all edges are equal and have central symmetry. It is also fits type C3C3C3C3C3C3: rotating an edge 120° creates a second edge, and then repeating the process with the second edge, etc., will from the complete figure. Finally, it fits TG1G1TG2G2.

A second way of arranging the tiles is not a TTTTTT pattern because the translation block is two, not one. It clearly can be a TCCTCC type, with the TT edges on the top and bottom. The shape is mirrored over the middle of the TT edges so it fits isohedral class IH13. It can also be formed as a TG1G2TG2G1 type.

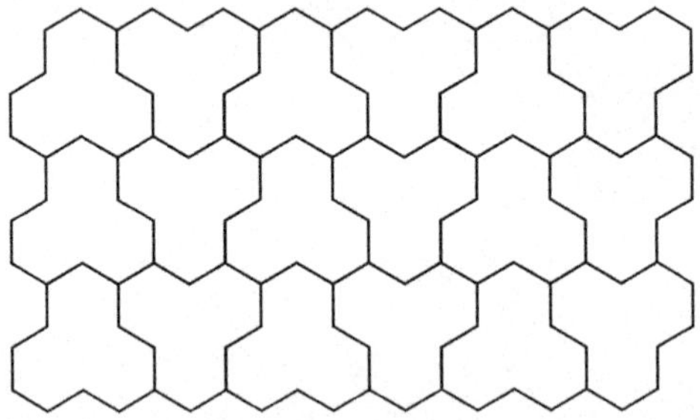

A third pattern using this tile is easily recognized as a TCCTCC type, with the TT edges being the two short edges connecting the tiles in a row. It could also be a TCCTGG type, with the GG edges being the two long edges that are adjacent to each other. One of the C edges would be short and one long. Type CG1CG2G1G2 also fits.

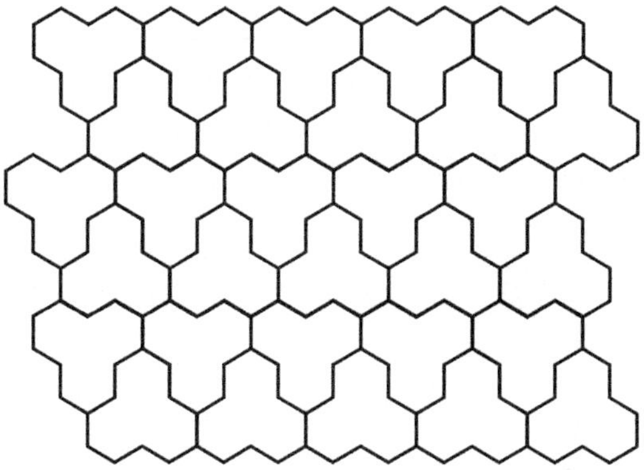

Finally, we have the pattern below. It cannot be a TTTTTT type because the translation unit is not one. What is it? There are long and short edges, and the sequence is SLSLLS or LLSSLS or several other sequences, depending on where one starts the sequence. (Some of the tiles are flipped, so will have the sequence in the reverse order.) That is the same sequence as in the pattern above, but the pieces are organized differently. I think there is only one thing it can be. My answer is below and if you want to come up with an independent answer, analyze it before you look at my answer.

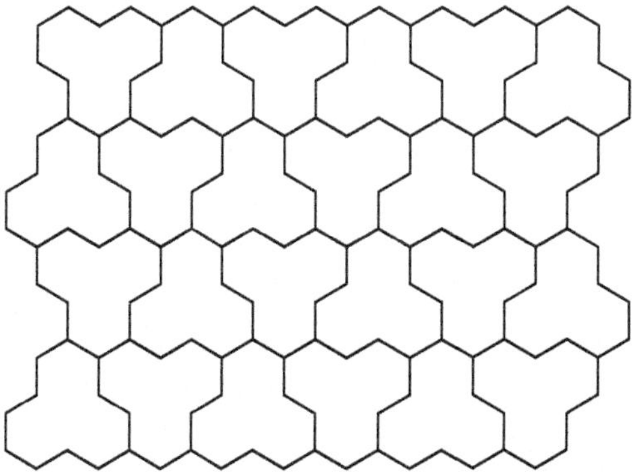

The tri-hex shape can be formed by a tiling that is C3C3C3C3C3C3.

In the tiling below six half-hexagon tiles form the tri-hex shape. I found this pattern in a picture of ceramic tiles on the Internet. It is an example of IH30, which is a bisection of IH16, which is a trisection of IH18. The half hexagon shape can be arranged in a variety of ways, but exploring its possibilities is beyond the scope of this book.

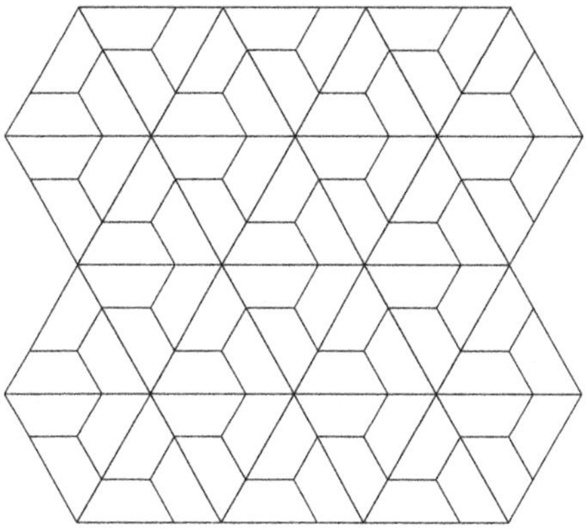

There are many other tilings that will yield the tri-hex shape by combining tiles. One is given as an example of isohedral class IH34.

My answer to the shape above: The translation block for the fourth pattern of the three fused hexagonal blocks is four. There are only two hexagonal types with a translation block of four, TCCTGG and CG1CG2G1G2. The TT edges will not fit the tile in this arrangement. However, CG1CG2G1G2 will align with a LLSSLS arrangement. G1 edges are long, G2 edges are short, and one C edge is long and the other short. The previous pattern could also be CG1CG2G1G2.

Tessellating Letters

In the late 1980s I discovered typography, the art of designing letters of the alphabet. The Macintosh was the first personal computer that supported different fonts and a few years after it was introduced, someone wrote a shareware or freeware bit-font editor that I downloaded and used to design a couple crude fonts. Soon after I purchased a copy of *Fontographer* and spent a number of years obsessed with type design. Given this background, it seemed natural to design mazes using letters as the decorative theme. I developed one book for young children and another, *Amusing Alphabet Mazes,* for an older audience. In the second book I used a number of tessellations, but most of the designs did not tessellate.

For reasons I no longer remember, I decided that it would be an interesting challenge to do a maze book with only tessellating letter mazes. I was not sure it was possible to find enough patterns to reach my goal of a 108-page book.* However, I not only found enough designs, but by the time I was finished, I was confident that I could produce a sequel, which I did. (For more about these books, *Puzzling Typography: Mazes with Letter Tessellations* and *Puzzling Typography A Sequel: Mazes with Tessellating Letters,* visit ingrimayne.com/mazes/mazeindex.htm.)

Attempting to reach a wider audience, I took many of the designs and made two books for a younger audience, *Tessellating Alphabet Mazes for Kids* and *The Tessellating Alphabet Coloring Book.* I also published most of the results in the form of several typefaces that are available on MyFonts.com. (Search for TessieDingie and Tescellations.) To let the reader see a typeface of tessellating letters, the rest of this section uses one that adds interior counters.

Until I began working on this book, I had never categorized these letter tilings by their Heesch type. By far the largest category is the TCCTCC type; no other type has even half as many entries. I also discovered that I had quite a few designs that did not fit the Heesch categories or even the isohedral classes. I had none that were based on triangular templates.

Let's take a look at some highlights, beginning with the alphabet done with TCCTCC tilings. Because there were so many options from which to choose, most letters show two examples. I have tried to include the best patterns; some others are included elsewhere in this book.

* Why 108 pages? Because CreateSpace charged a fixed rate for any book 108 pages or shorter. Each additional page after the 108th page added a couple cents to the cost of the book. It seemed wasteful not to fully utilize all 108 pages.

The TCCTCC Alphabet

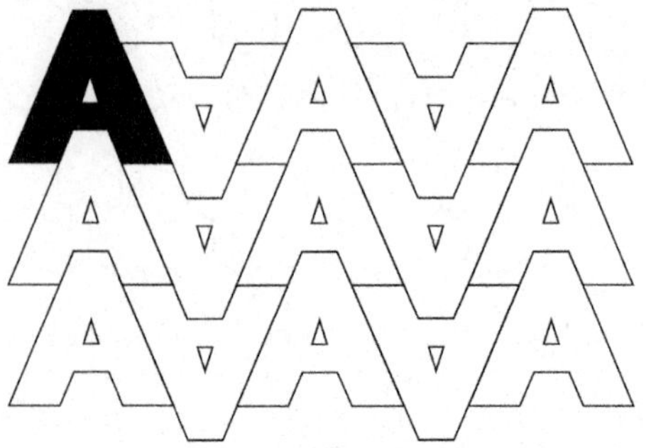

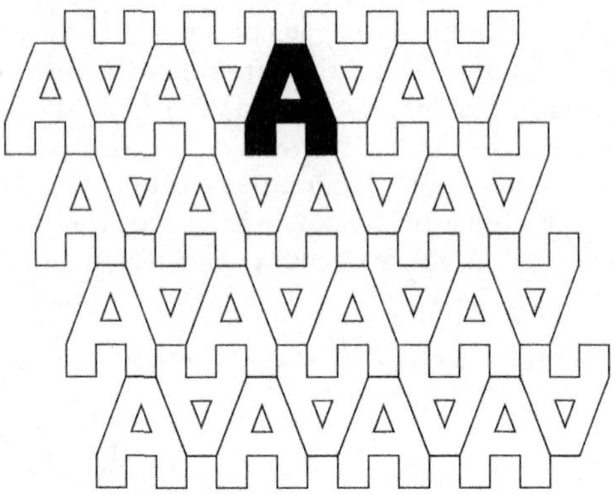

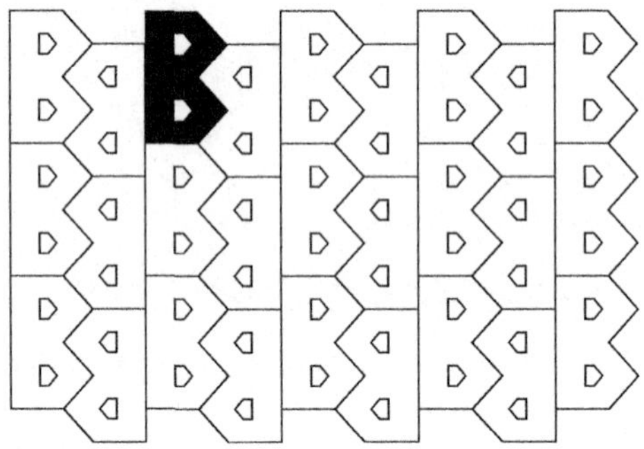

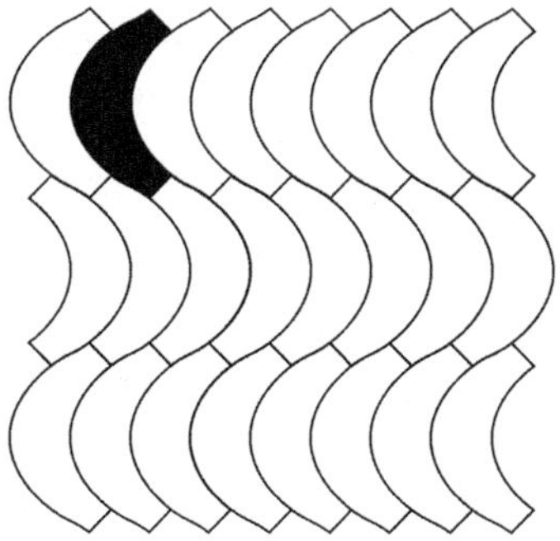

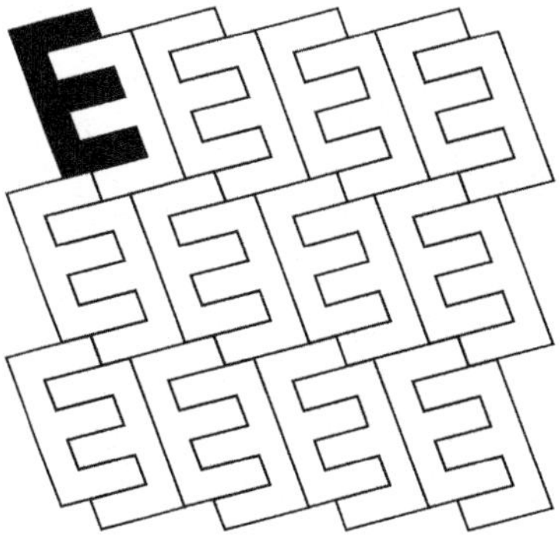

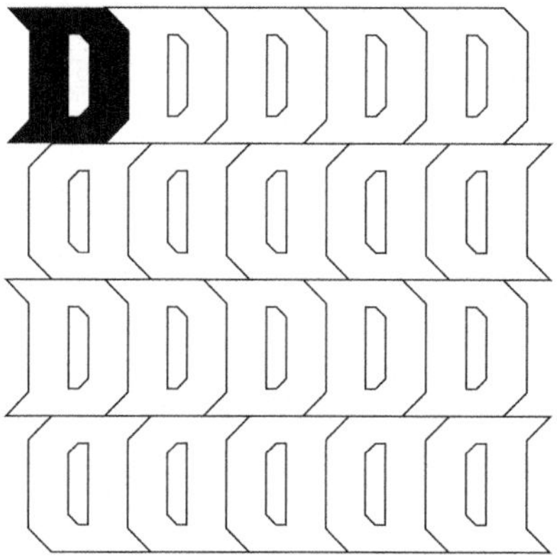

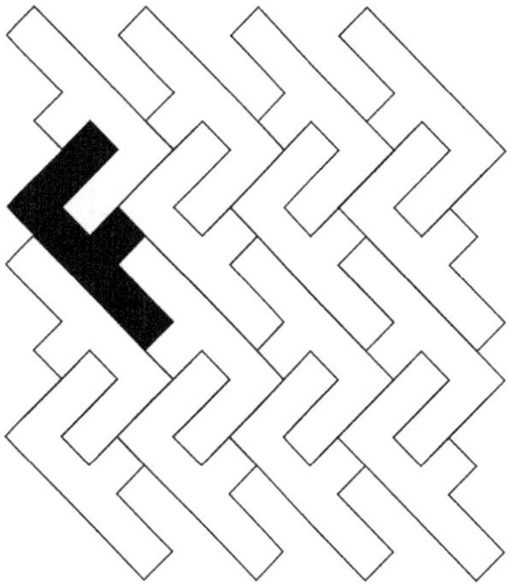

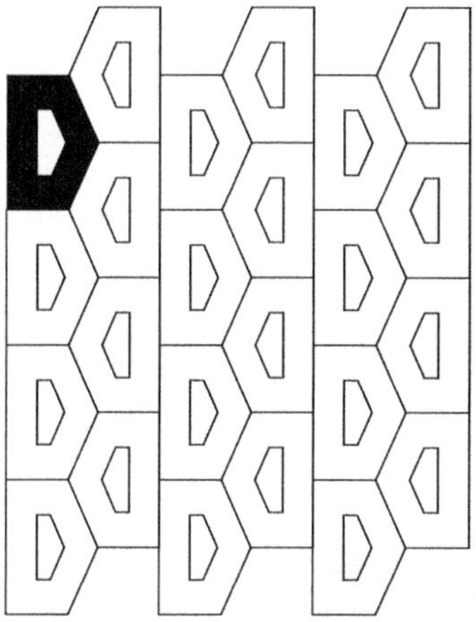

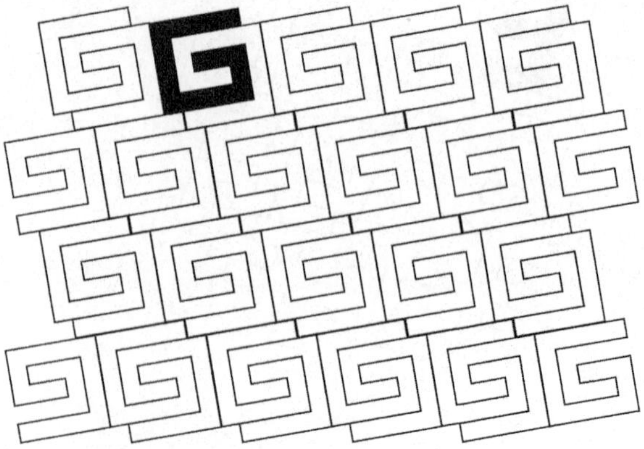

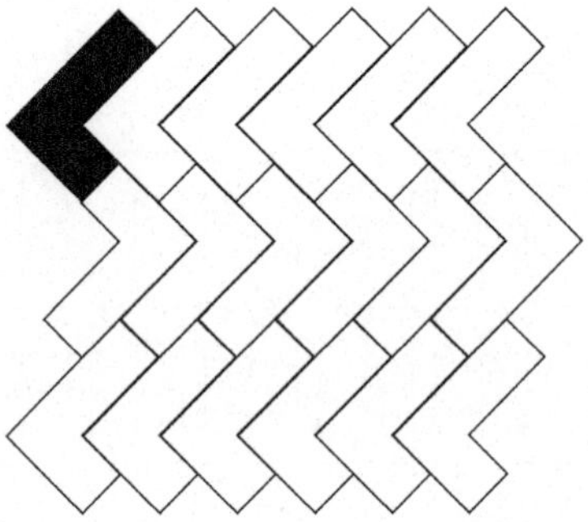

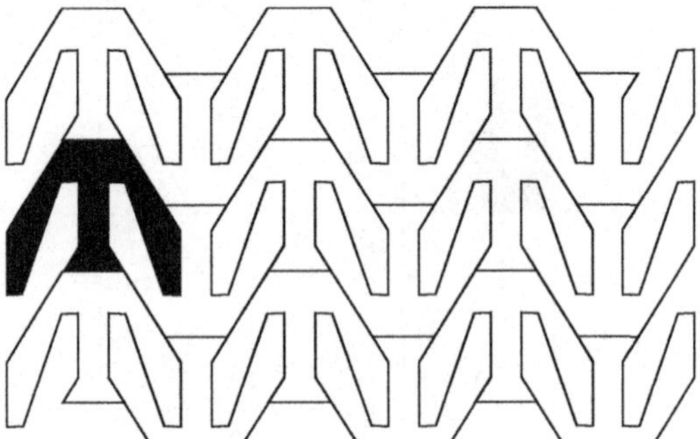

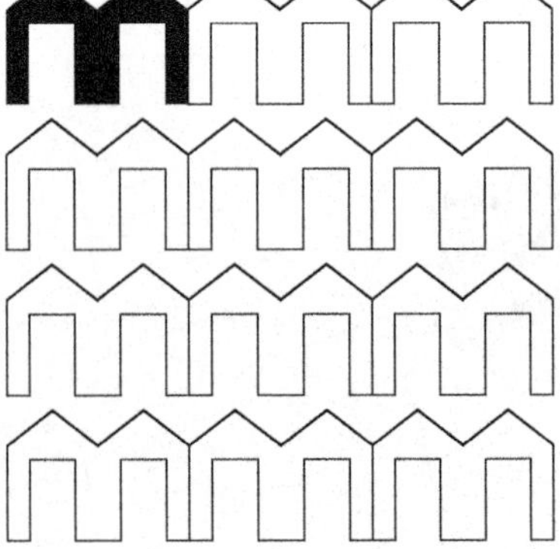

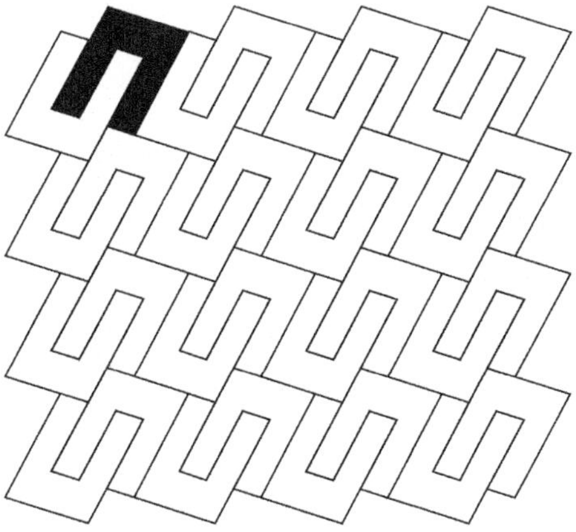

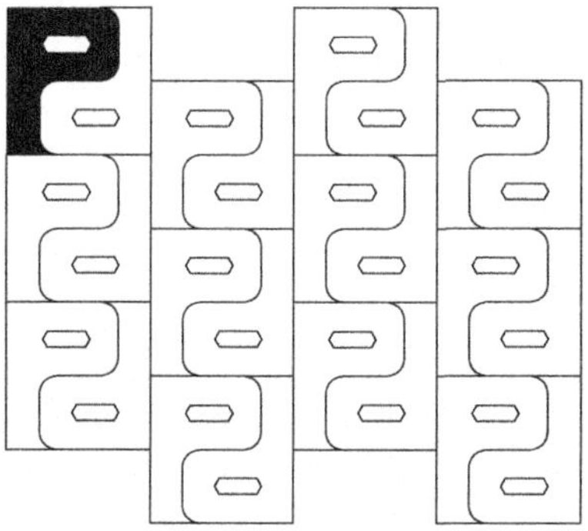

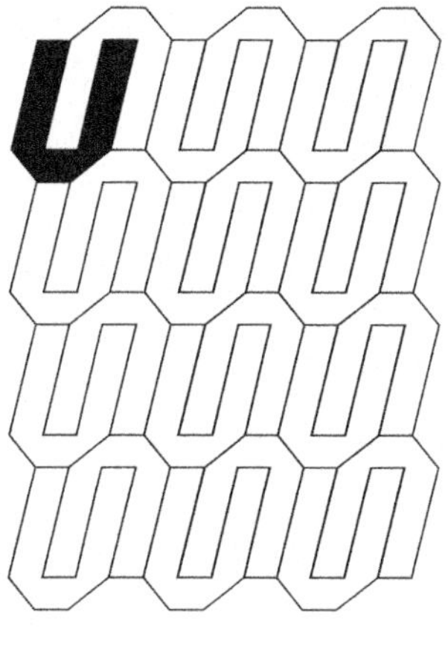

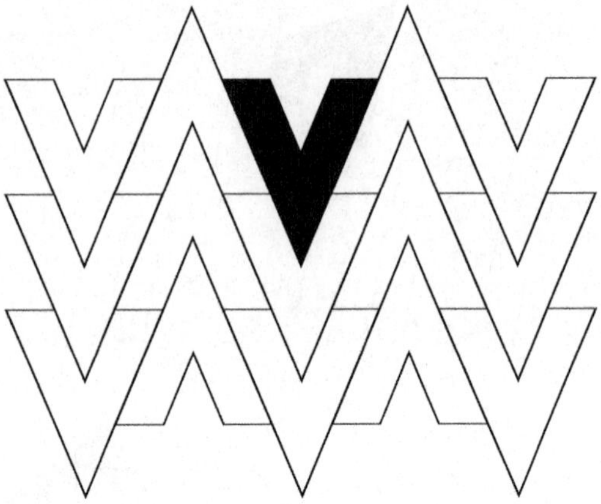

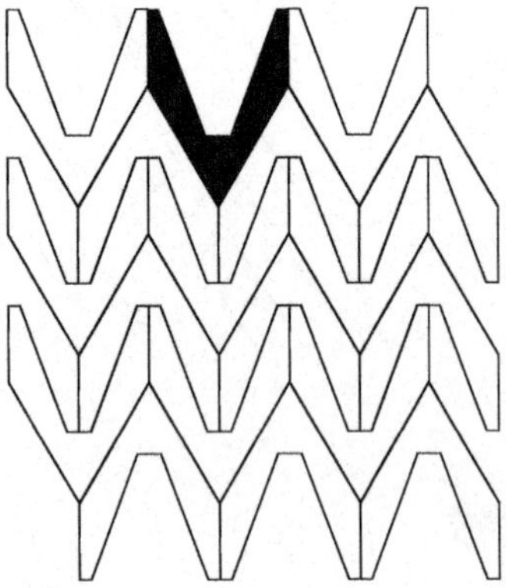

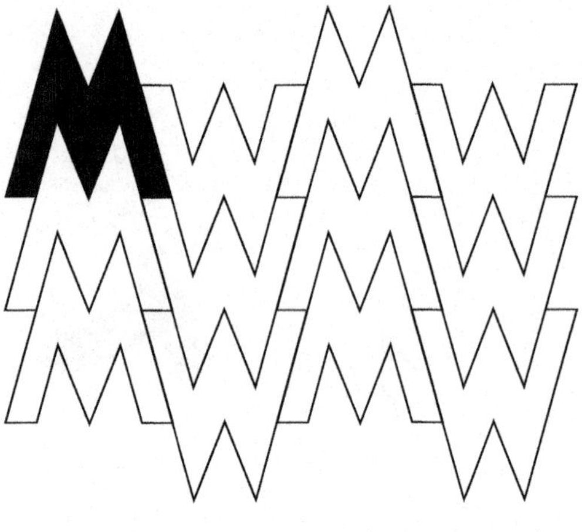

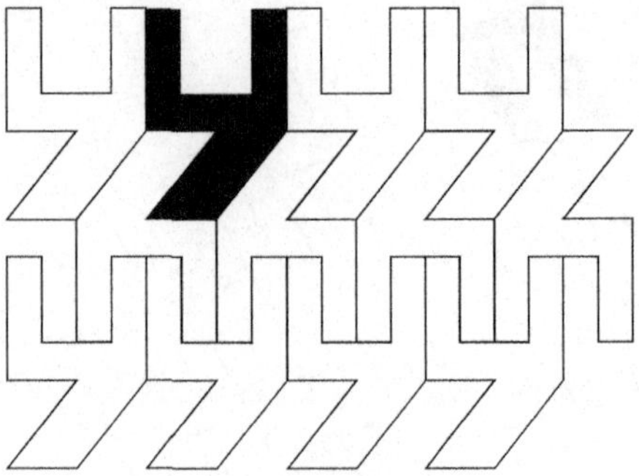

We are missing some letters, but they can be added with tiles that are both **TCCTCC** and **TTTTTT**, which means they fit into isohedral class **IH8** or **IH17**. The first H shape could also be an **I** shape if it is rotated **90** degrees.

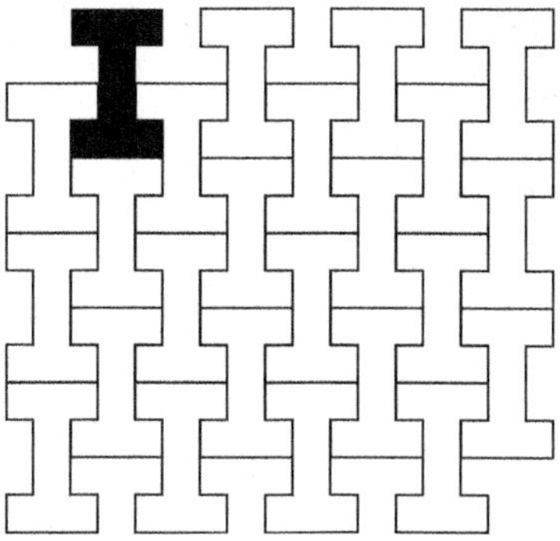

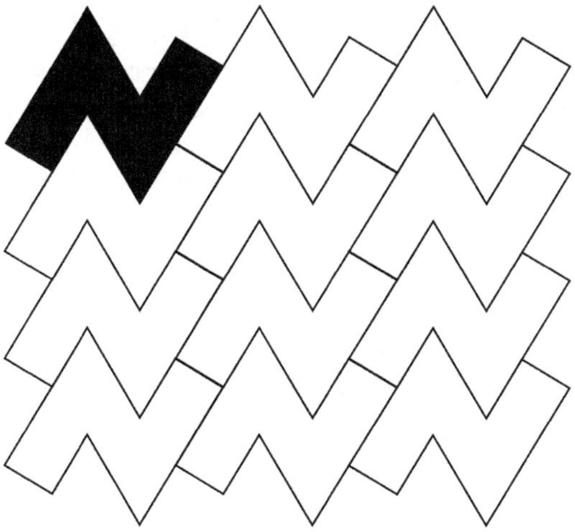

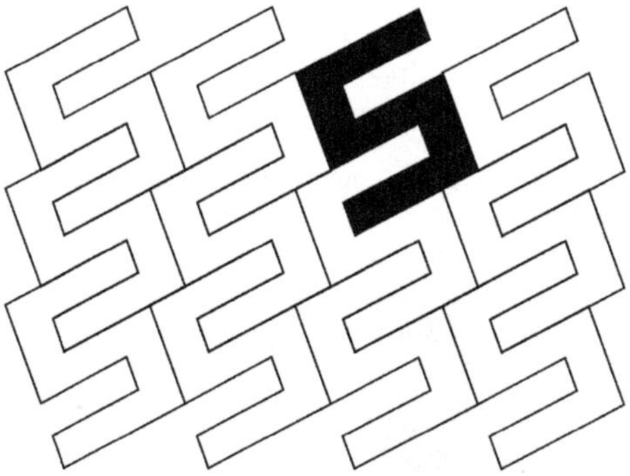

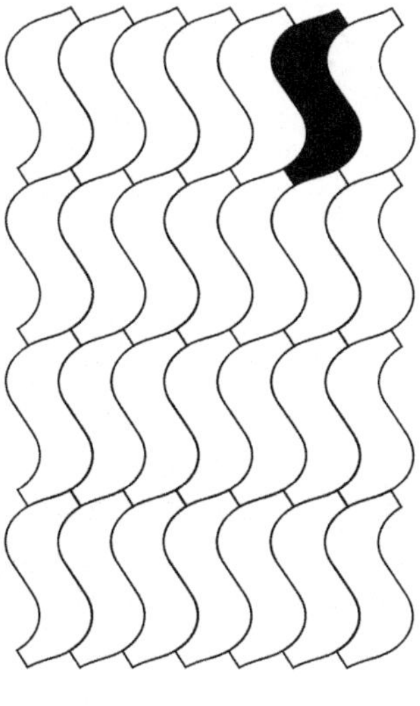

The next letter is supposed to be an **X** not a **T**.

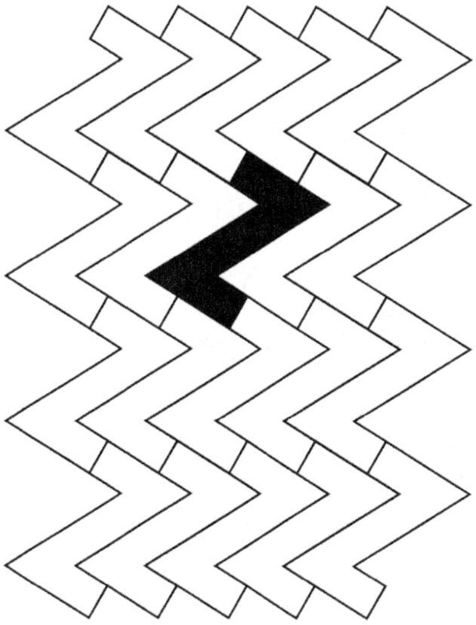

Finally the letter **O**, a challenging letter to tessellate. A pattern of elongated hexagons, which obviously is a type **TTTTTT** tiling but also fits all other hexagonal types except **C3C3C3C3C3C3** (as all **IH17** tilings do) was the best **I** could find.

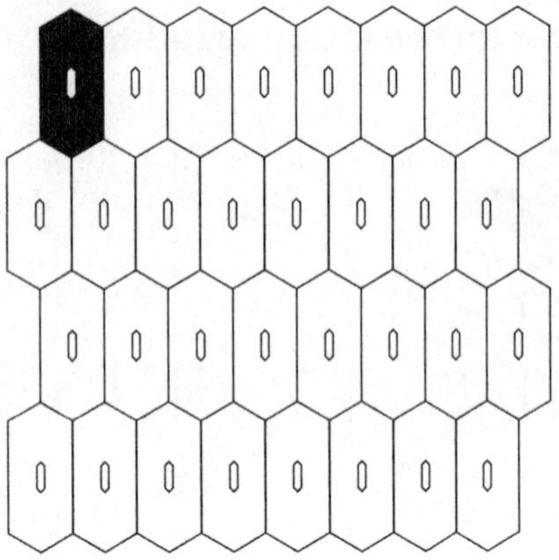

Other Types of Letters

The best tessellation of the letter A that I found was a mirrored CCCC or IH69 class tessellation. It could also be created as a CCGG type. The second A tiling is type CG1CG2G1G2.

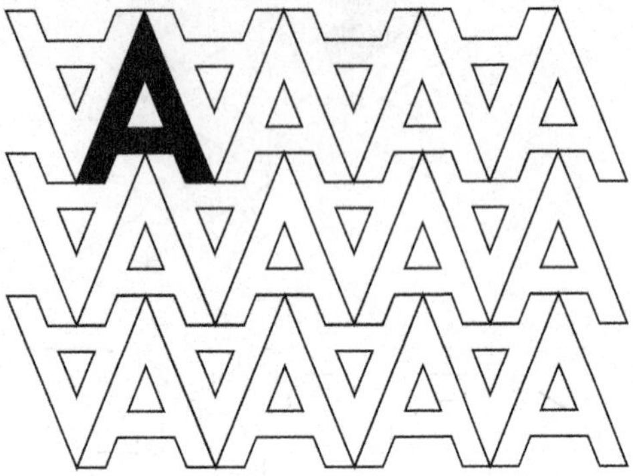

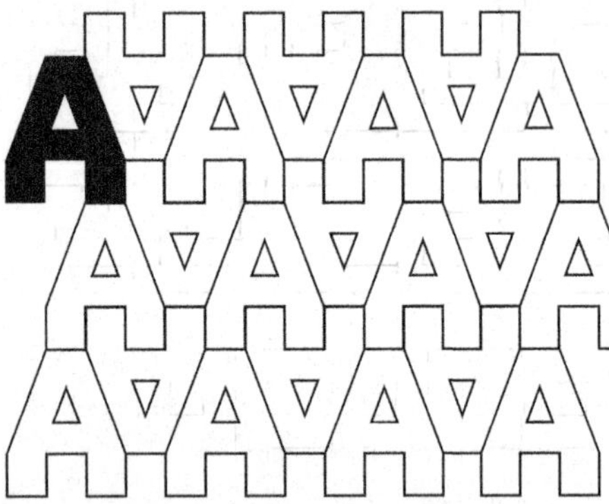

Although not nearly as common as the TCCTCC types, I found many TCTCC type letter patterns in what I had done. This pattern could be the lower case A or a lower case G, or if one is not too particular, can be arranged as a lower case E.

Most of my collection of letter tessellations are hexagonal types. This TTTTTT type has symmetry across one of the diagonals. It could also be formed as a TG1G2TG2G1 and the symmetry makes it appear as a TTTTTT. It is an example of class IH14.

Like one of the As above, this C is type CG1CG2G1G2.

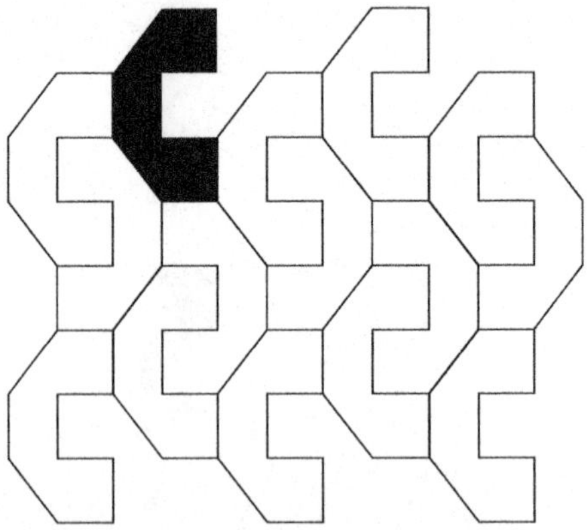

This simple shape is a TTTT type. It can also be classified as IH64, a highly restricted type of TTTT (or TGTG or TCTC). Two opposite sides are straight and unshapeable. The other pair is identical with central symmetry. The letter D shown next is also of this type and class.

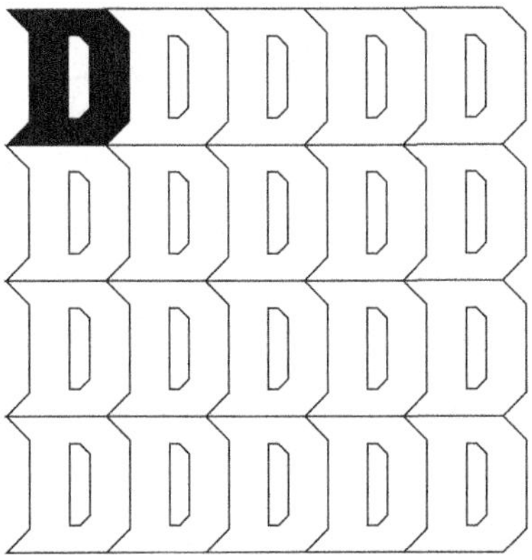

I was surprised to find a type **TCCTGG** tessellation in my collection of letter patterns. It is not a type that I find easy to use for mazes.

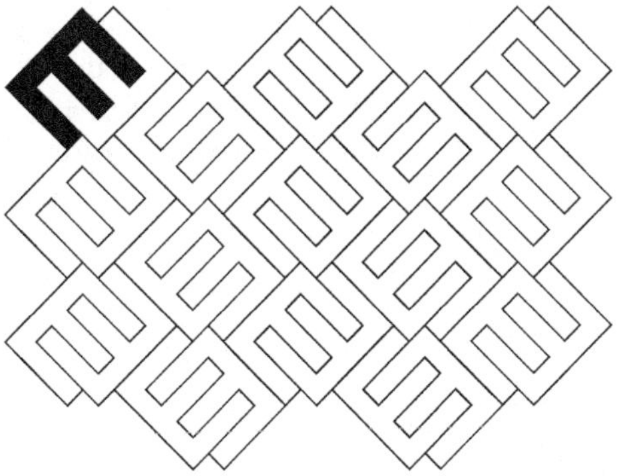

The same tile of the letter F fits into both a type **TCTCC** tiling and a type **CC4C4C4C4** tiling.

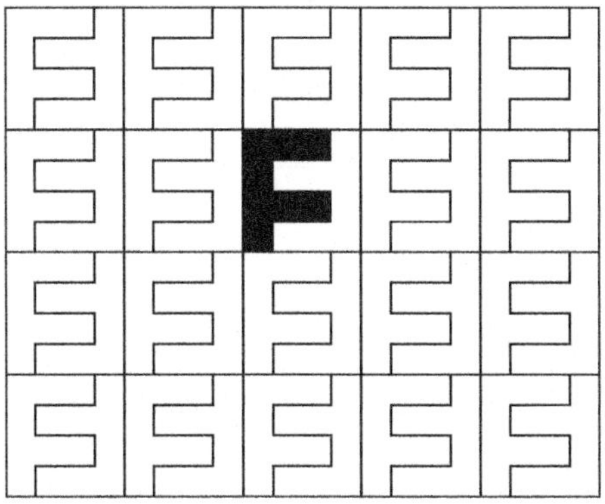

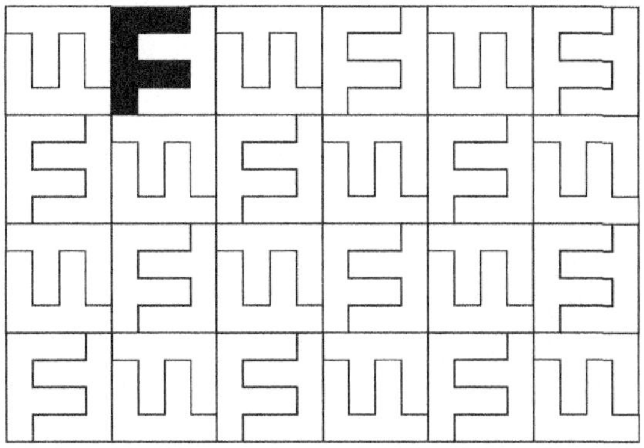

Type **TCTCC** was a productive source of letter tessellations, and contributed these tessellations of the letter G.

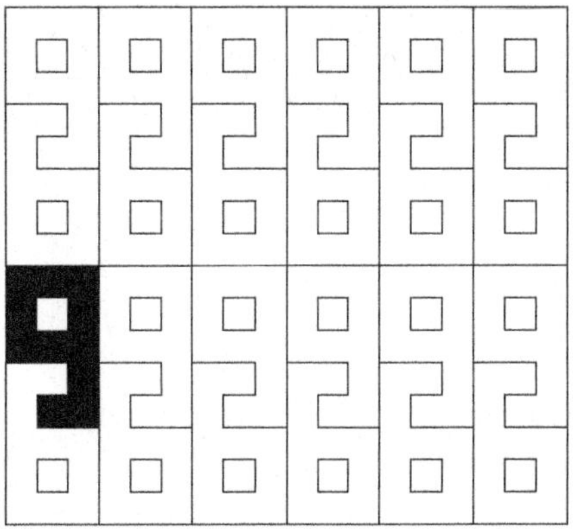

Here are two ways to tessellate the lower-case letter H. The first is type TTTTTT and the second TG1G2TG2G1.

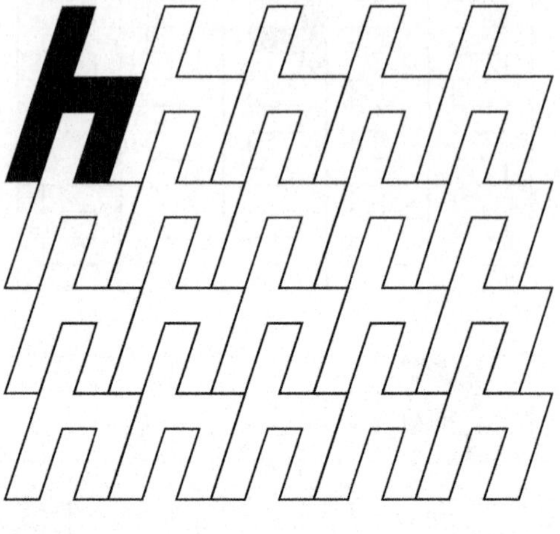

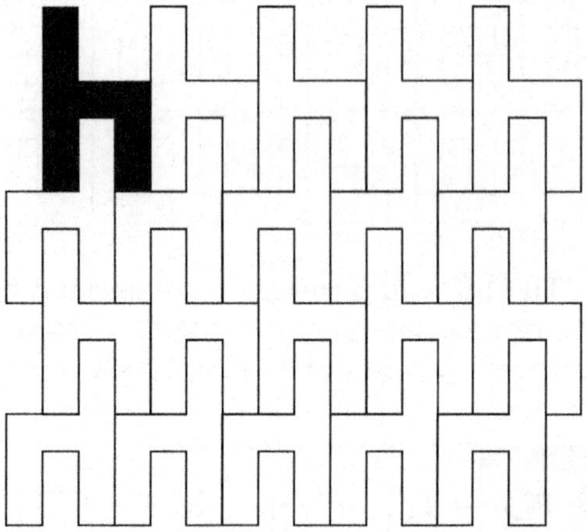

The commonest way to tessellate the letter I is with this type C4C4C4C4 with all edges shaped in the same way. It fits isohedral class IH73.

A pentagonal type TCTCC yields a convincing letter J.

The K is one of the most difficult letters to tessellate and I do not have a good example that is not TCCTCC. Below is the best I could find. It could be either TCCTCC or TG1G1TG2G2.

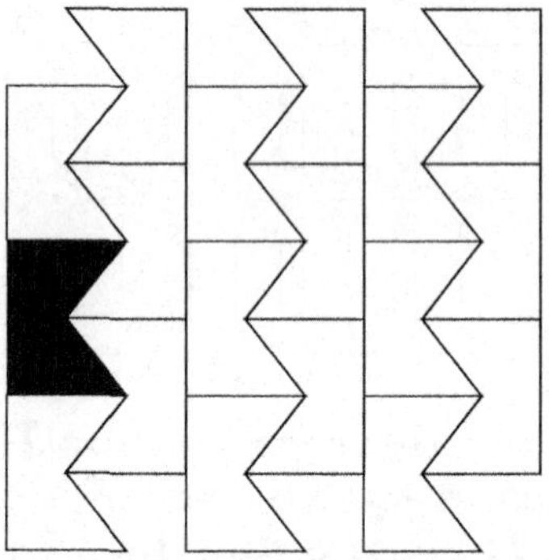

Others letters that are difficult are R and O. In contrast, the letter L is very easy to tessellate. I am pretty sure that there are an infinite number of ways to do it. Even confining oneself to ways that have small translation blocks of not more than 10, there are dozens. Both of these patterns of letter Ls are type TG1G2TG2G1.

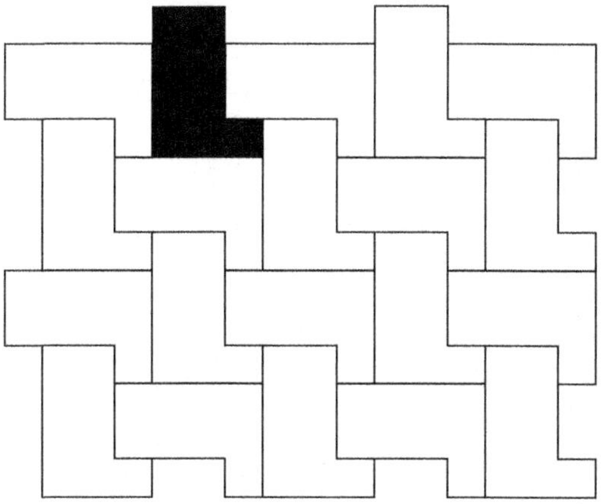

This letter M tiling is another example of class IH14, a special case of **TG1G2TG2G1.**

For the letter N see **U** or perhaps **Z.**

The **P** pattern below is **TG1G1TG2G2.** Rotated **180** degrees it can also be used for lower-case **B** and **D.**

This shape fits together in many ways. Below it fits as type **TCTCC.**

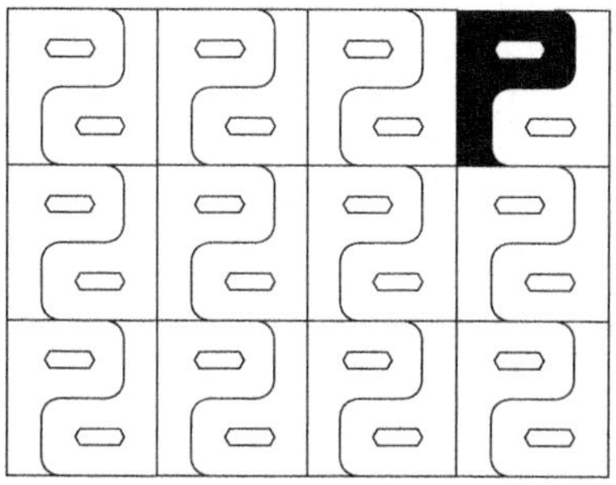

There are not a lot of ways to tessellate the letter **Q** but one of them results in a shape that is easily recognizable as a **Q.** It is an example of type **TTTT.** If top line is stretched, it can fit class **IH12,** which is a restricted case of type **TG1G1TG2G2.**

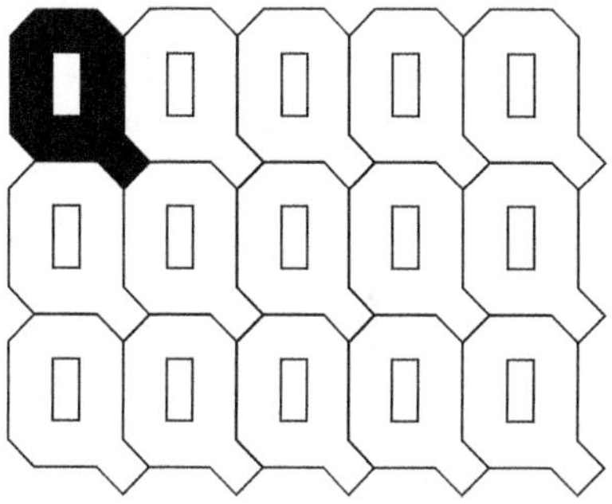

The shape below was the most realistic way to tessellate an upper-case letter **R** that I found. It is another example of **TCTCC.**

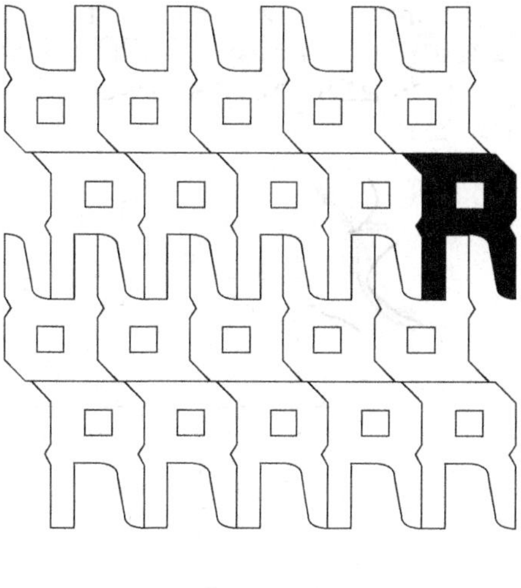

Less realistic is this **CCCC** version of the letter, slanted a bit to prevent drift.

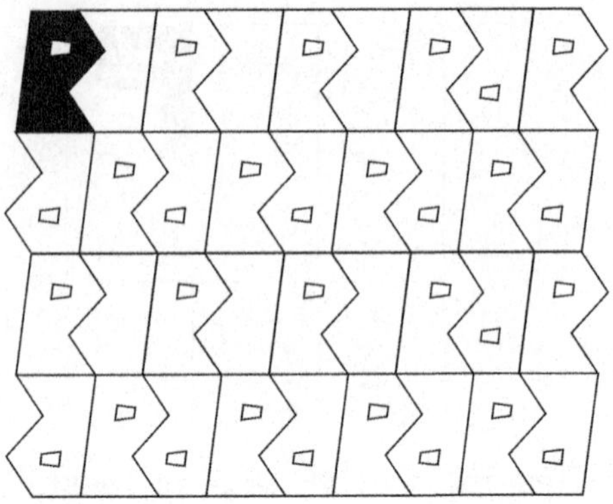

The first example of the letter **S** is type **TTTT** (though it could also be **TCTC** and thus also **IH57**) and the second is **G1G1G2G2** and **IH59**.

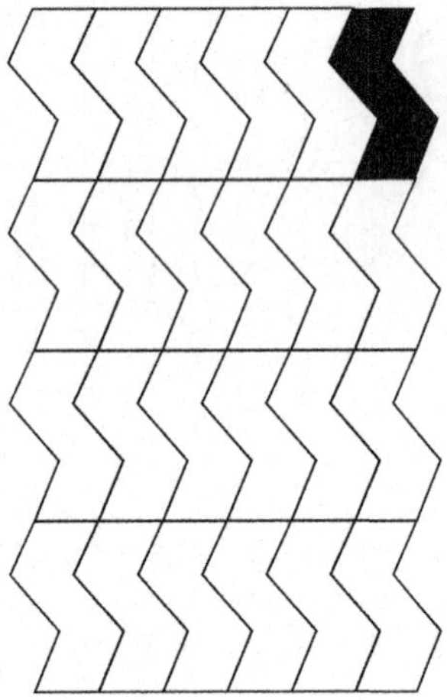

There are many ways to get patterns of tessellating letter **T**s. Here are examples of type **CC4C4C4C4**, a type that I have rarely used other than for tessellating letters, and type **CG1CG2G1G2**.

This crude letter **U** (or ***N***) is type **TCTCC**. With three edges held straight and the other two **CC** edges identical and mirrored, it fits isohedral class **IH26**. It is a bisection of an **IH17** tiling of the letter **H**.

The shape of the next **U** is the same as one that tiles as **TCCTCC** but here it is in a **CG1CG2G1G2** pattern.

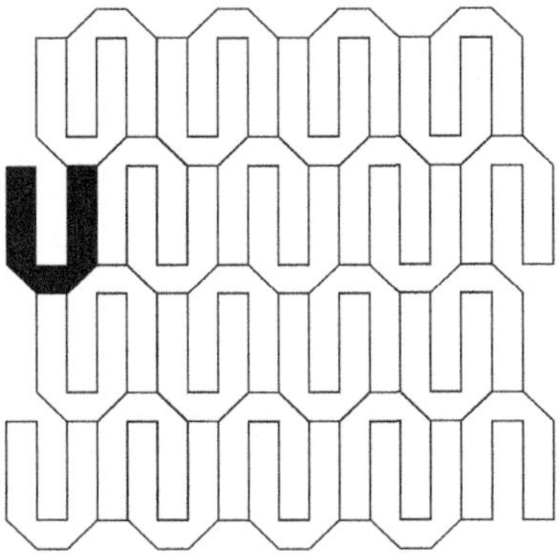

The letters V and W shown here are type **TTTT**. With straight sides and top and bottom with central symmetry, they fit isohedral class **IH64**.

The first letter **X** is type **TTTT**, **CCCC**, **TCTC**, and **C4C4C4C4** with all edges equal, which describes isohedral class **IH62**.

The second is a cross tessellation, type **TTTT**.

This letter **Y** is another example of isohedral class **IH64**, a restricted form of **TTTT**. Two opposite sides are straight and unshapeable. The other pair is identical with central symmetry.

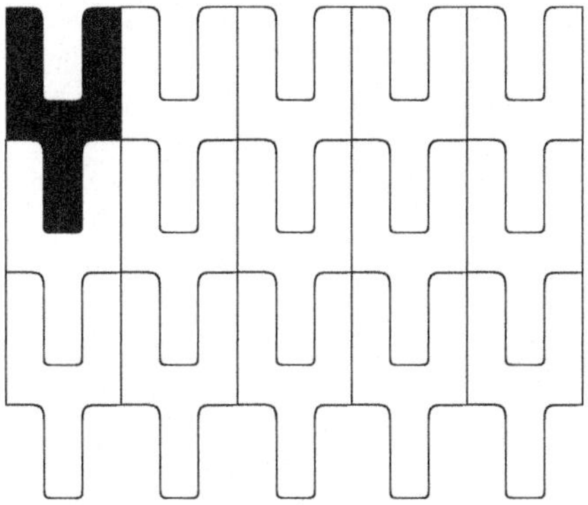

The first example of a letter **Z** tessellation is class **IH9**, a restricted type **TG1G2TG2G1**, and the second is class **IH34**, a restricted type **C3C3C3C3**.

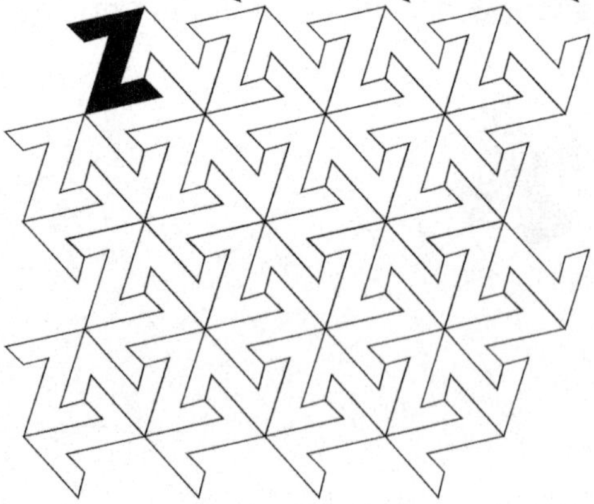

The Letter F

There are many ways to tessellate the letter F. Several shapes fit multiple tilings. For example, consider the shape and tiling below. It has six edges and because its translation block is one, it is TTTTTT. If you examine it carefully, you should see that it is also type TCCTCC. Isohedral class IH8 is a class that contains tilings that are simultaneously TTTTTT and TCCTCC.

elow is another tiling that initially may appear as if it is a different shape. It started as the same shape as above, but then I skewed it to make the rows perfectly horizontal and the columns perfectly vertical. Like the figure above, it also fits class IH8, but the edges are different.

This third tiling looks very much like the first one and you may guess that it too fits class IH8. However, it does not. Although it is type TCCTCC, it is not a type TTTTTT even though it appears that the translation block is one. Look at how the front of the letter fits into the back of the next letter. That long edge is an edge of center-point rotation, but it has no pair, and it must have a pair to be TTTTTT. The TT edges are the two edges that match, the angled surface. The translation block is two, not one.

This final pattern also has a translation block of two. It is Heesch type TG1G2TG2G1.

Another F shape that was interesting is shown below in a TCCTCC tiling.

When I was trying to determine the type of the tiling above, I thought it might be type CG1CG2G1G2. However, when checking it by trying to reproduce it in *TesselManiac!,* I realized that the pattern would be different for type CC1CG2G1G2, as shown below. Type CG1CG2G1G2 has a translation unit of four.

Below is a third pattern, also TCCTCC. Here the backs of the legs fit together rather than the fronts of the legs as in the two tilings above.

The power of type TCCTCC when tessellating letters is shown with a third way it can tessellate this tile.

Finally, below is a fifth tiling using the same shape. (The reason that these tiles do not look quite the same from pattern to pattern is that in order to make them line up in perfectly vertical columns and perfectly horizontal rows, I skewed some of them. For my way of making mazes, I needed to eliminate drift, where the pattern gradually shifts off to one side or the other.) Notice that the top of the letter F is in some rows placed next to the end of the crossbar of its neighbor, but in other rows it is nestled between the tops and the front of the crossbar. Also, those tiles with top front next to back crossbar have seven adjoining tiles while tiles with nestled fronts have only five adjoining tiles.

This tiling does not fit the Heesch types. Neither does it fit the Grünbaum and Shepard classification. The reason is that it is not an isohedral tiling; rather it is an anisohedral tiling. An isohedral tiling is a pattern in which each tile has the same shape and size and each tile plays the same role as every other tile. Playing the same role means that the way neighboring tiles fit the tile is the same for all tiles. If tiles fit their neighbors in more than one way, the tiling is anisohedral.

Mathematicians make a distinction between anisohedral tilings and anisohedral tiles. If a tile fits into an anisohedral tiling, it is still considered isohedral if it is capable of fitting into an isohedral tiling. Only a tile that cannot be fit into a isohedral tiling is considered to be an anisohedral tile. More information about anisohedral tiles and tilings can be found on the Internet. A site I found useful is www.angelfire.com/mn3/anisohedral/explain.html#aniso_tiling.

The notation that mathematicians have for classifying tilings has numbers before the words isohedral or anisohedral. Virtually all the tessellations in this book are isohedral and the vast majority are 1-isohedral. The 1 is usually dropped. The letter F tiling above is 2-isohedral. This tile is isohedral because it will fit into isohedral tilings as shown in the first four patterns.

The classification then looks at the number of neighbors a tile has in each of its roles, which in this case is five and seven. Finally, the number of neighbors with the same role and the number with a different role are counted. The five-neighbor tile has three neighbors that are unlike it and two that are similar and the seven-neighbor tile has three adjacent tiles that are unlike it and four that are similar.

According to the Wikipedia entry on anisohedral tiling, the first anisohedral tile was discovered by Heesch in 1935. Although I have found several anisohedral tilings of letters, none of the letter tiles is an anisohedral tile.

Easy Anisohedral Tilings

An easy way to build an anisohedral tiling is to mix two different isohedral tilings. For example, consider the two tilings of the letter L, which are the same except one is a rotation of the other. It is type TTTTTT.

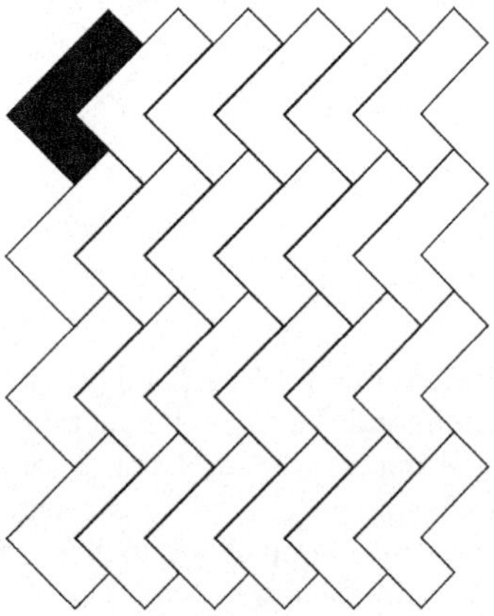

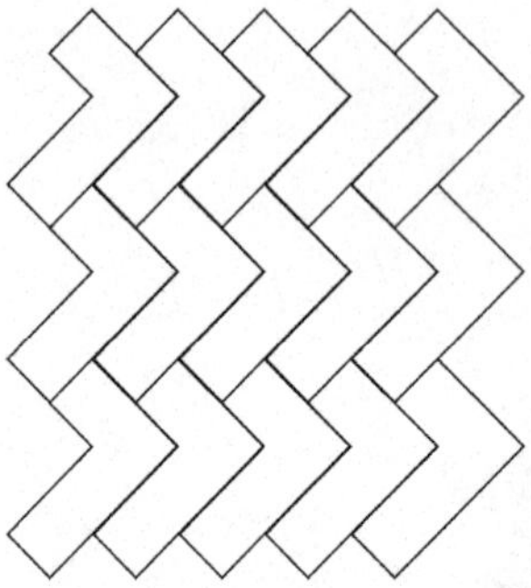

Alternating the rows still gives us an isohedral tiling, one that is TCCTCC.

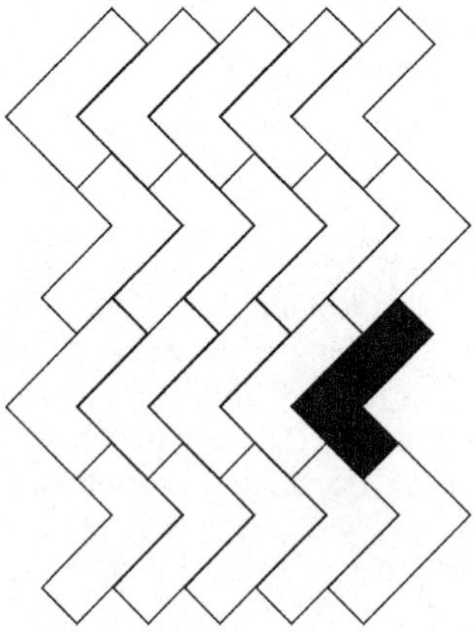

However, it we alternate every two rows we get a tiling that is not isohedral. Sometimes the tops of the letters meet other tops and sometimes they meet the side of the top.

Below is another example. These two tilings are CC4C4C4C4 and the second is simple a flip of the first.

If you mix these two patterns, you can get many other patterns, most or all of which will be anisohedral tilings.

Many of the anisohedral letter tilings I found are formed in this way.

More Anisohedral Tilings

I am way out of my depth in trying to make sense of anisohedral tilings and I would avoid the topic completely if I had not stumbled on so many of them when I was tessellating letters. I will attempt to make some sense of these tilings, but do not take my answers as authoritative because I have no expertise. Check my reasoning and counting and if you come to the same conclusion, we may both be right.

Subdividing squares and rectangles provide easy ways to get anisohedral tilings. In this first tiling the top of the P is either fit against the lower part of a neighbor's back or against the upper part of a neighbor's back.

Tessellation formed in the interior of a rectangle can be arranged in a great many ways. I can find three different positionings of the F in this pattern, some with five neighbors and others with six.

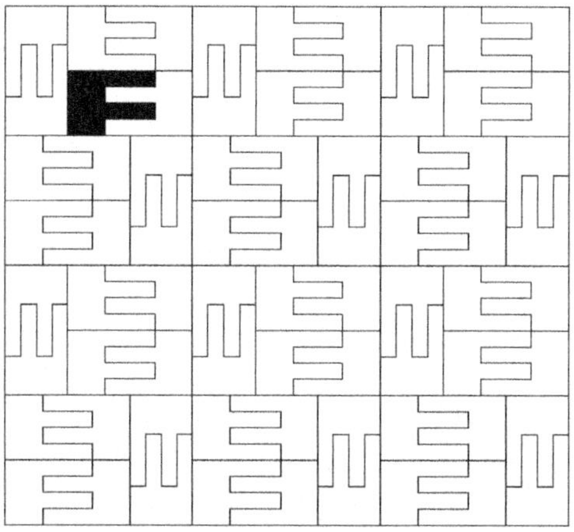

Below is a this tile in a Heesch TCTGG type showing that it is an isohedral tile.

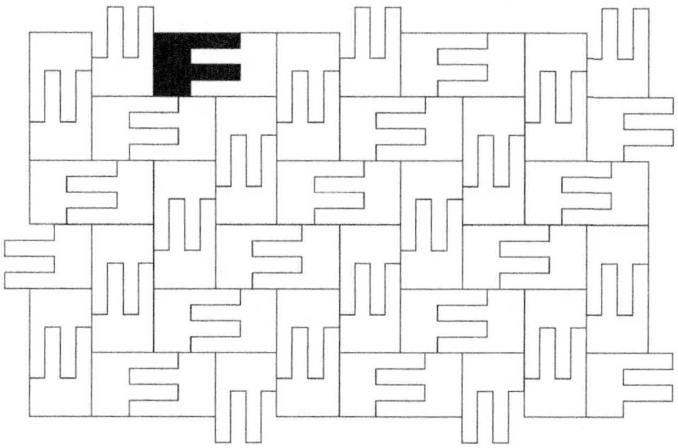

The letter L also fits nicely into rectangular blocks so there are many patterns one can build with it. In the next pattern I can see three different roles it plays, with four, five, and six neighbors for the various roles.

Here is another rearrangement of the blocks. I count three different roles and neighbors of five and six.

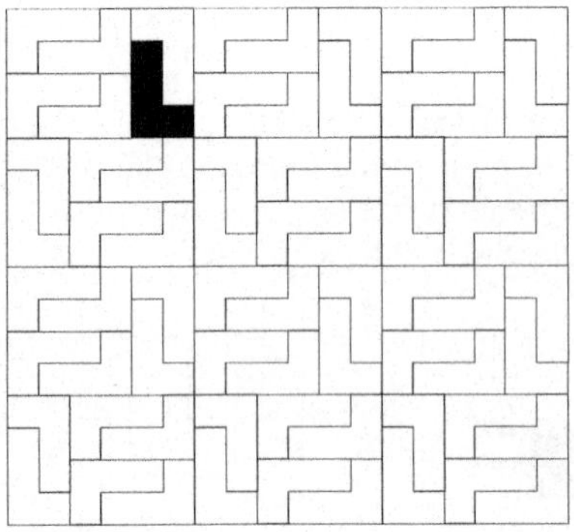

Below is one more arrangement of the blocks. I count two roles and neighbors of five and six.

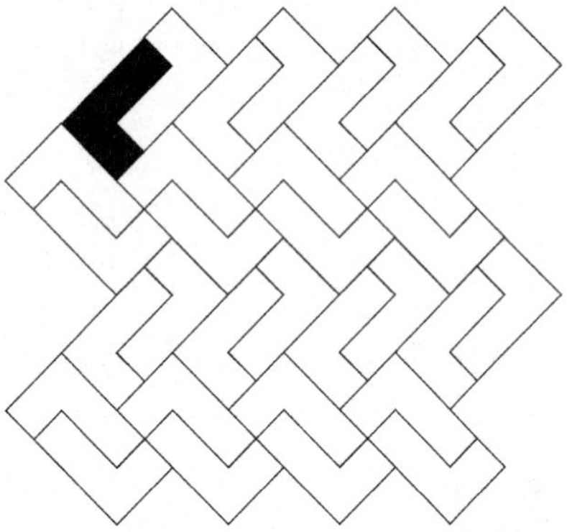

I think this is 2-isohedral.

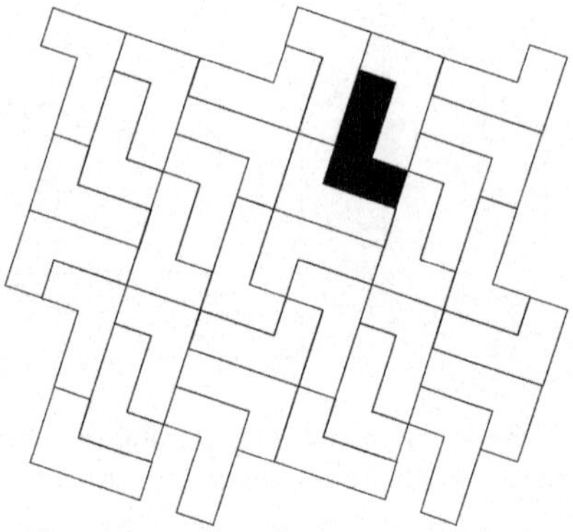

Below are three more arrangements of the letter L. In all of them I count two roles and in each some tiles have five neighbors and some have seven.

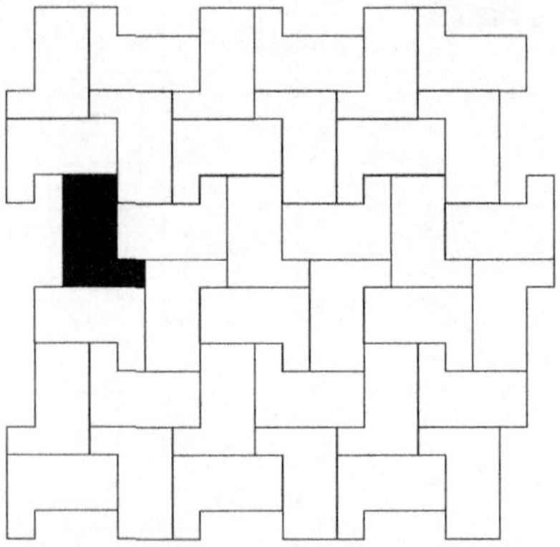

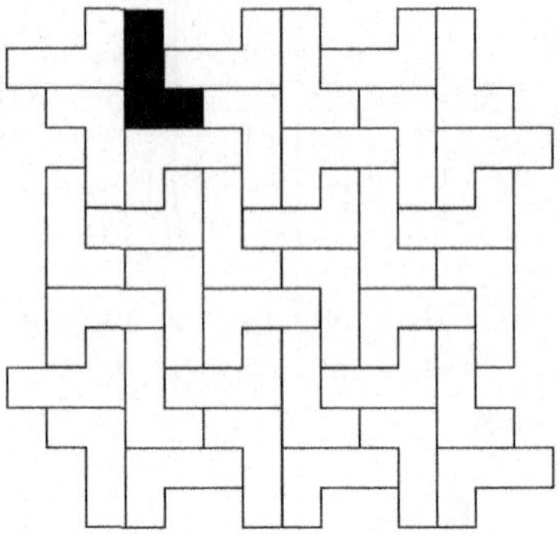

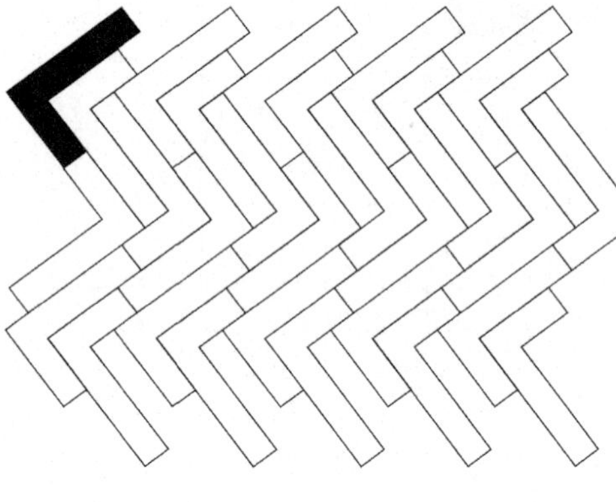

Likewise, some of these letter Es have five neighbors and some have seven.

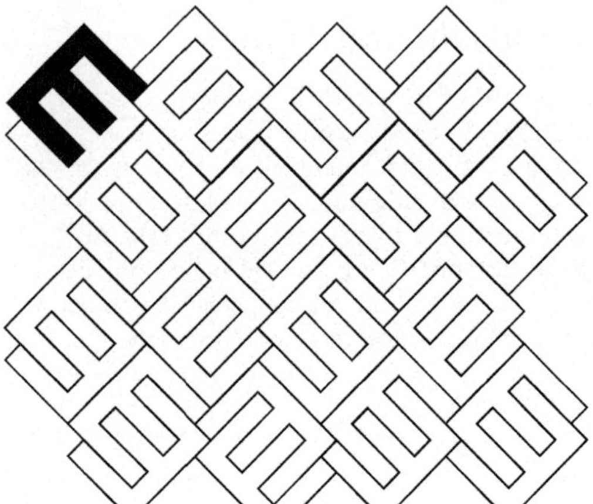

These tessellating letter Ls have a very simple pattern with a translation block of only two. Yet it is not an isohedral type as you can see from the bottoms of the L. They fit in two ways.

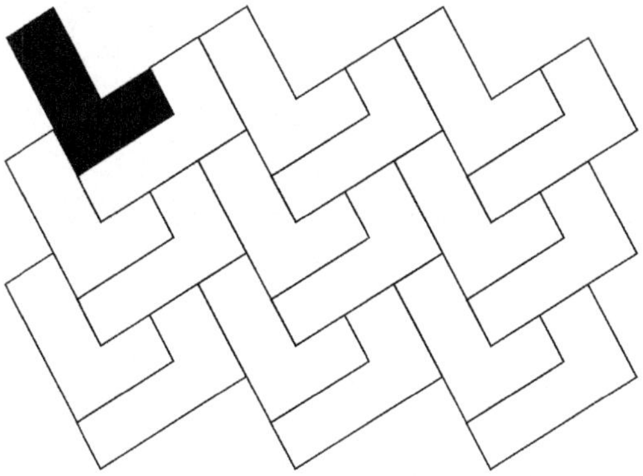

This pattern of letter Ts is another very simple pattern that is not isohedral. In one diagonal tops of the letter have three neighbors and in next row they have only two.

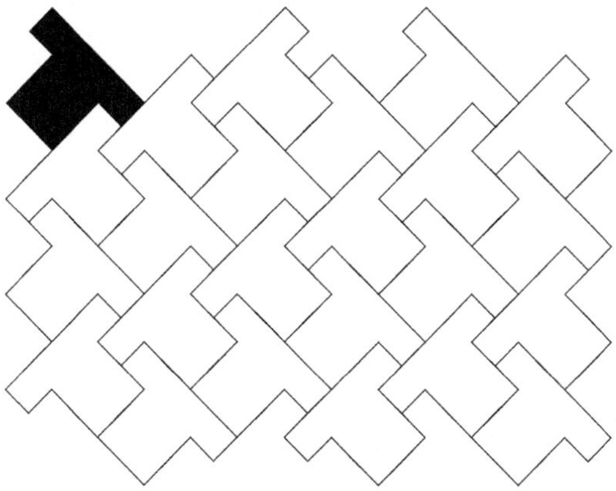

The letter F, which is fairly easy to tessellate, yielded some anisohedral tilings. Two are shown below, one of the left and the other on the right. Although they are arranged differently along their straight backs, they both have the fronts fitting together so that the crossbar in the left letter is not in the same position as the crossbar of the right letter.

Below the same tile fits into a Heesch type TCCTCC tiling.

The letter G is harder to tessellate than the letter F. If I analyzed them correctly, the first is 3-isohedral and the second it 2-isohedral.

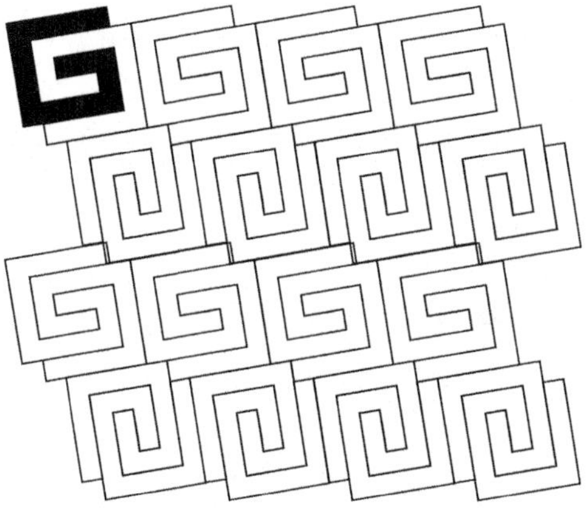

I count two roles and five and six neighbors for this pattern of the letter T, which is another letter with many tessellation possibilities.

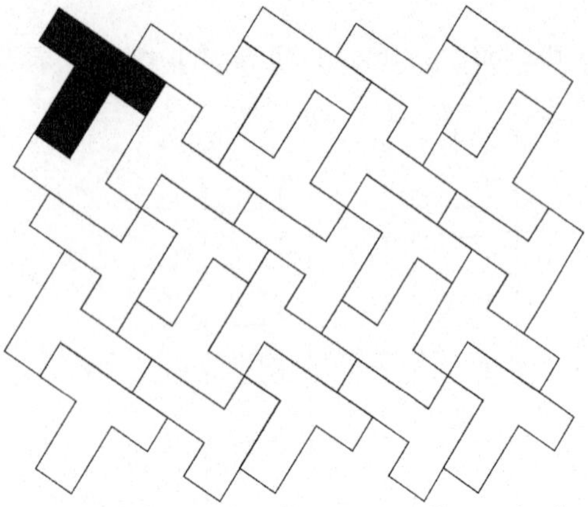

However, no letter tessellates as easily as the letter L. In this next example the shapes of the Ls have been distorted a bit because I skewed the pattern to make it line up horizontally and vertically. I count 2-isohedral with seven and five neighbors.

This appears to be 2-isohedral with 6 and 6 neighbors. It was formed by alternating two TCCTCC patterns.

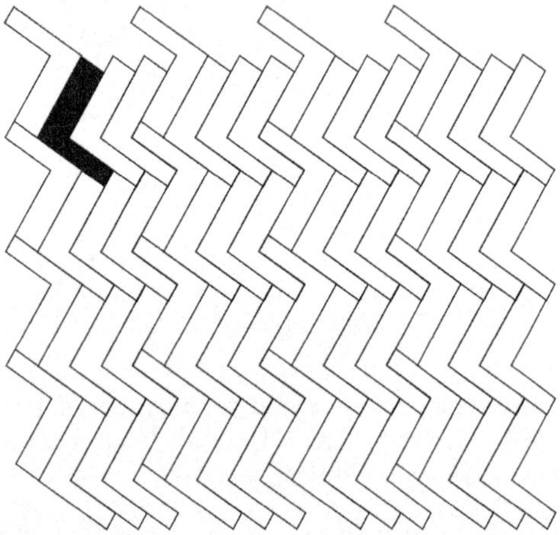

On these last two I count 2-isohedral with five and six neighbors. In the second pattern a block of four can be combined to form a tessellating letter S.

Notice the upper right part of the R shown below. Sometimes it is adjacent to itself as if it were a straight but center-point rotation side. In other places it is adjacent to the middle right part of another R.

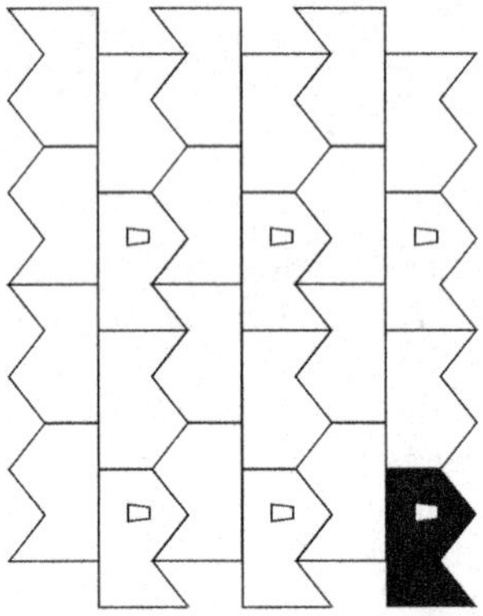

Below is a simple way to make an isohedral tiling with this shape. It fits the requirements for isohedral class IH49. It could also be arranged to fit class IH54.

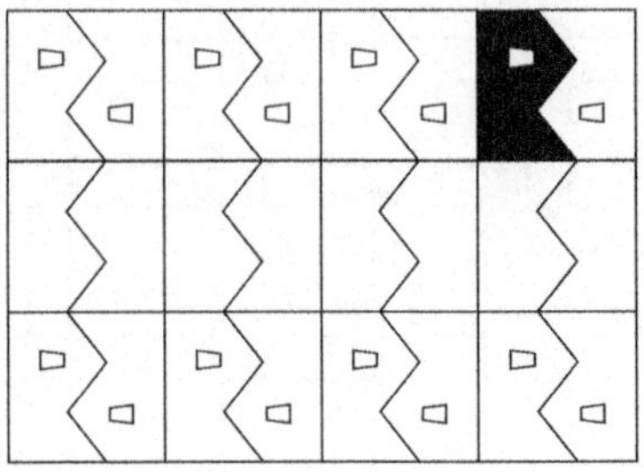

I would not be at all surprised if I made mistakes in classifying these tilings.

Anisohedral Tiles

The previous section had two tilings of letter F shown below, one on the right and the other on the left. (They differ in how the backs of the letter F are positioned.) As we saw there, they do not fit Heesch types and or any other isohedral classification. The tiles do not fit the adjacent tiles in the same way throughout the pattern—in some cases the top of the F fits between the top of a neighbor and the middle bar, and in other cases it fits above the top of a neighboring F. The requirement for an isohedral tiling is that a tile fit its neighbors in the same way throughout the pattern. Mathematicians call this type of tiling anisohedral and would say that the tiles belong to two symmetry classes.

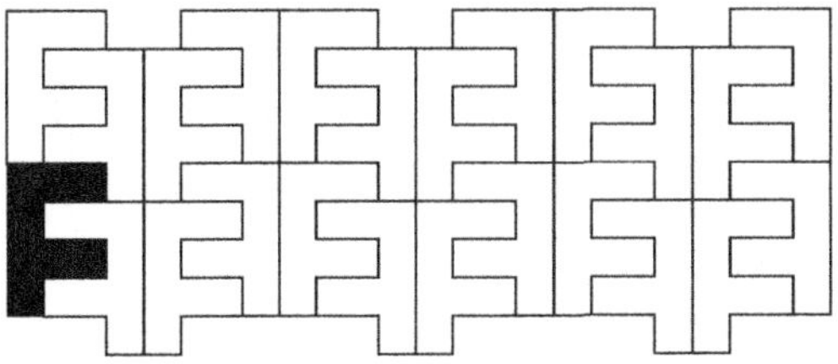

The website that I found very helpful in trying to understand anisohedral tilings is www.angelfire.com/mn3/anisohedral/index.html. Mathematicians make a distinction between anisohedral tilings and anisohedral tiles. The two patterns above are anisohedral tilings, which means they are not isohedral. However, the shape used for the letter F is not an anisohedral tile because it can be fit into an isohedral tiling, which was illustrated in the previous section.

As I sorted through the various letter tessellations, I found a number of examples of anisohedral tilings but no anisohedral tiles. However, I was very close. I needed only to put a slant on the ends of the bars of the letter F and they would no longer tile isohedrally. Below are two modified letter Fs that are anisohedral tiles. (The way the ends of the letters are sloped differs from right to left.)

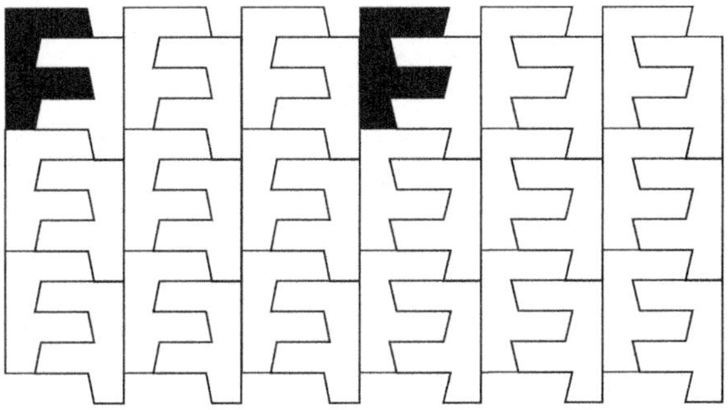

When I was doing letter tilings, I had no interest in this shape because it is an inferior way of representing the letter F compared to the shape in the first figure.

The website www.angelfire.com/mn3/anisohedral/criteria.html explains how to make anisohedral tiles by combining certain isohedral tiles and then splitting them. The site notes that the first anisohedral tile discovered, by Heesch in 1935, could be formed with this method. After playing with the directions a bit, I came up with a different way to get similar results that I call the three-glide method.

In the pattern above, we start with the bent line that makes up most of the very top of the letter F. We copy this line, flip it, and move it downward (shown below as 1). After connecting it to the original line, we copy it, flip it, and move it downward again (2). Again we connect this line that has been flipped twice (so it has the original orientation), then copy it, flip it and move it for one last time (3). When we connect this last line to the rest of the figure, we have formed the front part of the letter F (4). We have a shape that has been formed with three glides, a method that is the key element in many of the almost 150 anisohedral examples shown on the site mentioned above. (Note that in a true glide the segments would be moved downward until they connected. In the picture below they are move out of position to make the segments more visible.)

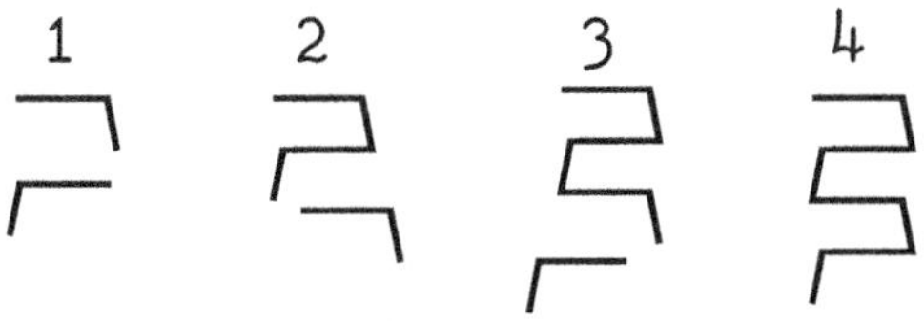

Below is another example of the three-glide method. To form the rest of the tile, I added two short edges with central symmetry that serve as TT edges and a final side that has not only center-point rotation, but central symmetry on each half of the center point. The result can be tiled in at least two ways, both shown in the figure below, one on the left where each tile has six neighbors and the other on the right where each tile has five neighbors. Both tilings are anisohedral and there is no tiling of this shape that is isohedral.

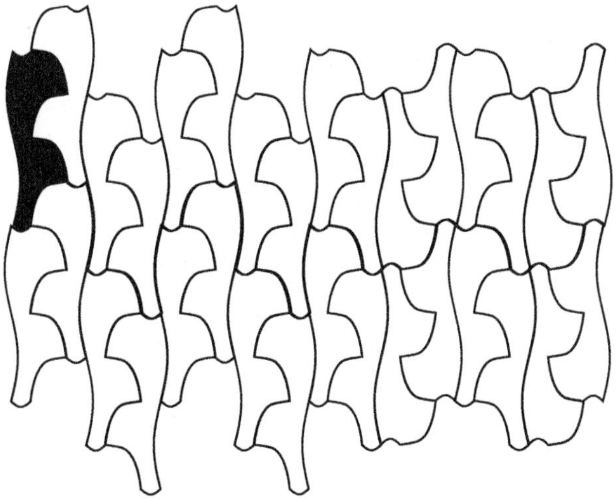

Both tilings are anisohedral because the top of the "F" shape sometimes fits under the top of itself and sometimes fits into the bottom of an adjacent "F" shape. In the jargon of mathematics, it has more than one symmetry class. In the six-adjacent tiling, four adjacents are in the same symmetry group and two are not. In the five-adjacent tiling, two are in the same symmetry group and three are not.

Using the same long side above but two straight lines as a backside gives the following tiling that is very similar to one that frequently has been used to illustrate anisohedral tilings. Each tile has four adjacents, all in the other symmetry group.

The angelfire site has instructions on making similar anisohedral tiles by combining tiles and cutting them. There are several ways to to this. I noticed that in an example I used to illustrate isohedral class IH12 there were four edges lined up with three glides. Combining two of the tiles and splitting them results in an anisohedral tile and tiling.

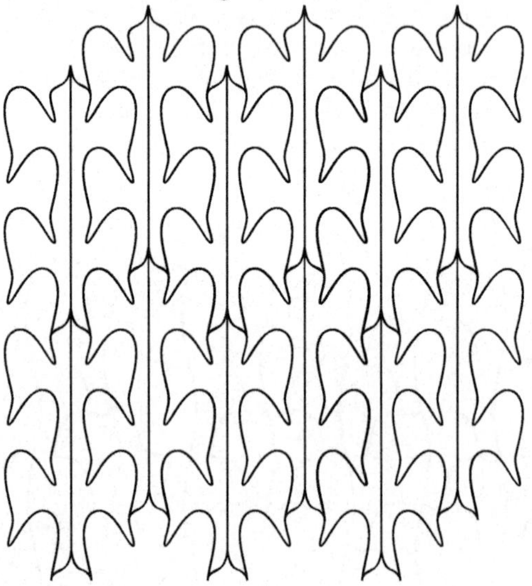

Unlike isohedral tiles that can be sorted into a limited number of types or classes, there is no catalog of classes for isohedral tiles. There may be an infinite number possible. Instead of classifying the patterns, mathematicians classify them by the number of roles the tile plays and the number of adjacents it has in each role. (A tiling in which the tile plays one role is isohedral.) In addition, the number of alike and unalike neighbors is counted. In the F example above that has anisohedral tiles, each tile has six adjacent tiles. Two of the adjacent tiles are alike and four unalike. The way this tile would be classified is $6_4 6_4$. The tilings with the curvy "Fs" are $6_2 6_2$ and $5_3 5_3$. The next tiling is $4_4 4_4$; all adjacent tiles are in the other symmetry group. In the doubled birds example each tile has five adjacent tiles. For each kind, three are alike and two are unalike, so the classification is $5_2 5_2$.

Some More Anisohedral Tiles

Another source of anisohedral tiles comes from dividing into equal parts symmetric tiles. A bisection of the peaked cross tile shown in the section "Crosses" is anisohedral as are some of the ways of dividing the cross in that section that fits IH17. These tilings are shown in the angelfire site mentioned in the previous section. Other tilings from the site that intrigued me are variants of the pattern shown below, classified as $5_4 6_4$.

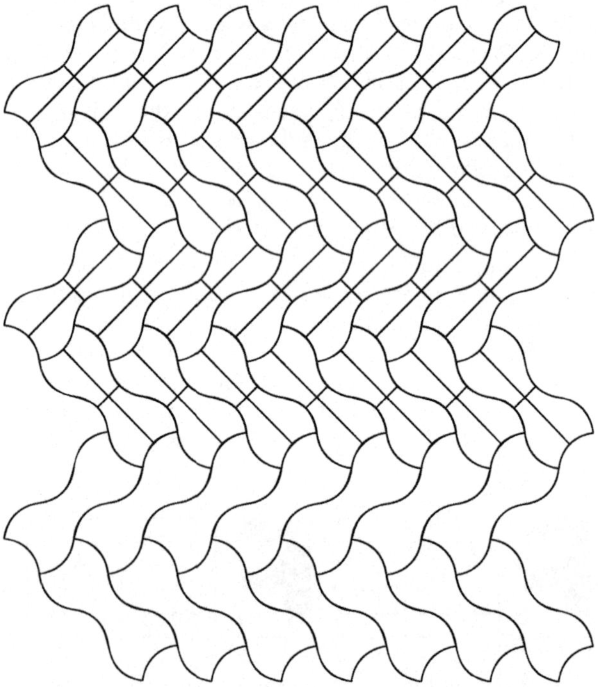

The base tile is shown in the last two rows. It is a TG1G1TG2G2 tile that has the pgg symmetry of a herringbone pattern with the long side three times as long as the short side. A short side is formed with central symmetry and then its copy is rotated 90° to start the long side. The rest of that side is formed with two glides, and then a copy of the two sides is rotated 180° to form the rest of the figure. It fits the requirement of IH9 and is a restricted case of that class. The tile itself seems to be hypersymmetric—it has symmetry that is not carried over into the tiling.

Bisections of the tile are isohedral. With the long line the result is CG1CG2G1G2, with the short TCCTGG.

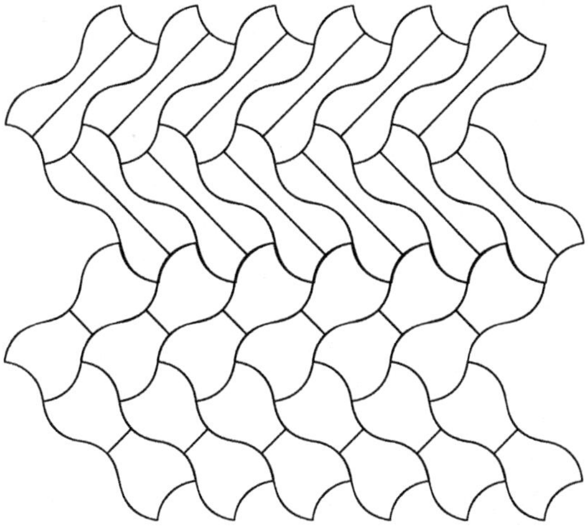

One of the examples of this pattern on the angelfire site has straight lines instead of curves. With straight lines the anisohedral tiles are convex pentagons and are one of the fifteen known types of convex pentagons that can tile the plane. It was one of four convex pentagons that tile the plane that was discovered by amateur mathematician Marjorie Rice.

Something else that is interesting about shapes formed in this way is that they can be formed from patterns of tiles in isohedral class IH73 by combining three tiles end-to-end.

Another way of combining groups of three tiles in the top of the figure above gives this tiling.

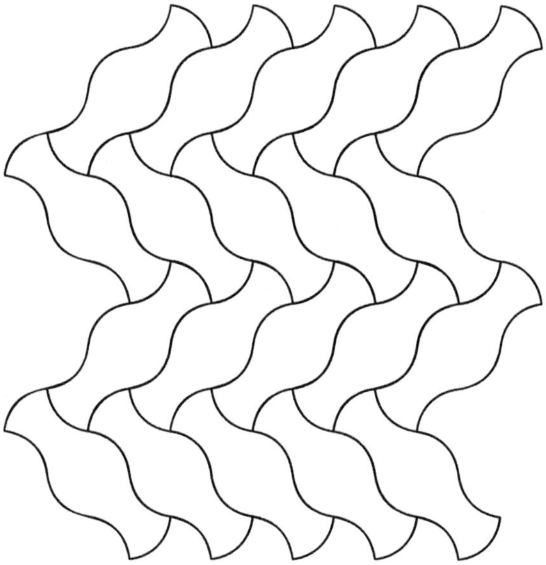

Combining this and the previous shape results in another IH73 tiling.

If the original IH73 tiling is made with straight sides and then it is bisected, the result is one of the 15 convex pentagons that tile the plane.

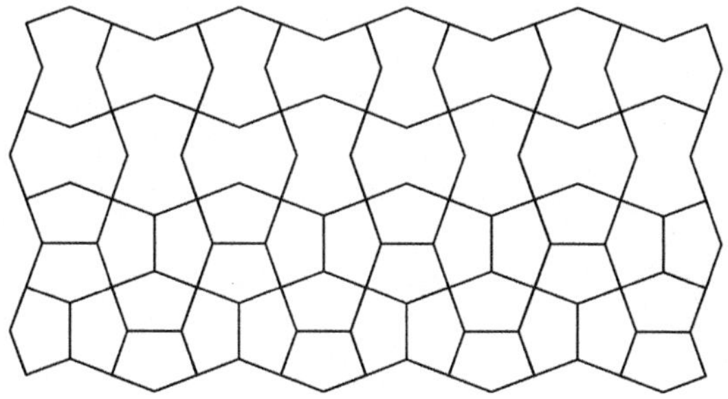

(Another form of tiling is an aperiodic tiling that lacks translation symmetry. This book has ignored them because the design tools that the author has cannot display them.)

V. Explorations One

After spending several months categorizing the various tessellations that I had developed for maze books and finding new ones to illustrate types and classes where I had no good example, I decided to see how many ways I could tessellate puzzle pieces, a shape I had used in several ways in maze books. That exploration revealed other areas that looked interesting. This chapter and the next describe what I found.

Puzzle Pieces

Puzzle pieces are an easy tessellation pattern to design and can provide a review of some of the classes discussed above. The tile above is a Heesch type CGG and you can see that the C edge is not a standard interlocking shape. However, both T and G edges can be, as can edges of corner rotations such as those in the C6C6C3C3 tiling shown below. A Heesch type CCC that is also IH90, a triangle type with all edges identical, can be formed by eliminating all the C3 lines, as the example shows.

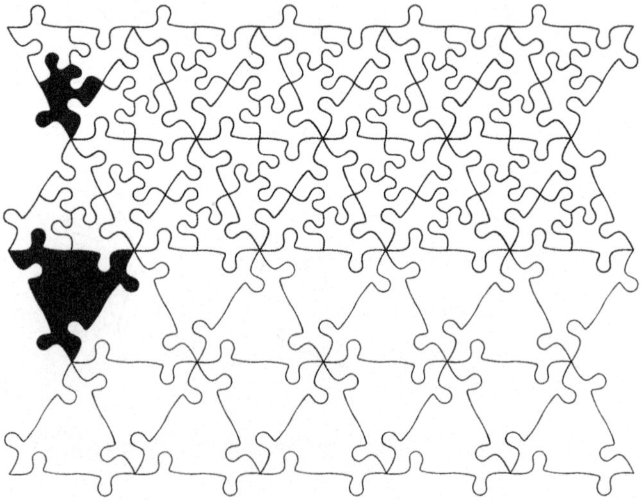

Puzzle pieces that look like real jigsaw puzzle pieces have four edges that interlock. What follows is an attempt to see how many different tilings can be made starting with one edge of a puzzle piece, an edge with asymmetry. The other three edges will use this same shape but can use it in different orientations. This exercise reviews some of the Heesch types and also some of the isohedral classes of Grünbaum and Shepard.

Forcing all edges to have the same shape, there are three different tilings possible for the TTTT type, two with symmetry and one without. Other shapes that can be formed are rotation or flips of these three so are not illustrated. The second two tilings, the ones with symmetry, also fit type G1G1G2G2 with all edges shaped the same and mirrored, or isohedral class IH68.

Using this edge I could find four different tilings that are TGTG types, shown below. All are asymmetric across the diagonal.

In addition to the two tilings above that are also G1G2G1G2, there are three other C4C4C4C4 tilings one can make using this edge. Only one of them is uniquely C4C4C4C4. The uniquely C4C4C4C4 tile is the tile below on the left and it also illustrates the class IH61 in which an edge is repeatedly rotated 90° until the shape is formed. The shape below and to the right was used in a TTTT tiling.

There are three different patterns based on this tile edge that fit together as type G1G2G1G2. The first two have symmetry across the diagonal and are examples of isohedral class IH71, a restricted Heesch type. Both of them are also examples of type C4C4C4C4.

The top three rows show a C4C4C4C4 tiling. If the second row is flipped as it is in row four, the tiling is anisohedral (discovered by a mistake).

Using this same edge, five different shapes can be formed as G1G1G2G2 types. Two of them were shown with the three TTTT tilings because as tilings that fit the IH68 class they also fit the TTTT type. The tiling below uses the tile immediately above but arranges it so the translation unit is two rather than four when it is in a C4C4C4C4 arrangement

The shape above is an example of the IH59 restricted class. Edge one is rotated and flipped to form edge 2, edge 2 is rotated and flipped to form edge three, and edge three is rotated and flipped to form edge four. Each tile is adjacent to four tiles that have been rotated and flipped.

Finally, the tile below can also be arranged to form a G1G2G1G2 pattern, which was shown above. The G1G2G1G2 pattern has a translation block of four unlike the translation block of two in the G1G1G2G2 tiling below.

If the puzzle edge has central symmetry rather than being asymmetric, the shapes from the previous illustrations will collapse to two tiles. Translations are not distinguishable from glides to the opposite edge, and glides and corner rotations are also identical. However, orientation still matters. Below we have a puzzle piece that resembles a turtle. Since the translation block in this pattern is one, we can call it a TTTT type. (It is also an IH68 class tiling so is also G1G1G2G2.) Below it is the same tile in a pattern that orients it in two ways with a translation block of two, which would make it type TGTG.

There is a second way to get a TGTG pattern, shown at the top of the next block. The same tile can also be part of a pattern in which it is oriented in four different ways, shown in the middle of the block, which would make it either a G1G2G1G2 or a C4C4C4C4 type. (It also fits the IH71 class.)

The second tile with this symmetrical edge is shown as the last pattern below. It could be either a C4C4C4C4 type or a G1G1G2G2 type. It is also a IH73 pattern.

The same one-eighth of a tile can produce five different patterns. Isn't central symmetry fun?

The same asymmetric edge makes very different looking patterns with the C3C3C3C3 type. The template shape is then a rhombus, not a square. The possible shapes are discussed later.

Identical Asymmetric Edges

The previous section examined puzzle pieces with identically-shaped edges. This section continues that exploration but with a different starting point.

There are four orientations that an asymmetrical line can have as an edge. They are shown in the figure below. Consider the first one to be orientation 0. When it is flipped over a horizontal line (a vertical flip), it forms a mirror image, shown as the second line, orientation 1. When it is flipped over a vertical line (a horizontal flip), it becomes orientation 2, the third line. Finally, when it is rotated 180° it becomes orientation 3, the bottom line. Further flips or 180° rotations of these lines will not produce any other orientations.

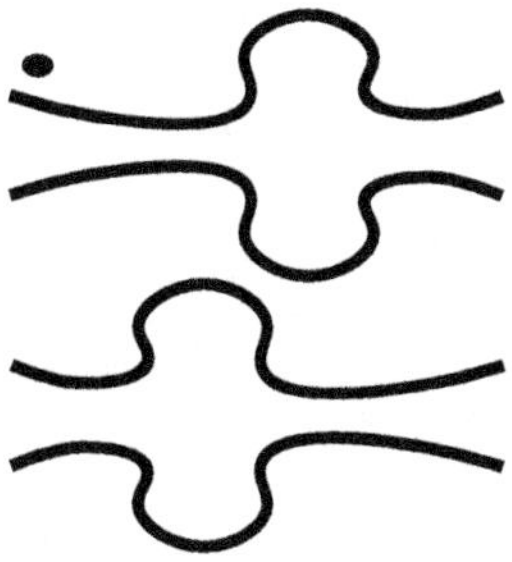

Rotating these orientations in 90° increments shows the options for the other three edges when the template shape is a square. In each case the order is the same, with the dot marking orientation 0. There are 4x4x4x4=256 different combinations of these edges. However, many of the shapes will not tessellate. In order to tessellate, a shape must have two edges with bumps (orientations 0 and 2) and two edges with indents (orientations 1 and 3).

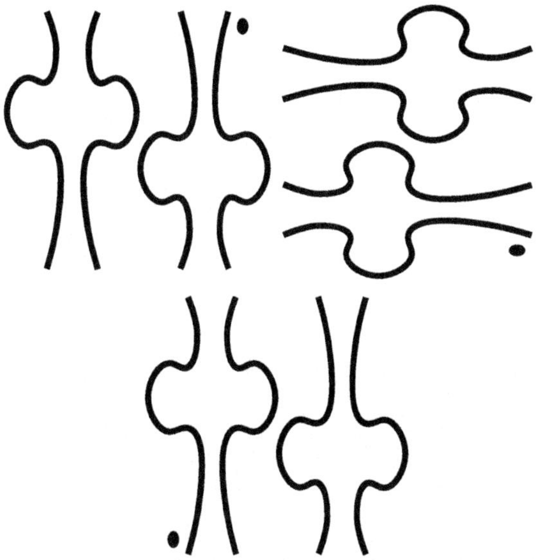

We can write out the possible shapes using base four numbers, starting with 0000 and ending with 3333. (This is the reason the orientations were labeled 0, 1, 2, and 3 rather than 1, 2, 3, and 4.) Any number with two even and two odd digits (two bumps and two indents) is retained and all the others are discarded, leaving 96 numbers. Some of these shapes are identical but are rotated. For example, because we have a square template a shape designated 1234 is the same shape as 2341, 3412, and 4123. Eighty-eight of the shapes can be consolidated to 22 groups. A shape designated as 1010 has only one alternate rotation, 0101. Eight more groups are consolidated to four groups, giving a total of 26 groups.

We can consolidate further because some shapes are flips of other shapes. Below are shapes 0011 and 2233. They are equivalent because a flip across the diagonal from lower-left corner to upper-right corner makes them identical.

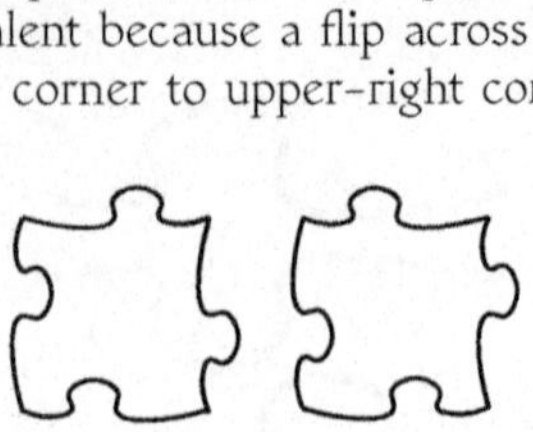

I could not find an easy way to consolidate the shapes by number so I printed examples of each of the 26 groups to determine how many unique shapes existed and which sequence of edges each of those unique shapes had. The table on the next page is a summary of what I found. There are 15 distinct shapes that will tessellate.

The previous section, "Puzzle Pieces," uses 13 different shapes, not 15, to form a variety of tilings, with some tiles capable of fitting in multiple patterns. The two missing shapes are the last two in the table. The images below illustrate them in the style used in "Puzzle Pieces."

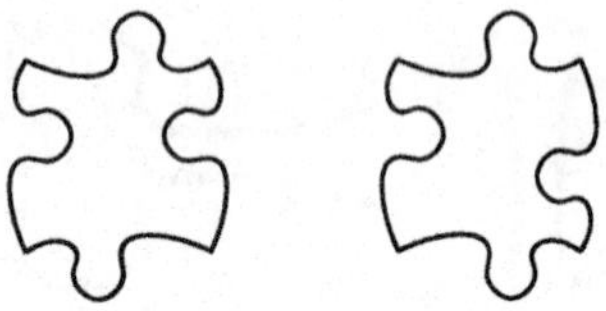

Below is a tiling of the right tile with the smallest possible translation block, which is a 4x1 block. It can be seen as either a row or a column.

No Heesch type has a 4X1 translation block that can be either a row or a column. No quadrilateral Heesch type has a 4x1 translation block. The tiling is not a Heesch type. It is not even isohedral.

An isohedral tiling has several characteristics. Its tiles are all identically shaped and have the same size. The tiling covers the plane without gaps or overlaps. And if we take any pair of adjacent tiles, the way their two edges fit together is consistent throughout the tiling. If an edge fits neighbors in more than one way, the tiling is anisohedral. If the tile in an anisohedral tiling can also fit into an isohedral tiling, the tile is considered an isohedral tile. However, if a tile in an anisohedral tiling fits no isohedral tiling, then the tile itself is anisohedral. There is a distinction between tilings and tiles; some isohedral tiles fit both isohedral and anisohedral tilings, but an anisohedral tile can fit only anisohedral tilings.

In the lower right of the illustration, the edges of the pieces are labeled. The edge labeled "1" sometimes fits the edge labeled "2" and sometimes fits the edge labeled "4". The edge labeled "3" also fits edges "2" and "4". Since the same part of the tile fits into two different parts an adjacent neighbor, the tiling is anisohedral.

Examining the way that the representative tile is formed shows why it is not a Heesch type. Start with the bottom edge in the picture of the representative tile. Rotating it 90° clockwise forms the right edge. Rotating the right edge 90° clockwise forms the top edge. How about the left edge? It can be formed with a reflection of the right edge, which is not allowed in a Heesch type. Or it can be formed as a glide from either the top or bottom edge. There is no group labeled GGC4C4. This is not only an anisohedral tiling but also an anisohedral tile. It is a bit odd that the first one that I find is a shape that is common in jigsaw puzzles.

The second "weird" shape also has a tiling with a 4x1 translation block, shown below. Notice that the diagonals from lower left to upper right contain the same orientation of the tile. Both of the "weird" tiles can also be arranged with a translation block of 16 with multiple arrangements of 16 possible.

Square Template Asymmetric Edges

Shape	Shape Codes	Shape	Shape Codes
	Group 1 0011 1100 0110 1001 2233 2332 3322 3223 (G1G1G2G2, G1G2G1G2)		Group 2 0033 3300 0330 3003 1122 1221 2211 2112 (TTTT, C4C4C4C4)
	Group 3 0112 1120 1201 2011 0332 3320 3203 2033 (TGTG)		Group 4 0211 2110 1102 1021 0233 2330 3302 3023 (TGTG)
	Group 5 0013 1300 0130 3001 1322 3221 2213 2132 (TGTG)		Group 6 0031 3100 0310 1003 1223 2231 2312 3122 (TGTG)
	Group 7 0213 2130 1302 3021 (C4C4C4C4, G1G2G1G2)		Group 8 0312 3120 1203 2031 (C4C4C4C4, G1G2G1G2)
	Group 9 0132 1320 3201 2013 (TTTT, G1G1G2G2)		Group 10 0231 2310 3102 1023 (TTTT, G1G1G2G2)
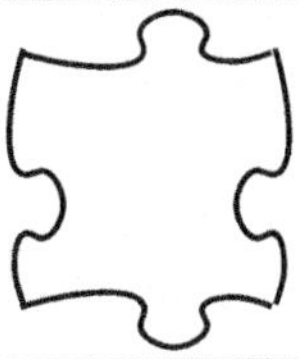	Group 11 0123 1230 2301 3012 0321 3210 2103 1032 (C4C4C4C4, G1G1G2G2)		Group 12 0101 1010 2323 3232 (G1G1G2G2)
	Group 13 0303 3030 1212 2121 (C4C4C4C4)	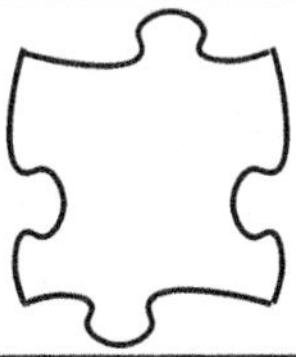	Group 14 0103 1030 3010 0301 1232 2321 3212 2123
	Group 15 0121 1210 2101 1012 0323 3230 2303 3032		

In conclusion, starting with a template shape of a square with all edges formed with the same asymmetric line, exactly 15 unique tiles can be formed that will tessellate, two of which will be anisohedral tiles. The anisohedral tiles in question would have three edges formed as C4C4C4 and the last edge formed with another C4 rotation and then flipped over its midpoint.

Using this procedure to form similar "weird" tilings from the tile that illustrates IH61 yields the following two tilings, each with the 4x1 translation block.

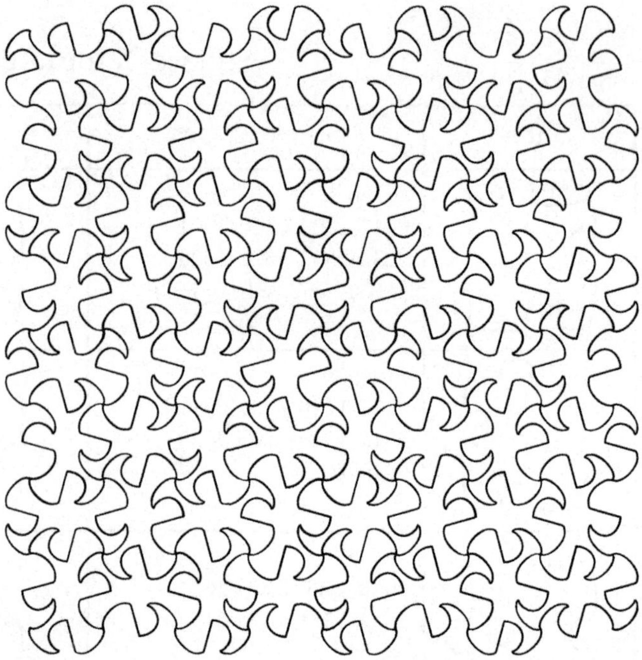

A Different Proof

I sent a draft of the previous section to Doris Schattschneider, an emeritus mathematics professor of Moravian College and a recognized authority on tessellations who has published extensively on the topic. She was not only kind enough to read what I wrote, but she provided an alternative proof for parts of it.

She noted that with the asymmetric edges, shapes formed on a square template would tessellate only if they had two edges that were "ins" and two edges that were "outs." Further, through rotations or flips, any shape with two "in" edges and two "out" edges can be arranged so that an "out" edge will be in a chosen fixed position. With one edge fixed, there are three ways that the other "out" edge can be positioned, and for each position it can have two orientations. Once the second "out" edge is fixed, there are two slots left for the "in" edges. Each of them can take two orientations. Thus there are 3x2x2x2 = 24 shapes that need to be considered. These twenty-four shapes are shown in the figure below as puzzle pieces with sides distinguished by letters.

When I examined these shapes to determine how they would be classified by Heesch type, I relied on what I had done in the earlier puzzle section. Dr Schattschneider used mathematical reasoning. She noted that there are six relevant isometries, a mathematical term of how tiles can be transformed so that the copy is congruent with the original, that relate edges.

A vertical glide-reflection interchanges top and bottom edges: a↔b, c↔d.

A horizontal glide-reflection interchanges left-right edges: e↔f, g↔h.

A 90° clockwise rotation transforms edges as follows: a→g, b→h, c→e, d→f, e→b, f→a, g→d, h→c.

A 90° counterclockwise rotation transforms edges as follows: a→f, b→e, c→h, d→g, e→c, f→d, g→a, h→b.

A diagonal glide reflection from bottom to right edge or left edge to top interchanges adjacent sides: a↔h, b↔g, c↔f, d↔h

A diagonal glide reflection from bottom to left edge or from right edge to top interchanges adjacent sides: a↔e, b↔f, c↔g, d↔e.

From this she identified the most obvious Heesch type, noting that some tiles fit more than one Heesch type and four were Not Heesch (NH).

Row 1: 1 TGTG; 2 G1G2G1G2; 3 TTTT; 4 TGTG; 5 G1G2G1G2; 6 TGTG; 7 TGTG; 8 TTTT

Row 2: 9 NH; 10 G1G1G2G2; 11 C4C4C4C4; 12 NH; 13 C4C4C4C4; 14 NH; 15 NH; 16 C4C4C4C4

Row 3: 17 TGTG; 18 G1G2G1G2; 19 TTTT; 20 TGTG; 21 G1G2G1G2; 22 TGTG; 23 TGTG; 24 TTTT

She then addressed the weakest part of my proof, the elimination of duplicates. She gave a signature to each of the shapes by listing the letters of their sides in clockwise order:

Row 1: beae, bfae, bebe, bfbe, beaf, bfaf, bebf, bfbf
Row 2: becg, bfcg, bedg, bfdg, bech, bfch, bedh, bfdh
Row 3: bgag, bhag, bgbg, bhbg, bgah, bhah, bgbh, bhbh

The square has eight symmetry transformations that map the square back onto itself. They are the identity (I); clockwise rotations of 90° (R1), 180° (R2), and 270° (R3); and flips over a horizontal line (H), over a vertical line (V), over the diagonal from the bottom right to the top left corner (DL), and over the diagonal from the bottom left to the top right corner (DR).

The listing and figure above have all possible sequences with a "b" on the top edge. If any of the sequences, when altered by one of these transformations, returns a sequence with a "b" on the top, it must be itself or a duplicate of another tile. We do not need to check all sequences with each transformation, only those that will result in a "b" on the top.

The eight transformations alter edges as follows:

I: sends each edge to itself. (Not very interesting, but mathematicians include it for completeness.)

R1: a→g, b→h, c→e, d→f, e→b, f→a, g→d, h→c
R2: a→d, b→c, c→b, d→a, e→h, f→g, g→f, h→e
R3: a→f, b→e, c→h, d→g, e→c, f→d, g→a, h→b
H: a→c, b→d, c→a, d→b, e→f, f→e, g→h, h→g
V: a→b, b→a, c→d, d→c, e→g, f→h, g→e, h→f
DL: a→e, b→f, c→g, d→h, e→a, f→b, g→c, h→d
DR: a→h, b→g, c→f, d→e, e→d, f→c, g→b, h→a

We can ignore the Identity transformation. The R1 transformation returns a "b" on top when an "e" is on the left edge. There are four in the first row, on tiles 1, 2, 3, and 4 with sequences beae, bfae, bebe, and bfbe. Applying the R1 transformation, they become bhbg, bhag, bhbh, and bhah. These sequences appear in the last row. Pairs are (1, 20), (2, 18), (3, 24), and (4, 22). Four tiles can be eliminated as duplicates.

The R2 transformation returns a "b" on top if a "c" is on the bottom, or tiles 9, 10, 13, and 14 in the second row with sequences becg, bfcg, bech, and bfch. Transformed, they become bfch, bfcg, bech, and becg. Duplicate pairs are (9, 14), (10, 10), (13, 13), and (14, 9). Two tiles are mapped to themselves and two tiles are mapped to each other. One tile can be eliminated.

The R3 transformation is a counterclockwise rotation of 90°. It will return a "b" on the top if an "h" is on the right side, or the four sequences bhag, bhbg, bhah, and bhbh, tiles 18, 20, 22, and 24 in row three. They map

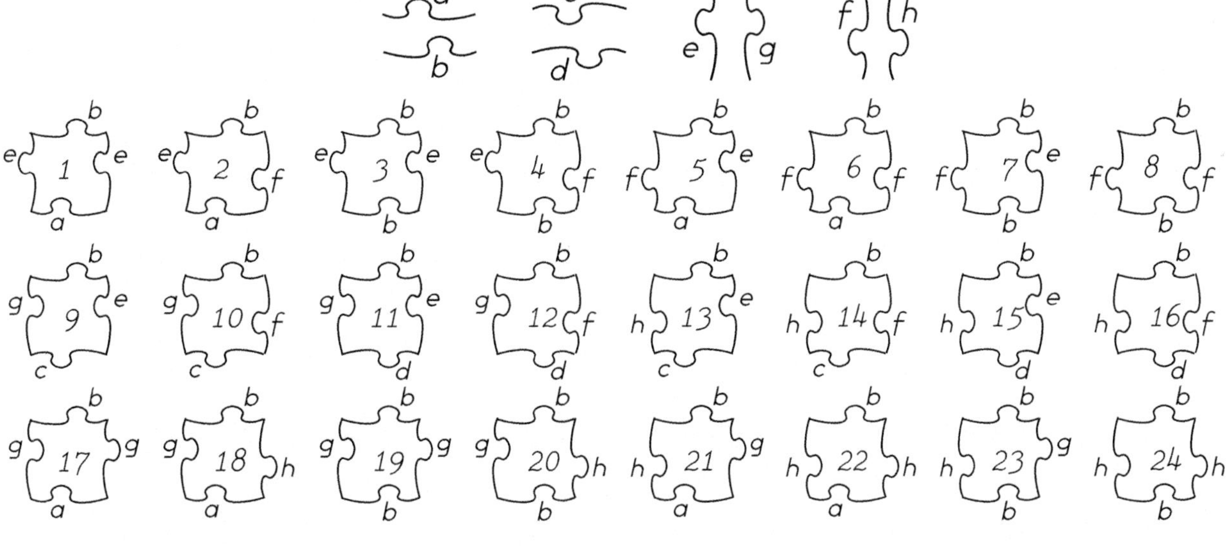

to bfae, beae, bfbe, and bebe. These tiles have already been paired and eliminated in the R1 transformation.

The H transformation flips bottom and top and changes the orientation on right and left, but leaves right side right and left side left. A sequence with a "d" on the bottom will become a sequence with a "b" on the top when flipped in this way. The tiles with a "d" on the bottom are 11, 12, 15, and 16 in row two, sequences bedg, bfdg, bedh, and bfdh. The transformation rule yields dfbh, debh, dfbg, and debg. However, transformations that flip the tile change the order of sides from clockwise to counterclockwise. The mapping is shown in an example below:

Correcting direction and putting the "b" on top yields bfdh, bedh, bfdg, and bedg. The pairs are (11, 16), (12, 15), (15, 12), and (16, 11). Two pairs are mapped to each other so two more tiles are eliminated as duplicates.

No tiles return a "b" with the V transformation.

The DL transformation puts a "b" on top if the left side is an "f". The sequences with an "f" on the left are 5, 6, 7, and 8 in the first row with signatures beaf, bfaf, bebf, and bfbf. Transformed they become bfae, bcbe, bfaf, and bfaf. Correcting the ordering, they become beaf, bebf, bfaf, and bfbf. The pairings are (5, 5), (6, 7), (7, 6), and (8, 8). Two tiles are mapped to themselves and two to each other. Another tile is eliminated as a duplicate.

Finally, the DR transformation puts a "b" on the top when the right edge is a "g". Four tiles are affected, tiles 17, 19, 21, and 23 in row three with sequences bgag, bgbg, bgah, and bgbh. The transformation yields bhbg, bgbg, bhag, and bgag, but again the order has been changed to counterclockwise. Correcting the order yields bgbh, bgbg, bgah, and bgag. Pairings are (17, 23), (19, 19), (21, 21), and (23, 17). Again two tiles are mapped to each other and two to themselves. One more tile is eliminated.

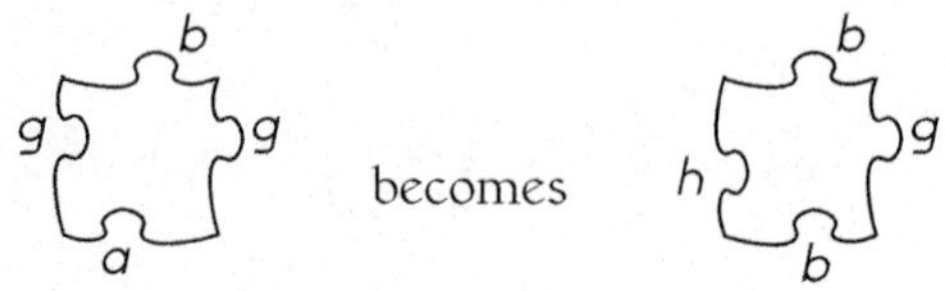

Applying the transformations reveals that nine of the 24 tiles are duplicates. Hence, exactly 15 distinct tiles can be formed on a square template with identical asymmetric edges. A list of unique tile shapes is 1, 2, 3, 4, 5, 6, and 8 in row one; 9, 10, 11, 12, and 13 in row two; and 17, 19, and 21 in row three. Thirteen of them tessellate isohedrally. The two that do not (9 and 12) will tile anisohedrally with a translation block of four (either vertically or horizontally) as the previous section has shown.

A note based on this section was published in the November 2016 issue of *Mathematical Gazette*.

A Third Way

If all edges placed on a square template are identical with mirror symmetry over the midpoint, there are two distinct shapes that will tessellate, one with two "outs" that are adjacent and one with two "outs" that are opposite. Note that the shape must have two "out" edges and two "in" edges; if the number of "outs" is not equal to the number of "ins", the pieces will not tessellate.

Suppose that the edge does not have the bump centered in the middle but rather offset to one side. How many distinctly different shapes with these identical asymmetric edges will tile the plane? One way to approach the question is to begin with the two orderings of "in" and "out" edges mentioned above. We need to determine the number of distinct shapes with each ordering and then test each of the distinct shapes to see if it tessellates.

To eliminate most of the duplication from rotation, we fix the orientation of each ordering so that the "ins" and "outs" are held in the same position. Each "in" and "out" edge can be fitted in two ways. The bump or indent can be high or low when the edge is vertical and to the left or to the right when the edge is horizontal. Thus, there are 2x2x2x2 = 16 possible shapes for each ordering to consider. The shapes for the ordering with adjacent "outs" are shown on the next page with edges labeled.

However, there are still duplicates because this ordering is symmetrical over the diagonal running from top left to bottom right. A flip over this diagonal, which turns the puzzle piece over, showing its back side and reversing the order of edges from clockwise to counterclockwise, interchanges edges as follows: a↔e and b↔f. Applying this transformation yields: 1 ebfa → faeb 16; 2 fbfa → fbeb 8; 3 ebfb → fafb 12; 4 fbfb → fbfb 4; 5 ebea → faea 14; 6 fbea → fbea 6; 7 ebeb → fafa 10; 8 fbeb → fbfa 2; 9 eafa → eaeb 15; 10 fafa → ebeb 7; 11 eafb → eafb 11; 12 fafb → ebfb 3; 13 eaea → eaea 13; 14 faea → ebea 5; 15 eaeb → eafa 9; 16 faeb → ebfa 1. Four shapes are mapped back to themselves and six pairs are mapped to each other. Six

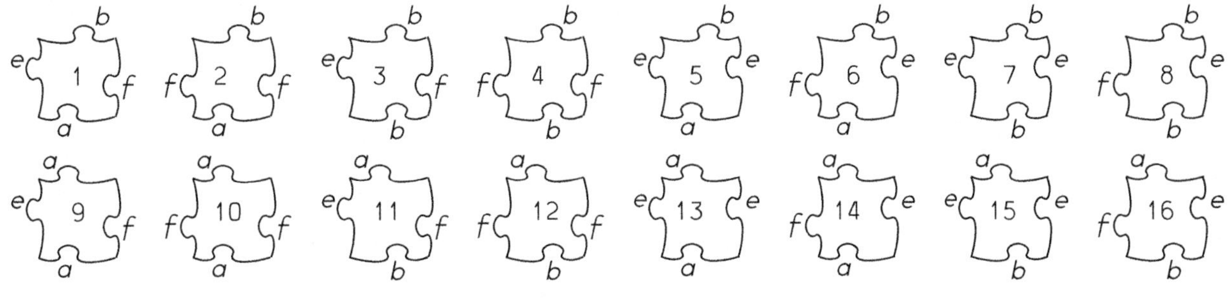

of the shapes are duplicates, so there are ten distinct shapes of this ordering of sides.

A quick (but incomplete) way to check if these shapes tessellate is to see if they fit Heesch types, a classification of ways that shapes with all edges shapeable can tessellate so that each edge fits in the same way throughout the tiling. When opposite edges are alike, the edges translate. When they are unalike, they glide-reflect. All these shapes tessellate in one of three ways: 1 G1G2G1G2; 2 TGTG; 3 TGTG; 4 TTTT; 5 TGTG; 6 G1G2G1G2; 7 TTTT; 8 TGTG; 9 TGTG; 10 TTTT; 11 G1G2G1G2; 12 TGTG; 13 TTTT; 14 TGTG; 15 TGTG; and 16 G1G2G1G2. Some of the shapes also fit as C4C4C4C4 (6, 7, 10, 11) or G1G1G2G2 (1, 4, 13, 16).

The second ordering also has sixteen possible ways to order edges, but because of the symmetry of the way the edges are placed, eight will be horizontal flips (flips over a vertical line) of the other eight. We can eliminate these duplicates by using only one of the two top edges. The results are shown below. (Because the ordering has both vertical and horizontal symmetry, we could as an alternative hold either the right or left edge fixed.)

Duplicates remain because if the bottom edge is a "d", a vertical flip will make it a "b" and if the bottom edge is a "c", a rotation of 180° will make it a "b". We need to examine these transformations to eliminate duplicates.

A flip reorders edges from clockwise to counterclockwise and swaps them as follows: d↔b, e↔f, h↔g. As a result: 3 gbfd → hbed 8; 4 hbfd → gbed 7; 7 gbed → hbfd 4; and 8 hbed → gbfd 3. Shapes 7 and 8 can be eliminated as duplicates. As for 180° rotations, c↔b, g↔f, and h↔e. The transformation are: 1 bfcg → bfcg 1; 2 bfch → becg 5; 5 becg → bfch 2; and 6 bech → bech 6. Two map to

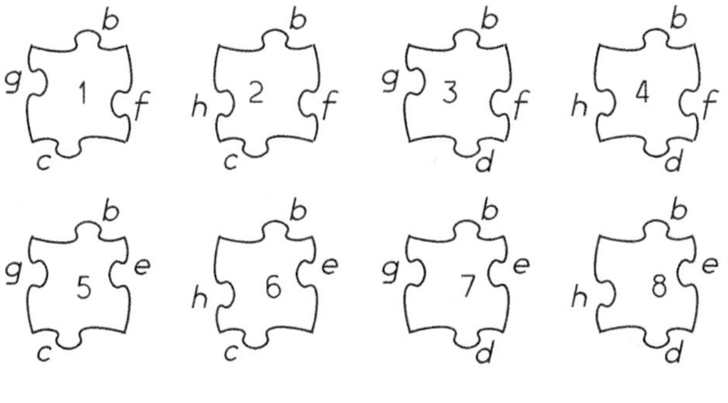

themselves and two map to each other. We can eliminated shape 5 as a duplicate. There are five distinct shapes of this ordering, which with the ten of the previous ordering make fifteen distinct shapes.

Shapes with this ordering of edges cannot tessellate as TTTT, TGTG, or G1G2G1G2. However, they may tessellate as G1G1G2G2 or C4C4C4C4. Because of the way the edges have been constructed and ordered, adjacent edges will fit either as C4C4 pairs or as GG pairs. If opposite corners have C4C4 pairs, the shape will fit as a C4C4C4C4 type. If opposite corners have GG pairs, the shape will tessellate as a G1G1G2G2 type. Starting at the top and going around each shape, we get the following: 1 GG GG GG GG, hence it fits G1G1G2G2 in two ways; 2 GG GG C4C4 C4C4, hence it fits neither type; 3 GG C4C4 C4C4 GG, hence it fits neither type; 4 GG C4C4 GG C4C4, hence it fit both types; and 6 C4C4 C4C4 C4C4 C4C4, hence it fits C4C4C4C4 in two ways.

Shapes 2 and 3 will tessellate, though not as Heesch types. All Heesch types are isohedral, that is, edges pair in the same way throughout the pattern. If edges fit in more than one way, the tiling is anisohedral. Below is an example of a tiling based on shape 2 with the edges labeled. Notice that edge A fits with edges D and B, B fits with edges A and C, C fits with edges B and D, and D fits with edges C and A.

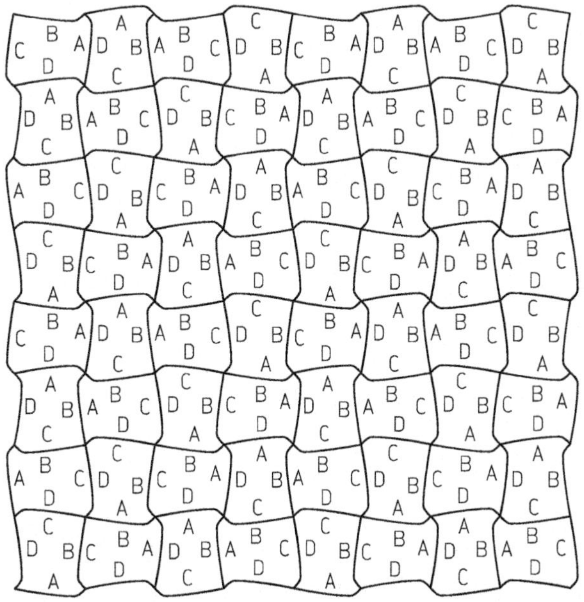

Shape 3 is an invert of shape 2, that is, it can be formed by switching bumps and indents. Because shape 2 tessellates, so must shape 3.

These two anisohedral tiles may be the easiest anisohedral tiles to form. Start with a tiling that fits isohedral class IH61, a C4C4C4C4 tiling with all sides shaped the same with asymmetric edges (shown below on the top left). If the edge between any two tiles is removed, the new tile will be of type TCTC (shown second and third on the top). If the edge between any two tiles is flipped over the midpoint of its vertices, the two new tiles will be the two anisohedral tiles discussed above.

Extending to The Rhombus Template

The square is both equilateral and equiangular. The quadrilateral that is only equilateral is the rhombus (a diamond), a parallelogram with four equal and parallel sides of which the square is a special case. The rhombus has less symmetry than the square. The square has reflection symmetry over four axes while the rhombus has reflection symmetry over only two, over its diagonals. The square has fourfold rotational symmetry while the rhombus has only twofold rotational symmetry. The square has all angles equal at 90° while the rhombus has opposite angles equal so that knowing just one angle determines the others.

The same 256 combinations of edges that are possible for the square template fitted with identical asymmetric edges are possible for the rhombus template fitted with the same asymmetric edges. As with the square template, 96 will have two knobs and two indents. However, with square templates all 90° rotations retain the shape. With rhombuses only 180° rotations preserve the shape. The fifteen distinctly different shapes become 30. A way of seeing why the rhombus template produces twice as many distinct shapes is to realize that there are two ways of flattening a square to get a rhombus. It can flatten so the NW-SE angles grow and the NE-SW angles shrink, or it can flatten so the NE-SW angles grow and the NW-SE angles shrink. The next table, which shows rhombus results, has illustrations of the 30 distinct shapes with the number codes for each group of shapes. Notice that each group from the table showing square results is split into two groups in the rhombus table.

There are at most only four orientations of sides for the rhombus when the template is in a fixed position. (See the table on the next page.) The original shape can be rotated 180°, flipped over its short diagonal, or flipped over its long diagonal. Any additional manipulation will reproduce one of these shapes. For example rotating the shape 180° and flipping it over its long diagonal produces the same result as flipping the shape over its short diagonal. If the tile itself has rotational or mirror symmetry as 12 of the groups in the table have, it will have only two orientations.

The square-based tiles tessellate as five Heesch types: TTTT, TGTG, G1G1G2G2, G1G2G1G2, and C4C4C4C4. Both the G1G2G1G2, and C4C4C4C4 types require a square template, so the rhombus based shapes cannot tessellate as these types. The groups in the square table that tessellate as TTTT and G1G1G2G2 produce groups in the rhombus table that also tessellate as TTTT and G1G1G2G2 and the pattern that they have is the rhombus pattern in which all rhombuses are similarly aligned, illustrated below.

Below is a rhombic tiling from group 1a in the table that tessellates as type G1G1G2G2.

The groups that tiled as TGTG in the square table also tile as TGTG in the rhombic table, but with a different configuration of rhombuses:

Rhombus Template Asymmetric Edges

Code	Sample Shape
1a 0011 1100 2233 3322 G1G1G2G2	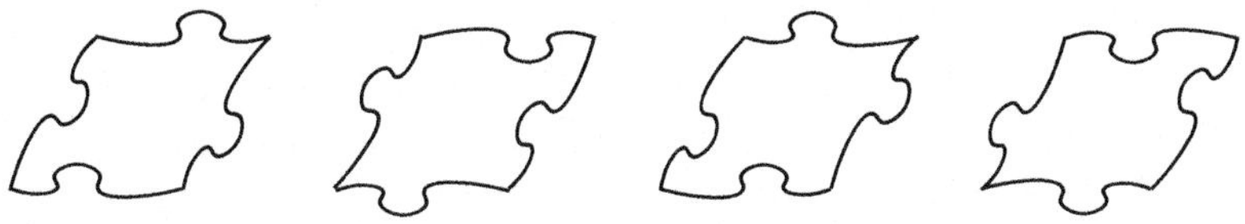
1b 0110 1001 2332 3223 G1G1G2G2	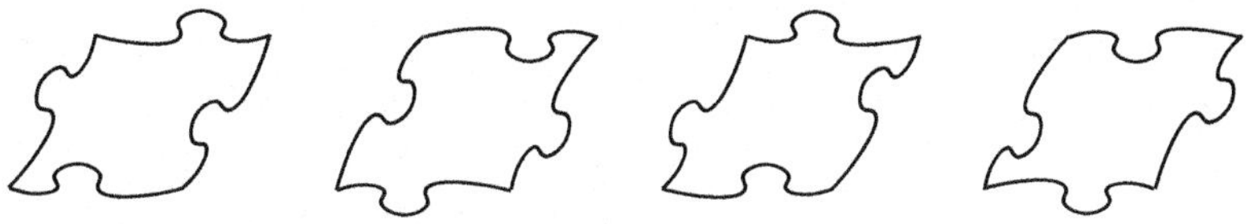
2a 0033 3300 1122 2211 TTTT; *(C3C3C3C3)	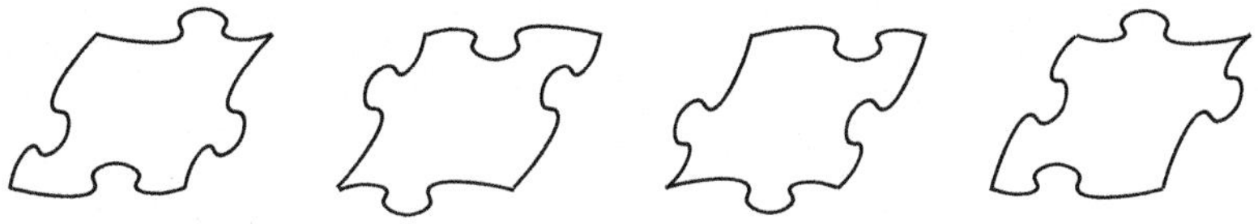
2b 0330 3003 1221 2112 TTTT; *(C3C3C3C3)	
3a 0112 1201 0332 3203 TGTG	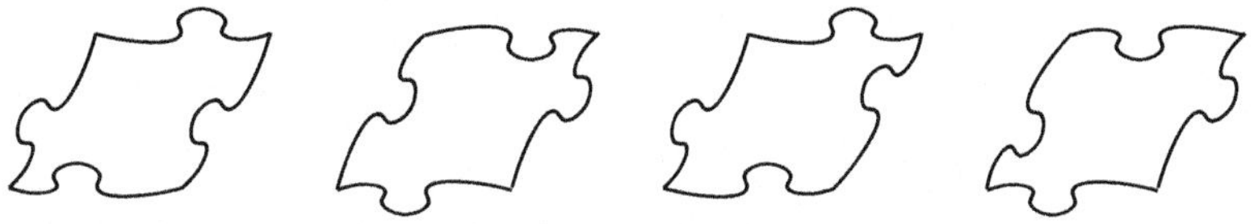
3b 1120 2011 3320 2033 TGTG	
4a 0211 1102 0233 3302 TGTG	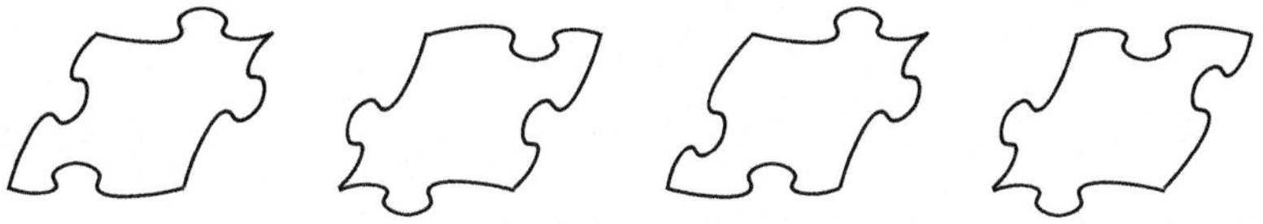
4b 2110 1021 2330 3023 TGTG	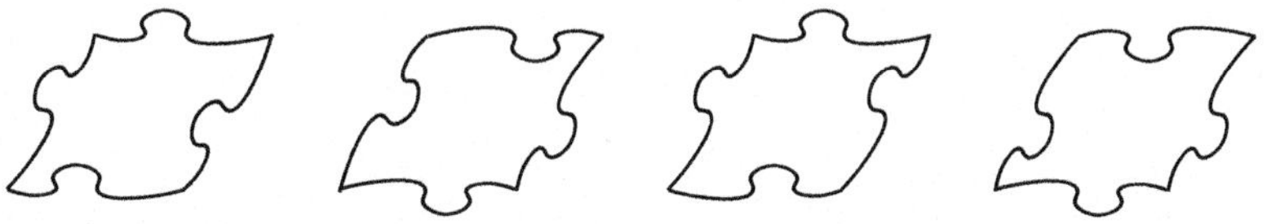
5a 0013 1300 1322 2213 TGTG	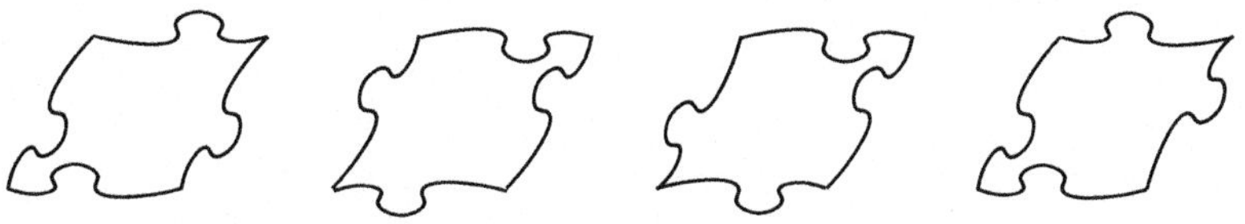
5b 0130 3001 3221 2132 TGTG	

Code	Sample Shape
6a 0031 3100 2231 3122 TGTG	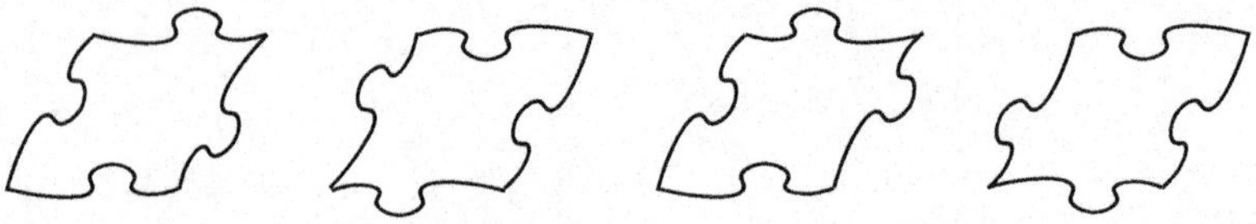
6b 0310 1003 1223 2312 TGTG	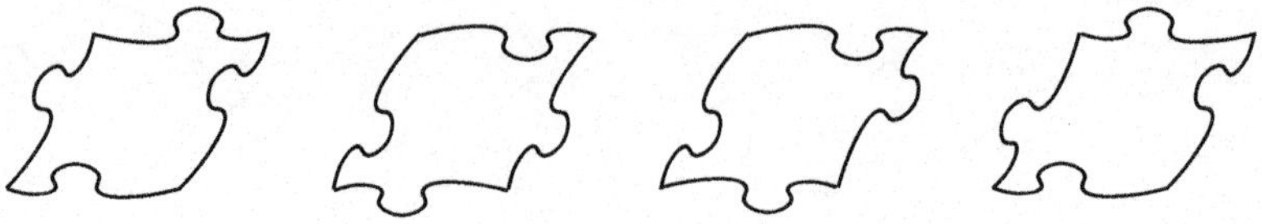
7a 0213 1302 *(C3C3C3C3)	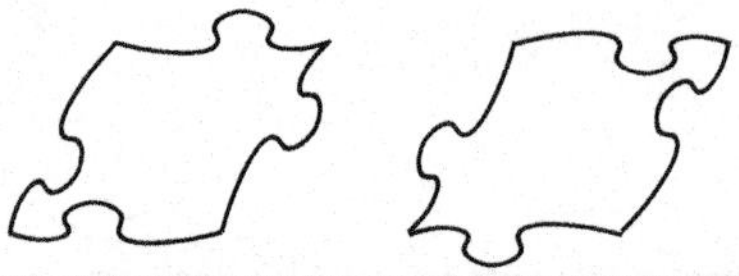
7b 2130 3021 *(C3C3C3C3)	
8a 0312 1203 *(C3C3C3C3)	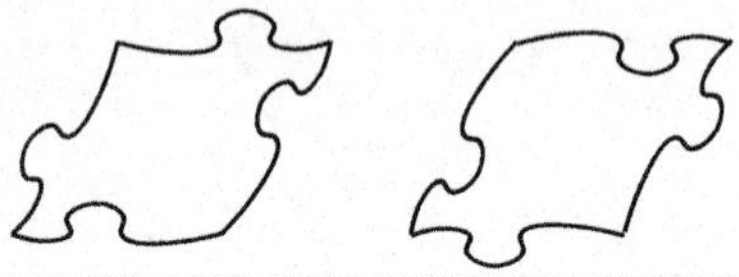
8b 3120 2031 *(C3C3C3C3)	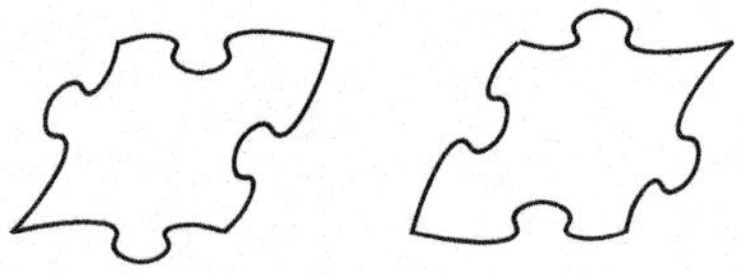
9 0132 3201 TTTT; G1G1G2G2	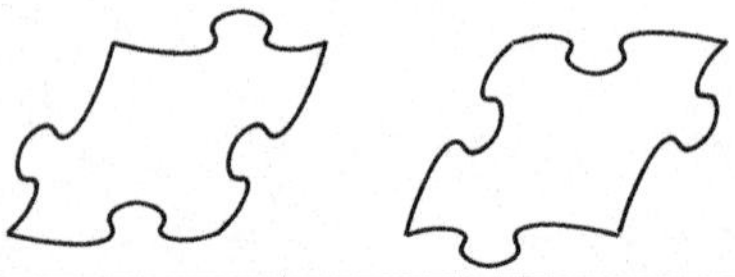
9b 1320 2013 TTTT; G1G1G2G2	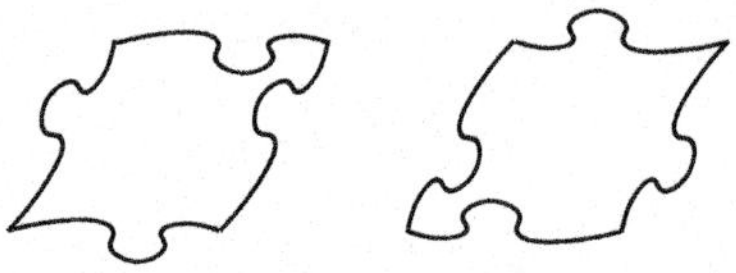
10a 0231 3102 TTTT; G1G1G2G2	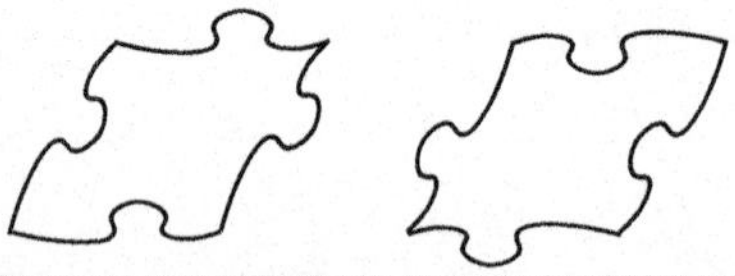
10b 2310 1023 TTTT; G1G1G2G2	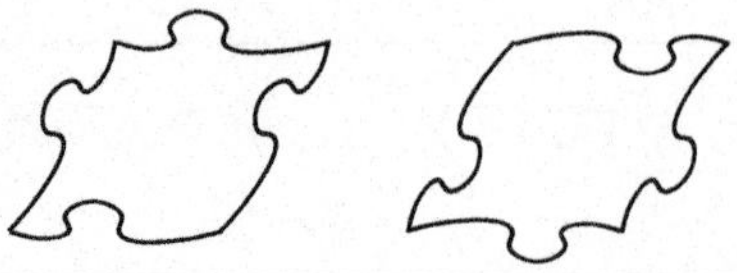

Code	Sample Shape
11a 1230 3012 0321 2103 G1G1G2G2; *(C3C3C3C3)	
11b 0123 2301 3210 1032 G1G1G2G2; *(C3C3C3C3)	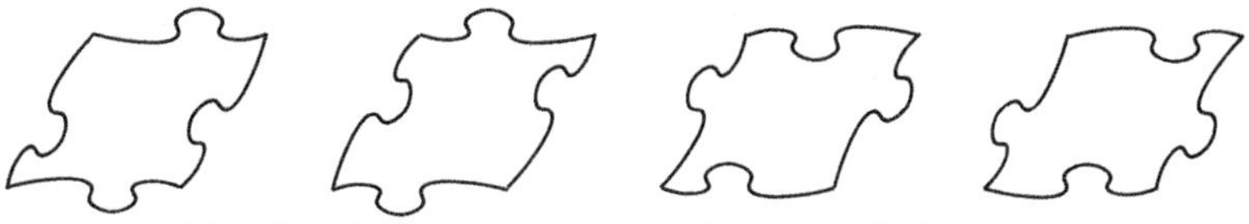
12a 0101 3232 G1G1G2G2	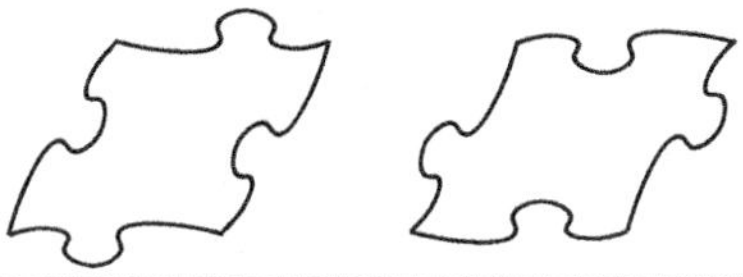
12b 1010 2323 G1G1G2G2	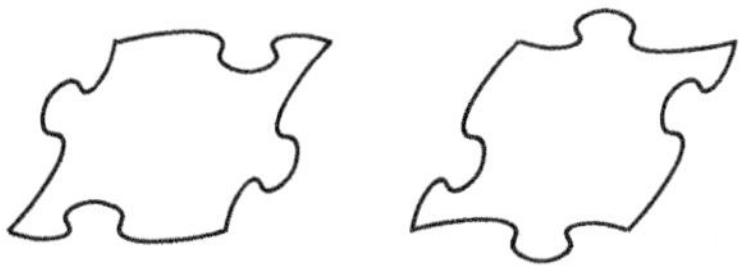
13a 0303 1212 *(C3C3C3C3)	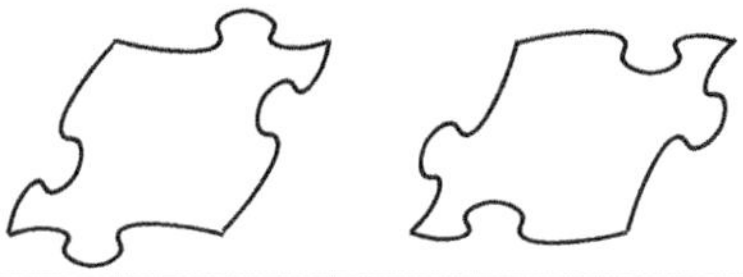
13b 3030 2121 *(C3C3C3C3)	
14a 0103 0301 1232 3212 ?	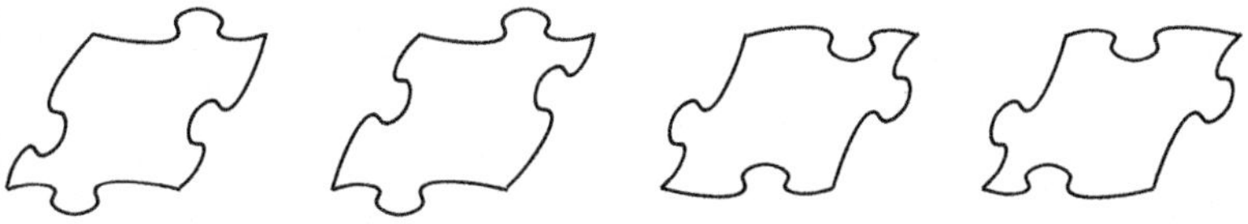
14b 1030 3010 2321 2123 ?	
15a 1210 1012 0323 2303 ?	
15b 0121 2101 3230 3032 ?	

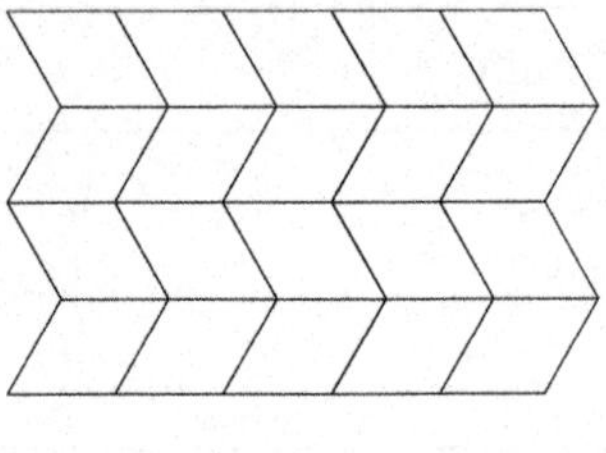

Below are examples from groups 3a and 5b.

The shapes on the square table that tessellate as type C4C4C4C4 have counterparts on the rhombus table that tessellate as C3C3C3C3 if and only if the rhombus template has angles of 120° and 60°. Below are examples from groups 13b, 13a, and 8b. The first two are examples of class IH34 and the third, the turtle shaped tile that has mirror symmetry, illustrates class IH36.

The square tiles the plane in only one way. The rhombus tiles the plane not only in the two ways illustrated above but in an infinite number of other ways that can be formed by combining strips of the first two patterns illustrated above. Below is a simple example with the strips two cells wide. None of the tiles in the rhombus table will fit in this pattern.

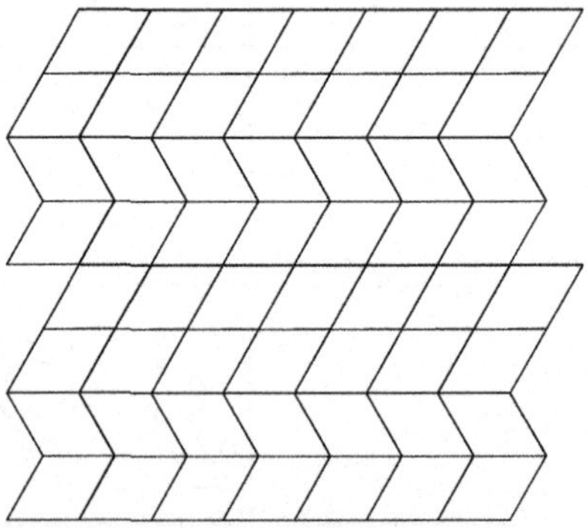

In conclusion, there are twenty distinct shapes of the rhombus template fitted with identical, asymmetric edges that will tile the plane.

Hexagonal Puzzle Pieces

A square template fitted with identical edges that mirror over the midpoint (each edge has mirror reflection) has only two possible shapes. One of them is a special case of both IH68 and IH71 but has no special isohedral class of its own. Depending on how it is fit together, it can form tilings of type TTTT, TGTG, G1G1G2G2, G1G2G1G2, or C4C4C4C4. The second distinct shape is IH73 and tiles in only one way that is simultaneously G1G1G2G2 and C4C4C4C4.

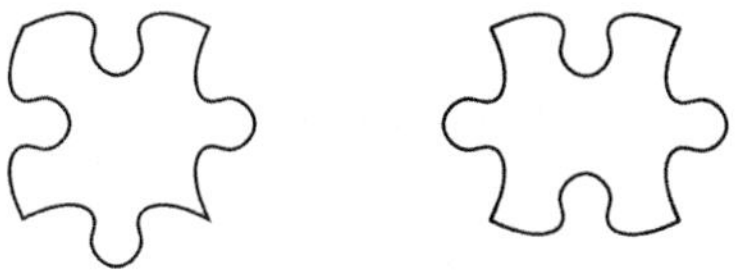

Except for the case in which all edges are straight lines, a triangle or a pentagon fitted with identical edges with mirror reflection cannot tessellate because the number of "in" edges does not equal the number of "out" edges. This is one way of seeing why all Heesch types based on triangles and pentagons have an odd number of edges with center-point rotation. An edge that has center-point rotation has mirror reflection only when it is a straight line.

When a regular hexagon is fitted with identical edges with mirror reflection, there are three distinct shapes possible. All three tessellate. One of the shapes has a special isohedral class, IH18. The shape has threefold rotational symmetry and reflective symmetry through the center of paired opposite edges. It tiles in only one way and that one way fits Heesch types TTTTTT, TG1G1TG2G2, and C3C3C3C3C3C3.

The second distinct shape has two adjacent "in" edges and two adjacent "out" edges. This shape has no rotational or reflective symmetry but satisfies Heesch types TG1G1TG2G2, TG1G2TG2G1, and C3C3C3C3C3C3. Each of these types has a different arrangement of tiles. They are illustrated below, first TG1G2TG2G1, then TG1G1TG2G2, and last C3C3C3C3C3C3.

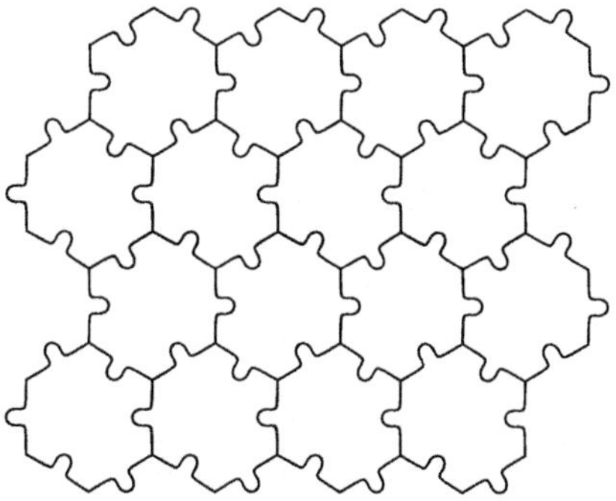

On the third distinct shape the three "in" edges are grouped together as are the three "out" edges. The shape has reflective symmetry over a line through the middle "in" and middle "out" edges. It satisfies types TTTTTT, TG1G1TG2G2, and TG1G2TG2G1 but not C3C3C3C3C3C3. The first tiling below is both TTTTTT and TG1G1TG2G2 (IH12) and the second is TG1G2TG2G1.

If we replace the symmetric edge with one that is asymmetric, the analysis gets far more complex. Previous sections showed that 15 distinct shapes can be formed from a square template fitted with identical asymmetric edges. All fifteen shapes tessellate, 13 of them isohedrally. The purpose of what follows is to extend this analysis to a template of the regular hexagon fitted with identical asymmetric edges.

My original attempt to analyzing the square template noted that the asymmetric edge could be fitted in four ways. With four edges to fit, each in four ways, there are 4^4=256 possible ways shapes can be formed. However, shapes that do not have two "in" edges and two "out" edges cannot tessellate and when they are eliminated, 96 shapes remain. Eliminating duplicates that are flips or rotations of each other leaves 15 distinct shapes. If this procedure is used for the hexagonal template, there are 4^6 = 4096 initial shapes.

In correspondence with me, Dr Doris Shattenschneider pointed to a different way to solve the problem. She noted that one edge could be fixed because any shape by flips or rotations can be positioned so one edge has a given, arbitrary orientation. Suppose that the arbitrary orientation is an "out" edge. There are three possible positions for the second "out" edge and the other two must be "in" edges. Once set as "out" or "in", each edge can have two orientations. Hence the starting point is 3*2*2*2=24 shapes. Nine of these are duplicates of other shapes, yielding 15 distinct shapes. Applying this method to the hexagons, the two additional "out" edges must be distributed in five positions. The combination formula shows there are ten ways to do this. Each of the five non-fixed edges can take two orientations, so we begin with 10*2*2*2*2*2 = 320 shapes.

These two procedures begin with a large number of shapes that must be checked for duplicates. However, I found a third approach to the problem as I began analyzing hexagons. As noted above, the square template allows only two ways to orient the "in" and "out" edges. Once the order of "ins" and "outs" is set, there are 2*2*2*2=16 ways to construct the shapes. With two orderings of edges, there are 32 shapes to check for duplicates. However, because of symmetry one half of the shapes in the ordering with opposite "out" edges will be flips of the other half. Eliminating them, we are reduced to a starting point of 24 shapes to examine

In the hexagonal case there are three ways to arrange the "in" and "out" edges. "Ins" and "outs" can alternate, two "ins" can be next to each other which forces two "outs" to be next to each other, or the three "ins" can be grouped together, which implies that the three "outs" are also grouped together. Once the order of "ins" and "outs" is set, there are 2^6=64 possible shapes. Since there are three orderings, we start with 3*64=192 shapes, which is preferable to 4096 or 320. Moreover, two of the orderings have reflective symmetry over midpoints of opposite edges, so the 64 shapes will include 32 that are flips of the other 32. Eliminating these gives us a starting point of 128. Although still a big number, it is manageable because the analysis is divided into three separate parts.

The First Ordering

The first table shows the 32 shapes that can be formed from the ordering in which "in" and "outs" alternate. Rotating the ordering clockwise or counterclockwise 120° reproduces the ordering, so we must check for duplicates with these rotations. A 120° clockwise rotation will move a "g" edge to the "a" position, and shapes with a "g" on the lower left need to be checked. The results of the rotation will be to move edges as follows: a→i, f→d, g→a i→g, l→f, and d→l. Applying this transformation yields the following:

(3 afiagi → agidgi 20), (4 afidgi→ agidgl 28),
(7 aflagi → agidfi 18), (8 afldgi→ agidfl 26),
(11 afiagl → afidgi 4), (12 afidgl → afidgl 12),
(15 aflagl → afidfi 2), (16 afldgl → afidfl 10),
(19 agiagi → agiagi 19), (20 agidgi → agiagl 27),
(23 aglagi→ agiafi 17), (24 agldgi → agiafl 25),
(27 agiagl → afiagi 3), (28 agidgl → afiagl 11),
(31 aglagl → afiafi 1), (32 agldgl → afiafl 9).

The counterclockwise rotation of 120° will move an "i" to the "a" position. A counterclockwise rotation reverses the clockwise rotation: i→a, a→g, d→f, f→l, g→i, l→d. Applying this transformation yields the following:

(1 afiafi → aglagl 31), (2 afidfi → aflagl 15),
(3 afiagi → agiagl 27), (4 afidgi → afiagl 11),
(9 afiafl → agldgl 32), (10 afidfl → afldgl 16),
(11 afiagl→ agidgl 28), (12 afidgl → afidgl 12),
(17 agiafi → aglagi 23), (18 agidfi → aflagi 7),
(19 agiagi → agiagi 19), (20 agidgi → afiagi 3),
(25 agiafl → agldgi 24), (26 agidfl → afldgi 8),
(27 agiagl → agidgi 20), (28 agidgl → afidgi 4).

Listing the shapes with their duplicates shows that twelve shapes can be eliminated:

Labelling of edges:

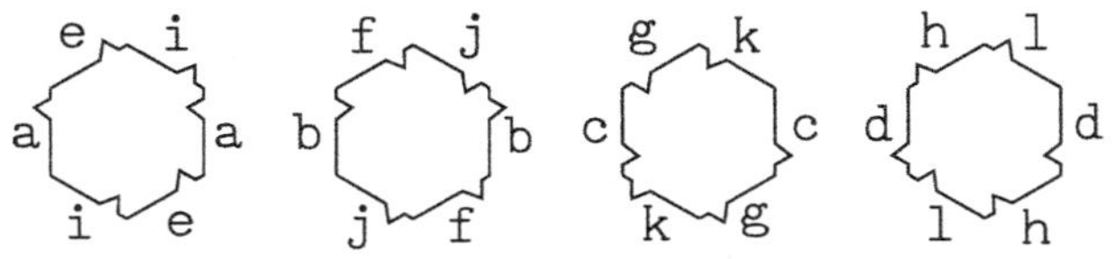

Thirty-Two Shapes from Ordering One. Gray shapes will be shown to be duplicates.

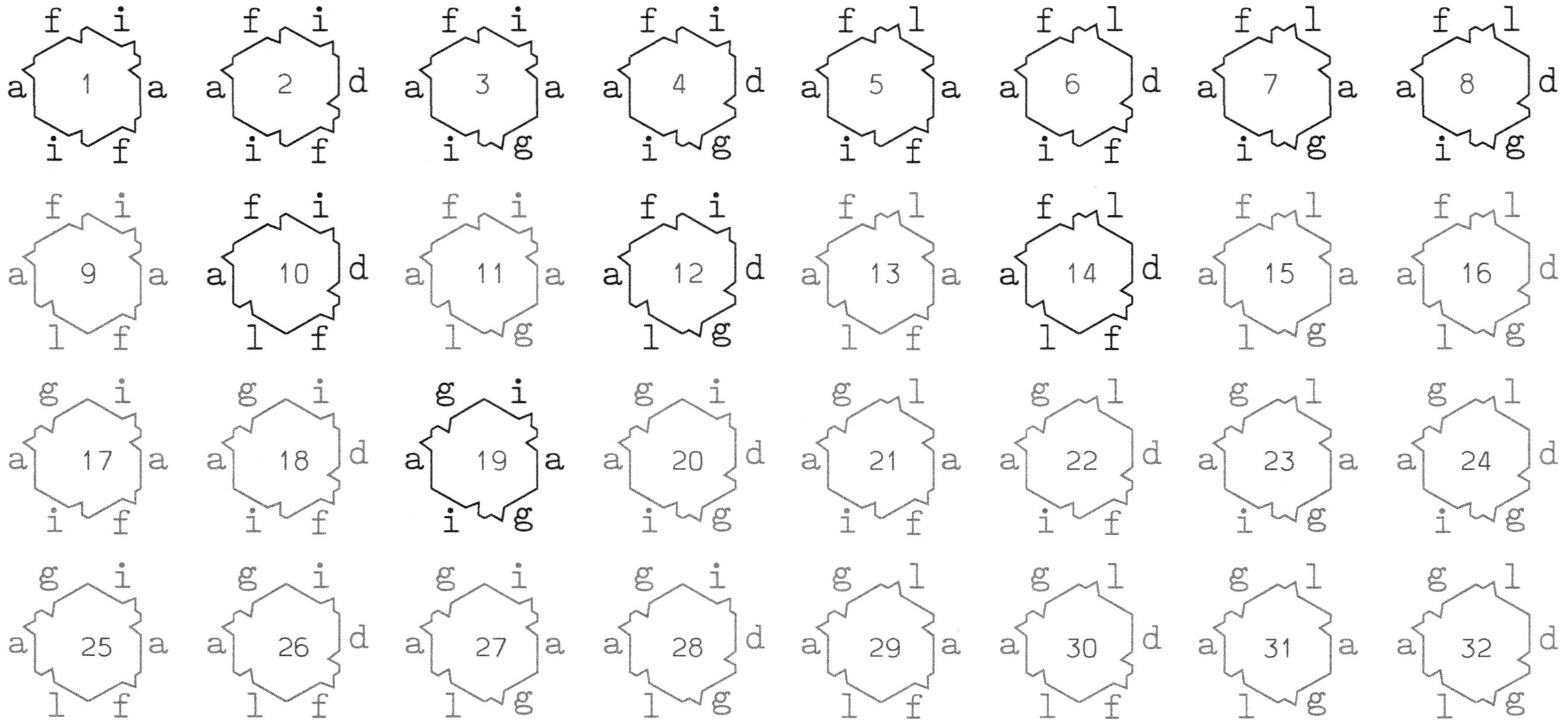

(1 - 31), (2 - 15), (3 - 27 - 20), (4 - 11 - 28), (5), (6), (7 - 18), (8 - 26), (9 - 32), (10 - 16), (11 - 28 - 4), (12 - 12 - 12), (13), (14), (15 - 2), (16 - 10), (17 - 23), (18 - 7), (19 - 19 - 19), (20 - 3 - 27), (21), (22), (23 - 17), (24 - 25), (25 - 24), (26 - 8), (27 - 20 - 3), (28 - 4 - 11), (29), (30), (31 - 1), (32 - 9)

The ordering also reproduces itself with a flip through the center of opposite edges. One of these flips has already been utilized to eliminate all the tiles that would otherwise have a "d" rather than the "a" on the right. Flipping over the il-il edges transforms edges as follows: i↔l, a↔f, d↔g. The flip also reorders edges from clockwise to counterclockwise. Applying this transformation to shapes that have an "f" edge on the lower right and have not already been eliminated, we get:

(1 afiafi → aflafl 13), (2 afidfi → aglafl 29),
(5 aflafi → afiafl 9), (6 afldfi → agiafl 25),
(9 afiafl → aglafi 5), (10 afidfl → aglafi 21),
(13 aflafl → afiafi 1), (14 afldfl → agiafi 17),
(17 agiafi → afldfl 14), (21 aglafi → afidfl 10),
(29 aglafl → afidfi 2), (30 agldfl → agidfi 18).

There are five pairings of shapes that have not already been eliminated: 1-13, 2-29, 5-9, 10-21, 14-17.

The flip over the midpoint of the fg-fg edges transforms edges as follows: f↔g, l↔a i↔d and changes order from clockwise to counterclockwise. Applying this transformation to shapes that have an "l" edge on the upper right and have not already been eliminated, we get:

(5 aflafi → agldgl 32), (6 afldfi → agldgi 24),
(7 aflagi → agldfl 30), (8 afldgi → agldfi 22),
(13 aflafl → aglagl 31), (14 afldfl → aglagi 23),
(21 aglafi → afldgl 16), (22 agldfi → afldgi 8),
(24 agldgi → afldfi 6), (29 aglafl → aflagl 15),
(30 agldfl → aflagi 7).

There are three pairings of shapes that have not already been eliminated: 6-24, 8-22, and 7-30. Thus, this ordering of "ins" and "outs" has only 12 distinct shapes.

The following tables help determine if a shape will tessellate isohedrally, that is, fit a Heesch type.

TT Edge Pairs	Pairings for TG1G1TG2G2	Pairings for TG1G2TG2G1
a-a, d-d, b-b, c-c	e-j, f-i, g-l, h-k	e-l, f-k, g-j, h-i
e-e, f-f, g-g, h-h	a-l, b-k, c-j, d-i	a-j, b-i, c-l, d-k
i-i, j-j, k-k, l-l	a-f, b-e, c-h, d-g	e-d, f-c, g-b, h-a

C3C3C3C3C3C3 pairs (need one in each box)

ag bh ce df	ia jb kc ld	ek fl gi hj

Because shape 1 has opposite edges that are identical, aa, ff, and ii, it will tile as type TTTTTT. It also tiles as TG1G1TG2G2 because in addition to the aa combination, its two edge combinations of fi in the first row of the second column indicate that they can be the glide edges for a type TG1G1TG2G2. None of the shapes of this ordering will tessellate as TG1G2TG2G1 because the ordering of "ins" and "outs" is incompatible with this type.

Examining the other shapes using these tables shows that shapes 1 and 19 fit type TTTTTT; shapes 6, 7, and 19 fit type C3C3C3C3C3C3; and shapes 1, 4, and 10 fit type TG1G1TG2G2. Six of the 12 unique shapes tile isohedrally.

Five of the six shapes that do not tile isohedrally will tile anisohedrally. (All the anisohedral tiles found in this exercise keep their edges so they can be labeled. Many anisohedral tiles alter edges depending on where they are in the pattern.)

Below is a pattern with a translation block of two for shapes 2, 15, and 29. The edges are labeled to show how they fit together. As the result of a flip, in some tiles the letters are clockwise and in others counterclockwise. Edges labeled A and D always pair. B fits E, which fits F, which fits C, which fits B.

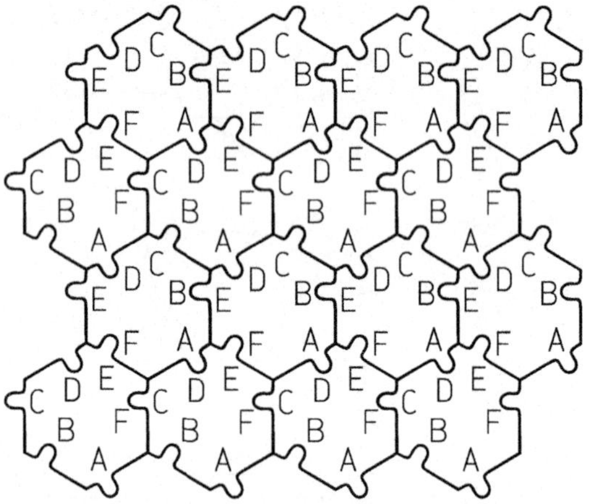

Shapes 5, 9, 32 also tile with a translation block of two. The way edges fit is identical because this shape is an invert of the previous shape. Take shape 2 and invert bumps so that "outs" become "ins" and "ins" become "outs". The result is shape 5 and its duplicates, shown below with the same lettering of edges.

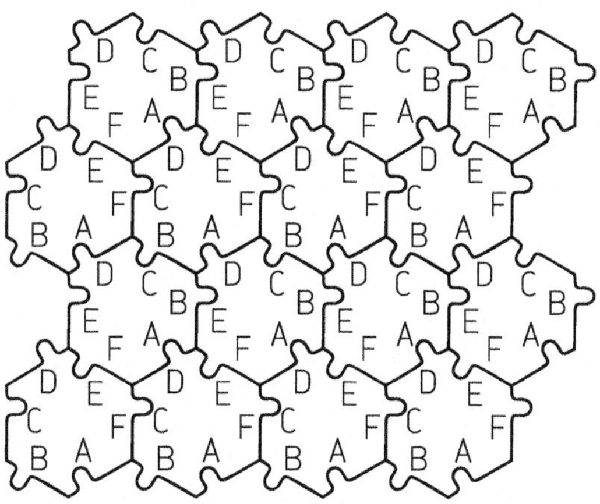

Rearranging the translation block of shapes 5, 9, 32 and combining it with the original arrangement forms a tiling with a translation block of four in a 4x1 alignment. A fits B fits E fits F fits C fits D fits A. Since it is an invert of the shape 2 group, members of that group will also tile in the same way.

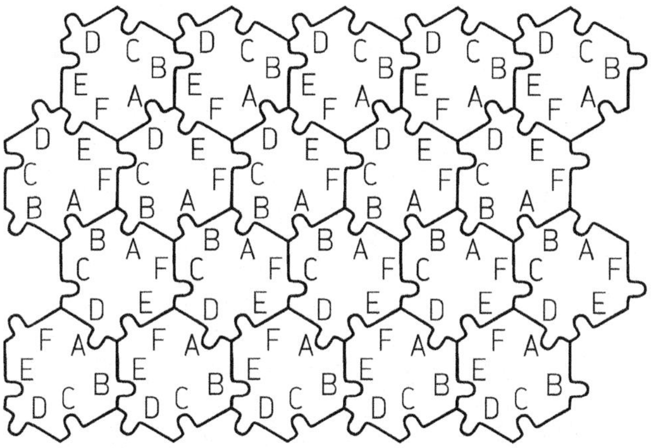

Shapes 3, 20, 27 have a translation block of four in a 1x4 alignment. A fits B fits C fits F fits E fits D fits A.

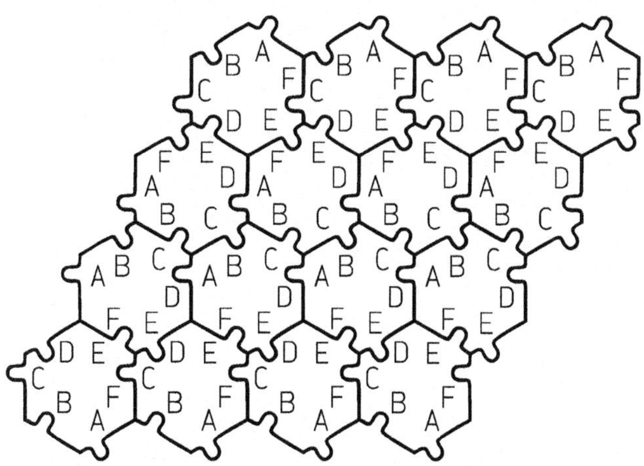

The invert of shape 3 is shape 14. Thus, shapes 14, 17, 23 tessellate, also with a translation block of four aligned 4x1. A fits B fits C fits F fits E fits D fits A.

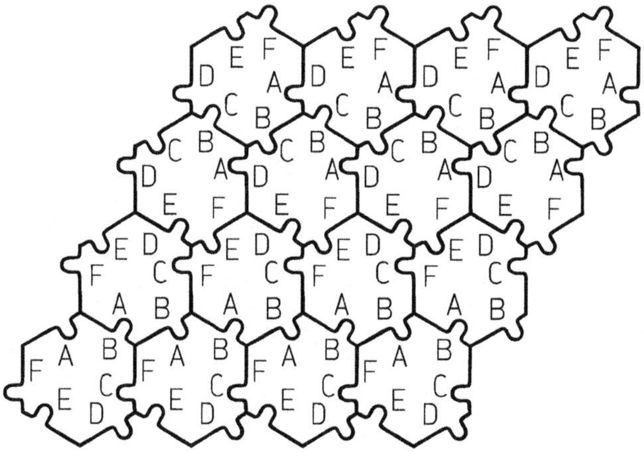

Shapes 8, 22, 26 tile with a translation block of four that is 2x2. A fits D fits E fits B fits C fits F fits A.

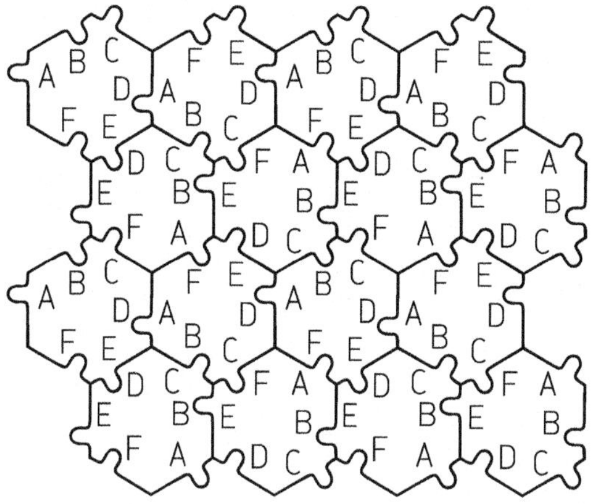

When shape 8 is inverted it gives back shape 8. All other anisohedral tiles in this exercise form invert pairs; shape 8 is the lone exception.

In some cases it is fairly easy to determine that the shape will not tessellate. Take a shape, fix its position, and select one edge. Suppose the chosen edge is an "out" edge. With rotation or flip each of the three "in" edges will fit this "out" edge in only one way. When the two pieces are fit, the space above and below the common edge will have two edges into which a third copy of the shape must fit. If the shape cannot fit into both of the two slots, this joining of the shape can be dismissed. If the same is true for the other two ways of fitting the selected edge, then the shape will not allow a tiling of the plane.

This procedure shows that shape 12 cannot tessellate. There are only two orientations of the shape because of its symmetry; all three possible ways of joining the two edges are identical. When they are joined, shown below, they form notches on the top and bottom that cannot be fit by the shape.

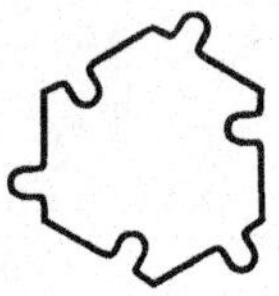

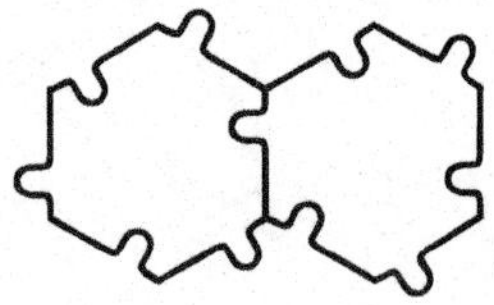

Of the twelve distinct shapes of this first ordering, six tile isohedrally, five anisohedrelly, and one does not tile:

1, 13, 31	TTTTTT, TG1G1TG2G2
2, 15 29	anisohedrel
3, 20, 27	anisohedrel
4, 11, 28	TG1G1TG2G2
5, 9, 32	anisohedrel
6, 24, 25	C3C3C3C3C3C3
7, 18, 30	C3C3C3C3C3C3
8, 22, 26	anisohedrel
10, 16, 21	TG1G1TG2G2
12	does not tile
14, 17, 23	anisohedrel
19	TTTTTT, C3C3C3C3C3C3

Shape 19 represents isohedral class IH10.

The Second Ordering

The second ordering has three "ins" adjacent and three "outs" adjacent. There is only one symmetry in the ordering, a reflective symmetry, and we use it to cut the count of shapes from 64 to 32. Since there are no other symmetries, none of these 32 can be eliminated as duplicates. The possible shapes as shown in the next table.

This alignment of edges does not allow any tile to fit the C3C3C3C3C3C3 type. Using the tables of paired edges reveals that four shapes fit Heesch type TTTTTT and four shapes fit type TG1G1TG2G2. Seven shapes fit type TG1G2TG2G1 with one of the seven fitting the type in two ways. Because three shapes fit more than one type, only ten of the 32 shapes tile isohedrally:

1 TTTTTT, TG1G1TG2G2, TG1G2TG2G1
4 TG1G2TG2G1
10 TG1G2TG2G1
11 TG1G1TG2G2
13 TTTTTT
16 TG1G2TG2G1
19 TTTTTT, TG1G2TG2G1 (two ways)
21 TG1G1TG2G2
28 TG1G2TG2G1
31 TTTTTT, TG1G1TG2G2, TG1G2TG2G1

The procedure mentioned above helped determine if an anisohedral tiling is possible. I checked the three ways of joining along a single edge to see if further tiling was possible. Below are three joinings of shape 30 with the left piece fixed.

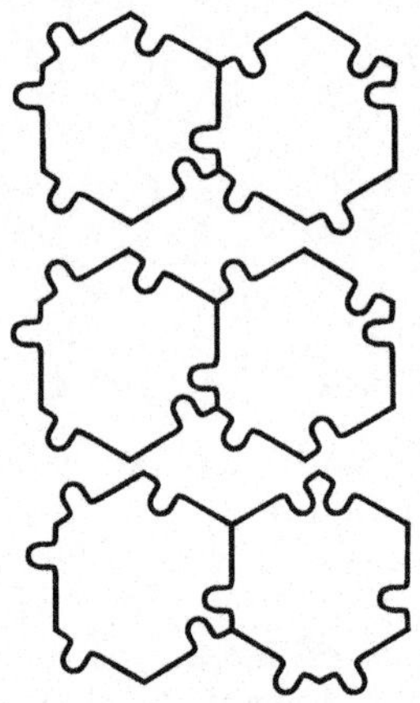

The bottom notch on the top two pairs requires an "in" and an "out" next to each other and that combination does not exist on this shape. The top of the bottom pair requires edges on which two "outs" are as far away from each other as possible and there is no edge pair with that combination. Hence, this shape cannot tessellate. In many cases this procedure quickly showed that no tiling was possible.

When notches could be filled, I filled them to see what edges additional pieces would need to fit. With some shapes, such as shapes 5 and 9, several pieces had to be fit before contradictions were revealed.

Using this procedure to examining the 22 shapes that do not tile as Heesch types, I found two shapes that tile anisohedrally, shapes 2 and 32. Both have translation blocks of two. Below is a tiling of shape 2. In it the edges labeled B and E always fit together. A fits F fits C fits D fits A.

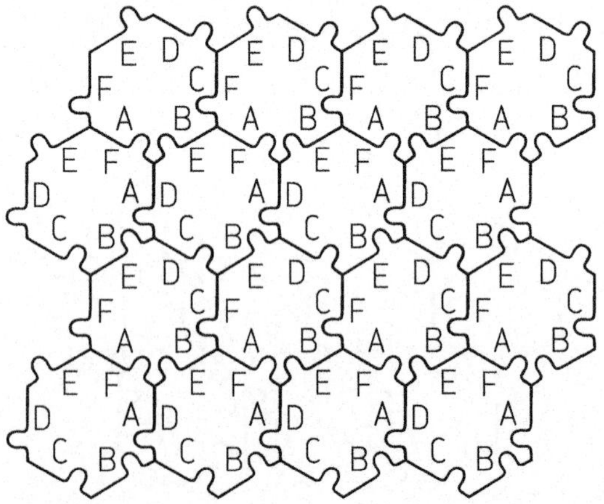

In the tiling of shape 32, A fits F fits C fits D fits A. Edges labeled B and E always fit together. The translation block is two.

Thirty-Two Shapes from Ordering Two

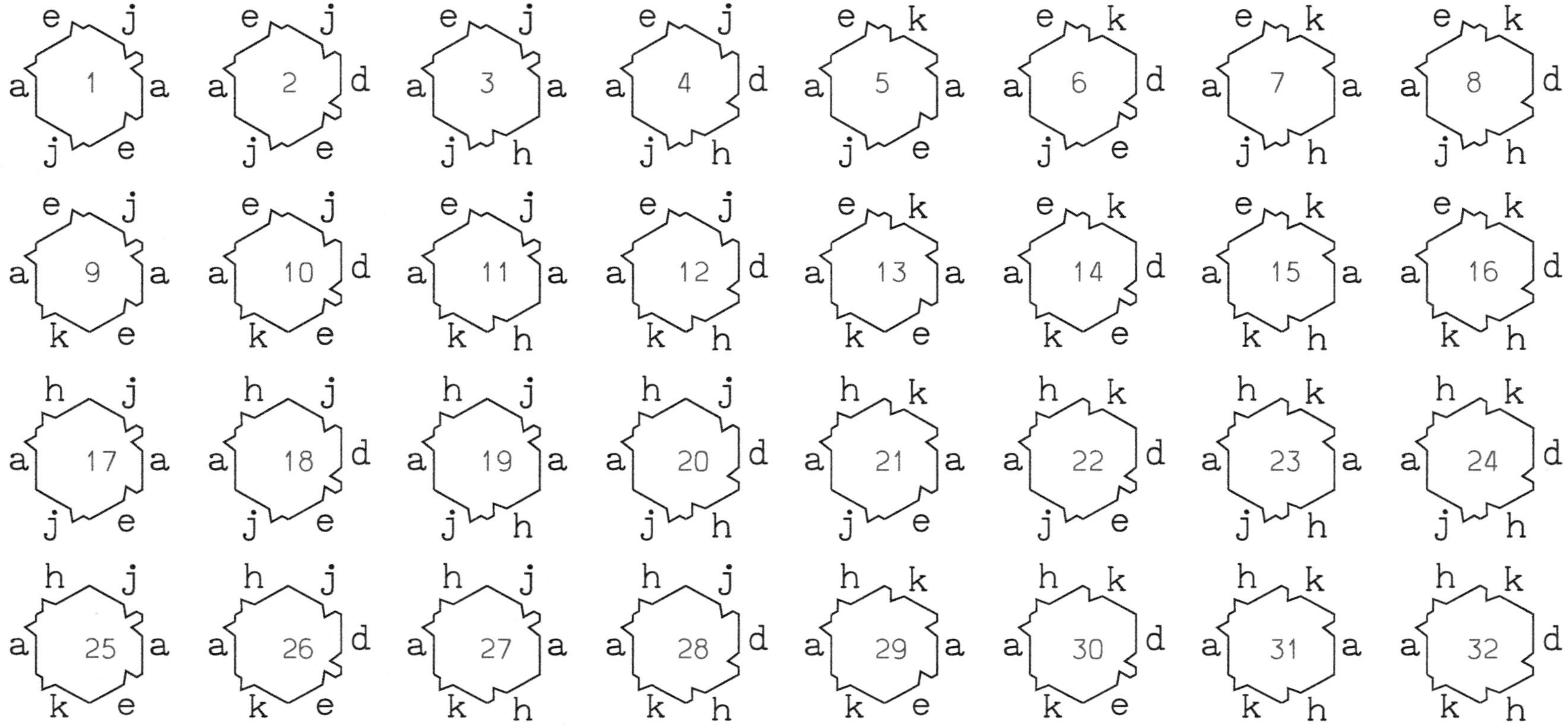

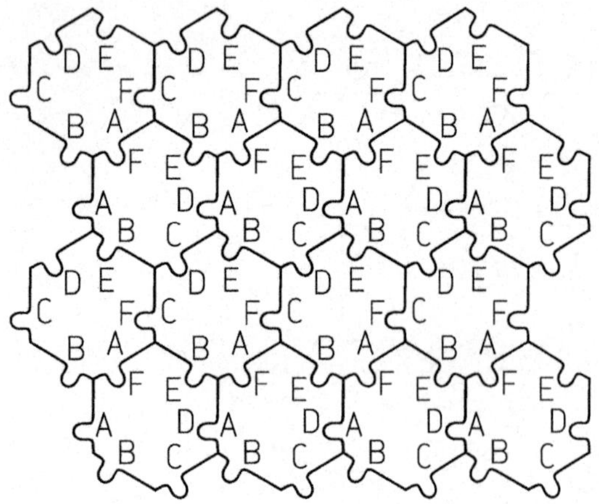

Shapes 2 and 32 tile in similar ways because they are inverts of one another. If the "out" edges of shape 2 are pushed in to make "in" edges and the "in" edges of are pushed out to make the "out" edges, the result will be shape 32.

Because these two shapes have some edges that pair and some that do not, a partial inverting of edges can maintain tessellation. Consider shape 2 of ordering 2. When the two paired edges are inverted, the "ins" and "outs" alternate and the new shape will be shape 32 of the first ordering. When the four edges that do not pair are inverted, again the "ins" and "outs" alternate and the new shape will be shape 2 of the first ordering. Similar results will hold for partial inverts of the other three anisohedral tiles that have two edges that pair.

In contrast to anisohedral tilings, isohedral tilings have pairs of edges that remain constant throughout the tiling. Shape 21 from ordering 2 tiles as a TG1G1TG2G2 type. It has a translation block of two and the shape is flipped to complete the tiling so some pieces have the edges in a clockwise order and others have them in a counterclockwise order. Notice that edge A always fits edge F, edge B always fits edge E, and edges C and D always fit together. This consistency in the way edges fit is a property of isohedral tilings.

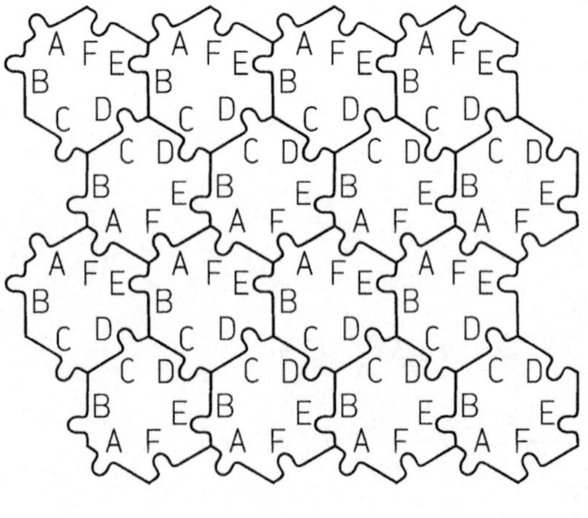

The Third Ordering

The third and final ordering with two "ins" adjacent and two "outs" adjacent has no symmetry so there are no duplicates to remove. The 64 possible shapes are shown in the last table, that with 64 shapes.

This ordering does not permit TTTTTT tilings but does contain eight TG1G1TG2G2 tilings, eight TG1G2TG2G1 tilings, and eight C3C3C3C3C3C3 tilings. Because six shapes fit more than one type, only 18 of the 64 tile isohedrally. The other 46 either tile anisohedrally or do not tile. The tiles that tile isohedrally and their types are listed below.

1 TG1G1TG2G2
6 C3C3C3C3C3C3
7 C3C3C3C3C3C3
11 TG1G1TG2G2, TG1G2TG2G1
13 TG1G2TG2G1
18 C3C3C3C3C3C3
19 C3C3C3C3C3C3, TG1G2TG2G1
21 TG1G1TG2G2, TG1G2TG2G1
31 TG1G1TG2G2
34 TG1G1TG2G2
44 TG1G1TG2G2, TG1G2TG2G1
46 TG1G2TG2G1, C3C3C3C3C3C3
47 C3C3C3C3C3C3
52 TG1G2TG2G1
54 TG1G1TG2G2, TG1G2TG2G1
58 C3C3C3C3C3C3
59 C3C3C3C3C3C3
64 TG1G1TG2G2

I found that two of the remaining shapes in the third ordering, shapes 2 and 63, tessellate anisohedrally. The tiling of shape 2 shown below has a translation block of four and it can be seen as a 4x1 arrangement or a 2x2 arrangement. A fits C fits D fits F fits B fits E fits A.

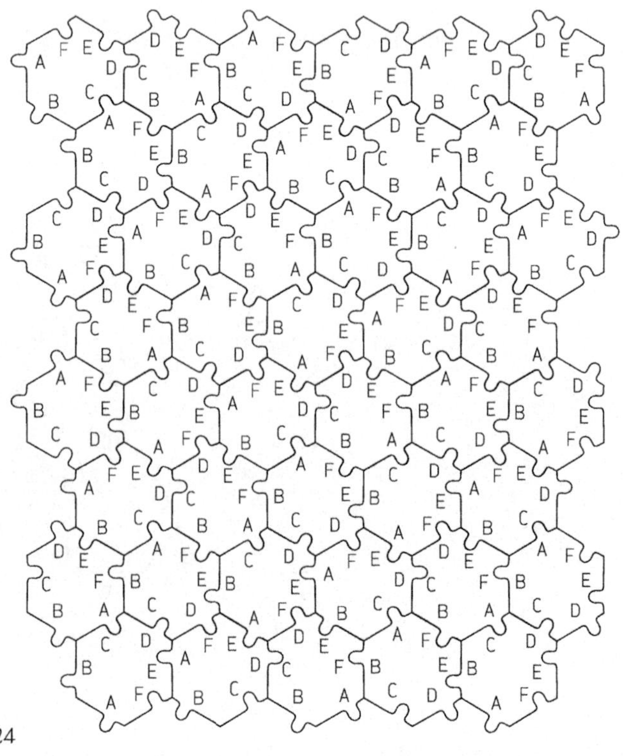

Sixty-Four Shapes from Ordering Three

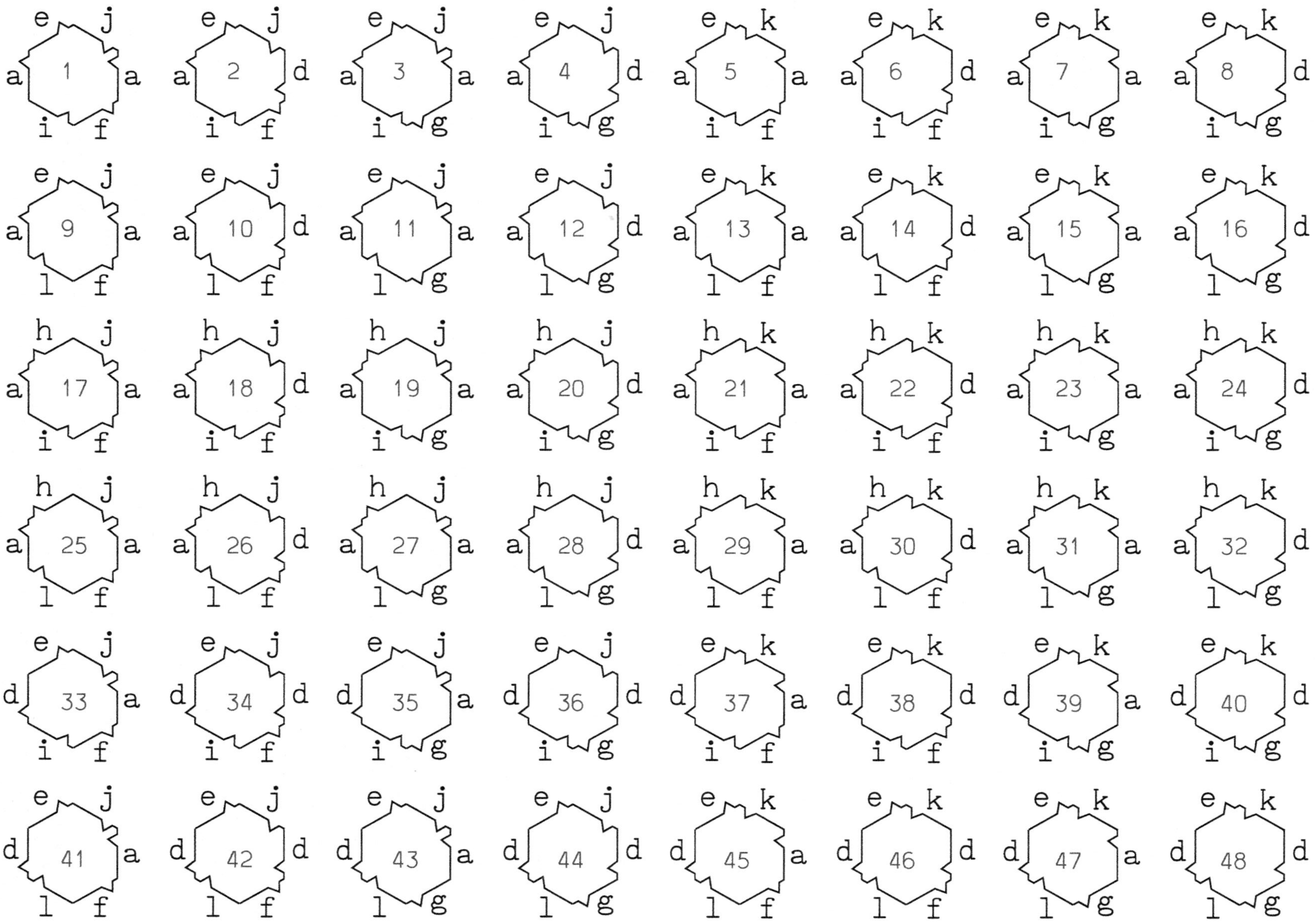

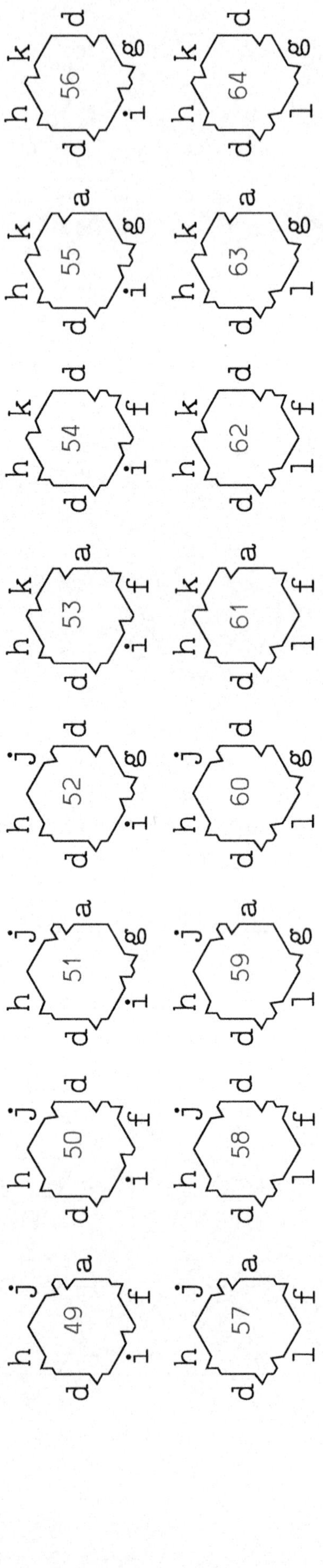

The invert of shape 2 is shape 63, and because it is an invert, it tiles in the same way as shape 2.

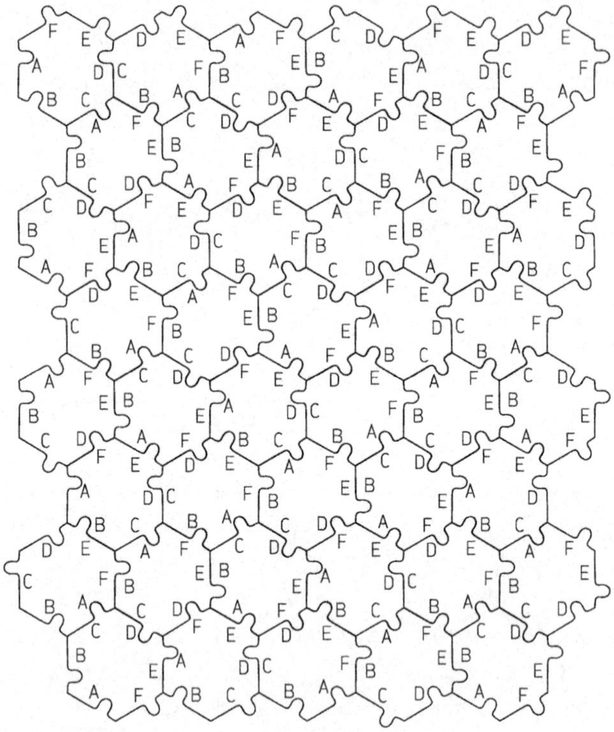

All inverts of shapes in this exercise, not just inverts of anisohedral shapes, will pair with another shape or self replicate. Finding the inverts of shapes that tile isohedrally is a check to see that all shapes that tessellate were found. Doing a quick check of those shapes reveals the following pairs and self-replicators.

Ordering One
- 1 self replicating
- 4–10
- 6 self replicating
- 7 self replicating
- 19 self replicating

Ordering Two
- 1–31
- 4–16
- 10–28
- 11–21
- 13 self replicating
- 19 self replicating

Ordering Three
- 1–31
- 6–47
- 7 self replicating
- 11–21
- 13–52
- 18–59
- 19 self replicating
- 34–64
- 44–54
- 46 self replicating
- 58 self replicating

Ten of the 34 isohedral tiles self replicate when bump and indents are inverted and 24 form pairs.

In summary, this analysis found 108 distinct shapes that have three "ins" and three "outs" when identical, asymmetric edges are fitted to the template of a regular hexagon. The shapes can be divided into three orderings of "in" and "out" edges. A total of 34 (6 + 10 + 18) tile isohedrally as Heesch types and another 9 (5 + 2 +2) tile anisohedrally. Sixty-five will not tile (1 + 20 + 44). The results are very different from those from the square template that has only 15 distinct shapes, 13 of which tile isohedrally and two that tile anisohedrally.

VI. Explorations Two

Identical Symmetric Edges

There are two types of symmetry that an edge can have, reflection symmetry and rotational symmetry. In reflection symmetry the right half of the edge is a reflection of the left half. In rotational symmetry the right half of the edge is rotated 180° to form the left half. The number of possible shapes when the edges have symmetry is far less than with the asymmetric edges.

When an edge has reflection or mirror symmetry, the four possible orientations are reduced to two.

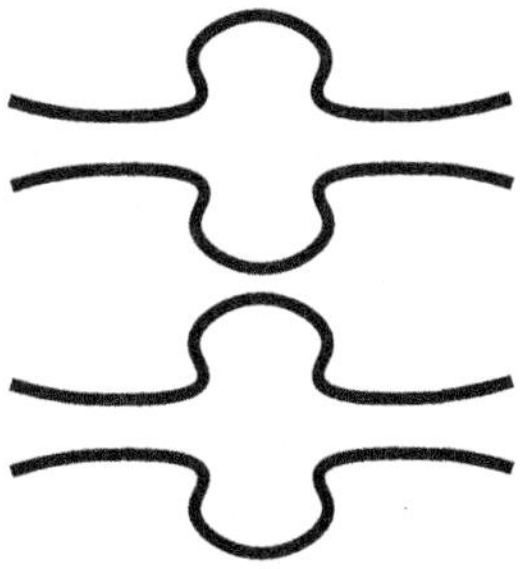

The original edge, orientation 0, is shown first. A flip over a horizontal line mirrors it, orientation 1. Orientation 2 is a flip over the vertical midpoint, and it returns the original shape. A rotation of 180° gives the same result as the flip over the horizontal line. Hence, we have only two orientations possible for each edge, or a total of 16 possible shapes. They can be indicated with the base-two numbers from 0 to 15. Again, we can eliminate shapes with an unequal number of indents and bumps. When we do this we get six possibilities.

0011, 0110, 1100, 1001

0101, 1010

The first four numbers represent rotations of the same shape and the second two represent rotations of a second shape. Hence, there are only two distinct shapes possible. Groups 1 to 10 in the table "Square Template Asymmetric Edges" collapse to one shape and groups 11 to 15 collapse to the other. Both shapes and ways that they tessellate were discussed in previous sections.

Below are the possibilities for the second sort of edge symmetry, central-rotation symmetry. Again, consider the first line the original or base line. Either a horizontal or vertical flip will produce a mirror image of the line. A rotation of 180° returns the original shape.

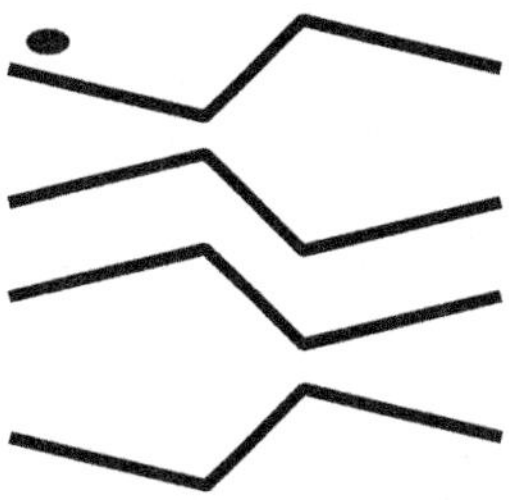

Again there are only 16 possible shapes, but with central rotation there are no bumps or indents to define the edges; each edge has both. Because edge faces edge, there are no items to eliminate because they will not tessellate. Grouping together the shapes that are simply rotations of one other, we get:

0000

0001 0010 0100 1000

0011 0110 1100 1001

0101 1010

0111 1110 1101 1011

1111

Flipping a tile swaps zeros for ones and ones for zeros. 0000 and 1111 are the same shape, as are 0111 and 0001. Swapping the zeros and ones in the two middle groups returns the groups. In conclusion, there are four distinct shapes with identically shaped edges of central rotation formed with a square template. From left to right below are examples of groups 0000, 0011, 0101, and 0001. Each of the first three differ in two numbers but the fourth differs from each of the other three in only one number. As a result the fourth shape shares three edges with each of the other shapes and differs on only one edge.

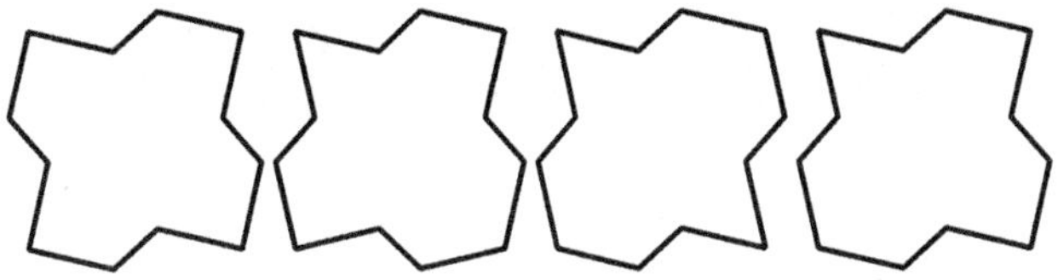

We have seen shapes with the same characteristics used as examples of several isohedral classes. The first from group 0000 fits into class IH62 and p4 symmetry.

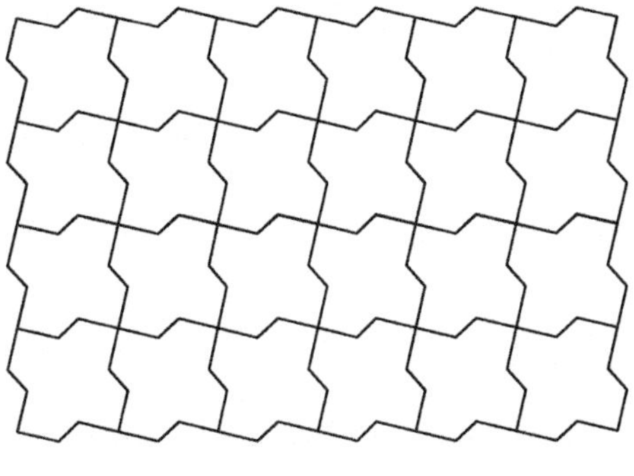

The second tile (group 0011) fits into class IH71 with p4g symmetry and also into an IH69 tiling with pmg symmetry. It is a more restricted form of each.

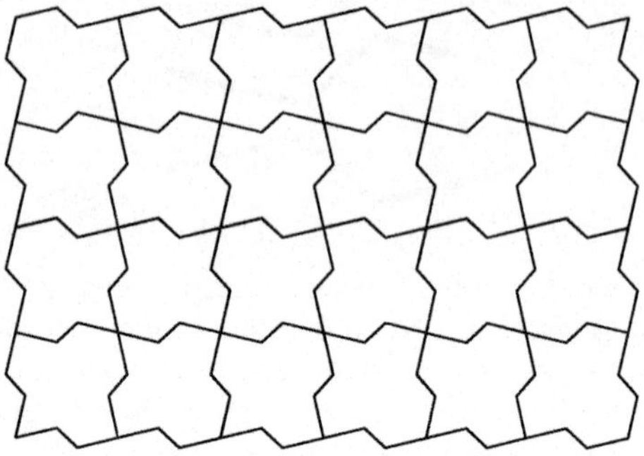

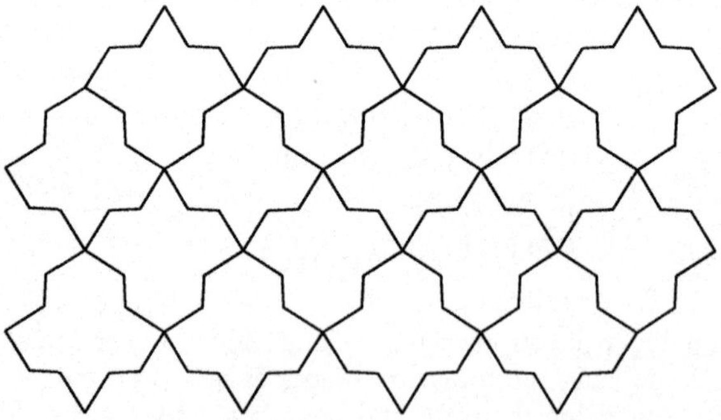

The third tile (group 0101) fits into an IH74 tiling with cmm symmetry.

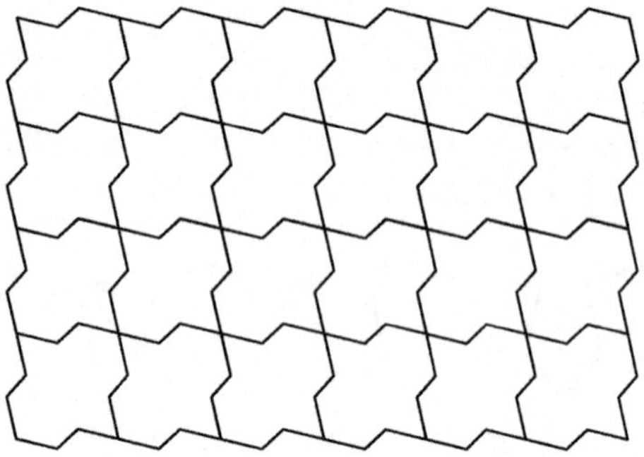

The fourth tile (group 0001) shows that having all edges identically formed does not guarantee a visually pleasing result. It fits no isohedral group other than that for CCCC, IH46 with p2 symmetry.

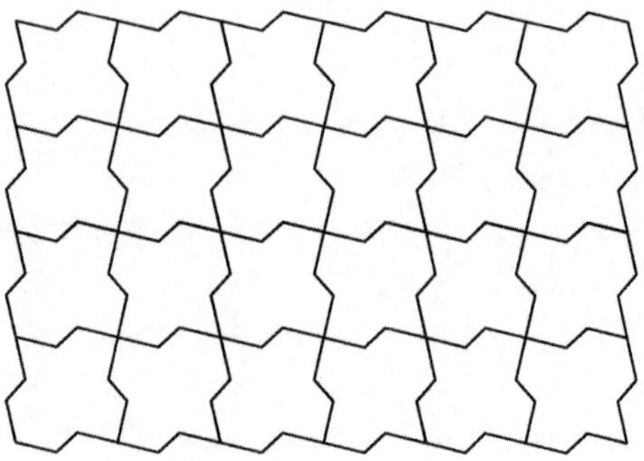

Below is an illustration using edges used earlier in the book to illustrate IH62, IH69, and IH74.

Because edges formed with center-point rotation need not play the role of a C edge but can play the role of any edge—T, G, C4, C3, or C6—these shapes fit nine of the eleven quadrilateral Heesch types. None can tessellate as C3C3C3C3 or C3C3C6C6 because these types are incompatible with a shape based on a square template. The table below has the criteria that these shapes must meet in order to satisfy the various Heesch types; the criteria apply only to shapes formed with identical edges of center-point rotation.

To fit together, edges must be alike, so a 0 edge must be adjacent to a 0 edge and a 1 edge must be adjacent to a 1 edge. Rotation does not change the edge numbers but does move them. Reflection or flipping changes not only the location of edges but also flips their numbers, with zeros becoming ones and ones becoming zeros.

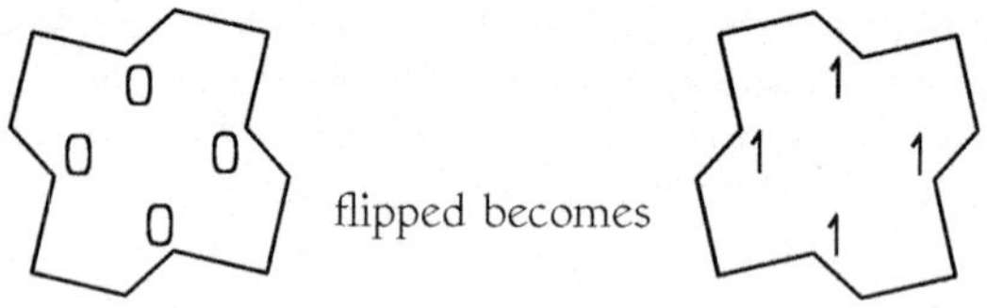

All four shapes will tessellate because all are CCCC types. The 0000 shape tessellates in only one pattern but that one patterns fits the criteria of four Heesch types as the table shows. When an edge is rotated 180° it reproduces itself but when it is flipped, it becomes the alternate form of the edge. Because a glide is a flip and will introduce ones into the shape, the 0000 shape cannot fit the Heesch types with glides.

The 0101 shape also tessellates in only one pattern. Translations, flips over the diagonal, and rotations of 180° reproduce the shape and the five types it fits have only these moves.

The 0011 group has opposite edges that are different so it does not fit the three Heesch types that have translations, which require opposite edges that are the same. Because of symmetry, three different patterns fit the six Heesch types that it satisfies. It will also tile anisohedrally, discussed below.

The final shape, represented by group 0001, fits five types and will also tile anisohedrally. It does not fit

Square Template Central-Rotation Edges

Heesch Type	Group 0000	Group 0001	Group 0011	Group 0101	Criteria
TTTT	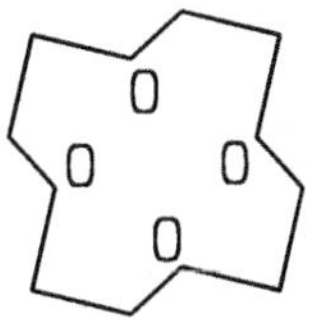			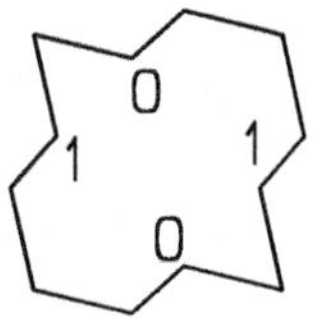	Both opposite edges the same
TCTC	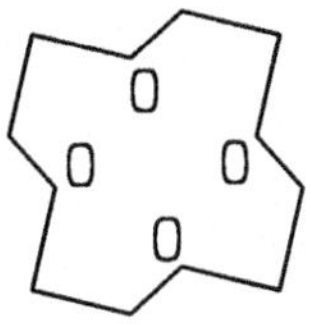	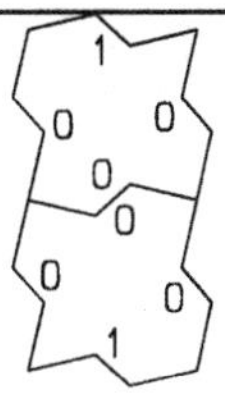		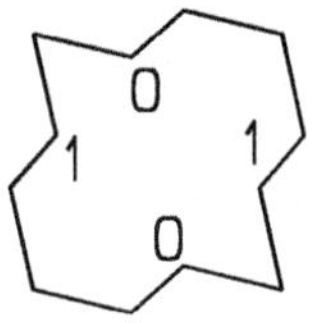	One set of opposite edges the same
TGTG		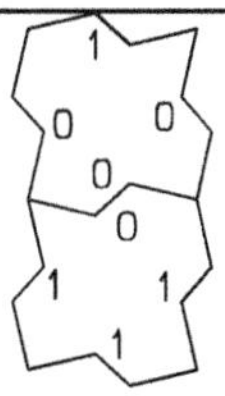			One set of opposite edges the same, one set different
CCCC	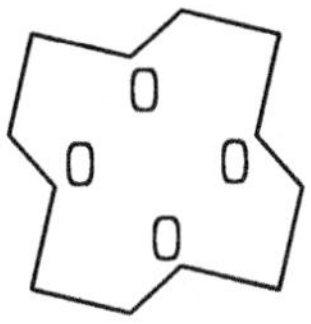	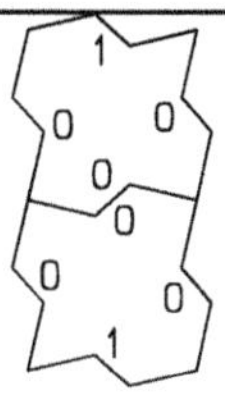	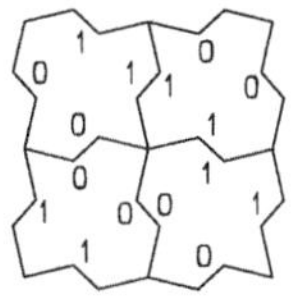	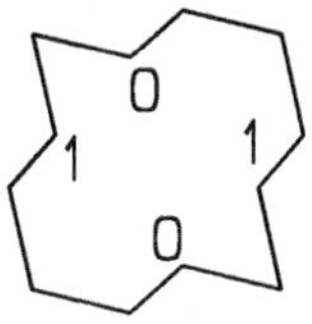	No restrictions
G1G1G2G2			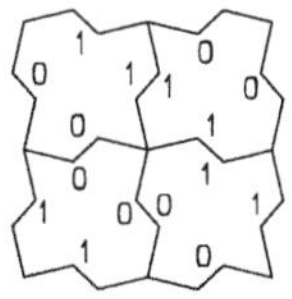	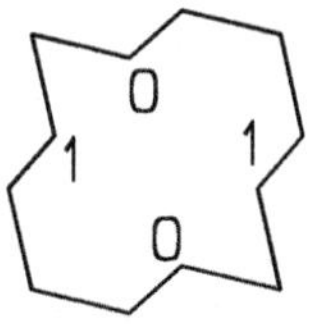	Adjacent pairs different
G1G2G1G2			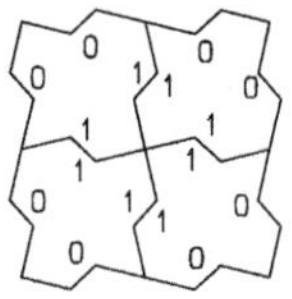		Both opposite edges different
C4C4C4C4	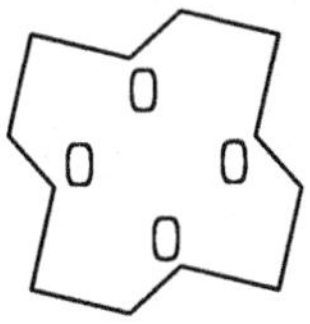		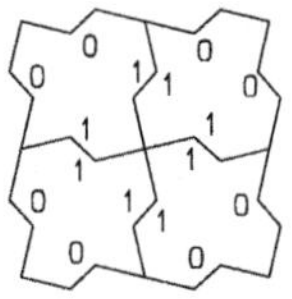		Adjacent pairs the same
CCGG		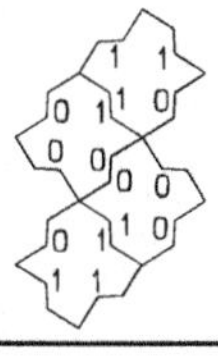	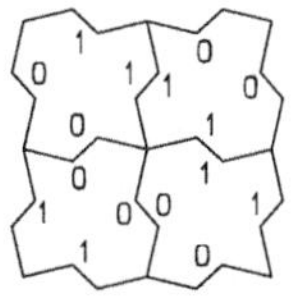	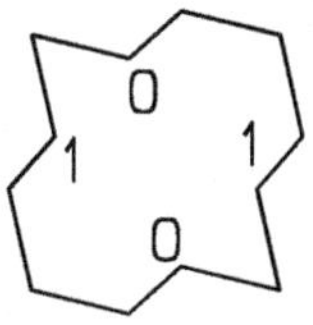	One pair of adjacents different
CGCG		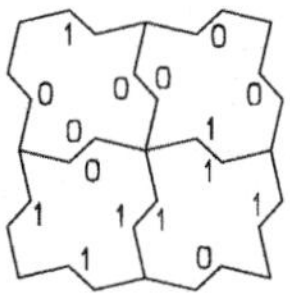	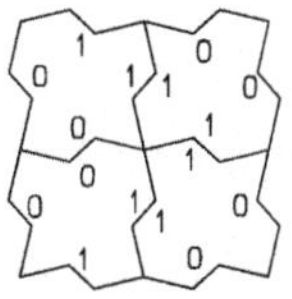		One set of opposite edges different

Heesch types that require even numbers of zeros or ones.

Below are two tilings that are not isohedral. The top figure shows a tiling of the 0001 shape and the bottom figure shows a tiling of the 0011 shape. In the top figure each tile has three adjacents that are of the same symmetry group and one of the other group and in the bottom figure each tile has one adjacent that is in the same symmetry group and three of the other group. Notice that sometimes the points of the tiles are pointed at another point and sometimes they are not. Each tiling has a translation block that is 4x1, though the bottom tiling also has a 2x2 translation block. In the bottom tiling there are groups of four that form a translation block of a C4C4C4C4 tiling but the blocks are not aligned in a way to make a C4C4C4C4 tiling. They are offset.

Below is a tiling that uses all eight orientations of the 0001 group. There are other tilings of these two shapes that are not isohedral.

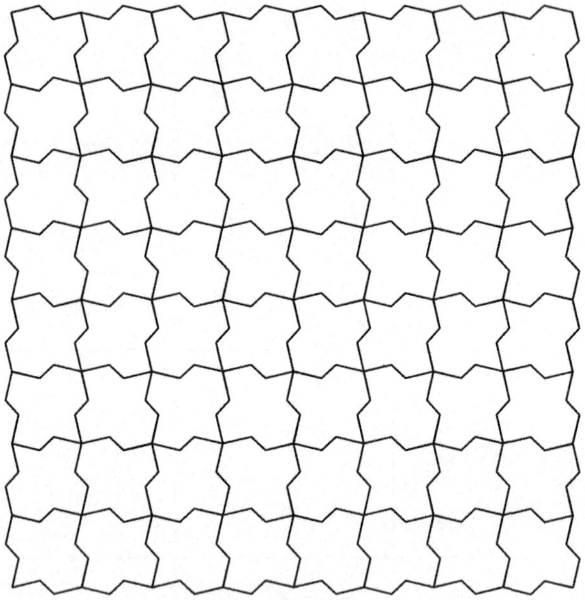

A Connection to Anisohedral Tiles

The discussion of identical asymmetric edges demonstrated a simple method of making anisohedral tiles, tiles that only could be fit into anisohedral tilings. It results in tilings like the following.

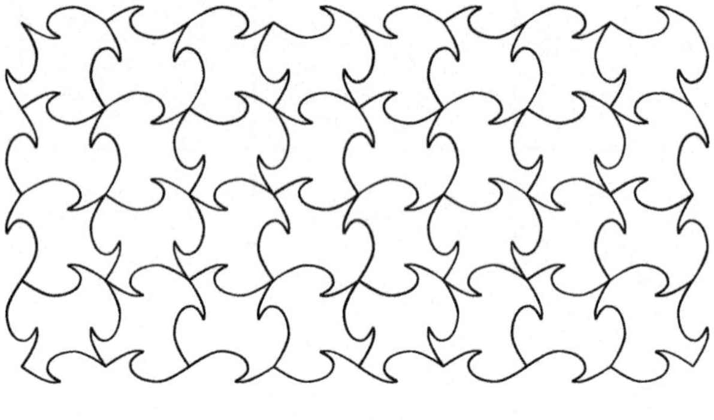

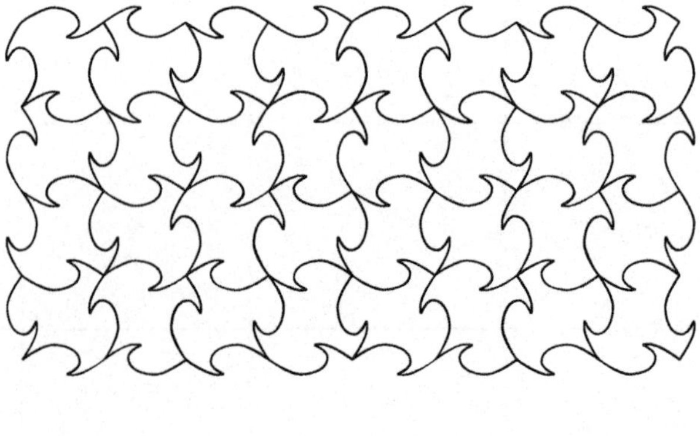

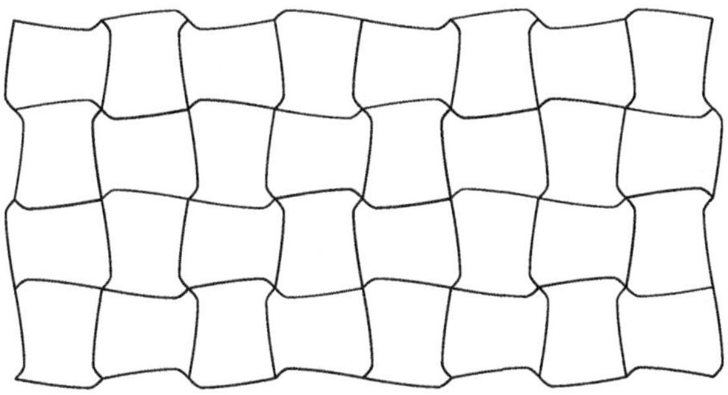

These tilings each have four neighbors, two alike and two not alike.

These tilings can be created by flipping one edge of an isohedral class IH61 tile, a C4C4C4C4 tile with identical asymmetric edges. The IH61 tiling from which the tiling above was derived is shown below.

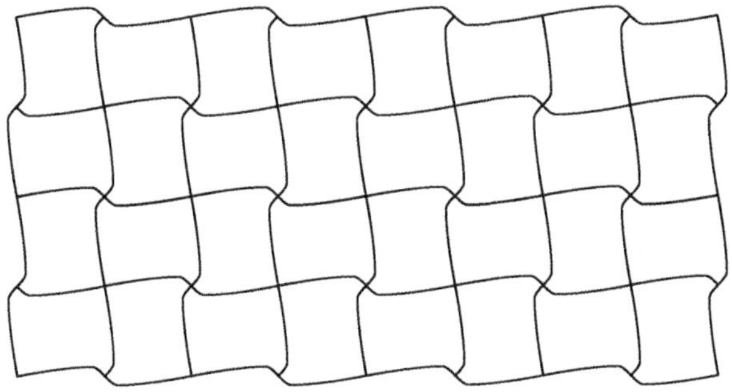

Notice that if we take a block of four we have a shape that has identical sides of central rotation or isohedral class IH62. That suggests that we can form anisohedral tiles from IH62 tiles. Below is an IH62 tile that I created for vertex-to-vertex patterns with edges extended as they would fit additional tiles. Taking this extended edge from its midpoint on the complete tile to its end and using it to subdivide the original tile produces a tiling of class IH61.

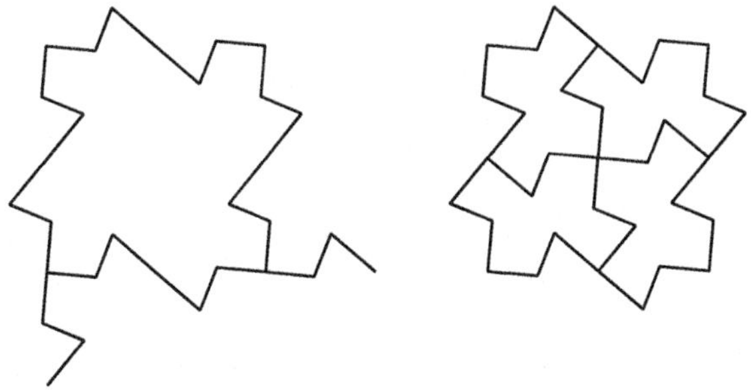

If we now take the top of the vertical divider and flip it over a horizontal line and do the same with the bottom half of the divider, we will get the figure below. It as two interior shapes, both anishedral tiles.

Below is the anisohedral tiling of one of the shapes.

At present anisohedral tiles and tilings are of interest only to a very few mathematicians. As far as I know, no one has created an Escher-like tiling with them and until someone finds a way to use some of them to make something other than abstract, geometric shapes, there will be little interest in them.

(Another form of tiling is an aperiodic tiling that lacks translation symmetry. This book has ignored them because the design tools that the author has cannot display them.)

Rhombuses Again

When the template shape is a rhombus instead of a square, the number of possible distinct shapes is seven in case of equally-shaped edges of central rotation. The tile corresponding to group 0000 has only one rhombus shape because it is identical when rotated at 90° increments. The isohedral class is IH57. With the square template it had p4 symmetry; with the rhombus it is p2.

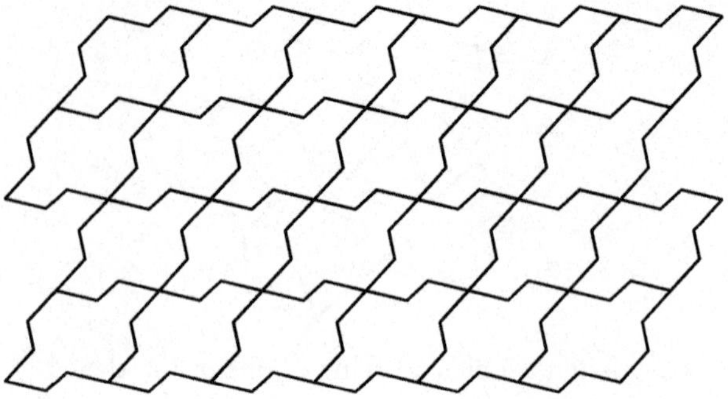

Group 0011 generates two shapes. Neither will tessellate as a C4C4C4C4 type, but both still fit the IH69 class with pmg symmetry.

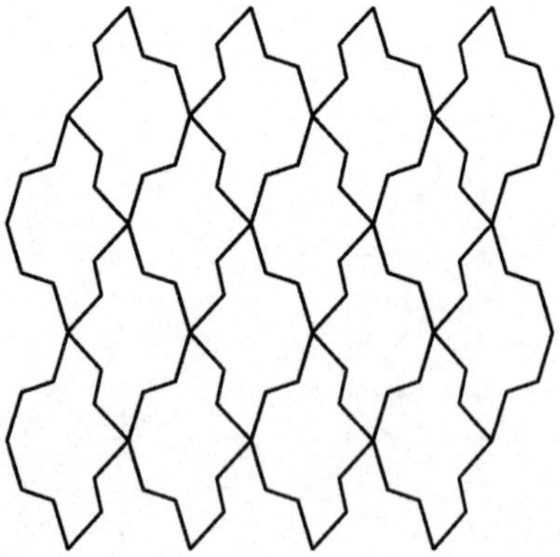

This second example is rotated 90° from the orientation of the tiling above.

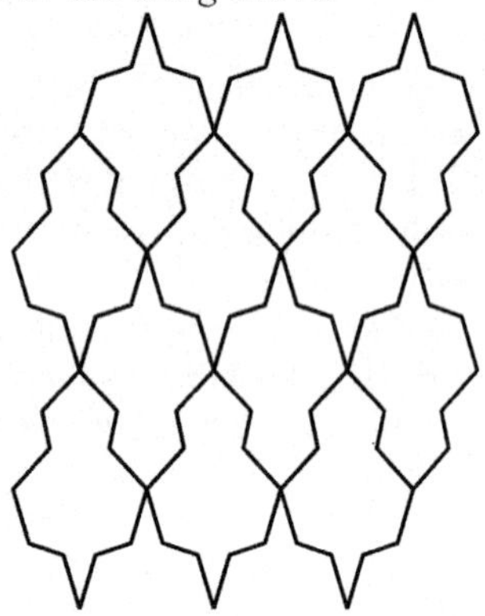

The rhombus shapes of the 0101 group remain examples of class IH74 because the IH74 class is based on a rhombus template. It takes two forms.

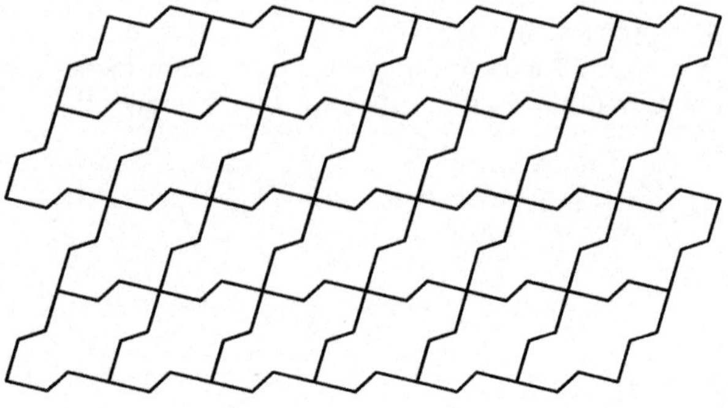

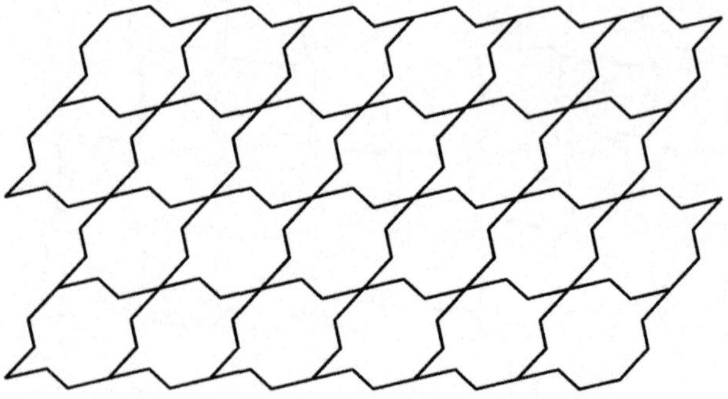

The two shapes representing group 0001 remain visually unappealing when based on a rhombus template rather than a square template.

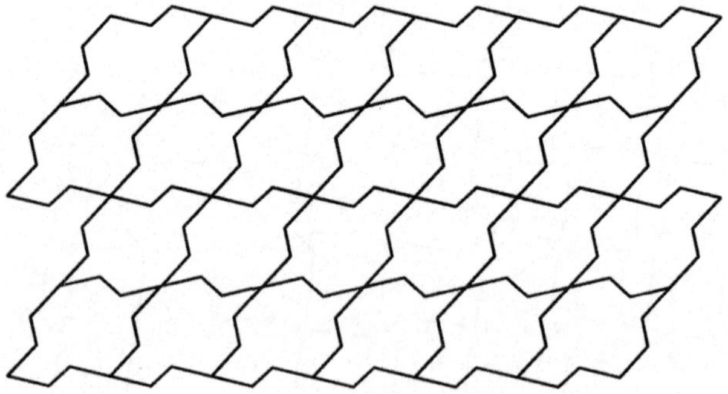

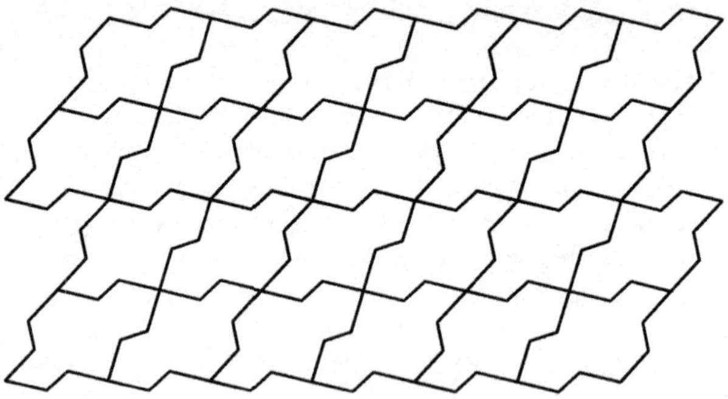

Only because of the angles chosen (a rhombus with 60° and 120° angles), two of these tiles can also be fit C3C3C3C3 tilings. The 0000 group shown below fits the IH34 class.

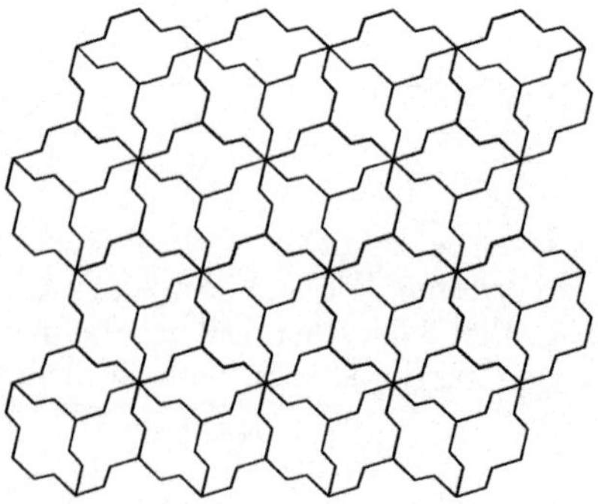

Rhombus Template Central-Rotation Edges

Heesch Type	Group 0000 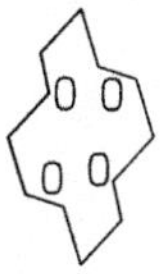	Group 1000 	Group 0001 	Group 1100 	Group 1001 	Group 1010 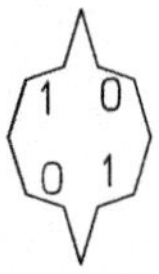	Group 0101 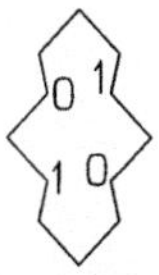	Criteria
TTTT	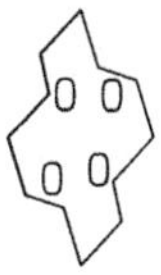					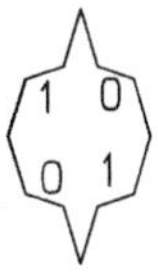	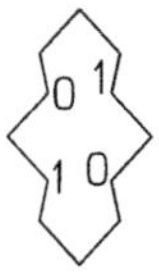	Both opposite sides the same
TCTC	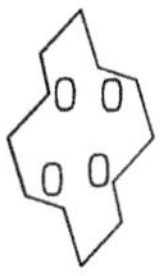	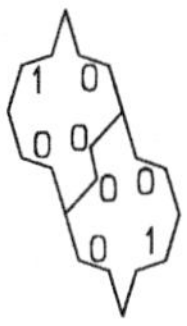	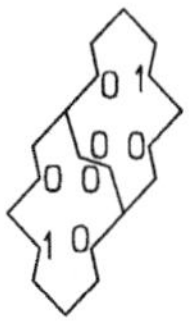			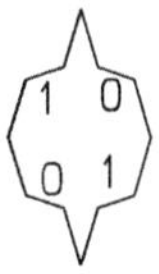	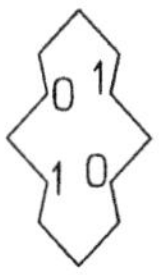	One set of opposite edges the same
TGTG		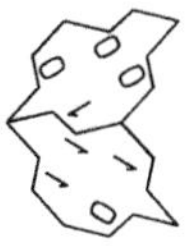	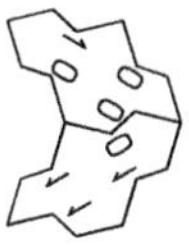					One set of opposite edges the same, one set different
CCCC	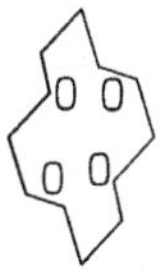	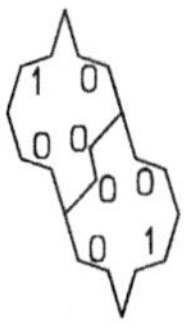	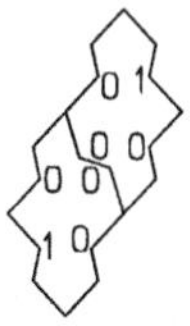	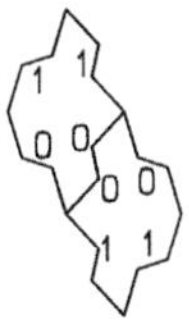	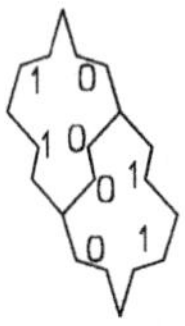	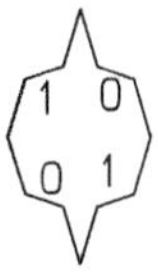	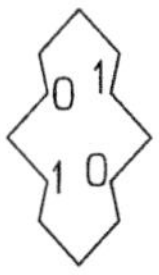	No restrictions
G1G1G2G2				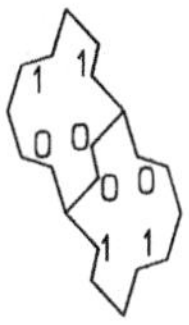	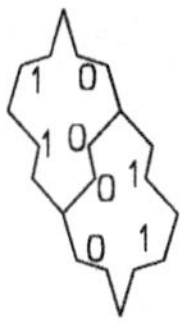	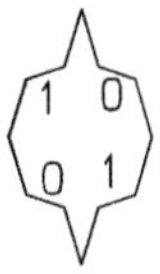	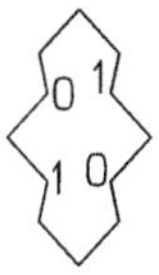	Adjacent pairs different
CCGG		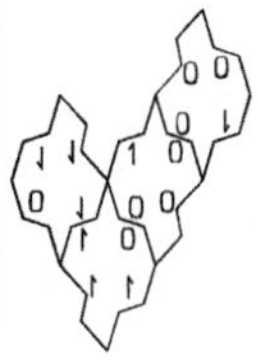	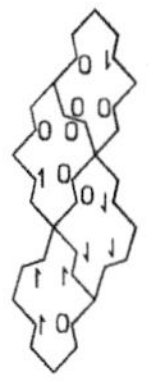	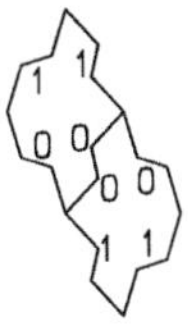	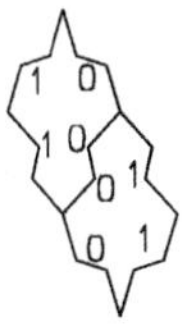	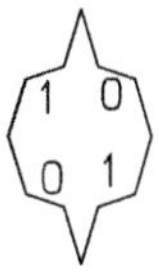	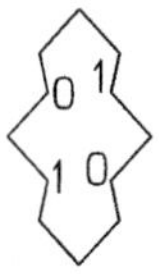	One pair of adjacents different
CGCG		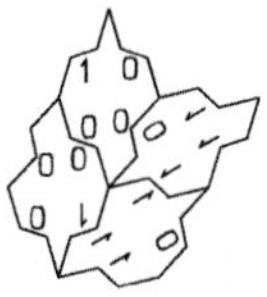	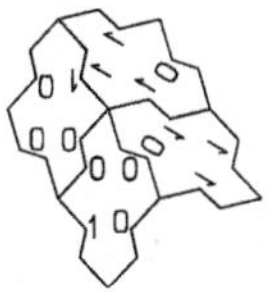	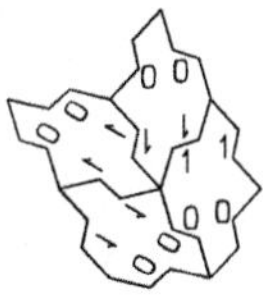	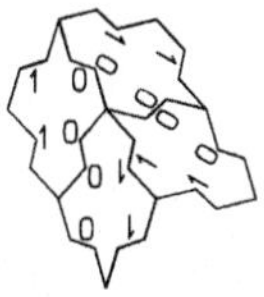			One set of opposite edges different

The 0011 shape also has an alternative representation and it fits class IH36. With both a block of three tiles combine to form an IH11 tiling

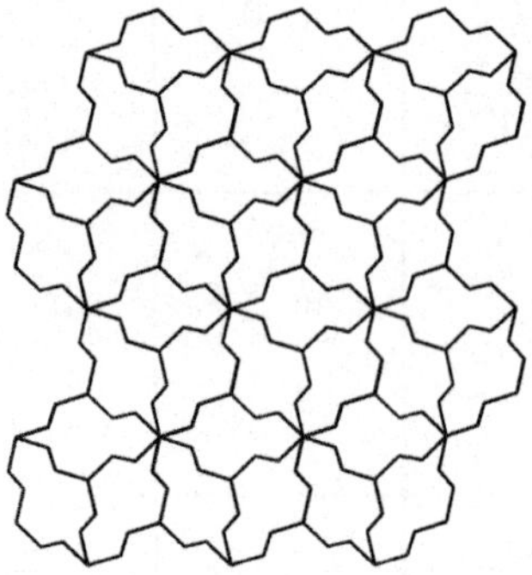

With any other angles, these two tilings would not be possible.

The table shows the Heesch types that these rhombus shapes can satisfy.

Equilateral Triangles

The previous sections examined tiles based on square and rhombus templates with identical edges formed with central rotation. What happens if we replace the square template with the template of an equilateral triangle? Using the same numbering used above, there are eight possible shapes—000, 001, 010, 100, 111, 110, 101, and 011. However, shapes 000 and 111 are reflections of each other and the other six are 120° rotations and/or reflections of each other. Therefore, for these triangular-based tiles only two distinct shapes are possible. One of the two shapes fits the criteria for isohedral class IH90. The other is formed by taking one edge of this shape and flipping it. To tile with equilateral triangles, the triangles must have two orientations, one a 180° rotation of the other. These two shapes form two sets of eight tiles. In each set of shapes, the IH90 shape has two orientations and the other has six. One set has its base on the bottom and the other is a 180° rotation of the first set. Below are examples of one set, with the IH90 shape in the first two positions.

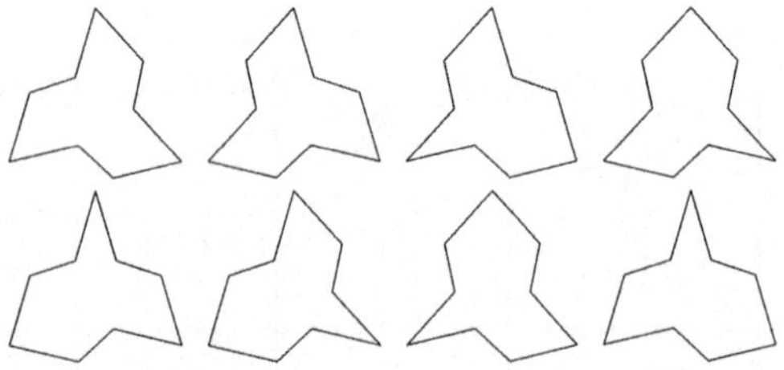

Here is the second set.

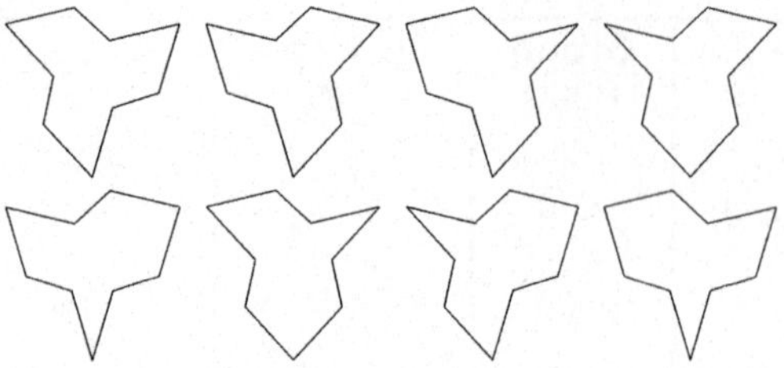

Of the five Heesch types using triangles, types CC4C4 and CC3C3 cannot be fit with an equilateral triangle. Because all sides are formed with center-point rotation, any tiling with these shapes will fit the CCC type. The CGG type requires that one side be a flip of the other two, so only the second shape will satisfy that requirement. The CC6C6 shape requires that one side be a rotation of an adjacent side, and because both shapes satisfy that condition, all tilings with these shapes will also fit the CC6C6 type. Hence, the only possible tiling with the IH90 shape will be both CCC and CC6C6 and the only possible tiling with the other shape will simultaneously be CCC, CGG, and CC6C6. An example of each tiling is shown in the discussion of IH90.

Regular Hexagons

The same numbering of edges that was used to analyze the square and triangular templates can be used to analyze the regular hexagon template. Each side of the template can be fitted with the edge in two ways. Let 0 represent the original edge and 1 represent the flipped orientation of that edge. There are 64 different codes or arrangements of edges but many represent rotations or flips of other arrangements/codes. Eliminating the duplicates leaves nine distinct shapes that can be formed with identical edges of center-point rotation when using the template shape of a regular hexagon. The table on the next page shows examples of the shapes with the codes that represent how the edges are formed. Rotating a shape by 60° changes the starting point of the sequence. For example, 000001 becomes 000010. Flipping a shape interchanges 0s and 1s and also changes ordering from clockwise to counterclockwise. We can also change the 0s to 1s and 1s to 0s by flipping each edge of a shape. In seven of the nine shapes, flipping edges gives the same result as flipping the shape. The two exceptions are the left two shapes in the bottom row of the table, shapes 7 and 8. Flipping the edges of shape 7 results in shape 8 and flipping the edges of 8 results in 7. In terminology introduced earlier, shapes 7 and 8 are inverts of one another while the other seven shapes self-replicate when edges are inverted.

When the square is fitted with edges of central rotation, all four possible shapes tessellated because there is a Heesch type CCCC. There is no Heesch type CCCCCC but edges of central rotation can play any role in a tessellation. How many of these nine shapes will tessellate and in which ways? We can use trial and error to determine which of the shapes tessellate, but we cannot

The Nine Hexagonal Shapes with Their Codes

Examples	Codes	Examples	Codes	Examples	Codes
	000000, 111111		000001, 000010, 000100, 001000, 010000, 100000, 111110, 111101, 111011, 110111, 101111, 011111		000011, 000110, 001100, 011000, 110000, 100001, 111100, 111001, 110011, 100111, 001111, 011110
	000101, 001010, 010100, 101000, 010001, 100010, 111010, 110101, 101011, 010111, 101110, 011101		001001, 010010, 100100, 110110, 101101, 011011		000111, 001110, 011100, 111000, 110001, 100011
	001011, 010110, 101100, 011001, 110010, 100101		010011, 100110, 001101, 011010, 110100, 101001		010101, 101010

be sure we find all possibilities. An alternative is to analyze them, asking which of the seven hexagonal Heesch types they fit. This procedure will give us the isohedral possibilities but will not tell us if the tiles will fit anisohedrally.

Edges that fit together must have the same number. An edge indicated with a 1 cannot be adjacent to an edge indicated by a 0. Also, the sequences are circular; the last number is adjacent to the first number in each sequence when it is part of a tile.

For a tile to fit the TTTTTT type, opposite edges must have the same number. Of the nine possible shapes shown above, only two meet this requirement, those represented by 000000 and 001001. Shape 000000 represents isohedral class IH11 class and shape 001001 fits the isohedral class IH8.

To fit into a TCCTCC tiling, all that is needed is a pair of opposite sides with the same number. Seven of the nine have them; the only exceptions are shapes represented by 010101 and 000111.

To determine what fits the C3C3C3C3C3C3 type, group the six numbers into adjacent pairs. If each of the three pairs has the same number, the shape will tessellate as C3C3C3C3C3C3. Shapes represented by 000000 and 000011 are the only shapes that fit this requirement.

For glide moves to align, paired glide moves must have different numbers. So for the TG1G1TG2G2 type there must be two opposite sides with the same number (the TT part) and the two pairs that are separated by these two opposite sides must have different numbers. Two shapes meet this requirement, those represented by 001010 and 001001.

The TG1G2TG2G1 must have a pair of opposite sides that have the same number. Then the two numbers adjacent to each of these two numbers must be different. Hence, only shapes represented by a sequence of four zeroes and two ones need to be checked. The shapes that satisfy this are represented by 000011 and 001001. Shape 001001 satisfies the conditions of isohedral class IH9.

The TCCTGG type requires that one pair of opposites be the same. The two sides represented by the CC part have no restrictions but the pair represented by the GG part must have one 1 and one 0. Five different sequences meet this requirement: 000001, 000101, 001001, 001101, and 001011.

Finally, in the CG1CG2G1G2 type the Cs can be any value because they will pair with themselves, but the G1G1 pair and the G2G2 pairs cannot contain the same numbers. Since there must be at least two ones, we can eliminate the 000000 and the 000001 shapes. We then check the others for sequences in which the second number and the fifth number are different and the fourth and six numbers are different. Five of the groups have sequences that fit this requirement: 000011, 010100, 001110, 001011, and 100110. The last item in the table, 010101 and the middle item in the table, 001001, will not fit the requirement.

Some of these shapes will also tile anisohedrally. The shape represented by 010101 will not tessellate.

Hexagon Template Central-Rotation Edges

Code	TTTTTT Block	TCCTCC Block	TCCTGG Block	C3C3C3C3 C3C3 Block	TG1G1TG 2G2 Block	TG1G2TG2 G1 Block	CG1CG2G1G2 Block
000000							
000001			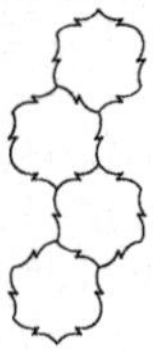				
000011							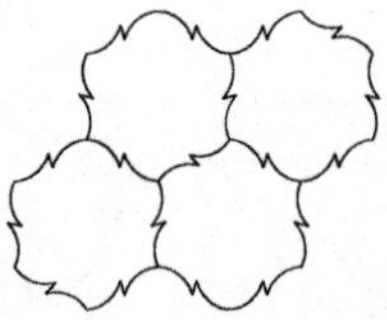
000101		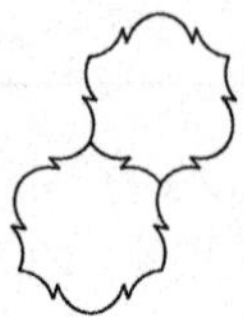	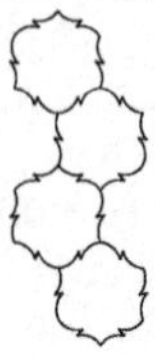				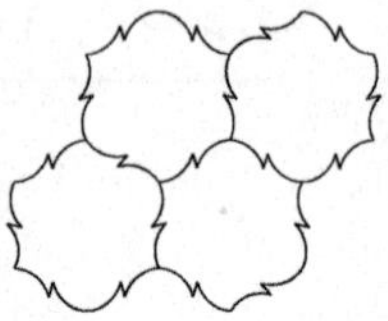
001001			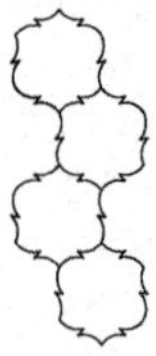		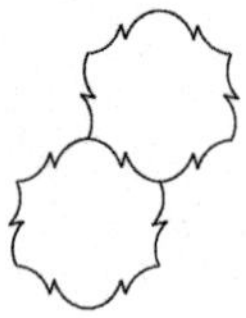		
000111							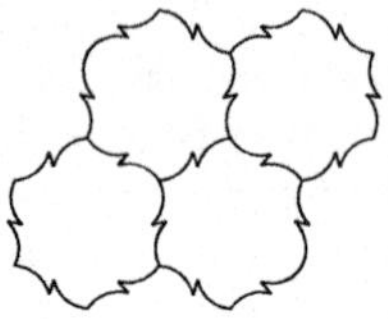
001011		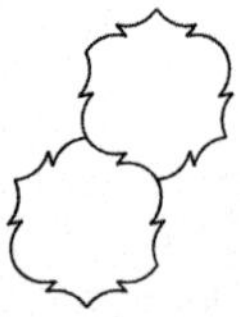	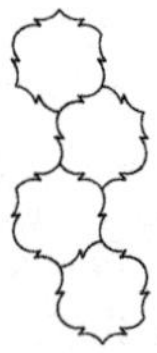				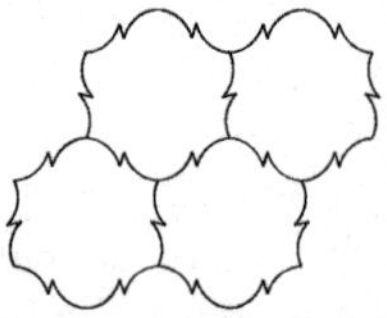
010011		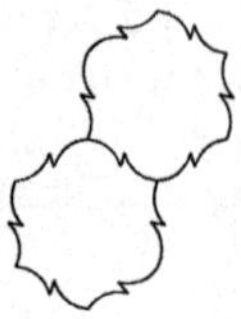	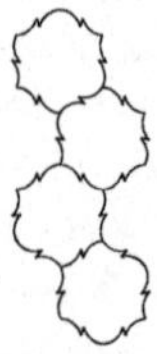				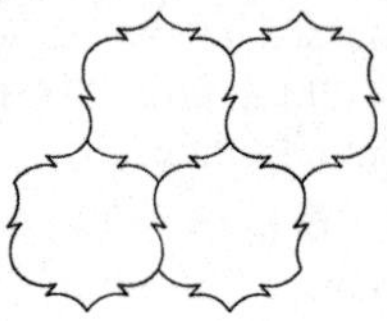
010101							

The table on the previous page reorganizes these results to show how each shape tessellates isohedrally. The table includes an illustration of a translation block for each tiling. Note that in two rows of the table the same block is in more than one cell. The 000000 group is an example of isohedral class IH11 and has sixfold rotational symmetry. Because rotating it 180° or 120° reproduces the original, the same tiling satisfies the conditions of TTTTTT, TCCTCC, and C3C3C3C3C3C3. The shape represented by 001001 is an example of isohedral class IH8 and because it has twofold rotational symmetry, the same tiling satisfies types TTTTTT and TCCTCC. Flips parallel and perpendicular to the sides serving as TT edges yield identical results so the same tiling satisfies types TG1G1TG2G2 and TG1G2TG2G1 and IH9. Two groups, represented by 010011 and 001011 have mirror symmetry over a diagonal but are not special types in the Grünbaum-Shepard classes. Their two classes with mirror symmetry over a diagonal have a pair of straight edges.

In addition to isohedral tilings, some of these shapes also produce anisohedral tilings. I suspect many are possible but do not know how to systematically search for them. Below are two examples I found by chance, both of group 000011. In both cases note that the peaked corner sometimes fits with another peaked corner and sometimes it does not.

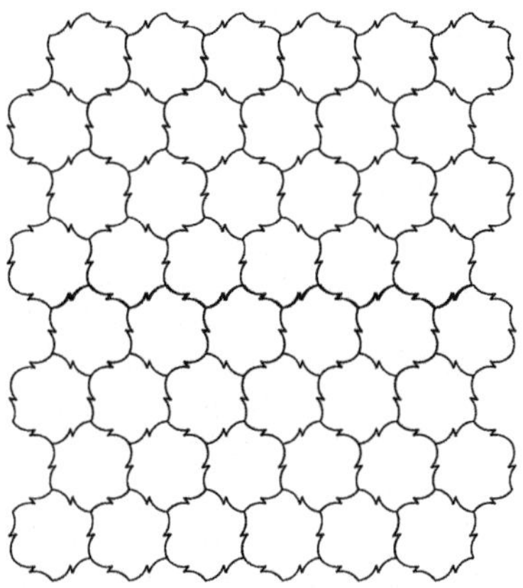

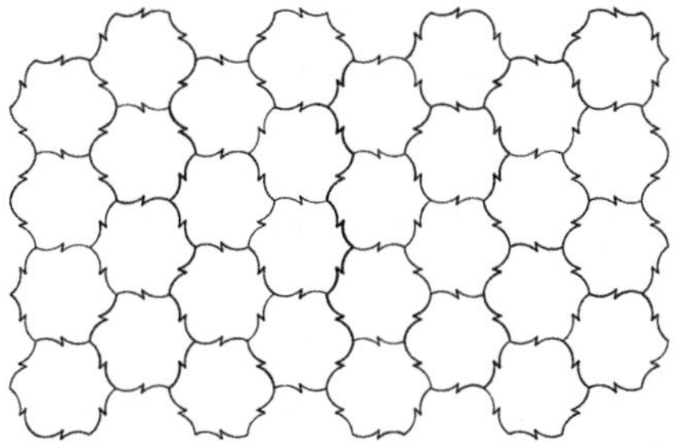

Five of the shapes that tessellate have either rotational or mirror symmetry and bisections of them will also tessellate. Three of these tilings are anisohedral, but because the bisected tiles can be seen as cases of the CCCC type, all can tile isohedrally.

When shape 001011 is bisected along the line of symmetry, the resulting tiling is anisohedral. However, the tile can be rotated 180° and the two halves will form a tile that is 001001. In this arrangement the bisected tile is isohedral.

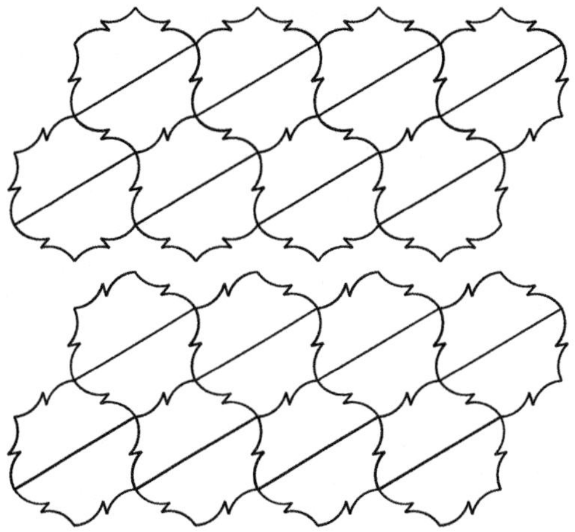

A bisection of shape 010011 also results in an anisohedral tiling, but the bisected tile can be rotated 180° and the two halves can be combined to form a tile that is 001001.

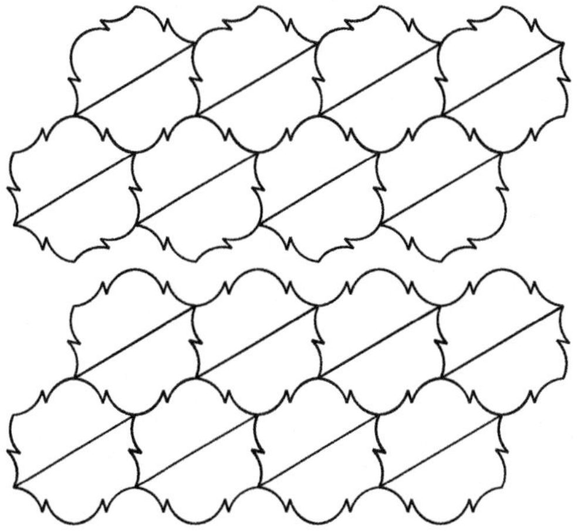

When the shape represented by 000111 is bisected along its line of symmetry, the new tiling is anisohedral. If the new tile is rotated instead of reflected, it will becomes a bisection of the group represented by 000000 and in this tiling it is isohedral.

the conditions of one of these three groups will not tile the plane.

Mathematicians are less interested in six-sided polygons that are not convex but that tile the plane. A hexagonal shape that has intrigued me is the chevron formed from a regular hexagon by inverting two adjacent sides, yielding an equilateral polygon with angles of 120°, 120°, 120°, 60°, 240°, and 60°. It will tile the plane in a number of ways, some of which are quadrilateral. One way was used as an illustration of the C3C3C6C6 type earlier in this book and it can also tile as TTTT and TCTC types. Another is anisohedral and still another is not periodic but spirals out from the center. However, if the chevron must have six neighbors, I can find only one tiling that it fits, shown below. This tiling is edge-to-edge, meaning that corners of the polygon are vertices of the tiling.

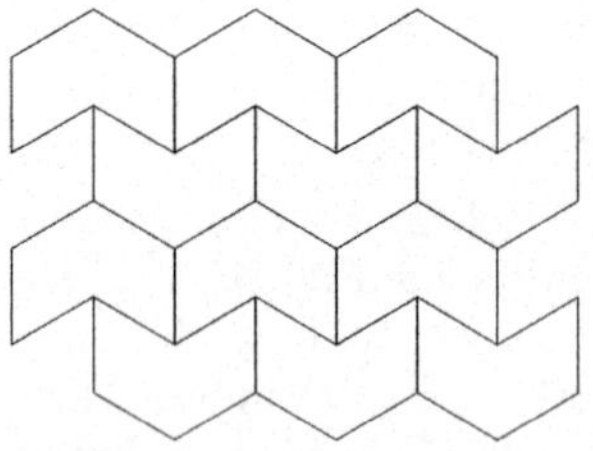

Because this tiling is equilateral, it can be used as a template on which identical sides of center-point rotation are attached. Analysis of shapes can be done with the same numbering that was used for regular hexagons with one difference. Cycling a set of numbers with the regular hexagon rotates the hexagon but retains the shape. Cycling a set of numbers with a chevron alters the shape. There are still 64 possible arrangements of sides, but only those in which the two opposite parallel edges allow translation will tessellate. The other four edges can have 16 different arrangements, from 0000 to 1111. If the opposite parallel edges do not have the same numbers, that is, they are 01 or 10, the shape will not tessellate. These parallel edges must be either 00 or 11. Hence, half of the possible shapes will not tessellate. However, any shape with opposite parallel edges 11 is a flip of another shape with the same edges 00. Therefore, there are sixteen distinct shapes that will tessellate and all of them will tessellate as TCCTCC types. The sixteen are shown in the table below with their number codes.

The equilateral chevron cannot tessellate as a TTTTTT type because the translation unit of its hexagonal tiling must be two. It cannot tessellate as C3C3C3C3C3C3 because every other angle cannot be 120°. Neither can it tessellate as CG1CG2G1G2 or TG1G2TG2G1 because neither type supports the shape. Trying to invert a corner with the TG1G2TG2G1 type results in an hourglass shape and the CG1CG2G1G2 type does not permit the obtuse angle to mirror the opposite acute angle.

For a tiling to be TCCTGG, the pair that is GG must be 01 or 10. The two TT sides must be 00 and the two CC sides can be 00, 01, 10, or 11. There are eight shapes that will tessellate when the GG sides are on the point of the chevron and eight that will tessellate when the GG sides

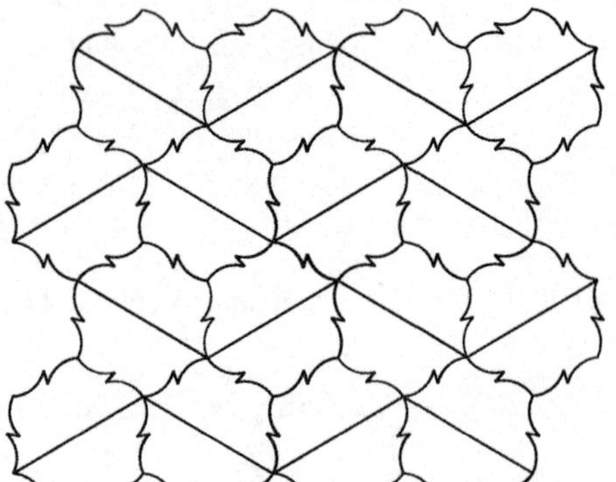

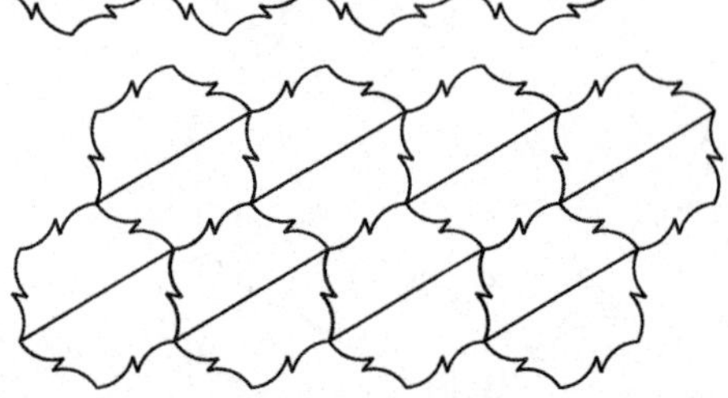

The shape represented by 010101 has threefold rotational symmetry and mirror symmetry over its three diagonals. The only hexagon with d3(l) symmetry that tessellates in Grünbaum and Shepard's classification is a marked regular hexagon, IH19. Although it does not tessellate, it can form patterns in which copies of it surround voids of shape represented by 000000.

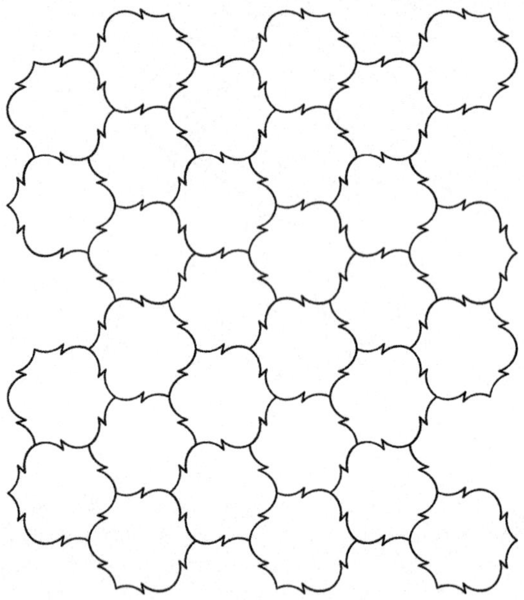

Equilateral Chevrons

All triangles and all quadrilaterals will tessellate but only some hexagons will. In his 1918 doctoral dissertation, Karl Reinhardt found that all convex hexagons (hexagons whose interior angles are less than 180°) that tessellate could be classified into only three groups. Hence, any convex hexagon that does not meet

Chevron Template Central-Rotation Edges

Code	TCCTCC Block	TCCTGG Block	TG1G1TG2G2 Block
000000	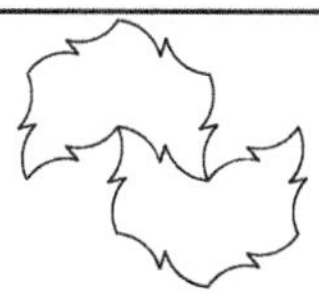		
000001	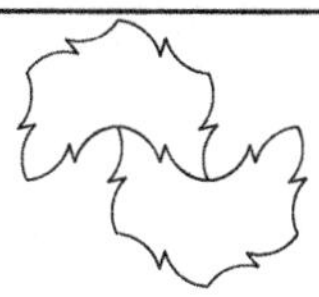	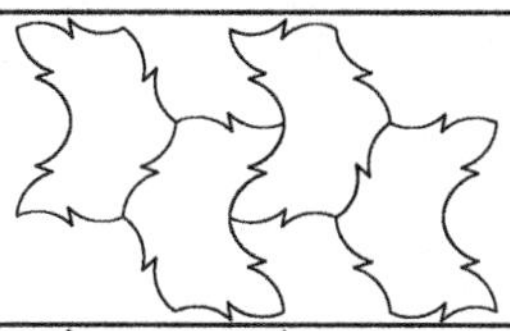	
000010	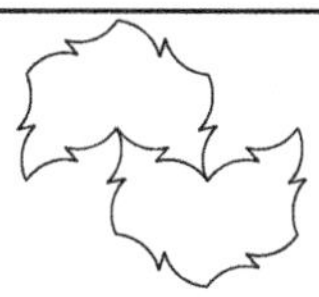	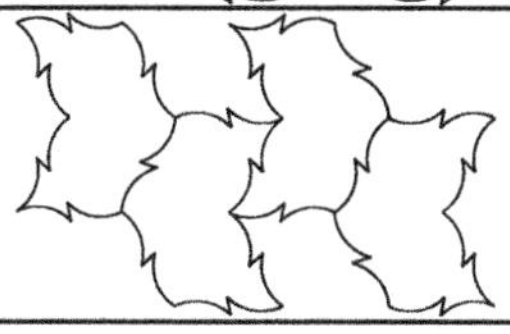	
000011	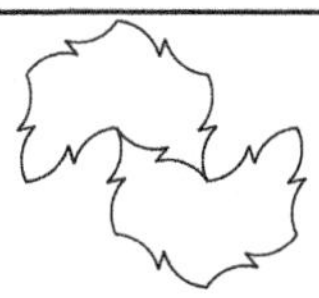		
001000	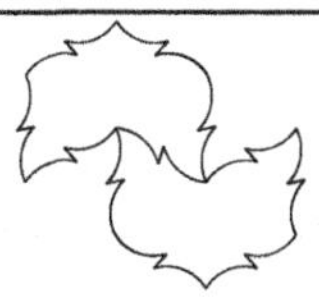	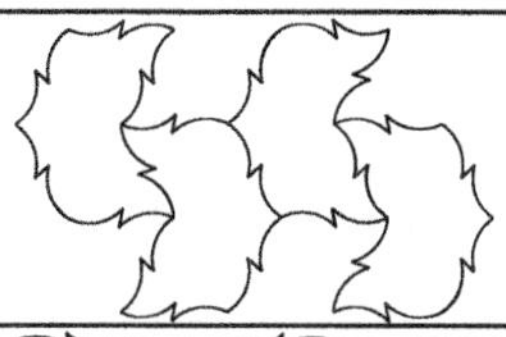	
001001	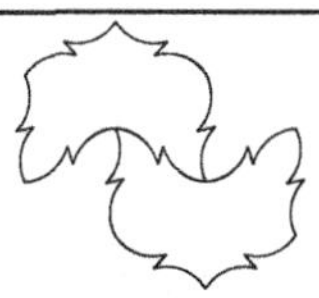	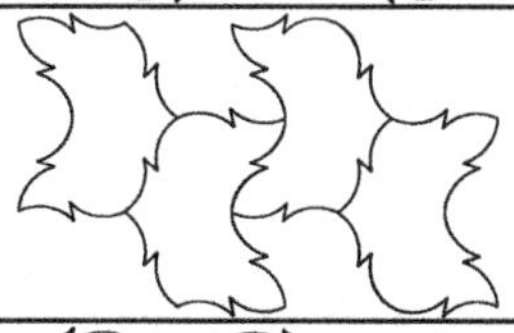	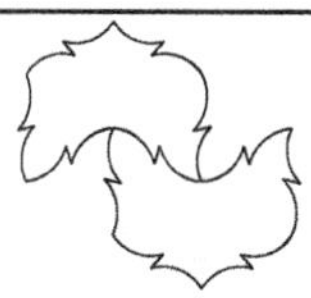
		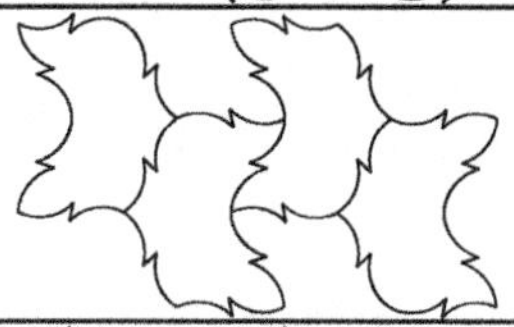	
001010	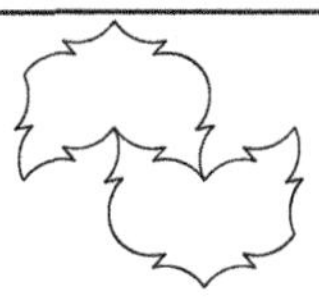	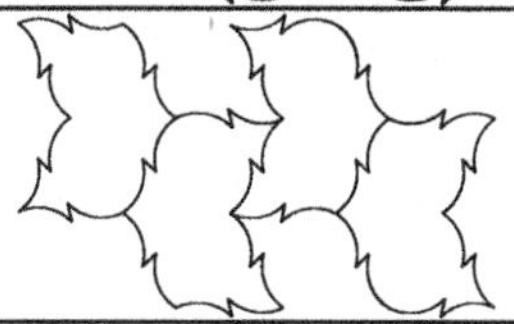	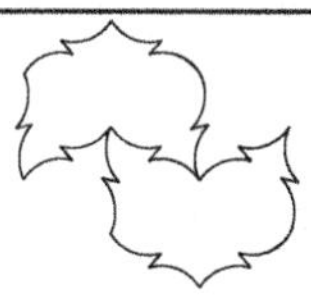
		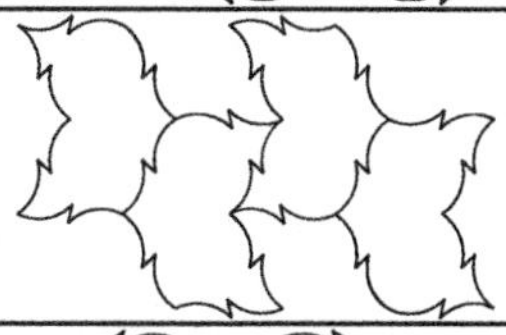	
001011	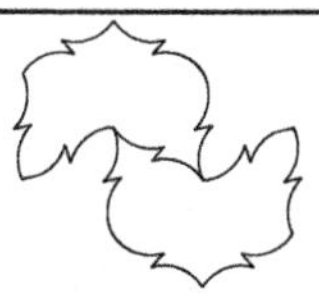	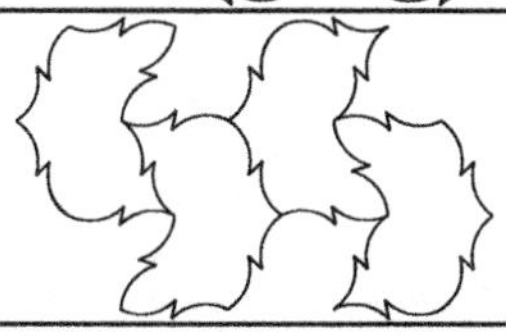	

Code	TCCTCC Block	TCCTGG Block	TG1G1TG2G2 Block
010000	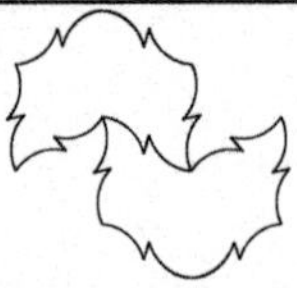	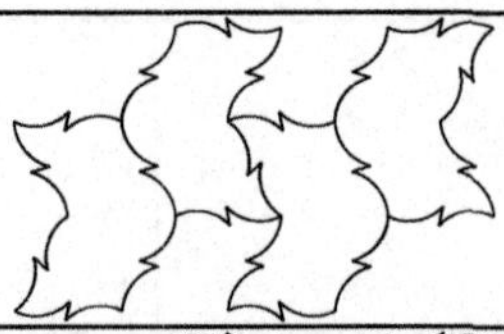	
010001	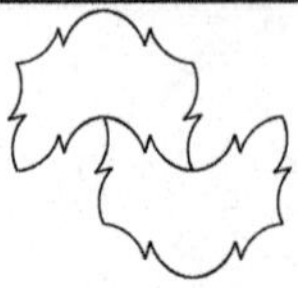	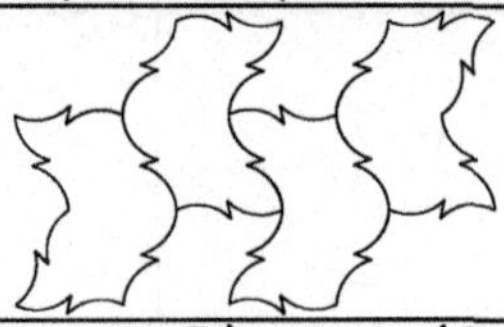	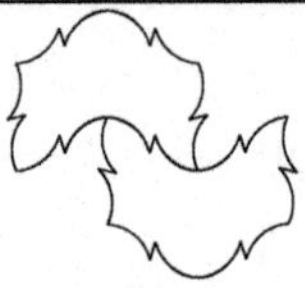
		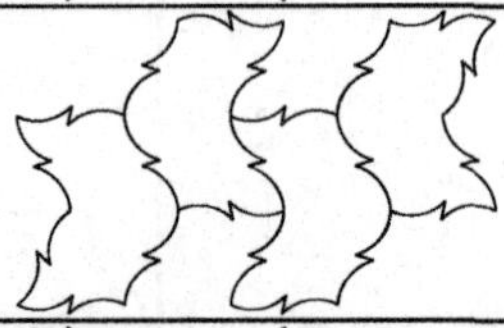	
010010	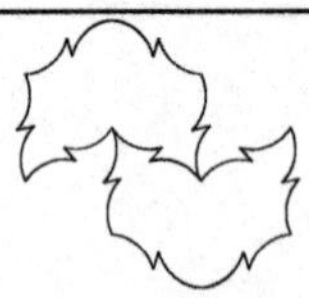	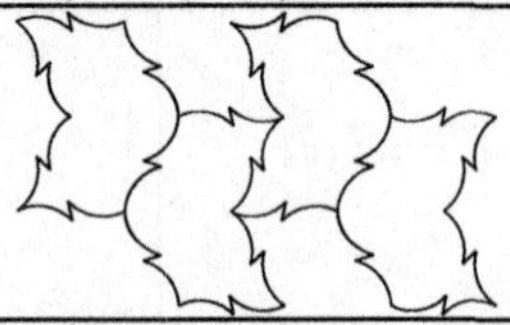	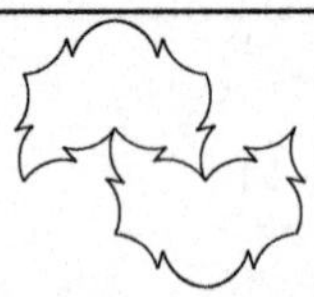
		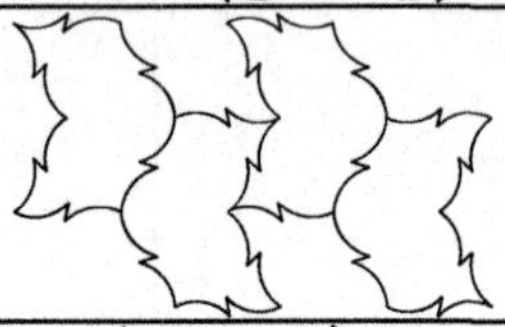	
010011	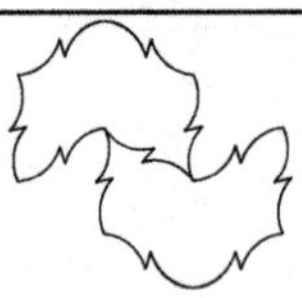	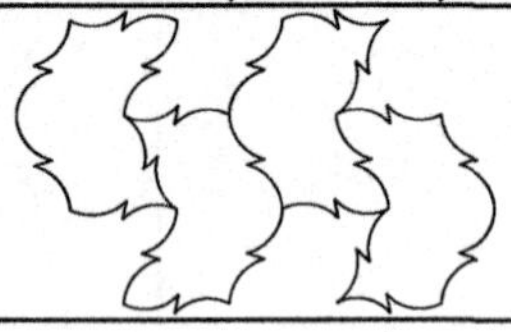	
011000	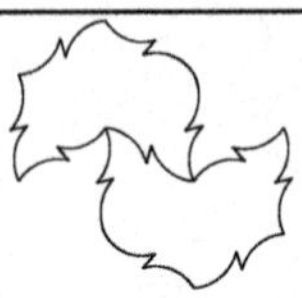		
011001	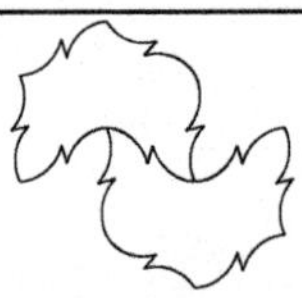	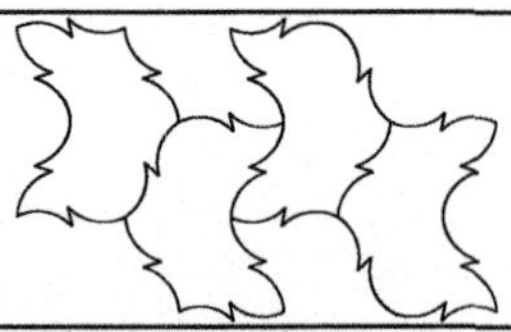	
011010	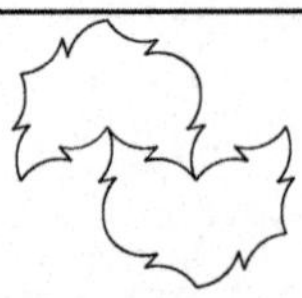	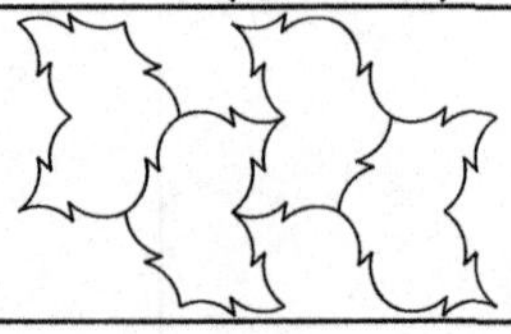	
011011	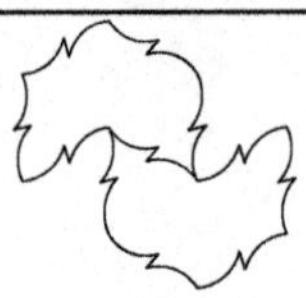		

are on the inverted sides. However, four of the shapes tessellate in both ways, so only twelve of the sixteen will tessellate as TCCTGG types. For a tiling to be TG1G1TG2G2, the G1G1 pair must be 01 or 10 and also the G2G2 pair must be 01 or 10. Only four of the sixteen meet this requirement.

The table shows how each of these 16 shapes tessellates. Note that swapping zeros and ones will flip the shapes, but these flipped shapes are not distinctively different. The four TCCTGG tilings in rows by themselves are the alternate ways of tiling the shape immediately above them.

Pentagonal Tilings

A feature of edges formed with center-point rotation is that they need not play the role of a C edge. They can play any role: T, G, C3, C4, or C6. Thus every Heesch type can be formed with tiles that have only edges with center-point rotation and, with only three exceptions, they can tile with identically-formed edges having center-point rotation. The exceptions are three Heesch types that cannot take the shape of an equilateral polygon, CC4C4, CC3C3, and C3C3C6C6.

An edge formed with center-point rotation can have only two orientations. A rotation of 180 degrees returns the original orientation. A flip over the line connecting the vertices of the edge or a flip over a line perpendicular to that line will give the same alternate shape. We can code the orientation of edges with two numbers, say 0 and 1.

For a tile with identical edges with center-point rotation to tile the plane, adjacent edges must have the same number. This puts restrictions on what Heesch types any particular tile can fit. For example, because a glide requires a flip, for any tile to fit into a Heesch type with glide edges, the two glide edges must be different numbers. On the other hand, translated edges must both have the same number (as must edges that are C3, C6, and C4). C fits with itself so it can be either number.

There are five pentagonal Heesch types and all of them can be formed from tiles with equally long edges. A pentagon formed as a square with an equilateral triangle attached is the template for two of the types.

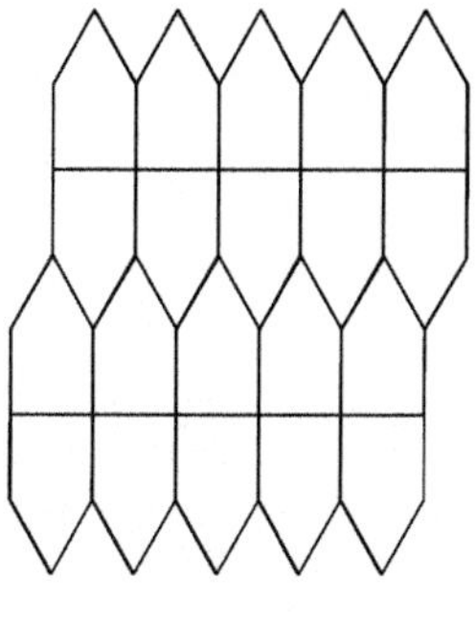

Another pentagon useful in this exercise has two angles that are 90°, two that are 114.295°, and a final angle that is 131.41°. There are other equilateral pentagons that tile, including some that are convex, but we do not need them for this exercise. (For a look at many of these shapes, see www.iread.it/lz/pentagons.html.)

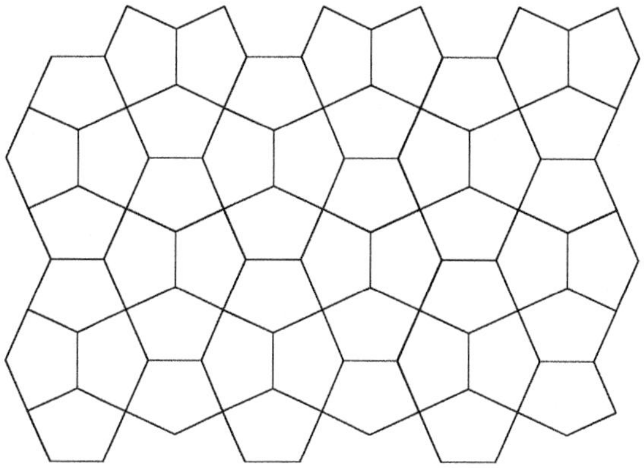

Next is an example of type TCTCC with identical edges with center-point rotation. The tile would be coded 00000.

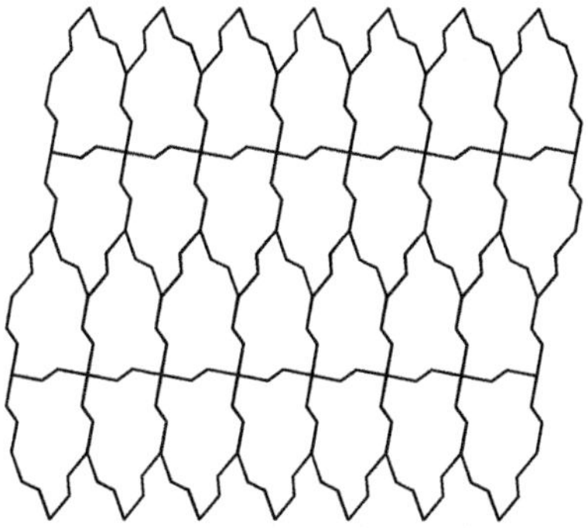

The example below of type TCTGG will also work as TCTCC. This type could be coded 00100. Only one edge has been changed from the above tile.

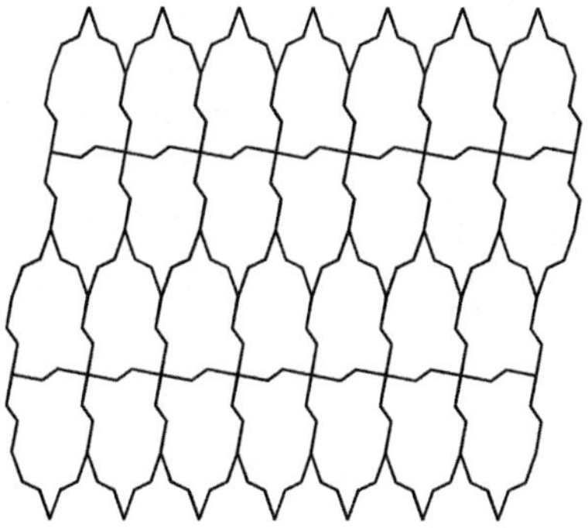

This type CC4C4C4C4 shown below would be coded 00000.

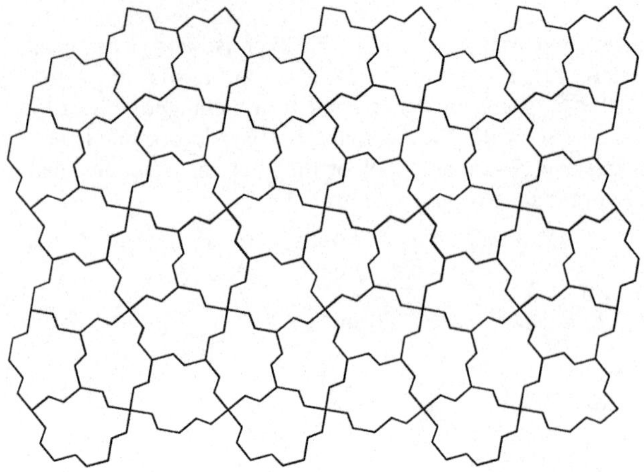

Finally, below is a type CG1G2G1G2 that could be coded 01001. Two of the edges of the tiles above have been flipped.

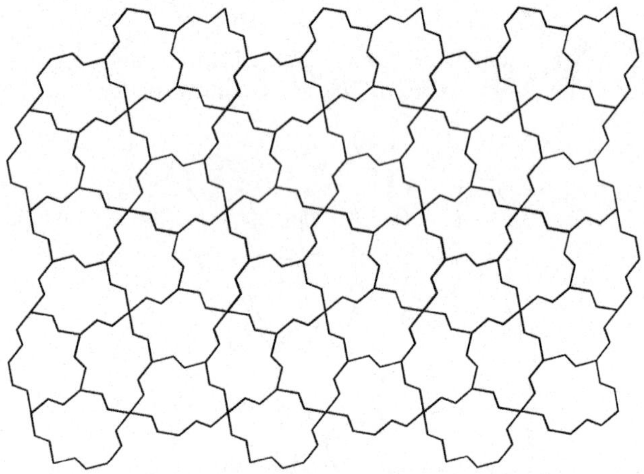

How many other arrangements of edges fit the two patterns above? To find the answer, we number the edges of the patterns used for the TCTCC and TCTGG types.

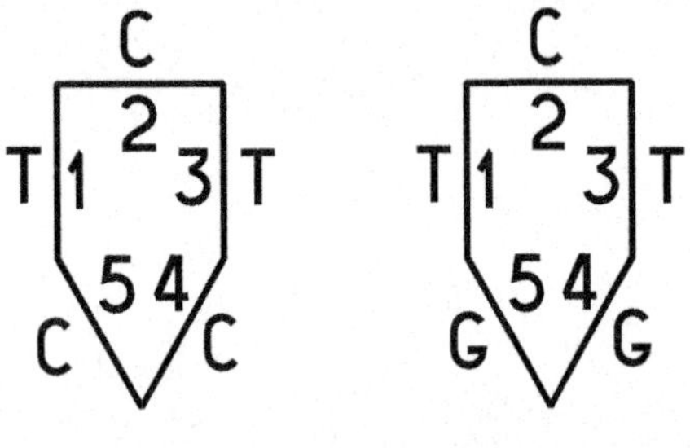

We then indicate what the orientation of edges is with the code numbers mentioned above. The TT edges (1 & 3) must have the same code number, indicating their edges are oriented in the same way. For the TCTCC tile, there are no restrictions on the other edges, but the TCTGG tile must have the two GG edges (4 & 5) with different code numbers. The resulting shapes that will tile are shown in the table below.

TCTCC & TCTGG	TCTCC only
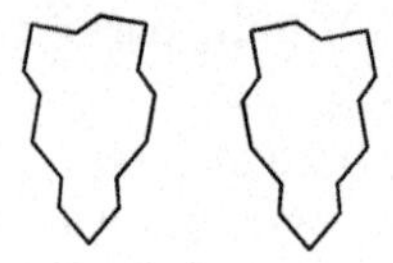 00001, 11110	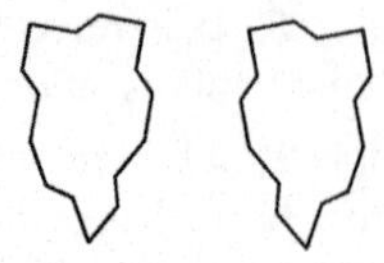 00000, 11111
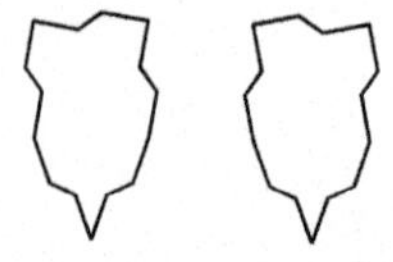 00010, 11101	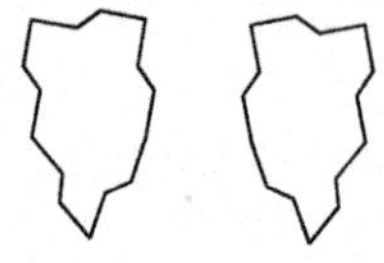 00011, 11100
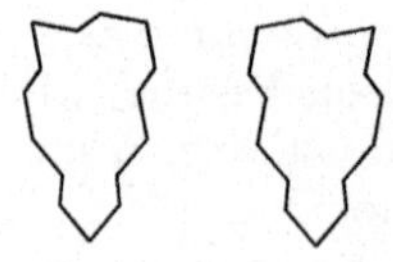 01001, 10110	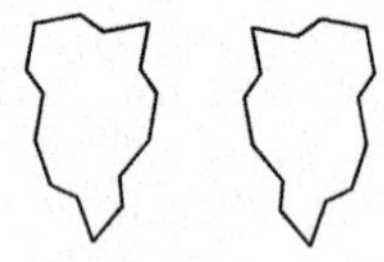 01000, 10111
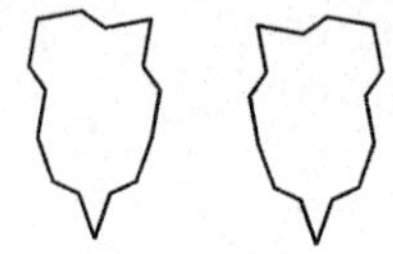 01010, 10101	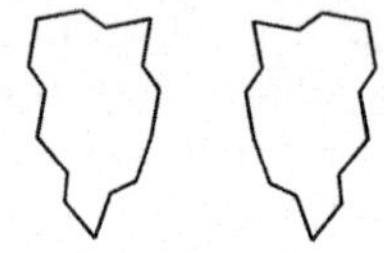 01011,10100
Edges 1 & 3 the same; edges 4 & 5 different	Edges 1 & 3 the same

Each cell has two shapes, one the flipped version of the other. Flipping changes ones to zeros and zeros to ones, reorders the edges, and changes the order from clockwise to counterclockwise. There are 32 possible arrangements of edges for a pentagonal-based tile. Half of them will not tessellate as TCTCC.

We can do the same for the second set of shapes.

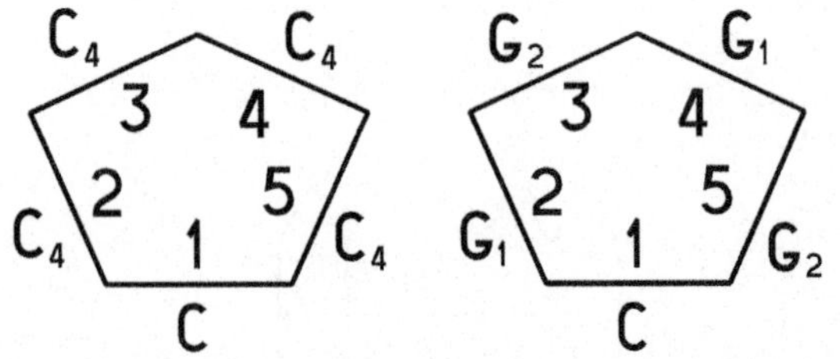

Paired C4 edges (2 & 3; 4 & 5) must have the same coded value in order to tile as CC4C4C4C4. Opposite G sides must have different coded values to tile as CG1G2G1G2. The results are shown in the table below. There are two cells that satisfy the requirements for both CC4C4C4C4 and CG1G2G1G2.

CC4C4C4C4 (edges 2 & 3 same, edges 4 & 5 same)	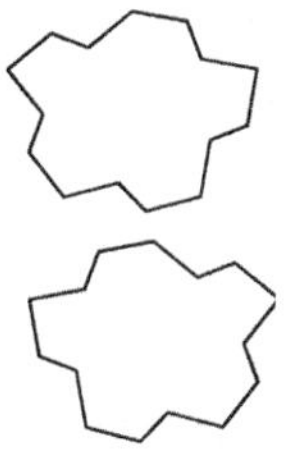 00000, 11111	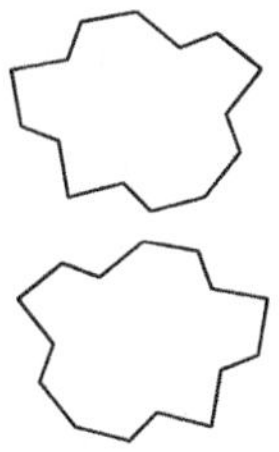 01111, 10000
CC4C4C4C4 & CG1G2G1G2	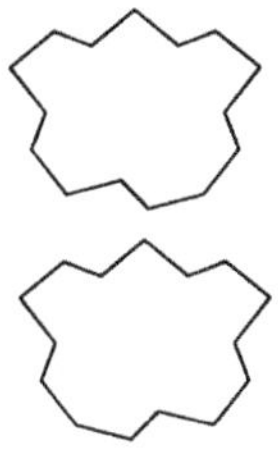 00011, 11100	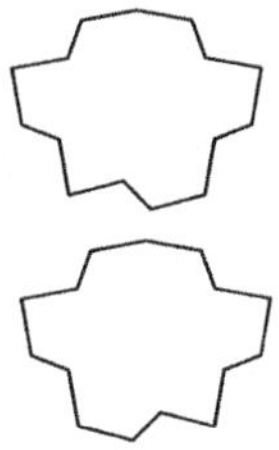 01100, 10011
CG1G2G1G2 (edges 2 & 4 different, edges 3 & 5 different)	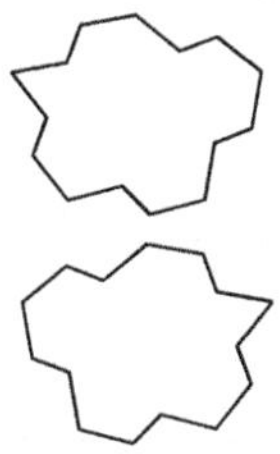 00110, 11001	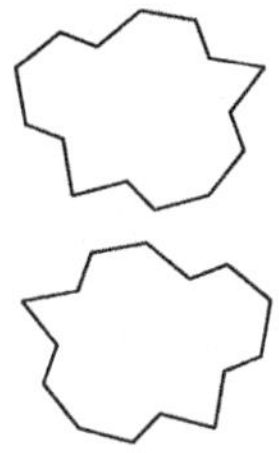 01001, 10110

Only twelve of the 32 arrangements of identical edges with center-point rotation will tessellate as either CC4C4C4C4 or CG1G2G1G2 tilings.

No true equilateral pentagon fits the CC3C3C6C6 type but the tiling can be formed from a trapezoid with five equally-long edges. (Perhaps it can be thought of as a pentagon with one corner having a 180° angle.) The tiling of the template and the numbering of edges are shown below.

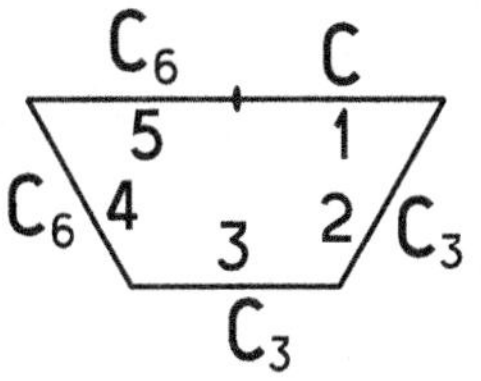

When the tile is flipped, the sides are reordered as shown in the next figure.

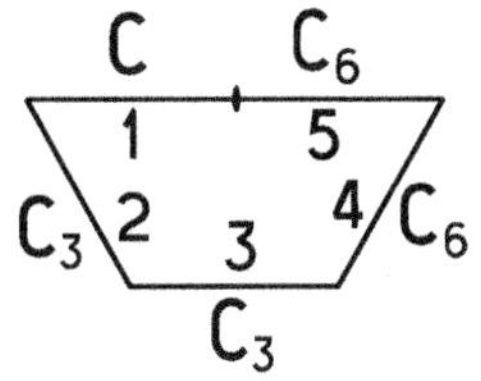

This trapezoid is formed by cutting a regular hexagon into two pieces. Alternatively, it can be considered the union of three equilateral triangles. For it to tile with identical edges with center-point rotation, edges 2 & 3 and edges 4 & 5 must have the same number code. These are the same requirements that the CC4C4C4C4 tiling had. There are four arrangements plus their flipped versions that satisfy these requirements, shown in the table below.

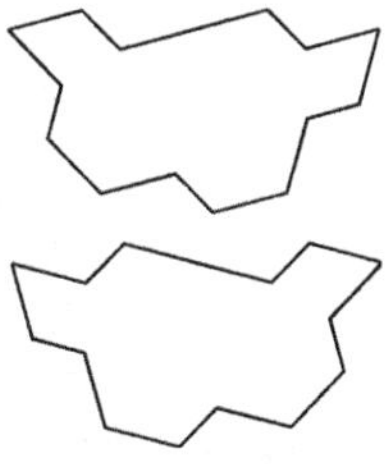 00000, 11111	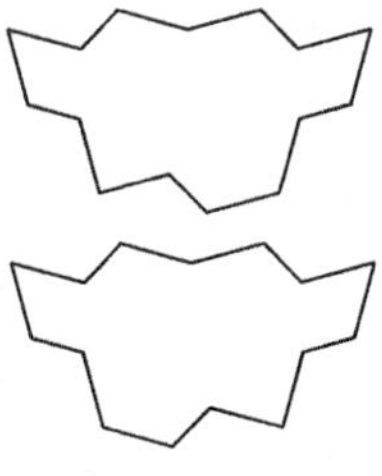 00011, 11100	CC3C3 C6C6 Edges 2&3 same; edges 4&5 same
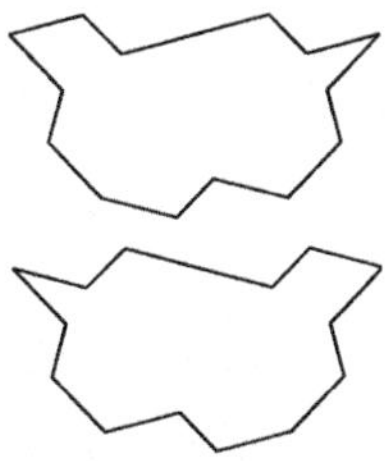 01100, 10011	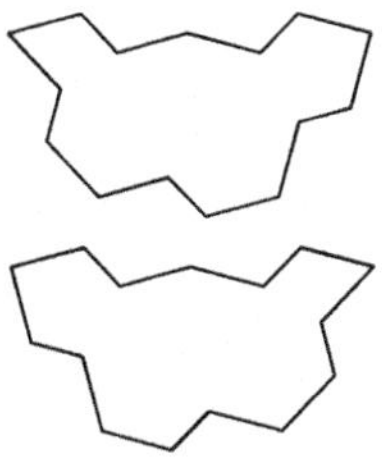 10000, 01111	

Below is an example of a tiling using the 00000 tile.

Here are the other three in the table.

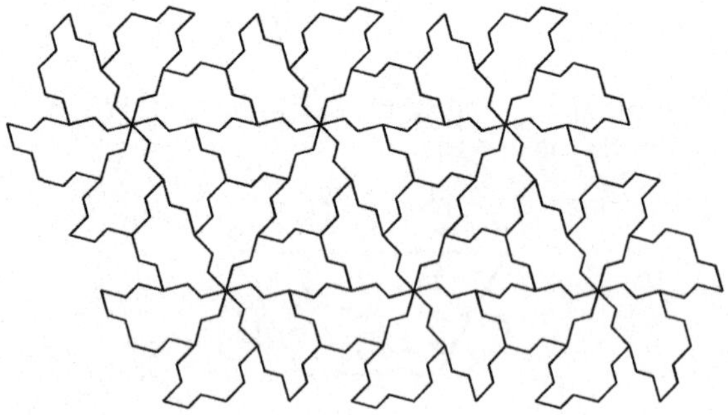

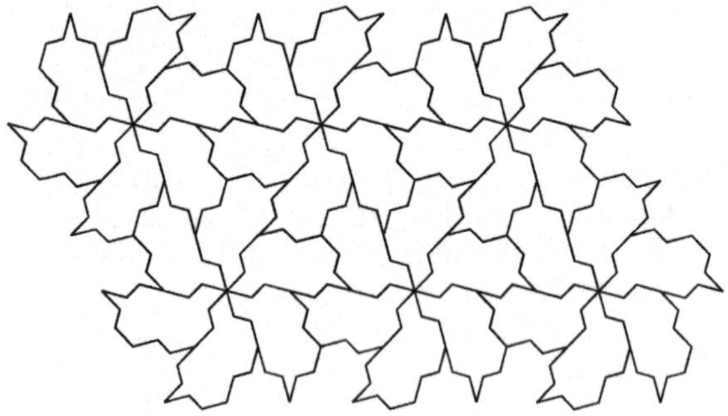

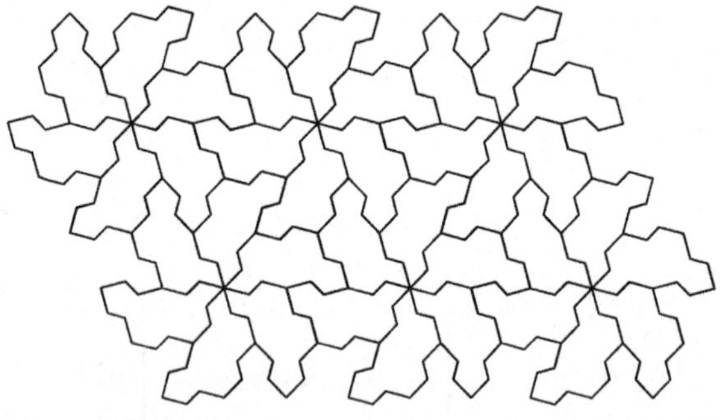

These pentagonal-based tilings do not seem to be as visually interesting as the quadrilateral and hexagonal-based tilings. None of pentagon-based tiles have reflection or rotational symmetry but many of the quadrilateral and hexagonal based tiles with identical edges with center-point rotation do have these symmetries.

Tiling Vertex to Vertex: The Square Template

The section "Identical Symmetric Edges" found four shapes formed on a square template with identical edges of central rotation. If these shapes are placed like the black squares of a checkerboard so that each vertex of a tile touches the vertex of only one other tile, a pattern of tiles and voids results. The voids must take the same four shapes that the tiles can have. There are many ways of fitting together the tiles and some ways give duplicate results. The patterns can be not just monohedral tilings but can also be two-, three-, and four-tile tessellations. Below are examples showing eleven different symmetry groups

The shape used below is the 0001 shape and this arrangement creates holes of the 0000 and 0011 shapes. Despite the symmetry of the holes, the pattern has only the translational symmetry of group p1.

My attempts to get a pg example using only one shape for black tiles resulted in single tile tessellations. However, I was able to get a pg example using two different shapes for black tiles.

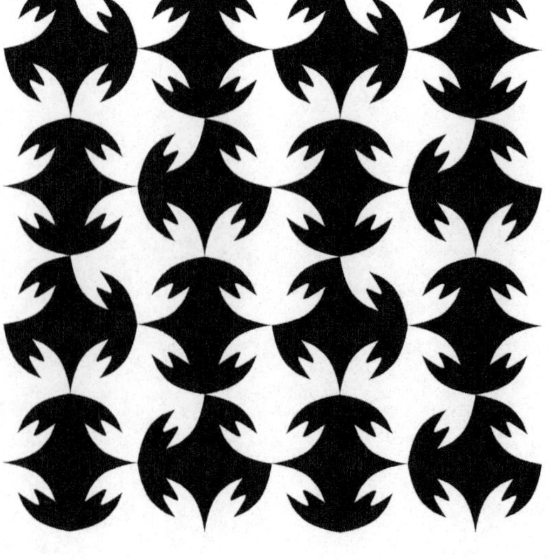

Below is a three-tile pattern that belongs to symmetry group pm.

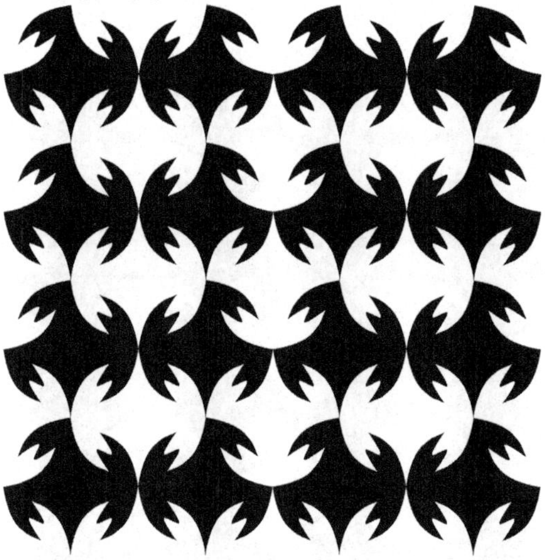

A shift in every other row results in a cm pattern.

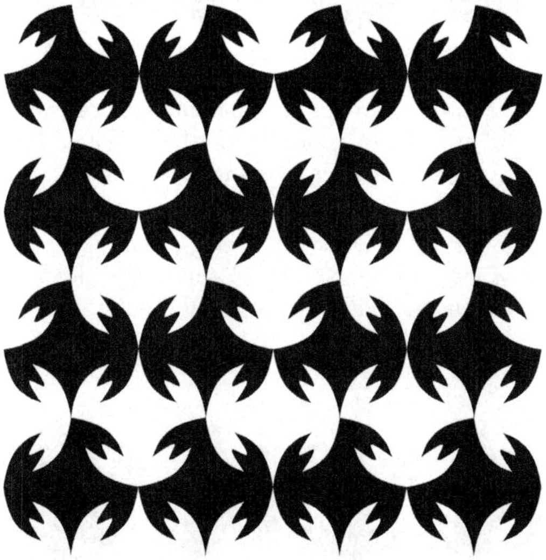

This next pattern uses all four shapes in both black and white tiles. It belongs to the p2 symmetry group.

The three-tile pattern below also belongs to symmetry group p2. Centers of rotation are along horizontal lines. Half are in the center of the white tiles and half are between these center where vertices meet.

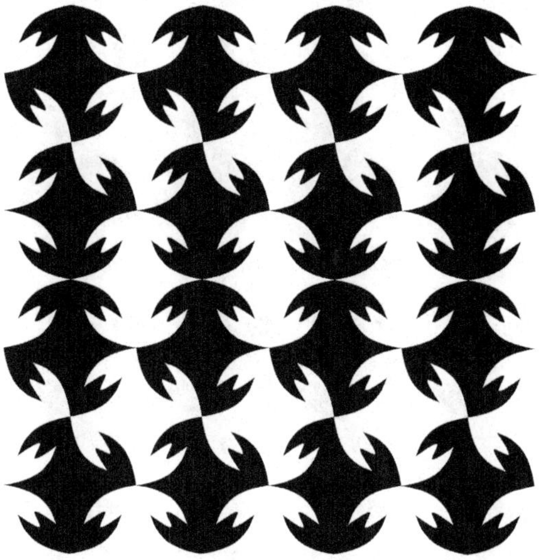

The same three tiles in a different arrangement fit into symmetry group pgg.

Why do the voids have the same four shapes as the tiles? The voids are surrounded by four black tiles and share their edges, each of which has the same shape with center-point rotation. Just as there are only four distinct shapes the black tiles can have when they have identical edges of center-point rotation, the voids must also have only those four shapes because they have the same edges as the black tiles.

In the pattern below there are horizontal lines of reflection and vertical lines of glide reflection. The pattern has pmg symmetry.

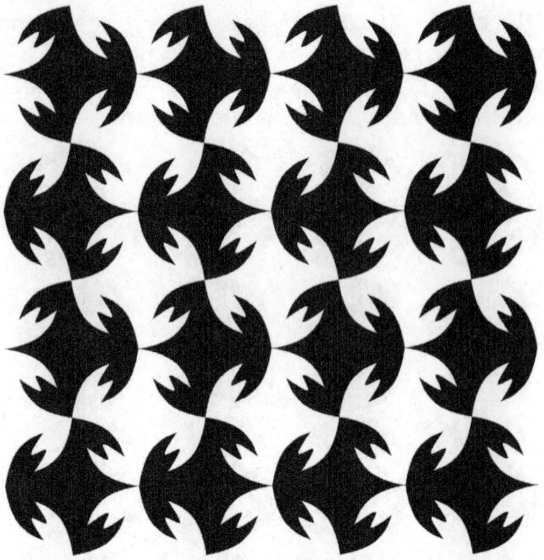

Next are two very different ways to get patterns with pmm symmetry.

In this second pattern of pmm symmetry, the black tiles have no mirror symmetry and the white 0101 tile is oriented three times more in one way than in the other.

A rearrangement of tiles so that the translation block of black tiles is 4x1 rather than 2x2 gives a very different pattern, one that is in symmetry group cmm.

These patterns use 16 tiles: two orientations of both the 0000 and 0101 groups, four orientations of the 0011 group, and eight orientations of the 0001 group. These are the 16 possible shapes given in the section "Identical Symmetric Edges".

Below is a three-tile pattern with p4 symmetry. Centers of fourfold rotation are in the white tiles of group 0000. In the middle of group 0101 tiles are centers of twofold rotations. The black tiles do not have a center of rotation within them.

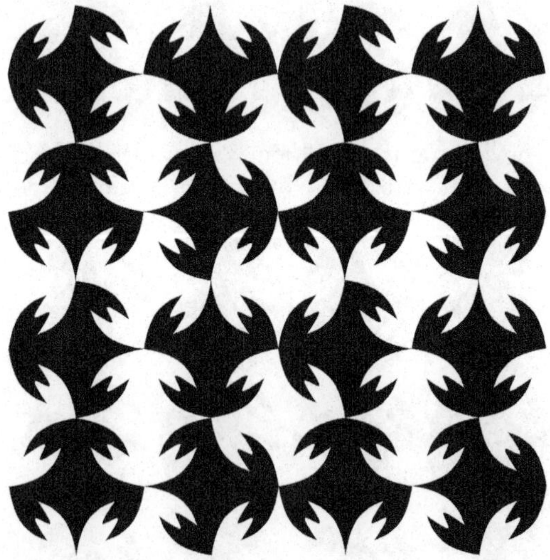

Finally the two-tile arrangement below has p4g symmetry. There are both horizontal and vertical lines of reflection that bisect the black tiles. The centers of fourfold rotation are in the centers of the white tiles.

Other sets of related tiles will make interesting patterns but none of them match what can be done with a set of four tiles formed on a square template with identical, central-rotation edges. All four shapes tessellate and all of the many patterns that can be constructed with them use only the four shapes as tiles. I suspect I have only scratched the surface of the design possibilities that these sets of four shapes offer. (Below is the same pattern as above but with a different edge.)

After I found this way of making patterns, I searched the Internet to see if others had found it. The closest I could find was this site in the UK, www.tess-elation.co.uk/birds---an-introduction/birds-1-1, which uses three of the four possible tiles for Escher-like tessellations. Perhaps there are others that could be found with the right search terms. I also could not resist looking at other possibilities, some of which are shown below with a sample that illustrates all four possible shapes.

(If you would like to explore these patterns, you can do so with the FabFours fonts available at MyFonts.com.)

One can get the same patterns with black and white tiles that are fitted edge to edge. The beauty of the vertex-to-vertex tiling is that one has complete freedom in placing the tiles and the voids are completely determined by the surrounding tiles. If the tiles are placed edge to edge, the selections of tiles is always constrained by the tiles that have already been placed.

There are other patterns that have square tiles arranged corner to corner. In the first example below each square touches only two other squares and leaves a void of stars with six rays. The stars have angles of 30° and 270°. The narrowness of the star rays would greatly limit how the edges could be altered. A similar pattern with rhombuses rather than squares is explored in the next section.

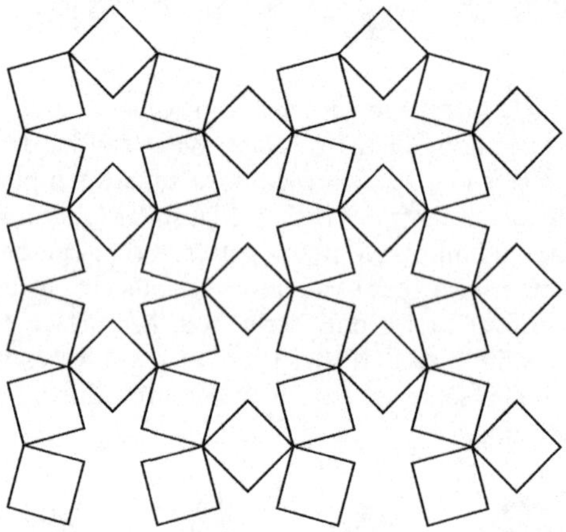

In the second example each square touches four other squares and the voids are rhombuses. This design will be explored further below in the section on rhombus templates.

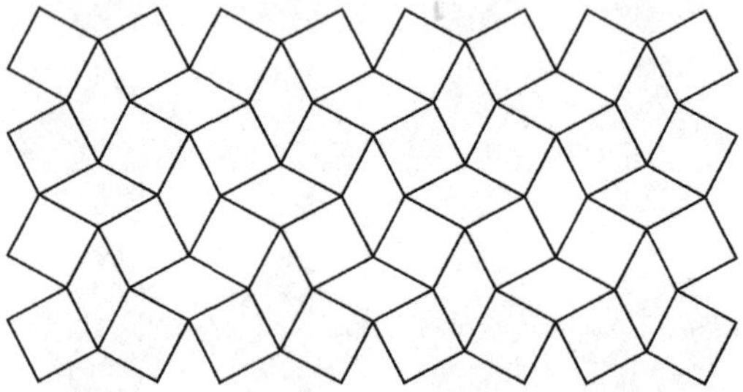

Some people have done very clever things that are similar to the above tilings. Search the Internet for "hinging tessellations" and check the images.

Tiling Vertex to Vertex: The Rhombus Template

A previous section showed that there were seven distinct shapes that can be formed with a rhombus template when fitted with identical sides that have center-point rotation. All tessellate; any quadrilateral with sides formed with center-point rotation will tessellate. This section considers patterns when these shapes are fitted vertex to vertex rather than edge to edge.

The most obvious way to tile rhombuses is in a matrix of diamonds, which has cmm symmetry when the rhombus sides are unshaped.

There are four symmetry transformation that map the rhombus with straight sides back onto itself: the identity, vertical flip, horizontal flip, and 180° rotation. Applying these transformations will tell us how many tiles can be used to replace the tiles in the figure above with our rhombus-based shapes. Two of the seven distinct shapes have both vertical and horizontal symmetry so all transformations map the shape back onto itself.

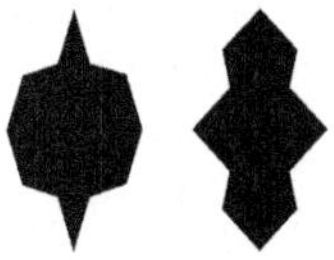

Two shapes have mirror symmetry on one axis. A flip over that axis returns the shape. A flip over the other axis yields the same result as a rotation of 180°.

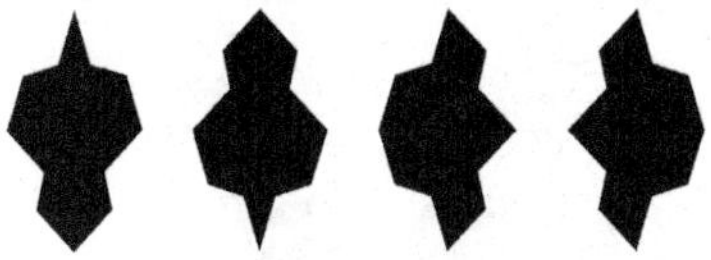

One shape has 180° rotational symmetry so rotation of 180° returns the original shape. Horizontal and vertical flips return identical results.

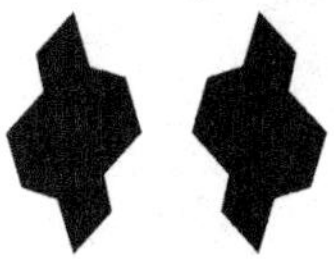

Two shapes have no symmetry and each transformation maps it to a new result.

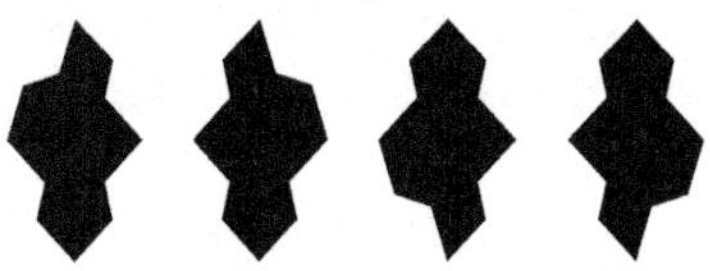

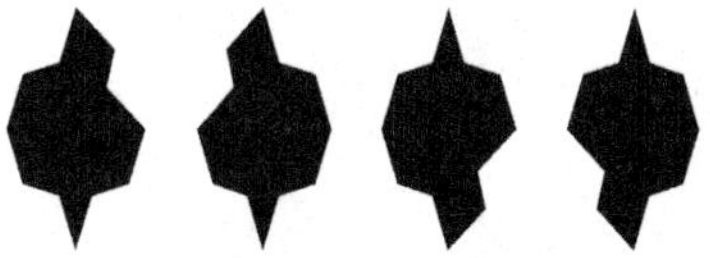

Hence, for any common edge, there are sixteen tiles that can be used to replace the regular tiles in the pattern above. Below is an example.

Another way to tile the plane with the rhombus is to flip alternate rows as in the pattern below. Fitted with tiles with center-point rotation, we get another way of tiling with voids from the same set of shapes as tiles.

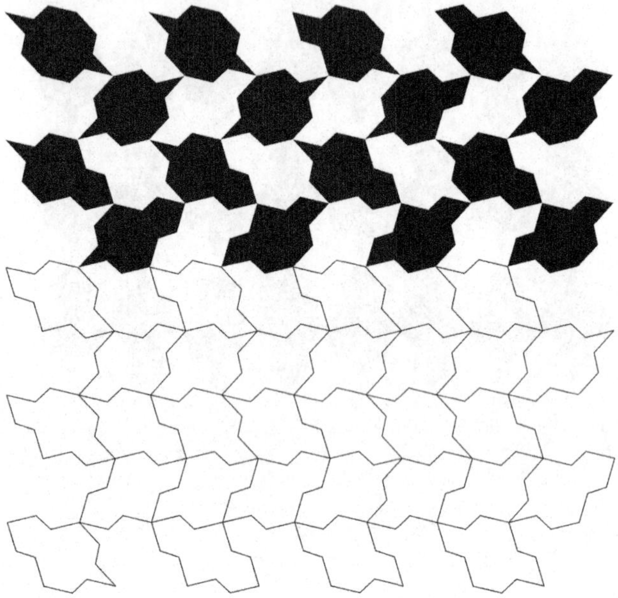

Another common pattern that has rhombuses tiled vertex to vertex rotates alternate tiles 90°, resulting in a pattern that has p4g symmetry. The voids in this arrangement are squares.

With the set of 16 tiles from our rhombus template, the voids must take the four shapes that were discussed in previous sections about square templates.

A fourth way of arranging these tiles vertes to vertex has the void filled with a six-sided star. When the rhombuses are formed with 60°/120° angles, the interior star could be filled with six additional rhombuses. The pattern belongs to symmetrical group p6m.

The regular tiles in this pattern can also be replaced with the set of 16 rhombus-based shapes, as the following figure illustrates.

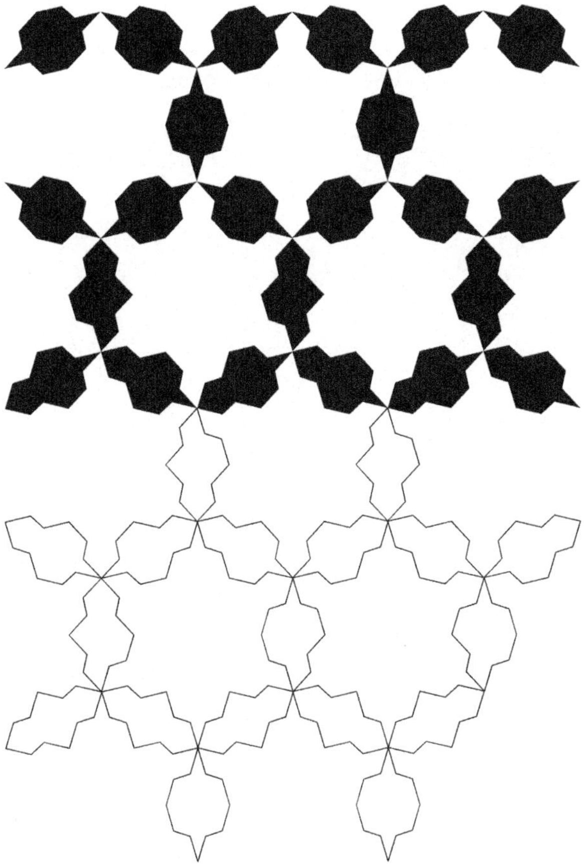

The second of these ways of tiling with rhombus-based shapes seems to offer the most visually attractive designs. Below are two examples using white tiles.

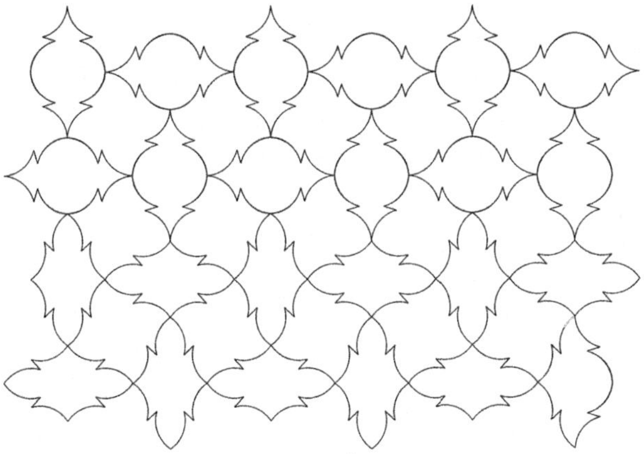

Tiling Vertex to Vertex: The Triangle Template

Many of the visually-interesting edges from the tiles with square templates will fail when put on the triangle template because adjacent edges will overlap. To prevent overlap in the case of the square template, the shape of the edge must be confined to a square with the edge as a diagonal. To prevent overlap in the case of a triangle template, the edge must be confined to a 60°/120° rhombus with the edge as the long diagonal. In the figure below the heavy lines show two adjacent template shapes with the shape of common edge confined to area within the thinner lines. Edges applied to a 60°/120° rhombus template will have the same shape area as the equilateral triangle.

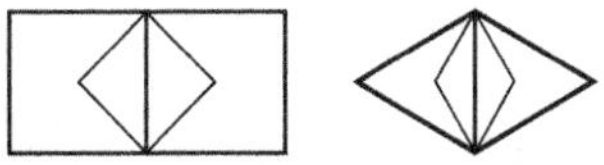

We have seen that files formed with the square template can take only four distinct shapes and these four shapes will, when arranged vertex to vertex, produce voids that must have the same four shape as the tiles. When shapes are formed with the template of an equilateral triangle, there are two sets of eight shapes. When tiling vertex to vertex, one set of eight is used and the other set forms the voids.

In the first example below the black tiles leave voids that have shape of the IH90 tile. Notice that the black tiles are from the set with the base of the triangle at the top and the voids are from the set with the base of the triangle at the bottom.

The next example uses white tiles, so the tiles are not readily distinguishable from the voids.

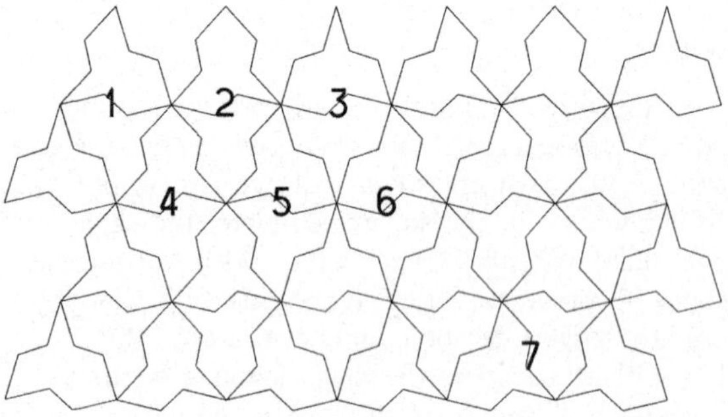

If a rhombus (diamond) is fitted with identical sides of center-point rotation, there are exactly seven distinct shapes that result. They were illustrated in the previous section. The pattern above from a triangle template has all seven shapes based on the 60°-120° rhombus if we can erase some of the lines that separate a tile and an adjoining void. (If we squeeze the rhombus template until it becomes a square, which is a special case of a rhombus, shapes 2 and 3 converge, as do shapes 4 and 6, and 5 and 7.)

Below are a several more examples with different edges and patterns.

The visual interest from patterns formed with tiles of these sets may be more in seeing these rhombus-based shapes than in the patterns of the triangular shapes.

Other interesting shapes result from combining blocks of six that share a common vertex and blocks of four centered on a middle tile.

Tiling Vertex to Vertex: The Hexagon Template

Patterns based on the square and triangular templates have an even number of lines meeting at each vertex, four and six. The allows the tiles and the voids to alternate, a TVTV or TVTVTV sequence. Patterns based on a hexagonal template have three edges meeting at each vertex, so the alternating sequence of tiles and voids that have the same shapes is not possible. In addition, all the shapes that can be formed with an identical side of center-point rotation using either a square or triangular template will tessellate. The same is not true when shapes are formed in the same way with a hexagonal template.

When regular hexagonal tiles are set vertex to vertex, the voids take the shape of equilateral triangles.

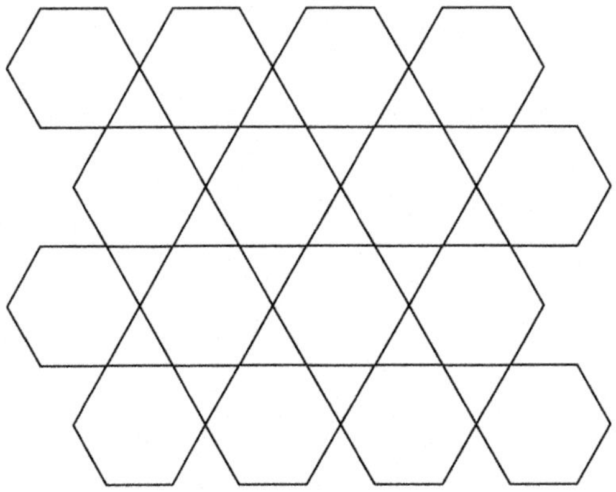

When the nine shapes described in the section "Regular Hexagons" replace the regular hexagons in the tiling above, the voids take the two shapes possible when the equilateral triangle template is fitted with identical edges of center-point rotation. Because the eight shapes have a total of 64 orientations, each of the hexagons can be replaced in 64 different ways, yielding a huge number of possible patterns. The figure below gives a small sample of what is possible.

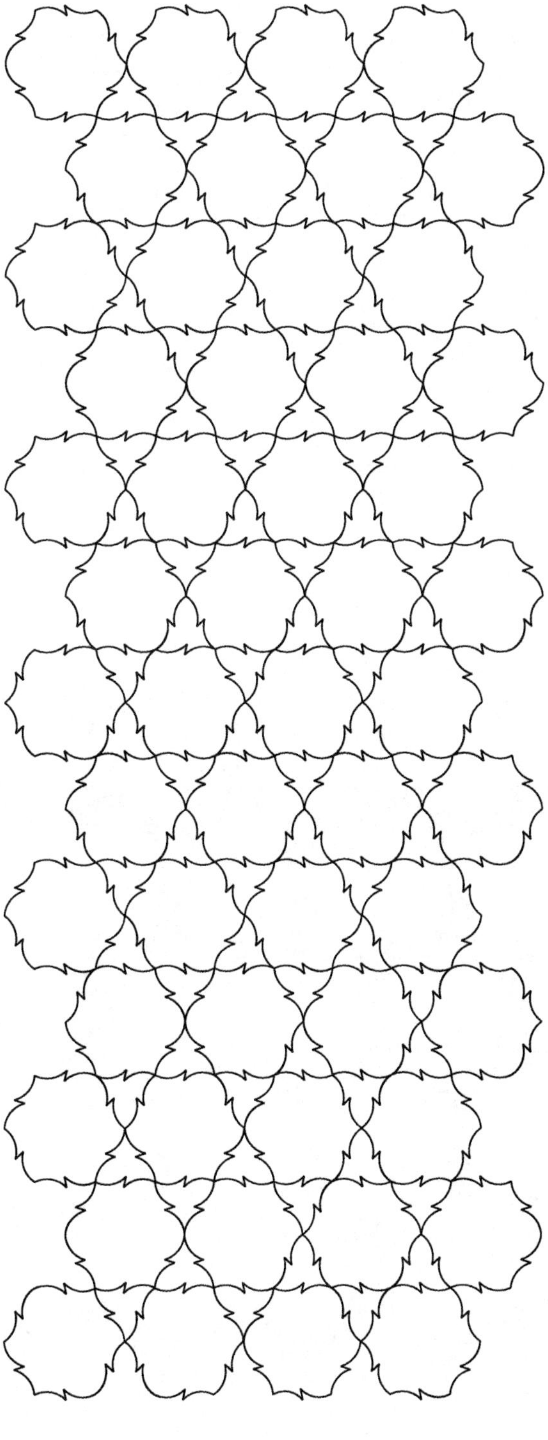

The same patterns can be obtained by using the shapes from the triangular template as the tiles, which results in the voids forming the various hexagonal-based shapes. Below is an example, with the tiles in black and the voids left white.

Below is the same pattern but with different common edges.

Despite the enormous number of possible patterns and the many way in which they can be displayed, these tilings do not seem to be as visually interesting as those based on the square template. In addition, some of the edges that work on the square template will overlap when formed with the hexagonal template and used in arrangements like those above.

A visually appealing tiling that has hexagons meeting vertex to vertex is one that has voids of squares and stars with four rays, shown below. Only four of the vertices meet. The rays of the stars have an angle of only 30° at the peaks, so the edges would have to be very limited in their shape area.

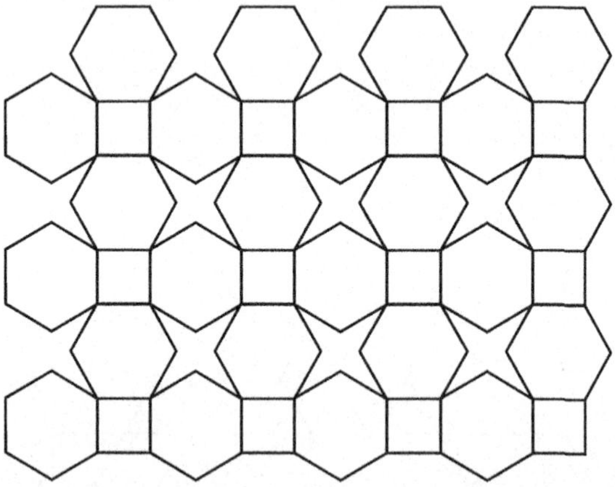

The regular pentagon with equal sides and angles does not tessellate, and placed vertex to vertex, it initially seems to produce interesting patterns, but those patterns do not form translation blocks. Below is the most visually pleasing pattern I found, but each pentagon has one corner that is not a vertex. Although the regular pentagons could be replaced with tiles with identical sides of central rotation, the narrowness of the rays of the star will result in very limited space in which to form those sides. All of the edges used in previous examples would overlap.

(If you would like more examples of tiling vertex to vertex, I used designs developed from these sections in *Delightful Designs: A Coloring Book of Magical Patterns*. It is available from the same places that this book is available.)

Vertex to Vertex with Chevrons

We havc seen how equilateral chevrons with six edges can tessellate and how the template of that equilateral template could be fitted with identical edges with center-point rotation. Tiles based on equilateral triangles, equilateral rhombuses, and regular hexagons with identical edges with center-point rotation can be placed so that only vertices meet and no edges, resulting in patterns of tiles and voids. There is no way that equilateral chevrons can be arranged so all six vertices of the chevron will meet with no common edges, but in the pattern below five vertices meet with no common edges. The tiles are equilateral chevrons and the voids are equilateral triangles and hexagons.

If the chevrons are replaced with tiles with identical sides with center-point rotation, patterns such as the following result. The voids are shapes with identical sides with center-point rotation formed on templates of equilateral triangles and regular hexagons.

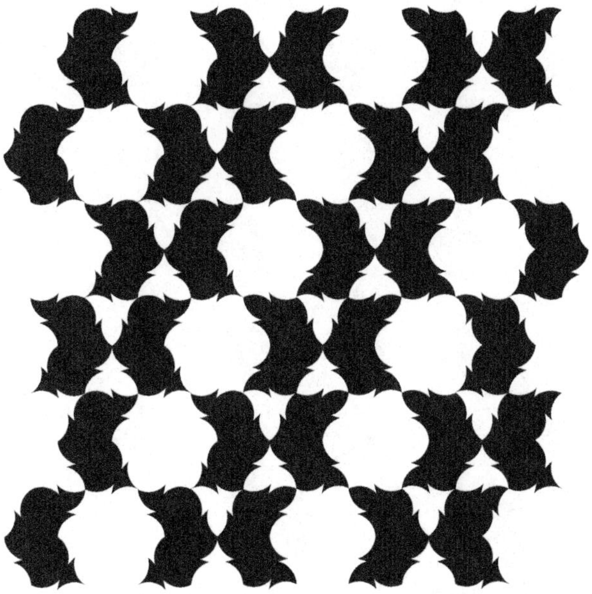

Below is another arrangement of chevrons with five corners touching. There are several others similar.

It is easy to arrange chevrons so that four vertices meet with no common edges and this pattern can be adapted to the chevron templates fitted with identical sides with center-point rotation.

The chevron pattern at the top fits Heesch types TCTC, CGCG, TGTG, or G1G2G1G2 while the template for the bottom fits TTTT or TGTG.

A more interesting pattern with four common vertices is one that uses a G1G1G2G2 arrangement.

Of the 64 possible tiles with the identical sides with center-point rotation, only eight shapes will form patterns that are true tessellations. All are shown below. Six tiles of each of the eight surround two voids of the same shape. Can you identify them?

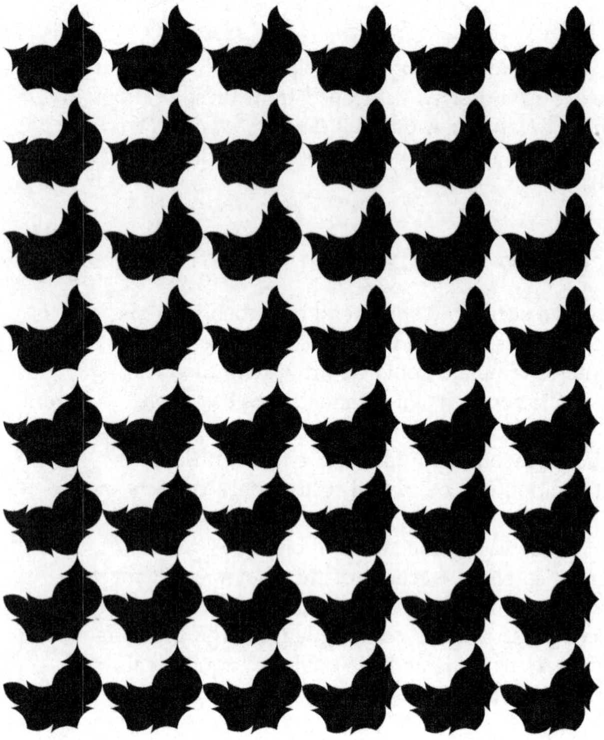

There are only eight because three of the sides of the chevron are determined by the other three. (The chevron template has six sides but only four edges in this configuration. An edge is the border with a neighbor and a side is a straight line in the template.) One G1 edge determines the other and one G2 edge determines the other. Each of the three sides that can be independently set can have two states, and 2x2x2=8. Fitting together other shapes results in voids that are different than the surrounding tiles.

Epilogue: Final Mazes

As mentioned in the Introduction, the book began as the result of a quest to see how many of the 28 Heesch types could produce recognizable birds standing on the backs of other birds. (For an early but not the earliest result of this quest, see the two posts made in April of 2015 on the mazepuzzles blog at mazepuzzles.blogspot.com/2015_04_01_archive.html.) When I decided to expand these posts into a book, my initial thought was to develop it as a maze book, a type of book with which I have had much experience. I quickly realized that a maze book was a poor vehicle for this project. A maze breaks up the pattern so that the tessellation shape is not the central focus, the maze is. My aim in this book was to focus on tessellations. In addition, the intended audience for this book is adults, adolescents, and perhaps precocious children. The appropriate mazes for them would be challenging mazes with small tiles, which again would de-emphasize the tessellations.

In the past I have attempted to reach those who might be interested in tessellations but not mazes by taking the tessellation patterns used in my maze books and using them to create two coloring books. One of them, *The Tessellating Alphabet Coloring Book,* is devoted solely to tessellating letters—my interest in typography led me to spend several months searching for ways to tessellate the letters of the alphabet. The other, *A Tessellating Coloring Book,* contains both tessellations that are geometric, abstract shapes and those that resemble people, animals, and other real-world objects. (For more about these books, visit ingrimayne.com/mazes/mazeindex.htm.) When I abandoned the idea of using a maze book for this project, I naturally thought of making it into a coloring book. It took several weeks before I realized that the coloring book format was also a bad idea. The book has too much text and the text is too technical to appeal to those who would find a coloring book interesting, and the coloring book format would be inappropriate for those who would appreciate the text.

Dropping the coloring book idea changed everything. There was no longer any reason to avoid using tessellations I had previously used in these two coloring books so there were many more tessellations I could use. On the other hand, I knew how to organize and format maze and coloring books but I had no model for a book that was neither.

I am unaware of anyone else who has been using and finding tessellation tiles for the purpose of making mazes. As mentioned earlier, most people interested in playing with programs like *TesselManiac!* are either tessellation artists who are following in the footsteps of M. C. Escher, teachers and students who are interested in teaching or learning a bit about geometry and visual design, or quilters, who have found that tessellation patterns can make beautiful quilts.

The next five pages end where I began this adventures, with mazes. Each page shows a different way to create mazes using tessellation patterns.

(I hope this book will be of some use to others. There is not much written that explores topics such as the isohedral classes, so perhaps this book may fill a gap. Or perhaps there is not much written because there is not real audience for the topic. Regardless, writing it has been useful to me as a way of organizing and directing my exploration of tessellations. I know that it contains errors both large and small that I have not found and corrected. I apologize to the reader for them.)

The computer program that generated this maze of a grid of triangles allows for connections downward only if the sum of the row and column is even. If it is odd, only a connection upward is allowed. The pattern used here a Heesch type CCC with all edges shaped in the same way. The tile is shown in six different orientations, two in the top six rows, two more in the middle six rows, and a final two in the bottom six rows.

The obvious way to have a computer generate a maze is to begin with a grid of rectangles and cut doors in their sides. I soon realized that the visual possibilities were much greater if I allowed cells in a block of four to each have a different shape. When I began using tessellations, this allowed for display of tessellation types that had translation blocks of two or four. The G design used here is actually hexagonal of type TCCTCC. Its complex shape confuses the eye and makes what is actually a simple maze a challenge to solve.

The hexagon, one of only three regular polygons to tessellate, is the basis for a making mazes in which each cell can connect to six neighbors. The tessellation used here belongs to isohedral class IH18.

The hexagonal framework used in the previous page does not allow for more than one shape. A way to display more complexity is to realize each cell can be formed with only three sides, allowing the cell's neighbor to provide the other three sides. A design with two different hexagonal shapes can thereby be displayed using only 16 patterns, and this is the trick used in this maze of the letter J, which is type TCCTCC and has a translation unit of two.

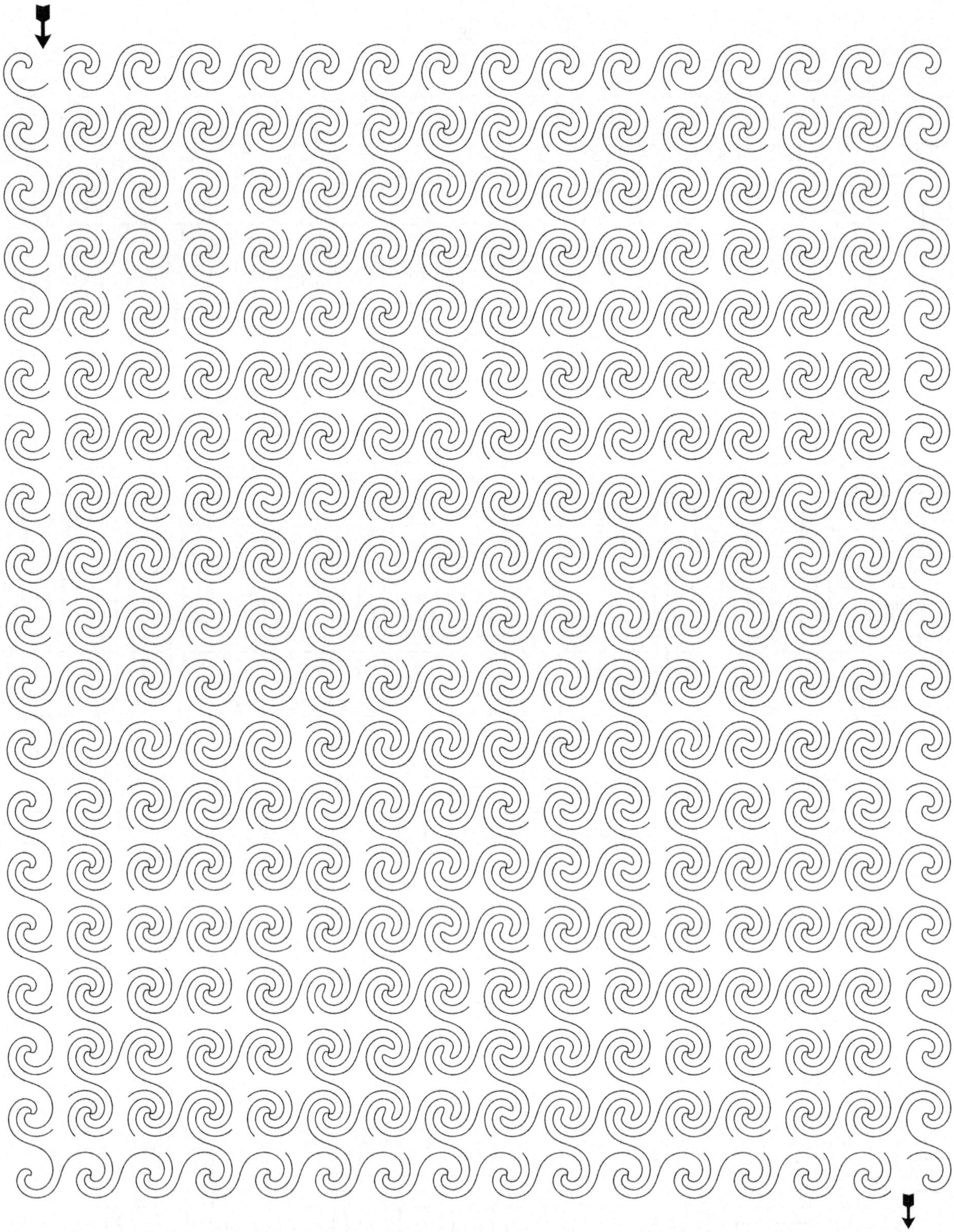

If a maze is made from a grid of rectangles, it need not be limited to vertical and horizontal passages. It can also have diagonal passages, so that a connection to any of eight neighboring cells can be made. The program making the maze must make sure that if a cell connects diagonally to the northwest, the cell to the west cannot connect to the northeast. With a maze limited to horizontal and vertical connections, there are 16 possible variations in the cells wall. When the diagonal connections are allowed, there are 256 possible connections, though connections to more than four cells are unlikely. Rather than design the typeface to display the result based on the cell, it is easier to design the typeface to display the corner, and that is what is done here. In this pattern the horizontal and vertical passages are easy, but the diagonal passages through the corners are very visually confusing.

Solutions

My maze generating programs solve mazes by blocking up dead ends and leaving only the path (or paths) that connect start to finish. The results are shown above. When I created my first book of mazes for Dover, my editor liked this way of displaying solutions but his superior did not and required that I redo them. However, for displaying mazes based on tessellations they have the virtue of emphasizing the pattern.

Partial Index of Types and Classes

Appendix 1

Summary of Relations among Isohedral Groups

Restricted Hexagons	Mirrored?	Center-Point Rotation	Straight Edges	Edges Mirror Symmetry	TTTTTT	TG1G1TG2G2	TG1G2TG2G1	TCCTCC	TCCTGG	CG1CG2G1G2	C3C3C3C3C3C3	Bisections, etc.	Degenerates	More Restricted	Symmetry Group
IH8	N	6			X			X					IH57	(IH11)	p2
IH9	N	2				X	X						IH59		pgg
IH10	N	0			X						X		IH34 (IH61)	(IH18)	p3
IH11	N	6			X			X			X		IH90 (IH62)		p6
IH12	Y	0		2	X	X						IH22	IH68		cm
IH13	Y	4		2			X	X		X		IH24	IH69 IH66		pmg
IH14	Y	0	2		X		X					IH45	IH68		cm
IH15	Y	4	2			X		X	X			IH49 IH58	IH69	(IH17)	pmg
IH17	Y	4	2		X	X	X	X	X	X		IH26 IH67 IH54	IH74		cmm
IH18	Y	0		6	X	X					X	IH16 IH30	(IH73)		p31m

Items in parenthesis have a different symmetry group than the row. Results are not guaranteed to be correct.

Summary of Relations among Isohedral Groups

Restricted Quadrilaterals	Mirrored?	Center-Point Rotation	Straight Edges	Edges Mirror Symmetry	TTTT	TGTG	TCTC	G1G1G2G2	CGCG	CCGG	G1G2G1G2	CCCC	C4C4C4C4	C3C3C3C3	Bisections, etc.	More Restricted	Symmetry Group
IH34	N													X			p6
IH36	Y													X	IH38		p31m
IH57	N	4			X		X					X				(IH62)	p2
IH59	N							X									pgg
IH61	N												X			(IH73)	p4
IH62	N	4			X		X					X	X				p4
IH64	Y		2	2	X	X									IH42		pm
IH66	Y	2		2		X	X		X		X				IH50		pmg
IH68	Y				X			X							IH83	(IH74)	cm
IH69	Y	4						X		X		X			IH85		pmg
IH71	Y										X		X		IH81		p4g
IH73	Y			4				X					X		IH29 IH56		p4g
IH74	Y	4			X		X	X		X		X			IH91 IH78		cmm

Items in parenthesis have a different symmetry group than the row. No items fit type C3C3C6C6. Results are not guaranteed to be correct.

Appendix 2: 29 Symmetrical Heesch-like Types

Heesch Type	Mirror Symmetry							Rotational Symmetry			
	D1	D1(s)	D2(s)	D3(s)	D1(l)	D2(l)	D2	C2	C3	C4	C6
TCCTCC		IH13			IH15*		IH17*	IH8			IH11
TCTCC	IH26*										
CCCC		IH67*			IH69	IH74		IH57		IH62	
TCTC		IH66									
CCC	IH91*								IH90		
C3C3C3C3C3C3				IH18	IH16*				IH10		
C3C3C3C3					IH36			IH34			
CC4C4C4C4	IH29*										
C4C4C4C4			IH73		IH71			IH61			
TG1G1TG2G2		IH12						IH9			
TG1G2TG2G1					IH14*			IH9			
G1G1G2G2					IH68			IH59			
TTTT		IH64*									

The 28 Heesch types require that all edges of a tile be shapeable and that the tiles themselves can be asymmetric. Another 29 of the isohedral classes of Grünbaum and Shepard that have at least one edge shapeable fit the edges of Heesch types but require that the tile have either mirror of rotational symmetry. They are shown in the table above. (Most of them have been called restricted Heesch types in this book.) Many fit more than one Heesch type.

Edges formed with central-point rotation can be used to fit T, G, or corner-point rotation edges, but the reverse is not true. The Heesch type given in the table is the one that best indicates how the edges must be formed. The column headings use the symbols of Grünbaum and Shepard. A "(s)" indicates the line of mirror reflection runs from edge to edge while a "(l)" indicates that the line of mirror reflection runs from vertex to vertex. (See the table at the end of Part III.) Items with an asterisk require at least one straight edge.

The text separated the 93 isohedral classes into 28 Heesch types, 20 restricted Heesch types, 24 classes with both shapable and straight edges, and 21 with only straight edges. This table suggests a different separation: 28 Heesch types, 29 symmetrical Heesch-like types, 15 non-Heesch types that have straight edges of reflection, and 21 with only straight edges.

The grouping of family members in the table suggests relationships. For example, IH69 lies beneath IH15, suggesting that if two of the edges of IH15 (in this case those serving as T edges) shrink away, the result will be a class IH69 tiling. Other relationships that the table reveals are IH16⇒IH36, IH13⇒IH66, IH14⇒IH68, IH9⇒IH59 and IH8⇒IH57. Less obvious are some other connections. If an edge has the line of mirror symmetry, when that edge shrinks away, the line of symmetry becomes a line from vertex to vertex. Examples are IH17⇒IH74, IH13⇒IH69, and IH12⇒IH68.

Appendix 3

Below are symmetrical Heesch-like tilings that will be incorporated into the text in some future revision. First column: IH17, IH90, IH36, IH34. Second column: IH11, IH61, IH71, IH73.

Printed in Great Britain
by Amazon

40212518R00097